PERSONALITY AND INDIVIDUAL DIFFERENCES

Sara Miller McCune founded SAGE Publishing in 1965 to support the dissemination of usable knowledge and educate a global community. SAGE publishes more than 1000 journals and over 800 new books each year, spanning a wide range of subject areas. Our growing selection of library products includes archives, data, case studies and video. SAGE remains majority owned by our founder and after her lifetime will become owned by a charitable trust that secures the company's continued independence.

Los Angeles | London | New Delhi | Singapore | Washington DC | Melbourne

PERSONALITY AND INDIVIDUAL DIFFERENCES

****REVISITING****
THE CLASSIC STUDIES

EDITED BY:
PHILIP CORR

SAGE

Los Angeles | London | New Delhi
Singapore | Washington DC | Melbourne

Los Angeles | London | New Delhi
Singapore | Washington DC | Melbourne

SAGE Publications Ltd
1 Oliver's Yard
55 City Road
London EC1Y 1SP

SAGE Publications Inc.
2455 Teller Road
Thousand Oaks, California 91320

SAGE Publications India Pvt Ltd
B 1/I 1 Mohan Cooperative Industrial Area
Mathura Road
New Delhi 110 044

SAGE Publications Asia-Pacific Pte Ltd
3 Church Street
#10-04 Samsung Hub
Singapore 049483

Editor: Becky Taylor
Editorial assistant: Katie Rabot
Production editor: Imogen Roome
Marketing manager: Lucia Sweet
Cover design: Wendy Scott
Typeset by: C&M Digitals (P) Ltd, Chennai, India
Printed in the UK

Introduction and Editorial Arrangement © Philip J. Corr 2019
Chapter 1 © Ian J. Deary 2019
Chapter 2 © Gerard Saucier 2019
Chapter 3 © John S. Gillis and Gregory J. Boyle 2019
Chapter 4 © Kieron P. O'Connor and Philip J. Corr 2019
Chapter 5 © John A. Johnson 2019
Chapter 6 © Michael W. Eysenck 2019
Chapter 7 © Neil McNaughton and Philip J. Corr 2019
Chapter 8 © Richard M. Ryan, William S. Ryan and
    Stefano I. Di Domenico 2019
Chapter 9 © Wendy Johnson 2019
Chapter 10 © Aurelio José Figueredo, Heitor B. F. Fernandes,
    Mateo Peñaherrera-Aguirre and Steven C. Hertler 2019
Chapter 11 © Margaret L. Kern 2019
Chapter 12 © Jeremy C. Biesanz 2019
Chapter 13 © John F. Rauthmann and Manfred Schmitt 2019
Chapter 14 © Virgil Zeigler-Hill and David K. Marcus 2019

First published 2019

Library of Congress Control Number: 2018943756

British Library Cataloguing in Publication data

A catalogue record for this book is available from
the British Library

ISBN 978-1-5264-1360-4
ISBN 978-1-5264-1361-1 (pbk)

At SAGE we take sustainability seriously. Most of our products are printed in the UK using responsibly sourced
papers and boards. When we print overseas we ensure sustainable papers are used as measured by the PREPS
grading system. We undertake an annual audit to monitor our sustainabiliy.

Contents

About the Editor

Philip J. Corr is Professor of Psychology at City, University of London, and previously he held professorial positions at the University of East Anglia and Swansea University. Philip's main research interests are in individual differences, especially personality factors and processes – he is most known for his work on the Reinforcement Sensitivity Theory (RST), a topic on which he edited a book in 2009. Philip has written and edited several other books, including *Understanding Biological Psychology* (2006), the *Cambridge Handbook of Personality Psychology* (2008; second edition 2019), a scientific biography of one of the leading personality psychologists in the world, *Hans Eysenck: A Contradictory Psychology* (2016), and along with Anke Plagnol, *Behavioural Economics: The Basics* (2018). Philip has several other ongoing book writing projects and has published more than 150 peer reviewed scientific articles. In 2009 he co-founded the British Society for the Psychology of Individual Differences (BSPID) in the UK; and he is a past President (2015–17) of the International Society for the Study of Individual Differences (ISSID). In 2017 he established a new journal, *Personality Neuroscience*, published by Cambridge University Press.

About the Contributors

Jeremy C. Biesanz is an Associate Professor of Psychology at the University of British Columbia and Director of Quantitative Methodology at the Department of Psychology. A graduate of Cornell University, New York, he received his PhD from Arizona State University and has taught at the University of Wisconsin–Madison. He is the recipient of the 2000 J. S. Tanaka Personality dissertation award and the 2006 Cattell early career award for contributions to multivariate experimental psychology. A former associated editor at *Personality and Social Psychology Bulletin*, his research interests include personality, accuracy, person perception, models for interpersonal perception, and quantitative methodology and statistics.

Gregory J. Boyle is an Honorary Professorial Fellow at the University of Melbourne, and a Fellow of both the Australian Psychological Society and the Association for Psychological Science. He is a recipient of the Buros Institute of Mental Measurements Distinguished Reviewer Award. His sustained contributions to the evidence-based psychological literature have been acknowledged with conferral of a Doctor of Science degree from the University of Queensland. He is co-author of the book *Elementary Statistical Methods: For Students of Psychology, Education and the Social Sciences,* co-editor of the book *Measures of Personality and Social Psychological Constructs*, co-editor of *The SAGE Handbook of Personality Theory and Assessment (2 vols.)*, and co-editor of the following *SAGE Benchmarks in Psychology series: Psychology of Individual Differences (4 vols.), Psychological Assessment (4 vols.)*, and *Work and Organisational Psychology (5 vols.)*.

Ian J. Deary is Professor of Differential Psychology at the University of Edinburgh. He is a graduate of Psychology and Medicine from the University of Edinburgh, where he also took his PhD. He practised psychiatry in London and Edinburgh before moving to academic psychology. His principal research interests are: human mental abilities, personality traits, the effects of ageing and medical conditions on cognitive functions, and the impact of cognitive ability on people's lives. Ian is founding Director of the Medical Research Council-funded University of Edinburgh Centre for Cognitive Ageing and Cognitive Epidemiology. He is Director of the Lothian Birth Cohort studies. He is co-author of *Personality Traits* (2009, Cambridge University Press).

Stefano I. Di Domenico is a postdoctoral fellow at the Institute for Positive Psychology and Education, Australian Catholic University. He received his PhD from the University of Toronto (2016). His doctoral and postdoctoral research have been funded by the Social Sciences and Humanities Research Council of Canada. Stefano uses a multi-method approach to research basic questions within the fields of motivation and individual differences. His current work examines the measurement and neurobiology of autonomous motivation, the relationships between personality traits, cognitive abilities and motivational processes, and the ways in which people's motivation and health are influenced by socioeconomic conditions.

Michael W. Eysenck is Emeritus Professor and Honorary Fellow at Royal Holloway, University, and is currently Professorial Fellow at Roehampton University, in London – he is the son of H. J. Eysenck. Michael is one of the most prolific British psychologists, with over 50 books and in excess of 200 articles and book chapters, including the best-selling *Cognitive Psychology: A Student's Handbook*, which is now in its seventh edition. Michael is a renowned cognitive psychologist with major research interests in the field of anxiety and cognition – two of his central ideas are that anxiety impairs processing efficiency more than performance effectiveness and that many adverse effects of anxiety involve inefficient attentional control systems.

Heitor B. F. Fernandes is a PhD candidate in the Anxiety Research Group and the Ethology and Evolutionary Psychology Laboratory within the Cognitive and Neural Systems Program at the University of Arizona. He focuses on anxiety, personality and life history socioecology, but has also published on mating strategies and intelligence.

Aurelio José Figueredo is Professor of Psychology and Director of the Ethology and Evolutionary Psychology Laboratory at the University of Arizona. Past research centres on evolutionary psychology, life history strategy, intelligence, sex and violence in human and nonhuman animals. Recent academic efforts include pioneering the nascent field of *Social Biogeography*.

John S. Gillis is a Research Professor of Psychology at St Thomas University in Fredericton, New Brunswick, Canada. He has written books and articles about a wide variety of topics, including game behaviour, personality assessment, human height, intelligence, genetics, dyslexia, creativity, bullying, cancer immunology and avian flu vaccines. His most recent book is a biography, *Psychology's Secret Genius: The Lives and Works of Raymond B. Cattell*.

Steven C. Hertler is a licensed examining psychologist. Past research centres on personality, using behavioural genetics, evolutionary biology and behavioural ecology to alternatively explain classic character types; more recent writings centre on life history evolution, comparative psychology, cross-cultural psychology, biome distribution and climate effects on evolved human nature and behaviour.

John A. Johnson is Professor Emeritus of Psychology at the Pennsylvania State University. He has published numerous journal articles and book chapters on the personality and evolutionary psychology of moral and educational development, career choice and work performance, and is a recognized expert on computerized psychological measurement. Over a million people have completed his online personality test, which was designated a Yahoo! Incredibly Useful Site of the Day. John currently helps manage the International Personality Item Pool website and co-edited a book published by the American Psychological Association, *Advanced Methods for Conducting Online Behavioral Research*. He also has an interest in psychology and the arts and has co-authored a book published by Palgrave, *Graphing Jane Austin: The Evolutionary Basis for Literary Meaning*. John has taught more than 20 different courses in psychology and the humanities, and is the recipient of a number of excellence in teaching awards.

Wendy Johnson is a Professor, with a Chair in Differential Development, at the University of Edinburgh. Her research interests focus on gene–environment interplay in development, especially involving cognitive abilities, personality and 'successful ageing'. She authored the 2014 book *Developing Difference*, served as Editor of the *European Journal of Personality* and has published widely in developmental psychology, behaviour genetics, and personality and cognitive journals.

Margaret ('Peggy') L. Kern is a senior lecturer at the Centre for Positive Psychology within the University of Melbourne's Graduate School of Education. Her research focuses on understanding, measuring and supporting optimal functioning across the lifespan. Peggy incorporates a lifespan perspective, mixed methodologies and interdisciplinary collaboration, and works with schools and workplaces to consider strategies for bridging gaps between research and practice.

David K. Marcus is Professor and Chair of the Department of Psychology at Washington State University. Much of his research focuses on psychopathy and other dark personality traits. He is currently the editor of *Group Dynamics: Theory, Research, and Practice* and co-edited *The Dark Side of Personality: Science and Practice in Social, Personality, and Clinical Psychology* (2016). He is a fellow of the American Psychological Association.

Neil McNaughton is a Professor in the Department of Psychology at the University of Otago and a Fellow of the Royal Society of New Zealand. He graduated in Psychology and Philosophy from the University of Oxford and obtained his PhD in the Department of Physiology and Biochemistry at Southampton University. A

30-year collaboration with Professor Jeffrey Gray resulted in a detailed theory of the neuropsychology of anxiety (in the 2000 second edition of *The Neuropsychology of Anxiety: An Enquiry into the Functions of the Septo-hippocampal System*). Neil is currently testing this theory into the clinic with a human anxiety disorder biomarker derived from a highly successful rodent model of anxiolytic action.

Kieron P. O'Connor is a Professor at the Department of Psychiatry, University of Montreal, and director of the obsessive compulsive spectrum group of the research centre at the University Institute of Mental Health at Montreal. He is interested in the evaluation and treatment of obsessions compulsions, tics and Tourette disorder, body focused repetitive disorders, as well as hoarding disorder and eating disorders, and has received several research grants from the Canadian Institute of Health Research. Kieron has developed several innovative treatments focusing on individual differences in the psychophysiological, emotional and behavioural processes underlying tic and obsessional problems. His most recent books include: *A Clinician's Handbook for Obsessive Compulsive Disorder* (2012); *A Constructivist Clinical Psychology for Cognitive Behaviour Therapy* (2015); and *Managing Tics and Habit Disorders* (2017).

Mateo Peñaherrera-Aguirre is a graduate student in the Anxiety Research Group and the Ethology and Evolutionary Psychology Laboratory within the Cognitive and Neural Systems Program at the University of Arizona. He is interested in the socioecological correlates of life history strategy, coalitions and alliances, and lethal conflict in human societies.

John F. Rauthmann is Professor of Personality Psychology and Psychological Assessment at the University of Lübeck. He studied at the University of Innsbruck, earned his PhD at the Humboldt-University of Berlin, and worked as an Assistant Professor at the Wake Forest University. His interests lie in personality structure and processes; psychological situations (their conceptualization, taxonomization and measurement); and person–situation transactions (e.g., how people perceive, navigate and shape situations). He serves as an associate editor of the journals *Personality and Individual Differences, European Journal of Psychological Assessment, British Journal of Psychology* and *Frontiers: Psychology*. He is currently editing the Elsevier *Handbook of Personality Dynamics and Processes* and, together with Ryne Sherman and David Funder, the *Oxford Handbook of Psychological Situations*.

Richard M. Ryan is a clinical psychologist and Professor at the Institute for Positive Psychology and Education at the Australian Catholic University and in the Department of Psychology at the University of Rochester. He is co-developer of Self-Determination Theory (www.selfdeterminationtheory.org), an internationally recognized framework for the study of human motivation. Ryan has received several distinguished career awards and fellowships, and he has authored over 400 papers and books in the areas of motivation, mindfulness, personality development and well-being.

William S. Ryan is a research consultant and lecturer at the University of Toronto. He received his PhD in Psychological and Brain Sciences from the University of California, Santa Barbara in 2017. Will's research examines the question of how social contexts and interactions support and thwart health and wellness among members of stigmatized groups. Utilizing a Self-Determination Theory framework, his current work examines identity development and disclosure among LGBTQ individuals. Will is also interested in psychophysiological methodology and developing and testing new methods for assessing cardiovascular reactivity.

Gerard Saucier is a Professor of Psychology at the University of Oregon. His major research interests are the generalizable structure and optimal assessment of personality attributes and of beliefs and values, including thinking patterns related to mass violence. He received the Cattell Award from the Society of Multivariate Experimental Psychology (1999), is a Fellow of the Association for Psychological Science, and is past Associate Editor for the *Journal of Research in Personality* and for the *Journal of Personality and Social Psychology*.

Manfred Schmitt is Professor of Personality and Psychological Assessment at the University of Koblenz-Landau, Germany. He also heads the Centre for Methodology, Assessment and Evaluation at his university. His research interests cover individual differences in various domains, especially in justice beliefs and justice sensitivity, personality processes with a focus on dual-process models of information processing and behaviour, latent state-trait theory and research and the effects of teacher personality on the quality of teaching processes and outcomes. He has served as associate editor of *Psychologische Rundschau, Diagnostica, Social Justice Research*, the *European Journal of Psychological Assessment* and the *European Journal of Personality*. Together with Clara Sabbagh, he has edited the *Handbook of Social Justice Theory and Research*. He has also served as president of the Individual Differences, Personality and Psychological Assessment Division of the German Psychological Association.

Virgil Zeigler-Hill is a Professor in the Department of Psychology at Oakland University. Much of his research focuses on the darker aspects of personality (e.g., narcissism, spitefulness), self-esteem, or interpersonal relationships. He is currently associate editor for the *Journal of Personality*, the *Journal of Personality Assessment* and *Self and Identity*. He has edited eight books, including *The Dark Side of Personality: Science and Practice in Social, Personality, and Clinical Psychology* (2016), *The Sage Handbook of Personality and Individual Differences* (2018) and *The Evolution of Psychopathology* (2017).

Introduction

Revisiting Classic Studies in Personality and Individual Differences

Philip J. Corr

P ersonality psychology and related individual differences have become more prominent in scientific psychology over the past few decades, and their utility in applied fields (e.g., occupational selection) has remained undiminished – of course, these aspects of psychology have long fascinated wider society. As evidence of the vitality of the field, there are now quite a few dedicated journals as well as national and international societies and conferences. Reflecting the age of sophisticated genetics and brain imaging technology, it is no surprise that personality and individual differences are increasingly being studied within a neurophysiological framework, informed by evolutionary considerations, and aided by major computational advances which were unknown even a few years ago. The research field is now underpinned by some very impressive empirical studies entailing, in the case of the molecular genetics of personality, hundreds of thousands of participants. In recognition of these developments, there is now a journal, *Personality Neuroscience*, published by Cambridge University Press, devoted specifically to the field – founded and edited by the present author.

Yet, despite its prominence, the student of personality and individual differences – whether starting out or established in the profession – struggles to make sense of the vast and disparate literature that confronts them. It is often seen as far too multifaceted and complex to play effectively the central role it deserves in general psychology – this is its Achilles' heel. (It also reflects the 'two schools' of psychology – experimental/cognitive and correlational/differential – that have long militated against a unified psychology; see Corr, 2016, pp. 42–43.) This impression is unfortunate because the field has the potential to serve as a major unifying force to fuse theoretical, empirical and applied psychology – indeed, the field may well be said to be the principal bulwark against the fragmentation of psychology that, if anything, is worsening. Given this state of affairs, it seems appropriate to stand back and take historical account of the classic studies that have contributed so much to defining the field – they help to uncover the major themes that characterize personality and individual differences today.

ABOUT THIS VOLUME

The 14 classic studies revisited in this volume are ones that have, over many years, echoed down university research corridors, as well as informing and influencing applied (e.g., occupational) studies and practices. Few experts would look back on them and say that they have not been highly influential in shaping the field, especially as to how people *think* about the central issues that inform their own research and practice. A distinguishing feature of these classic studies is how far ahead of their time they were – beating a path through dense conceptual, theoretical and empirical undergrowth, enabling others to follow with greater ease, and sometimes greater acclaim – the studies that followed may well be more sophisticated in methodology and statistics (how could they not be?) but typically they have been less ground-breaking and much more incremental in their contribution. In this respect, classic studies are prescient, if not perfect.

CRITERIA FOR A CLASSIC STUDY

The choice of which classic studies to include in this volume was made no easier by the existence of two facts.

First, the field of personality and individual differences touches on so many other areas of psychology; and it goes from (distal) evolution, DNA, neurophysiology, through (proximal) developmental, cognitive and social processes, all the way up to the collective behaviour of society (e.g., political attitudes) – and in doing this it is required to encapsulate both individual and societal features. (In addition, the wide-ranging implications of the field means that it connects with some big societal issues; for example how organizations, both commercial and political, should use social media data to target the consumer and voter with specific persuasive campaign messages based on personality, 'psychographic', profiling.) Of course, no single volume can possibly do justice to this vast expanse of research; this needs something else, which has already been provided in the form of *The Cambridge Handbook of Personality Psychology*, edited by Philip Corr and Gerald Matthews (Cambridge University Press, 2008, 2nd edition, 2019).

The second fact relates to what the prominent personality psychologist Charles Carver noted to me when I was enquiring about the classic studies in the field: 'I think of shaping of the field in terms of bundles of literature, rather than specific studies.' This comment is an accurate reflection and it is, indeed, appropriate to acknowledge that personality psychology is characterized by the *accumulation* of research findings and, typically, it is difficult, if not outright invidious, to point to any single study as being the crucial one responsible for notable scientific progress. However, to conclude that there are no such seminal studies is itself a partisan position to adopt, and a vexatious one to defend. With the above caveats in mind, there clearly are classic studies that characterize the development of the field.

The final selection of 14 classic studies in this volume – which was arrived at only after a number of iterations, informed by experts – span the very diverse topics that define the field of personality and individual differences. (Although sometimes intelligence and cognitive abilities are included under the rubric of 'personality', this volume focuses on the non-cognitive literature – there are many classic studies from intelligence research that deserve their own volume.) However, it quickly became all-too-evident that many more studies could have been selected, but a decision had to be made: many were called, but few were chosen. This decision was guided by a number of inclusion criteria.

First, the focus was on those studies within mainstream personality psychology, as recognized by university researchers and teachers. This focus excluded those studies that may popularly be regarded as belonging to personality psychology but which have not shown sufficient evidence of 'progressive science'; that is, stimulation of empirical progress (psychodynamic notions fall into this category). Related to this first point, secondly, the studies chosen either report empirical data or set the theoretical stage for empirical research. An example of the latter is Jeffrey Gray's (1970) theoretical paper, which summarized extant empirical findings to recast Hans Eysenck's then-dominant biological theory of personality in a new scientific light (Chapter 7). Much the same may be said of David Buss's (1991) paper on evolutionary considerations which stimulated considerable empirical research and much debate (see Chapter 10). Even negative accounts of personality psychology – in this case, Mischel's (1968) critique of the entire field – provided the impetus that led to much-needed theoretical and empirical advances that served the field very well in the years that followed its publication (see Chapter 6). A third criterion laid emphasis on the degree of consensus among current personality researchers. Many of them were asked to nominate what they considered to be classic studies, and all came back with a long list – fortunately, many contained the same studies – that after some toing-and-froing resulted in the long list being whittled down to the 14 chapters that comprise this volume.

CLASSIC STUDIES NOT INCLUDED IN THIS VOLUME

The relatively small number of classic studies chosen meant the exclusion of purely theoretical contributions, as well as some highly influential books and monographs. Examples that readily spring to mind include: Hartshorne and May's (1928) *Studies in the Nature of Character (Vol. 1), Studies in Deceit*; Gordon Allport's (1937) *Personality: A Psychological Interpretation*; Henry Murray's (1938) *Explorations in Personality*; Murray and colleagues' (1948) *The OSS Assessment Staff, Assessment of Men: Selection of Personnel for the Office of Strategic Services*; and Jack Block's (1971) *Lives Through Time*. Also omitted are some influential papers, such as Cronbach and Meehl's (1955) paper on construct validity, and Guion and Gottier's (1965) influential occupational testing review that had a demonstrable impact on applied psychological research (e.g., personality and occupational selection/performance; e.g., Barrick & Mount, 1991).

REVISITING THE CLASSIC STUDIES

History has value in its own right: it is interesting to know the various ways in which the current psychological landscape has been shaped by past thinking and research. But, more importantly for a scientific perspective, it is essential that we *learn* from the past – learn in the sense of getting an insight into what constitutes the types of *thinking* that are destined to have long-term impact. What we really need to know is how classic studies broke new ground given the *conditions of their time*. This is the real value of any reconsideration of classic studies.

OVERVIEW OF CHAPTERS

The classic studies chosen are all different, in content and form, but also intention and impact. This fact presents a challenge to any volume that aims to achieve a modicum of coherence – and reader convenience – while at the same time being sympathetic to the varied nature of the studies. To help overcome this obstacle, contributors were asked to adhere to the following structure, as best they could, and to modify it where necessary: (1) background to the classic study; (2) detailed description of the classic study, including theory, methodology and findings; (3) impact of the classic study; (4) critique; (5) conclusions; and (6) further readings. Contributors rose to their task admirably.

Chapter 1 (**Webb, 1915**) presents the first major attempt to study personality in a way that is easily recognized today – it may be said to have empirically wrenched personality away from theoretical philosophy. It is arguably where modern personality psychology started. As Ian Deary notes, researchers in the psychology of individual differences take for granted that people can sensibly be described in terms of a limited number of personality traits. However, before Webb's time, the study of personality was little more than descriptions of how people differ – more literature than science. Webb's (1915) paper is specifically important because it was the first study to identify a personality trait by the use of methods now in widespread research use. Following a very rigorous data collection phase – itself served to inform future research – and in addition to a factor of intelligence, Webb extracted a non-cognitive personality factor which comprised 'persistence of motives', meaning consistency of action resulting from deliberate volition, or *will* – this Webb labelled w. This factor has much in common with the Big Five factor of Conscientiousness (see Chapter 5) but maybe others too.

Chapter 2 (**Allport & Odbert, 1936**) provides the first major classification of (17,953) English 'trait-name' words – previously non-comprehensive examinations were attempted (e.g., by the Victorian polymath and cousin of Darwin, Sir Francis Galton). As Gerard Saucier observes, this study made a number of significant contributions (e.g., highlighting that normal human life seems to depend on notions of personality and, thus, deserve serious scientific attention). As Allport and Odbert reflected, even psychologists hostile to the very idea of personality would not hesitate to write a reference letter in support of a student which is sprinkled with trait-like adjectives such as 'diligent', 'honest', 'friendly', and so on. This classic study formed the foundations for all subsequent lexical and factor analytical work in personality psychology, and like no other delineated the questions that personality psychologists should be answering.

The influence of Allport and Odbert's work is seen in Chapter 3 (**Cattell, 1943**), where the sophisticated statistical analysis of trait-names began in earnest. As highlighted by John Gillis and Gregory Boyle, Cattell set out to provide a comprehensive map of human personality, in both the normal and abnormal spheres – his tool of choice was the newly developed advanced statistical technique of factor analysis. This was not only a great personal undertaking but a major scientific achievement, and the enormous proliferation of factor analytical studies of personality that followed can trace their origins, and many of their techniques, directly to Cattell's early work.

Chapter 4 (**Eysenck, 1944**) takes a different approach to understanding the structure, and by inference causation, of personality. As discussed by Kieron O'Connor and Philip Corr, Hans Eysenck adopted that idea that normal and abnormal personality are located on the same (statistically described) dimensions – defined in factor analytical terms. Eysenck reasoned that by studying a clinical population (in his case, 700 'war neurotics' during World War II), normal traits of personality would be 'writ large' and, thus, could be identified and defined. From an analysis of a medical checklist, Eysenck identified the personality factors of Introversion–Extraversion and Stability–Neuroticism – we would be hard-pressed today to find a descriptive model of personality that does not contain these two factors in some form! (In 1952, Eysenck isolated a third factor, Psychoticism, which is similarly found, in some form, in modern-day descriptive models of personality.) Attendant with Eysenck's statistical work was a deeper understanding of the true dimensional nature of mental illness, and it is this very idea that increasingly is being applied to research and clinical psychology/psychiatry. In addition, in 1944 Eysenck was beginning to think about the biological nature of these personality dimensions – he discusses the work of Freud, Jung and Pavlov – which later he would transform into a fully-fledged neurophysiological model, which was to inspire others to follow in his footsteps (e.g., Jeffrey Gray; see Chapter 7).

Building on the earlier statistical work, Chapter 5 (**Tupes & Christal, 1961**) discusses the first major articulation of what was to become the, so-called, consensual model of personality: the Big Five. As John Johnson makes clear, Tupes and Christal wanted to find out why Donald Fiske (1949), when factor-analysing scores from a personality rating form very similar to the one used by Cattell, repeatedly found five broad personality factors rather than the 11 or 12 personality factors that Cattell led us to believe existed. Using real-world military samples, Tupes and Christal found, as they put it, 'five strong and recurrent personality factors'. In addition to Introversion–Extraversion and Stability–Neuroticism, the three other factors are: Conscientiousness and Agreeableness (seemingly opposite poles to Eysenck's Psychoticism), and Openness to Experience.

But trait psychology was never going to have it all its own way, and it did not, especially in the heyday of behaviourism and, related, social constructivism.

As presented in Chapter 6 (**Mischel, 1968**), this fact manifested itself in the form of a full-frontal critique from social (situationist) psychology which opposed the very notion that stable traits exist, let alone are responsible for driving behaviour. As Michael Eysenck (Hans Eysenck's son) discusses, Mischel's critique highlighted some very real methodological limitations of the empirical personality psychology literature. Mischel also highlighted what he saw as quite a few theoretical weaknesses; however, as discussed by Michael Eysenck, there was always something of a Straw (Wo)Man argument around this issue. Nonetheless, along with better designed and conducted personality studies, theoretical clarification came and, ironically perhaps, Mischel's main impact was to lead to improvements in research that considerably strengthened the field of personality psychology.

Now, a major problem of personality psychology has always been its very descriptive, correlational-statistical, nature. In comparison with the emerging experimental and computational advances of cognitive psychology, personality psychology seemed too vague, lacking *causal-process* models. Although Hans Eysenck promulgated the idea of 'experiments in personality' (e.g., by the use of drugs to move the individual along personality dimensions; e.g., caffeine leading to over-arousal and making, typically under-aroused, extraverts more like introverts), it was not really until Jeffrey Gray's work that a proper neuropsychological approach was advanced. Chapter 7 (**Gray, 1970**) traces his critique of Hans Eysenck's then-dominant biological model of personality. As a former student of Eysenck and highly versed in his work, Gray introduced the idea that underlying the major dimensions of Introversion–Extraversion and Stability–Neuroticism are individual differences in sensitivities to reward and punishment. Gray's early work was a wholesale importation of learning/behavioural theory into personality psychology, which included findings from elegant experiments in rodents (using drugs and neuroscience techniques to dissect behaviours into various classes that reflected the operation of separate reward and punishment systems in the brain), as well as evidence from human patients. This work led to the Reinforcement Sensitivity Theory (RST) of personality, which today is one of the major neuroscience theories of personality. But, as Neil McNaughton and Philip Corr show in their chapter, one major resistance to Gray's approach is its complexity, entailing unfamiliar and (sometimes exotic) behavioural phenomena (e.g., frustrative non-reward and the fear=frustration in the case of depression). To this day, Gray's work is not appreciated fully in personality psychology – this chapter explains why.

Chapter 8 (**Deci, 1971**) takes a very different view to the psychological consequences of reinforcement. As discussed by Richard Ryan and colleagues, Deci made a clear distinction between intrinsic and extrinsic motivation, and by so doing challenged the prevailing notions of behaviourist-based reinforcement theories – as well as neoclassically-inclined economic notions of the power of financial incentive. Specifically, Deci's theory challenged the view that external sources of reward lead to motivation. Among other things, this conventional view fails to account for spontaneous play and exploration occurring without *obvious* external reinforcement – the 'weasel' idea in behaviourism is that there *must* always be an influence of prior reinforcement, however difficult it is to identify (for an example of this reasoning malady, see Skinner, 1974). Deci's seminal study revealed the counter-intuitive finding that increasing external reward may lead only to short-lived (extrinsic) motivation and a decrease in longer-lasting (intrinsic) motivation. Deci argued for the importance of the satisfaction of the *basic psychological needs*: competence, autonomy, and relatedness. This early work flowered into an enormous research literature, leading initially to self-determination theory (SDT) and then to a number of related sub-theories.

Chapter 9 (**Bouchard et al., 1990**) moves us into a different area of personality psychology, namely the roles played by genes and the environment, and how these processes can be understood within an evolutionary framework. As detailed by Wendy Johnson, although genetic influences on behaviour and psychological characteristics are now widely accepted – they are supported by a wealth of empirical research – this was very far from being the case for most of the 20th century. With a few exceptions (e.g., Hans Eysenck), most psychologists held firm to the belief that our personalities are shaped by experience – this was the mantra of behaviourism, *for everything*. Bouchard's classic study revealed to us that the world does not conform to this tenaciously held belief – many psychologists were proved plain wrong. There is little doubt that this classic study represents a major turning point in psychological science. It encouraged subsequent research which has opened the scientific floodgates to both behavioural/statistical and molecular studies of psychological phenotypes, including personality and individual differences.

A related issue to psychogenetics are the roles played by evolution in shaping the human mind. As discussed by Aurelio Jose Figueredo ('AJ') and colleagues, Chapter 10 (**Buss, 1991**) shows the fundamental significance of evolution in personality psychology. Buss sets about dispelling many myths surrounding this topic and makes the positive case for taking evolutionary theories seriously. Specifically, Buss asked: 'Why does personality psychology need evolutionary theory?' The answers he gave proved highly influential and propelled the field forward. In particular, Buss saw their value as a way to address one of the less appealing features of personality psychology, namely to 'circumvent the plethora of seemingly arbitrary personality theories' (p. 3) – a problem facing the field to this day.

But, personality psychology is interested not only in theoretical matters and, what some might see as ivory-tower research, but also very real-world applications, as shown in Chapter 11 (**Friedman et al., 1993**). Margaret ('Peggy') Kern summarizes the results and implications of a seminal study that highlights the long-term effects of personality on health outcomes. At a time when many wondered if there was such a thing as 'personality', the Friedman et al. (1993) study looks beyond cross-sectional and short-term associations to consider long-term effects. The study examines child personality traits as predictors of mortality risk across seven decades. The resulting effects are small and correlational, but the findings suggest that traits are more important than previously thought. It triggered numerous longitudinal studies using archival data, which together have led to a greater understanding of life course processes. It has since been found that individual differences influence multiple mechanisms, which accumulate and interact across the lifespan ultimately to impact, in both positive and negative ways, meaningful life outcomes. A large literature in personality and health psychology now suggests that personality is not only of theoretical significance, but of considerable practical utility in terms of the length and quality of life.

Chapter 12 (**Funder, 1995**) addresses a major problem in personality research that has perplexed researchers, namely how to measure constructs accurately, especially as they tend to be abstract, 'theoretical', and often hard to pin down. Scientific research requires the operationalization of these constructs, and some form of measurement system is needed. Jeremy Biesanz discusses how Funder's work refreshed this field and reignited interest, even among those psychologists who were losing hope that much more advance was possible. In particular, in this theoretical paper, after a detailed review of history of accuracy research and the intensifying focus on error and bias, Funder outlines the Realistic Accuracy Model (RAM). As discussed by Biesanz, this model has a wide range of practical applications.

Now, another of the major challenges facing the field is how to account for *inter*-individual (between people) differences, as measured by personality *traits*, and *intra*-individual (within-individual) variations that characterize the *state* fluctuation of a person's behaviour (and thoughts, feelings, desires and so on) over time (ranging from minutes to years) – and, importantly, how states and traits relate to one another. This is an important issue because state variations are large, and, in fact, can be larger than the trait differences observed between people. John Rauthmann and Manfred Schmitt in Chapter 13 (**Fleeson, 2001**) summarize how traits and states can be reconciled in terms of 'density distributions': these summarize *individual* within-person trait-expressions in states (several intra-individual density distributions from single individuals can be aggregated to form an inter-individual density, trait-like, distribution). In this way, inter-individual traits may be seen to come from the density of intra-individual states. One positive outcome of this view is the widescale adoption of experience sampling, which is made easier and more sophisticated by mobile technology. Fleeson's work made us think about, and then research, the fundamental connection between these very different levels of abstraction and measurement, which hitherto seemed, if not irreconcilable, very difficult to unify within a common theoretical and measurement system. As a direct consequence of Fleeson's work, it is possible to resolve a number of long-standing debates (e.g., consistency/stability vs. variation, and structure vs. processes).

Finally, Chapter 14 (**Paulhus & Williams, 2002**), concerns itself with the 'dark' side of personality which has had a major impact on how we think about and research the opposite of the 'bright' side of personality. As discussed by Virgil Zeigler-Hill and David Marcus, this classic study focuses on the, so-called, 'Dark Triad: narcissism (grandiosity, unjustified entitlement and undeserved superiority); psychopathy (callousness, impulsivity and interpersonal antagonism); and Machiavellianism (devious, harm inflicting and manipulativeness). Zeigler-Hill and Marcus note that these dark aspects of personality have attracted a tremendous degree of empirical attention since the early 2000s and this owes much to the pioneering work of Paulhus and Williams. It is perhaps surprising that the importance of these dark aspects was not appreciated sufficiently before – although they have long been in the literature (most notably, Cleckley, 1941) – especially as their negative effects are played out in every quarter of life, often to a degree that is hard to ignore (see Babiak & Hare, 2007).

ORDER OF CHAPTERS: HOW TO READ THIS VOLUME

C hapters are presented in chronological order. This is more than mere convenience; it affords a temporal perspective that goes to show just how studies, even seminal ones, are built upon the foundations of previous work – this reflects Isaac Newton's own views on science as expressed in a letter to Robert Hooke (5 February, 1676): 'If I have seen a little further it is by standing on the sholders of Giants [*sic*]' (Some people think this was an insult to Hooke who was both diminutive in stature and physically deformed – if true, then a reflection on Newton's own, it must be admitted, peculiar, personality!).

However, chronology can be misleading with regard to the true course of scientific progress. For example, Webb's (1915; Chapter 1) study of personality had relatively little impact during the early years, but today it is seen as a major achievement; Allport and Odbert's (1936; Chapter 2) work clearly influenced R. B. Cattell's sophisticated factor analytical work (1943; Chapter 3), but neither seems to have had much of an impact on Hans Eysenck's own factor analytical work (1944; Chapter 4). What we now see as Tupes and Christal's (1961; Chapter 5) 'Big Five' personality description had much less traction at the time than Norman's (1963) work, which was along the same lines but which enjoyed the advantage of being published in the mainstream psychology literature rather than being buried in an inaccessible US Air Force report. In contrast, chronological progression can more readily be seen in Jeffrey Gray's (1970) classic paper which could not have been conceived without the prior work of Hans Eysenck. When viewing this history, we must be wary of falling into the trap of what might be coined *hindsight consistency bias*: looking back and seeing purpose and order in how things unfolded over time– the true nature of scientific progress is rarely so neat, almost always messier, and all the more interesting.

INTENDED READERSHIP

B efore agreeing to the commission of a new book, the publishing company will ask, 'What is the readership?', by which they mean, 'Who will buy it?' This is a fair question. *This* volume will be of value to psychology undergraduate and A-level students, who want a deeper understanding of the classic studies that underpin the field of personality and individual differences – such in-depth coverage is simply not permissible in standard textbooks. In addition, it will be of value to graduate students, researchers and those with applied psychological interests.

But it is not only for these target markets. As the book progressed, it became clear that classic studies are not well understood even by professors in the field. This was brought home by Chapter 7, in which Neil McNaughton and Philip Corr discuss Jeffrey Gray's (1970) seminal paper. Despite McNaughton being a long-standing research colleague of Gray's and Corr's PhD having been supervised by Gray on the very topic of his personality theory, it soon became apparent that the implications of Gray's (1970) paper were far from obvious. This was unexpected: we thought we knew the paper inside-out! This realization attests to the importance of revisiting classic studies in order to understand them fully in the light of current understanding. As world-leading experts have contributed to this book and have clarified the true significance of these classic studies, even seasoned professionals in the psychology business will gain new insights from revisiting them.

Any published book requires a dedicated editorial and production team. I gratefully acknowledge Luke Block, the commissioning editor who saw the value of this volume, and Lucy Dang, Becky Taylor and Katie Rabot – they have great personalities!

REFERENCES

Babiak, P., & Hare, R. D. (2007). *Snakes in suits: When psychopaths go to work.* London: HarperBusiness.

Barrick, M. R., & Mount, M. K. (1991). The big five personality dimensions and job performance: A meta-analysis. *Personality Psychology, 44,* 1–26.

Cleckley, H. (1941). *The mask of sanity: An attempt to clarify some issues about the so-called psychopathic personality.* Oxford: Mosby [www.cix.co.uk/~klockstone/sanity_1.pdf].

Corr, P. J. (2016). *Hans Eysenck: A contradictory psychology.* London: Palgrave.

Cronbach, L. J., & Meehl, P. E. (1955). Construct validity in psychological tests. *Psychological Bulletin, 52,* 281–302.

Eysenck, H. J. (1952). *Scientific study of personality.* London: Routledge & Kegan Paul.

Fiske, D. W. (1949). Consistency of the factorial structures of personality ratings from different sources. *Journal of Abnormal and Social Psychology, 44,* 329–344.

Guion, R. M., & Gottier, R. F. (1965). Validity of personality measures in personnel selection. *Personnel Psychology, 18,* 135–164.

Norman, W. T. (1963). Toward an adequate taxonomy of personality attributes: Replicated factor structure in peer nomination personality ratings. *Journal of Abnormal and Social Psychology, 66,* 574–583.

Skinner, B. F. (1974). *About behaviorism.* London: Cape.

1

Assessing and Enumerating Personality Dimensions

Revisiting Webb (1915)

Ian J. Deary

BACKGROUND TO THE STUDY

Today, researchers in the psychology of individual differences almost take it for granted that people can usefully be described in terms of a limited number personality traits (Matthews, Deary, & Whiteman, 2009). These traits are non-cognitive aspects of character on which people differ, usually with a normal (bell-shaped) distribution in the population. Traits are often derived from questionnaires using multivariate statistical methods. Prior to the scientific study of personality characteristics, there were descriptions of human personality for millennia. For example, Theophrastus's *Characters* was written in the 4th century BCE (Rusten & Cunningham, 1993; Diggle, 2004). Edward Webb's (1915) paper is important because it was arguably the first study scientifically to discover a personality trait using recognizably modern methods. Toward the end of the empirical part of his study of human character differences, Webb concluded as follows:

> We therefore venture to suggest (tentatively and with much desire for further evidence) that the nature of the second factor [after general intelligence], whose generality would appear to extend so widely in character, is in some close relation to 'persistence of motives.' This conception may be understood to mean consistency of action resulting from deliberate volition, or will. (For convenience, we shall in future represent the general factor by the symbol 'w'.) (p. 60)

Today, the leading model in the scientific study of personality traits is the Five-Factor Model (or 'Big Five') (Matthews et al., 2009). That is, there is much evidence, from lexical and questionnaire-based studies, that people differ with respect to neuroticism, extraversion, conscientiousness, agreeableness and openness (see Chapter 5). There is a broad consensus that these five traits usefully describe important aspects of human psychological variation (i.e., systematic and measurable differences between people). They are moderately stable across decades of adult life, are partly heritable (between about 30% and 50%), are found in different cultures, and predict important life outcomes such as mental and physical health. Of course, there are disputes. Some favour more (see Chapter 3) or fewer (see Chapters 4 and 5) dimensions. Some prefer to study narrower (e.g., sensation seeking) or broader (e.g., a general factor of personality) traits. Some personality schemes render and name the traits slightly differently. There is still no validation of the nature and number of these traits in terms of brain structure and function (Deary, 2009). Nevertheless, the Five-Factor Model is the currently best-agreed scientific model with which one might compare a classic study.

Several histories of the Five-Factor Model have been written (e.g., Digman, 1990; Goldberg, 1993; McCrae & John, 1992; Deary, 2009). Most acknowledge the work of R. B. Cattell (e.g., 1945, 1947; see Chapter 3) in taming, culling and organizing the huge number of trait terms listed by Allport and Odbert (1936; see Chapter 2). Their work leads into both questionnaire and lexical approaches to personality traits that have a lineage to today's understandings of the nature and number of human personality trait differences. The importance of Webb's (1915) classic study is that it was arguably the first to use recognizably modern methods to find a trait like conscientiousness. Moreover, although he did not appreciate it, we shall see later that Webb produced a dataset in 1915 that contained components resembling most of the five factors that are recognized today.

DETAILED DESCRIPTION OF THE STUDY

Webb's (1915) study was his Doctor of Science thesis for the University of London. A request for the thesis from the university brings a bound copy of the article. It was published as a Monograph Supplement to the *British Journal of Psychology*, a format that the journal did not continue for long. The article, with its preface included, is over 100 printed pages long, and has some large fold-out sheets containing correlation matrices. Webb's (1915) paper is similar in page-numbers length to Charles Spearman's (1904) paper in which the latter discovered general cognitive ability (usually known as *g*). That is relevant, because Spearman was Webb's doctoral advisor and is mentioned often in the article, the statistical methods are Spearman's, and the article may be seen as the discovery of the first general psychological (personality) factor after Spearman's *g*. There are several remarkable things about Webb's study, in addition to its length, namely its style, the study design, the data collected, the statistical analyses, the results and its latent content. Each of these is now described and discussed in turn.

STYLE

There are enjoyable literary and historical allusions throughout Webb's (1915) article. For example, the Preface addressed potential critics of the seemingly intractable topic of human psychological variation using Tennyson's 'Flower in the crannied wall'. Later, in excoriating pre-scientific conceptions of personality, Webb uses concepts from Francis Bacon's 17th century *Novum Organum*. For these and other literary-historical references, Webb does not mention the original authors; he expects the reader to know them. In several places, Webb's (1915, p. 23) writing explicitly recognized that he was taking the study of personality from pre-science to science: 'The present work is guided by the principle that neither casual observation nor dialectical discussion can furnish the groundwork of any empirical science, the decision between the conflicting opinions of descriptive psychologists must rest with definite, and as a rule, quantitative evidence.'

Webb's (1915) writing often has a critic clearly in mind, and is therefore reminiscent of Spearman's style (see Spearman, 1927). For example, as Webb (1915) moved to the very important Chapter V in his paper – 'A Second General Factor' – he had by that stage reviewed past efforts, had collected data and had analysed the intelligence variables (finding g, of course). He was then ready to look for any further general aspects of psychological variation, probably in non-intellectual traits. He wrote (p. 52) as follows:

> A few of these unwarranted generalisations [concerning human psychological variation, by past writers] which have been put forward are passion, will, pleasures and pains and their corresponding interests; strength and weakness of activity; speed of activity; vitality (sanguine, choleric, etc.); primary and secondary functions; spontaneity; easy and difficult reactibility ... But all that these writers have really done is to observe a person's actions to have certain characteristics under certain particular conditions. They have never produced, nor even tried to produce, any evidence of the same person exhibiting the same characteristics generally, that is to say, under varied conditions.

That last sentence is a pretty good approximation to what personality traits are. In this part of his paper Webb makes the connection with Spearman clear by stating that the clarity that his own work brings to personality research is like the clarity that the discovery of general intelligence (g) brought to the study of cognitive differences.

Toward the end of Chapter V, Webb (1915) stated his main discovery as an hypothesis, as follows: 'The evidence thus appears to be decisive; and we therefore venture to put forward the hypothesis: *That a second factor, of wide generality, exists; and that this factor is prominent on the "character" side of mental activity (as distinguished from the purely intellective side'* (p. 58, italic in the original). Also in this chapter were things one would expect to see in a modern Discussion section (i.e., a reflection on how the research integrates with and develops previous work, and some practical application). Indeed, the practical application is rather fun; it applies Webb's newly discovered general personality factor of 'w' (persistence of motives) to two highly intelligent thinkers: Isaac Newton (1642–1726/7; a high scorer on w, Webb reckons) and Francis Bacon (1561–1626; a low w scorer, Webb reckons). And Chapter VI continued the 'Discussion section' by addressing limitations in the research undertaken.

In summary, Webb's (1915) over-100-year-old (at the time of this writing) paper is a good read. It has the excitement of someone writing with awareness that he was among the first to conduct adequate-quality empirical research on important aspects of personhood. It is perhaps expected that one would have to make allowances for limitations in such an old paper in terms of its design, data and analyses. However, bearing in mind how the majority of personality trait studies are conducted today, allowances for limitations mostly would have to be afforded by Webb to today's researchers, and not vice versa. Early in the Preface Webb quoted Galton's (1883) urging that character should be studied more and that schoolmasters might be well placed to make assessments: 'It would be necessary to approach the subject wholly without prejudice, as a pure matter of observation, just as if the children were the flora and fauna of hitherto undiscovered species in an entirely new land' (p. v). What did Webb do?

DESIGN

In Webb's (1915) review of previous scientific studies of personality, his style was reminiscent of Spearman's (1904) review of previous work on intelligence. That is, Webb quite thoroughly described and assessed (as inadequate) prior work on personality. The review included historically important studies by Heymans and Wiersma (1909), and Pearson. Pearson's (1906) paper was rather dominated by head size, but did contain some modern-sounding personality traits. In essence, Webb started all over again, as follows.

Webb's (1915) study participants were 194 men, about age 21 years, who were students at a training college for teachers. About half were observed and tested between January and July 1912, and the other half between January and July 2013.[1] Each participant was assessed by two judges working independently. The judges were prefects from the training college, who also had dining-room and social duties. Each judge was allocated 20 or 19 subjects, selected so that they were persons with whom the judge was not especially friendly or the reverse.

From January until the Easter break, the judges were asked to make notes on each of their allotted subjects, having been encouraged to make these as widely as possible, in all work and social settings and on all aspects of behaviour: 'any ability, habit, tendency or quality is worthy of notice' (Webb, 1915, p. 11). They were asked to be unobtrusive and secret, and were given written assurance that everything they observed and noted would be strictly confidential, and that nothing would be used to the detriment or advantage of anyone. In the Easter break each judge was asked to write a full character-sketch of each of his subjects. All of this was preparatory work only; this work was not used as data. After the Easter break, each judge was given a 'Schedule of Qualities' on which to rate each of his subjects, again, over a college term.

DATA COLLECTED

The good aspects of Webb's (1915) design would not deliver good results if the data collected were inadequate. Beginning the work in 1912, Webb would have had few antecedents in terms of collecting personal qualities. He described his choice of the qualities to be rated on each person as follows:

The lists adopted in this work were made independently of these [clinical psychology records for psychiatric hospitals and prisons, with examples in a footnote] and were not (like the lists referred to in the footnote) casual collections of qualities, but were deduced on principle, and therefore—within the range contemplated—systematically complete. Qualities were included if they could be conceived as having a general and fundamental bearing upon the total personality, while other qualities which were obviously offshoots of these and dependent upon them were omitted. (p. 12)

There were 39 qualities (24 for the study of schoolboys) to be rated on each person; each was a sentence or short statement (see Figure 1.1 here). They were listed in the paper as: Emotions, Self Qualities, Sociality, Activity and Intellect; five items were added later. The judges were not given the names of these groupings. During and after the ratings, additions were made concerning physique (by a doctor and a physical exercise lecturer), athletics, general excellence of character (separately by the two judges, after ratings were complete, and by two members of the college staff), college examination results, and tests of intelligence. Five months after the ratings were complete, each judge was asked to write in detail about how they understood the meaning of each of the qualities they had been asked to rate. Webb (1915) summarized these reports in his Appendix II, and stated that there was good cross-judge agreement. Where there was less agreement, Webb stated (p. 17, footnote) that these tended to be instances where there was poor intra-pair reliability, and these data were discarded.

LIST OF QUALITIES USED IN SCHEDULES FOR STUDENTS

Emotions

1. General tendency to be cheerful (as opposed to being depressed and low-spirited).
2. Tendency to *quick* oscillation between cheerfulness and depression (as opposed to permanence of mood).
3. Occasional liability to extreme depression.
4. Readiness to become angry.
5. Readiness to recover from anger.
6. Occasional liability to extreme anger.

Self Qualities

9. Desire to excel at performances (whether of work, play or otherwise) in which the person has his chief interest.
10. Desire to impose his own will on other people (as opposed to tolerance).
11. Eagerness for admiration.
12. Belief in his own powers.
13. Esteem of himself as a whole.
14. Offensive manifestation of this self-esteem (superciliousness).

Sociality

15. Fondness for large social gatherings.
16. Fondness for small circle of intimate friends.

(Continued)

17. Impulsive kindness (to be distinguished from No. 18).
18. Tendency to do kindnesses on principle.
19. Degree of corporate spirit (in whatever body interest is taken, e.g. college, school, country, native place, etc.).
20. Trustworthiness (keeping his word or engagement, performing his believed duty).
21. Conscientiousness (keenness of interest in the goodness and wickedness of actions).
22. Interest in religious beliefs and ceremonies (regardless of denomination).
23. Readiness to accept the sentiments of his associates.
24. Desire to be liked by his associates.
25. Wideness of his influence (i.e. the extent to which he makes his influence felt among *any* of his fellows whenever he speaks or acts).
26. Intensity of his influence on his special intimates.
27. Degree of 'tact' in getting on with people.

Activity

28. Extent of mental work bestowed upon usual studies.
29. Extent of mental work bestowed upon pleasures (games, etc.).
30. Degree of bodily activity during business hours.
31. Degree of bodily activity in pursuit of pleasures (games, etc.).
32. Degree in which he works with distant objects in view (as opposed to living 'from hand to mouth').
33. Tendency *not* to abandon tasks in the face of obstacles.
34. Tendency *not* to abandon tasks from mere changeability.

Intellect

35. Quickness of apprehension.
36. Profoundness of apprehension.
37. Soundness of common-sense.
38. Originality of ideas.

And, added subsequently:

7. Degree of aesthetic feeling (love of the beautiful for its own sake).
8. Degree of sense of humour.
47. Degree of strength of will.
48. Degree of excitability (as opposed to being phlegmatic).
39. Pure-mindedness (extent to which he shuns telling or hearing stories of immoral meaning).

Figure 1.1 Webb's (1915, pp. 13–14) list of 39 qualities on which students were rated by prefects over a college term.

Webb (1915) instructed the judges to ask him if they had any doubts about the meaning of the qualities. Each quality was rated on a seven-point scale, from −3 to +3. The judges were instructed on approximately how many students should receive each score among their allotted subjects, so as to form a normal distribution.

STATISTICAL ANALYSES

Prior to substantive analyses, Webb (1915) checked the reliability of each pair of judges for each of the qualities in the schedules. He rejected data from pairs of judges where the reliability was not above about 0.3. The overall judge–pair reliability for all rated qualities for the students was 0.47, including those data that had low reliabilities and were later rejected. In fact, 87% of the data were usable, with a mean reliability of 0.55. He used the mean estimates of reliability for each quality (i.e., the mean of the reliability across all judges whose data were of acceptable reliability) to correct correlations in later analyses. He presented raw as well as corrected correlations in those analyses.

Webb (1915) took the pooled estimate of the two judges and then calculated the correlations between all pairs of qualities. He provided probable errors of each of the coefficients and also calculated the corrected correlations after taking into account the reliability with which each quality was estimated. Here, Webb was taking pains that one rarely sees in studies today.

Toward the end of the statistical methods chapter – which was quite concerned with reliability and producing correlations (raw and corrected) among the qualities, and with checking aspects of the intelligence tests – Webb (1915) moved to a new-ish method. Spearman had already used this method with cognitive tests (Hart & Spearman, 1912). This new method drove the rest of the analyses and produced the main findings on personality. Just as an example, he created two columns of correlations, one for the rated quality 'Profoundness of apprehension' and one for 'Originality of ideas'. The rows of each column were these qualities' correlations with all the other qualities. Webb (1915, pp. 32–33) explained:

> Each of these coefficients represents the extent to which high (or low) degrees of each of these qualities tend to be accompanied by high (or low) degrees of each other quality in the list. But quite obviously these two columns are themselves series of numerical values assigned to the two qualities, and the correlations between these is a further source of information to us. This coefficient represents not so much the extent to which the two qualities tend to occur in the same individuals as the extent to which they may be regarded as possessing, or not possessing, the same common elements from among the other qualities, and the same errors in the estimates thereof. Thus the coefficient of +.99 between 'profoundness of apprehension' and 'originality of ideas,' in becoming +.73 by this new method of calculation—the correlation of correlations—reveals the fact that the two qualities, in the minds of the judges, have many elements in common, and some, though few, not common ... If 'profoundness of apprehension' and 'originality of ideas' were exactly similar in nature we should expect that the correlation of their correlations would be +1; it is therefore easy to examine the columns and see which of the values are most responsible for producing the discrepancy (in this case between +.73 and unity). We thus have a means of analysing the 'build' of a quality in terms of other qualities.

Webb then presented a table (XIII) of 'correlations of the correlations' for 16 of the qualities for the students, and for all 28 qualities used in the schoolboys' sample. (This lengthy quote is important because it is the intellectual-methodological heart of Webb's paper – the point at which the then-quite-new correlation coefficient was used to move toward something more profound: the cleaving of a personality trait from these intelligence-personality data.)

RESULTS

The results of Webb's (1915) Chapter IV were largely about intelligence test data. Webb, like Spearman (1904) – but this time with a variety of cognitive tests – found a general cognitive factor among the cognitive tests. He computed, using partial correlation methods, the 'saturation' of each specific test with the general factor (g). It is important to recall that, at that time, there were few cognitive tests – Binet's tests, for example, were first translated into English in 1908. Therefore, Webb's (1915) results with the complex cognitive tests were quite novel, though incremental to Spearman's results with simpler tests (e.g., Hart & Spearman, 1912). Webb reported a correlation of 0.67 between the g extracted from the five intelligence tests given to the 1913-tesed students and their college examination results. This theoretically and statistically significant result alone would merit a substantial publication in recent times.

The correlations between g and the personal qualities were computed by Webb (1915), and one notable result was a correlation of −0.39 between g and ratings of 'quick oscillation between cheerfulness and depression, as opposed to permanence of mood'. Webb (1915, p. 42) concluded, with respect to intelligence-personality correlations: 'Collecting these observations, we may say that the possession of a good degree of "g," i.e., of pure intellectual ability (the general factor—whatever it may eventually prove to be—which produces the correlation between dissimilar tests) ... tends to occur in persons with stability of emotions, some cheerfulness added to a fair degree of sociality, with marked application to duty and some foresight and perseverance.' However, it was the preponderance of small and 'insignificant' correlations between g and the personal qualities that most interested Webb, and he concluded that that lack of association, 'furnishes some indication of the purity of "g" as a mental constant' (p. 43). An amusing (no pun intended) finding was that the only-moderate correlations between prefects' ratings of their participants' intelligence qualities were biased by their ratings of humour, something that had almost no correlation with measured intelligence. In ratings of intelligence qualities, Webb found some evidence for separation of other personal qualities, i.e., there are those that related more strongly with people thought to be high on 'quickness of apprehension', and 'originality of ideas', and those that related more strongly with those rated highly on 'profoundness of intelligence', and 'common sense' (pp. 43–50).

Webb's (1915) main novel results appeared in 'Chapter V: A Second General Factor' (pp. 51–66). He stated:

> There is no a priori ground either for affirming or denying the existence of further general factors [in addition to g], but the definite system revealed above in relation to the two-fold aspect of intelligence (as estimated) at least suggests the possible existence of another. These differences are chiefly related to character, and they seem to point to some degree of generality on this side of the mind also. (p. 51)

Therefore, he obtained his clue to there possibly being a general 'character' factor from the finding that ratings of intelligence-related qualities cleave with respect to their association with other personal qualities. What Webb emphasized and repeated in this part of the paper was that it is important to move away from a priori verbal generalizations that bring together character qualities as if they were linked to some broader general category. Rather, he was trying to find some empirically derived latent trait (he did not call it that) that provided what he calls a 'functional generality' among seemingly diverse character qualities, by analogy with what g does among diverse cognitive performances.

By applying Hart and Spearman's (1912) method of analysing the correlations of the columns of correlations between variables with other variables – with an additional step in the student sample of partialling out measured intelligence – Webb (1915) reported finding a general factor in character among those traits that are differentially correlated with quick- and profound-estimated intelligence. The qualities contained in this factor were as follows: it had positive loadings on 'Tendency not to abandon tasks from mere changeability', 'Tendency not to abandon task in the face of obstacles', 'Kindness on principle', 'Trustworthiness' and 'Conscientiousness'; and it had negative loadings on 'Readiness to become angry', 'Eagerness for admiration' and 'Bodily activity in pursuit of pleasure (games, etc.)'. In discovering this, Webb made the point (p. 60) that these qualities appeared from diverse over-arching character qualities, yet they are bound – in his terms, they have a 'functional relation' (p. 60) – with an underlying general trait, as follows:

> the persistence of a motive in consciousness, and its power to appear in consciousness at any time, even when the field of ideas occupying consciousness at the moment is little, if at all, related to it, seems quite reasonably to be at the base of moral qualities. Trustworthiness, conscientiousness, kindness on principle, fairplay, reliability in friendship, etc. are lessons derived from social education. These lessons will be learnt more effectively in proportion as they persist long and recur readily.

> Further, this theory—that of regarding all these qualities as being in some functional relation to 'persistence of motives'—seems to be in good accordance with the system of relations we have shown to be exhibited by the two aspects of intelligence. For 'profound' intelligence, as distinguished from mere 'quickness,' may be regarded as being a steadier and more stable grasp of the mental content ... [This continues on to the quotation at the start of the background section.] (p. 60)

There are three characteristics of this articulation of the discovery that resemble how Spearman dealt with the discovery of g: first, there was the method applied to finding the factor; second there was the search for an appropriate name and abbreviation for the factor; and, third, there was the seeking after a mechanism that explained the associations among diverse qualities.

Following the discovery Webb (1915) discussed in detail how others' ideas about personality had found similar types of variation. The longest section was devoted to some similarities in the empirical work of Heymans and Wiersma (e.g., 1909). The closest agreement was seen with Ach's idea of 'will'. The final words of Webb's (1915) study – before the Appendices – were a good summary of the main results:

> Turning now to our main thesis, we have been able to demonstrate the existence of a second factor exerting a widely-ramifying influence on the side of character.
>
> (a) Its generality has been demonstrated.
>
> (b) It markedly dominates all the correlations yielded by the estimates of moral qualities, the deeper social virtues, perseverance and persistence; also, on the negative side, qualities related to instability of the emotions and the lighter side of sociality.
>
> (c) *Its nature is best conceived*, in the light of our present evidence, to be in some close relation to 'persistence of motives'; i.e., *to depend upon the consistency of action resulting from deliberate volition, i.e., from will*. It thus appears to coincide more with Ach's conception of will than with either 'perseveration' or the 'secondary function.' Further evidence is necessary. (p. 76)

LATENT CONTENT

On the penultimate page of the main body of the paper, before the Appendices, Webb (1915, p.75) wrote:

> The investigation returned such an abundant harvest of results that it became necessary to limit the present report to certain broad features of character in general. It is apparent, however, that the material could be profitably examined in further detail—each quality is shown in its relations to all the others, and consequently a study of any one quality is assisted.

And 'profitably examined in further detail' it has been, for at least eight decades, as we see in the following sections.

IMPACT OF THE STUDY

We must beware of slipping into a counterfactual history of personality here, and over-stating the influence of the paper, especially after it was revealed what lay in the data (Deary, 1996). Although Webb's (1915) study is a classic in personality research, one would also be justified in viewing it as not very influential. The facts are: that personality assessments did not learn from Webb regarding the pains that should be taken to make individual assessments of traits; that methods of extracting multiple factors from psychological trait data grew elsewhere and did not follow directly from Spearman's/Webb's methods; and that the modern-seeming solution in Webb's data was not

appreciated until several decades later (Deary, 1996), when personality psychology already had that solution from multiple other sources. We saw above
that, although opinions differ as to how *w* fitted in terms of more modern personality schemes, some thought it was the first extraction of a conscientiousness
factor of personality.

RE-ANALYSES OF WEBB'S DATA

On the other hand, Webb's (1915) study was not ignored. Other researchers
appear to have agreed with Webb's statement: 'the material could profitably be
examined in further detail' (p. 75). Garnett (1917–1919) thought there were factors of *g* and cleverness (*c*) in Webb's data, and a third factor of purpose. Eysenck
(1953/1970) thought that *c* was more like extraversion than an ability factor.
McCloy (1936) reanalysed 31 qualities in Webb's data using Thurstone's multiple
factor analysis. This found four factors: (a) social qualities versus antisocial qualities; (b) positive action tendency versus negative action tendency/submission;
(c) individual qualities versus a tendency to merge with the group; and (d) positive
attitudes. Elsewhere (Deary, 1996), I judged that McCloy's analyses were unsatis-
factory because there were low loadings on factors after the first one, there were
items like 'physique' and 'athletics' included, and important-seeming items such as
'liability to severe depression' loaded no higher than .34 on any factor. Reyburn
and Taylor (1939–1940) applied multiple factor analysis with rotation to 19 of
Webb's items and extracted four factors. Factor 1 was 'akin to Cattell's Surgency–
Desurgency ... It can perhaps best be described by the antithesis between
light-heartedness and serious-mindedness' (p. 162), Factor 2 was called
Perseverance, Factor 3 *Charity* and Factor 4 *Social Sensitiveness*. Eysenck
(1953/1970) thought only the first two of these were meaningful, representing
extraversion and negative neuroticism. I agreed with the first but not the second
of these judgements (Deary, 1996).

I reanalysed Webb's (1915) data on the 39 qualities rated on the 194 training
college students (Deary, 1996). A longer description of the rationale, method and
results is given in my paper. I gave five reasons for re-analysing. Briefly: Webb had
left a high-quality dataset that had not, by then, been analysed adequately; histories of the Five-Factor Model had not seen such a structure before the 1930s/1940s;
Webb's study was the first factor-analytic-type study of traits beyond cognitive
ability; there was disagreement about what Webb had found; and Webb's design
and data were free from prior knowledge of the 3-, 5- and 16-etc. factor models of
personality. I applied principal component analysis (PCA) to Webb's correlation
matrix of qualities rated on the teaching trainees. I used the 45 × 45 matrix of
uncorrected correlations in Webb's (1915) Table IV, inserted between pages
26 and 27 of his paper. Items 40–45 were not used; some were not personality-
related and some were not provided by the raters. Therefore, the variables for the
analyses were the 39 personality traits (Figure 1.1), rated by prefects who had
been observing the students for several months. Six components appeared above
the scree slope (which is one criterion for knowing how many components to

extract) and these were then rotated using varimax rotation (ensuring that the components were independent of each other, i.e., orthogonal). My summaries of the six rotated components were as follows:

1. 'This factor emphasizes assertiveness, expressive anger, self-esteem, and a lack of concern for the opinions of others' (p. 997). I concluded that this appeared to be like an aspect of (low) agreeableness in the Five-Factor Model.

2. 'This factor incorporates the pursuit of pleasure, sociability, and gregariousness' (p. 997). I concluded that this appeared to be like extraversion in the Five-Factor Model.

3. 'This factor includes traits that are related to conscientiousness, perseverance, planning, serious mindedness, prudishness, will to achieve, and high principle' (p. 997). I concluded that this appeared to be like conscientiousness in the Five-Factor Model.

4. 'This factor appears to be associated with a search for popularity amongst others' (p. 997). I concluded that this appeared to be like an aspect of agreeableness in the Five-Factor Model.

5. 'This factor has facets of intelligence, originality, humor, and influence on others' (p. 997). I concluded that this appeared to be like culture/intellectance and openness to experience in the Five-Factor Model.

6. 'This factor is primarily relevant to the tendency toward negative moods and mood variability' (p. 998). I concluded that this appeared to be like neuroticism in the Five-Factor Model.

I submitted this study for publication. One referee made the suggestion that, in addition to my opinions, it would be good to have the opinions of other experts in the field. Twenty-eight international personality experts were approached, and 15 replied. The following agreed to help: Alois Angleitner, Peter Borkenau, Nathan Brody, Boele de Raad, John Digman, Vincent Egan, Hans Eysenck, Filip De Fruyt, Willem Hofstee, Paul Kline, Gerald Matthews, Ivan Mervielde, Robert McCrae, Robert Stelmack and Guus van Heck. Raymond Cattell sent a detailed letter. Raters were sent my rotated principal components solution with the full text of all 39 of Webb's (1915) items, and items' component loadings given to two decimal places (Table 1 in Deary, 1996). They were told that the analysis was based on an 80-year-old dataset and that the ratings were of trainee teachers. They were told nothing about my interpretations of the components. They were asked to estimate the correlation between each of Webb's components and the dimensions of the Five-Factor Model (FFM), Eysenck's three-factor model, and the five super-factors from Cattell's 16PF (I do not discuss these latter results here). For the major results, 10 of the raters provided full data. Table 1.1 here shows strong associations, as follows: Webb Factor[2] 1 (see above for the list of factors I obtained from Webb's data) with agreeableness (–.63) and psychoticism (.60); Webb Factor 2 with extraversion (.58 FFM, .60 Eysenck); Webb Factor 3 with conscientiousness (.61); Webb Factor 5 with intellectance/culture (.53); and Webb Factor 6 with neuroticism (–.57 FFM, –.60 Eysenck). Webb Factor 4 had its strongest association with agreeableness (.36). These were similar to my own judgements. They supported the view that Webb's dataset from 1915 contained factors that resembled all of the dimensions of the Five-Factor Model and Eysenck's three-factor model, all of which had emerged long after Webb's paper. Two of the raters, who did not contribute to Table 1.1's data here, independently took on the job of locating each of Webb's items in Big Five space, according to the lexical model. They then used Tucker's phi coefficients to calculate the correlations between Webb's components and the Five-Factor Model's factors (Deary, 1996, Tables 3 and 6). They were not dissimilar to the results in Table 1.1 here, though they found strong correlations between Webb's Factors 1 and 4 and agreeableness (all > 0.5).

Table 1.1 Means of 10 expert personality psychologists' ratings of the correlations between the six personality components found in Deary's (1996) analysis of Webb's (1915) data in Table IV and the dimensions of the five-factor model and Eysenck's three-factor model.

Personality model	Dimension	Webb factor 1	Webb factor 2	Webb factor 3	Webb factor 4	Webb factor 5	Webb factor 6
Five-factor	Neuroticism	.08	–.05	.02	–.01	–.10	**–.57**
	Extraversion	.15	**.58**	–.27	.09	.20	.16
	Openness	–.08	.04	.18	.10	.29	.06
	Agreeableness	**–.63**	.17	.18	**.36**	.19	.06
	Conscientiousness	.–23	.01	**.61**	.04	.10	.11
	Intellectance/ Culture	–.01	–.01	.24	.02	**.53**	.04
Eysenck	Neuroticism	.10	–.07	–.06	–.03	–.12	**–.60**
	Extraversion	.17	**.60**	–.26	.16	.24	.12
	Psychoticism	**.60**	–.00	–.26	–.21	–.05	–.08

Note: This table was re-drawn as an extract of some results in Table 2 from Deary (1996) *Journal of Personality and Social Psychology*, 71, 992–1005.

Although 'factor' is used as a column header the analysis was of principal components with varimax (orthogonal) rotation.

CRITIQUE OF THE STUDY

P art of the critique of the study was done by Webb (1915) himself, in 'Chapter VI: Consideration of the errors involved in estimates of character-qualities'. Here, as some more modern authors do, he managed to slip in some strengths while considering limitations:

> We all can and do form such estimates frequently under infinitely less favourable conditions than those of the present investigation—our personal adaptation to the social environment depends largely upon our ability to do this. In ordinary life, for instance, we meet a stranger at dinner, and after an hour's conversation we have made more or less decided judgments of him with reference to many qualities, such as candour, discretion, personal vanity, tact, humour, even honesty and conscientiousness. These 'first impressions' are very frequently, though not always, confirmed by subsequent further acquaintance. Our judges on the other hand were definitely and deliberately keeping their subjects under close daily observation for six months with the express purpose of making such estimates to the best of their ability. Further, the stranger we met at dinner is very probably aware that he is 'making an impression,' our subjects were utterly ignorant of the fact that they were under observation at all. Still, putting aside the question of exaggeration, there must be errors, and these are large as compared with measurements of material things. (p. 68.)

This eight-page chapter addressed problems due to: random errors; bias in the minds of all observers; problems with observers taking different points of view; and other irrelevant factors. Webb (1915) discussed how the checks on reliability and the detailed scrutiny of what each judge understood by the character qualities answered and mitigated these. He summed up by concluding that there had been a good check on possible errors, that some did not exist, that some that were found were put to his advantage, and that undiscovered errors could not upset the main findings.

Of course, it is a limitation that no women were studied, and that the social and educational background of the rated subjects and their raters was limited. Webb (1915) acknowledged that the people involved were well educated. Because it was at the heart of the study, the list of rated qualities could have had more description and justification, not least regarding their origins.

Commentators have pored over Webb's (1915) results through the years, trying to understand Webb's w and fit his data into their own personality schemes. Eysenck (1953/1970) thought w was the opposite pole of emotionality, as discovered by Heymans and Wiersma (1909). Walton (1959, p. 360) also interpreted w as the 'opposite pole of the neuroticism factor'. In this interpretation, w contributed knowledge to a subsequently discovered major factor of personality.

A second interpretation of Webb's (1915) w agreed with the above in thinking that the statistical methods were valid, but disagreed that a specific personality factor *per se* had been identified. Instead, w was interpreted by some as a nonspecific general indicator of how some people are seen as being generally good or the reverse. Thus, Burt (1940, p. 7) thought it was a 'general moral factor'. Others thought Webb had found results relevant to the so-called 'positive halo error' (Saal, Downey, & Lahey, 1980; Jacobs & Kozlowski, 1985; Fisicaro, 1988).

A third set of views on what Webb (1915) found in *w* aligns it more or less with conscientiousness in the Five-Factor Model, although the terms they used vary a bit. Tupes and Christal (1961/1992; see Chapter 5) thought it was like their 'Dependability', containing traits such as orderliness, responsibility, conscientiousness, perseverance and conventionality. They thought it was akin also to French's (1953) dependability and Fiske's (1949) conformity. Similar suggestions for the interpretation of *w* were as follows: 'perseverance–industry–tenacity' (Brierley, 1961, p. 274); 'persistence … thought to comprise component traits such as reliability, tact, and persistence of motives' (Feather, 1962, p. 97); a persistence factor (Battle, 1965); and, similar to the Conscientiousness dimension of the Big Five (Digman, 1990). However, Digman was inclined to use Will to Achieve or just Will (Digman & Takemoto-Chock, 1981); he judged that Webb had discovered this factor.

CONCLUSIONS

You should read Webb's (1915) study, long as it is. It is well written and fun to read, both in its style and its literary allusions. The design and methods are undertaken almost ex nihilo; this was the genesis of personality research. You will wonder – but not find out – how Webb's list of items turned out to be so good. The design and methods are thorough, and should shame the few minutes that most personality trait researchers spend in issuing and then collecting-in self-report questionnaires to/from their study participants. You will marvel at how much work Webb's raters did for him. The statistical analyses were very new – developed in the same lab, by Spearman – and following how he used these now-very-crude tools cleverly to extract factors from the rich and well-collected data is a joy.

My conclusion (Deary, 1996) from my re-analyses of Webb's (1915) data, and what the world's top personality psychologists thought of the results was as follows:

> It has been demonstrated that the latent structure of Webb's correlation matrix can justifiably be interpreted in terms of currently accepted major personality dimensions … The discovery that the data contain something akin to a model of personality that is broadly accepted today pushes back the 'discovery' of the Five-Factor Model by decades. That such a discovery, even if it was only latent in the original publication, should come from the laboratory that discovered the general factor in human intelligence, and which is the acknowledged home of differential psychology, underscores the historical importance of Spearman's influence in the study of individual differences. Further importance accrues to Webb's data because of the fact that it cannot possibly have been influenced by current knowledge of the Five-Factor Model of human personality. Therefore, it provides a blind test of Goldberg's (1993) claim that any adequate sampling of human personality terms will tend to contain about five broad factors.

That is why Webb's (1915) paper is a classic in personality psychology.

NOTES

1. There were also 140 schoolboys, approximately 12 years old, from four different schools. However, the results from the two groups are similar and I will mostly concentrate on the student sample.
2. They are components, not factors, but the use of 'factor' in this situation is common.

FURTHER READING

Deary, I. J. (1996). A (latent) big five in 1915: A re-analysis of Webb's data. *Journal of Personality and Social Psychology, 71*, 992–1005.

Deary, I. J. (2009). The trait approach to personality. In P. J. Corr & G. Matthews (Eds.), *The Cambridge handbook of personality psychology*. Cambridge, UK: Cambridge University Press.

Matthews, G., Deary, I. J., & Whiteman, M. C. (2009). *Personality traits* (3rd ed.). Cambridge, UK: Cambridge University Press.

REFERENCES

Allport, G. W., & Odbert, H. S. (1936). Trait-names: A psycho-lexical study. *Psychological Monographs, 47* (1, Whole No. 211).

Battle, E. S. (1965). Motivational determinants of academic task persistence. *Journal of Personality and Social Psychology, 2*, 209–218.

Brierley, H. (1961). The speed and accuracy characteristics of neurotics. *British Journal of Psychology, 52*, 273–280.

Burt, C. (1940). *Factors of the mind*. London: University of London Press.

Cattell, R. B. (1945). The description of personality: Principles and findings in a factor analysis. *American Journal of Psychology, 58*, 69–90.

Cattell, R. B. (1947). Confirmation and clarification of primary personality factors. *Psychometrika, 12*, 197–220.

Deary, I. J. (1996). A (latent) big five in 1915: A re-analysis of Webb's data. *Journal of Personality and Social Psychology, 71*, 992–1005.

Deary, I. J. (2009). The trait approach to personality. In P. J. Corr & G. Matthews (Eds.), *The Cambridge handbook of personality psychology*. Cambridge: Cambridge University Press.

Diggle, J. (2004). *Theophrastus: Characters*. Cambridge, UK: Cambridge University Press.

Digman, J. M. (1990). Personality structure – emergence of the five factor model. *Annual Review of Psychology, 41*, 417–440.

Digman, J. M., & Takemoto-Chock, N. K. (1981). Factors in the natural language of personality – re-analysis, comparison, and interpretation of 6 major studies. *Multivariate Behavioural Research, 16*, 149–170.

Eysenck, H. J. (1953/1970). *The structure of human personality* (3rd ed.). London: Methuen.

Feather, N. T. (1962). The study of persistence. *Psychological Bulletin, 59,* 94–115.

Fisicaro, S. A. (1988). A re-examination of the relation between halo error and accuracy. *Journal of Applied Psychology, 73,* 239–244.

Fiske, D. W. (1949). Consistency of the factorial structures of personality ratings from different sources. *Journal of Abnormal and Social Psychology, 44,* 329–344.

French, J. W. (1953). *The description of personality measurements in terms of rotated factors.* Princeton, NJ: Educational Testing Service.

Galton, F. (1883). *Inquiries into human faculty and its development.* London: Dent.

Garnett, J. C. M. (1917–1919). General ability, cleverness and purpose. *British Journal of Psychology, 9,* 345–366.

Goldberg, L. R. (1993). The structure of phenotypic personality traits. *American Psychologist, 48,* 26–34.

Hart, B., & Spearman, C. (1912). General intelligence, its existence and nature. *British Journal of Psychology, 5,* 51–84.

Heymans, G., & Wiersma, E. (1909). Beitrage zur apeziellen Psychologie auf Grund einer Massenuntersuchung [Contributions to differential psychology based on a large scale investigation]. *Zeitschrift fur Psychologic, 51,* 1–72.

Jacobs, R., & Kozlowski, S. W. J. (1985). A closer look at the halo error in performance ratings. *Academy of Management Journal, 28,* 201–212.

Matthews, G., Deary, I. J., & Whiteman, M. C. (2009). *Personality traits* (3rd ed.). Cambridge, UK: Cambridge University Press.

McCloy, C. H. (1936). A factor analysis of personality traits to underlie character education. *Journal of Educational Psychology, 27,* 375–387.

McCrae, R. R., & John, O. P. (1992). An introduction to the five-factor model and its applications. *Journal of Personality, 60,* 175–215.

Pearson, K. (1906). On the relationship of intelligence to size and shape of head, and to other physical and mental characters. *Biometrika, v,* 105–146.

Reyburn, H. A., & Taylor, J. G. (1939–1940). Some factors of personality: A further analysis of some of Webb's data. *British Journal of Psychology, 30,* 151–165.

Rusten, J., & Cunningham, I. C. (Eds.) (1993). *Theophrastus: Characters.* Cambridge, MA: Loeb Classical Library/Harvard University Press.

Saal, F. E., Downey, R. G., & Lahey, M. A. (1980). Rating the ratings: Assessing the psychometric quality of rating data. *Psychological Bulletin, 88,* 413–428.

Spearman, C. (1904). 'General intelligence' objectively determined and measured. *American Journal of Psychology, 15,* 201–293.

Spearman, C. (1927). *The abilities of man.* London: Macmillan.

Tupes, E. C. & Christal, R. E. (1961/1992). Recurrent personality factors based on trait ratings. *Journal of Personality, 60,* 225–251.

Walton, D. (1959). A children's apperception test: An investigation of its validity as a test of neuroticism. *Journal of Mental Science, 105,* 359–370.

Webb, E. (1915). Character and intelligence: An attempt at an exact study of character. *British Journal of Psychology Monograph Supplements, 1* (III), i–iv and 1–99.

2 | Classification of Trait-Names

Revisiting Allport and Odbert (1936)

Gerard Saucier

BACKGROUND TO THE STUDY

I n 1936, *Psychological Monographs* published an extended-length (171-page) article by Gordon W. Allport and Henry S. Odbert, entitled 'Trait-names: A psycho-lexical study'. The essence of the work was a classification of 17,953 English 'trait-name' words (terms distinguishing the behavior of one human being from another) into four categories. The first of these categories, dubbed as stable personal traits, was emphasized as the most immediately relevant for the study of personality. The study turned out to be enormously consequential for personality psychology.

Why did Allport and Odbert devote so much attention to extracting and cataloging all those terms in a language that might denote personality tendencies? Well, from a scientific standpoint, some of the most basic personality attributes might be discovered from studying conceptions implicit in use of the natural language. If a distinction is highly represented in the lexicon – and found in any dictionary – it can be presumed to have practical importance. Accordingly, folk concepts of personality (Tellegen, 1993) provide basic but not exhaustive (necessary but not sufficient) components for a science of personality attributes (Goldberg & Saucier, 1995). This is because *the degree of representation of an attribute in language has some correspondence with the general importance of the attribute in real-world transactions*. Therefore, when a scientist identifies personality attributes that are strongly represented in the natural language, that scientist is simultaneously identifying what may be the most important attributes. This would be a good basis on which to build basic tests of personality.

Application of this lexical principle had an important, beneficial effect on the science of personality at a key juncture in the 1980s and 1990s. Previous to this time, literature on the structure of personality characteristics was a maelstrom of competing inventories, mostly commercially sold (and so, expensive and inconvenient for researchers), embedded in a large mass of mutually isolated research measures. Application of this lexical principle has brought more order and

efficiency to the field, by enabling a consensual organization of personality concepts based on what is found important in the natural language.

Although Allport and Odbert's monograph reflected the most complete and
ambitious collection and classification of personality-relevant terms from *any* language up to that time, it was not the first. In an 1884 article on the measurement
of character, Sir Francis Galton (1884) – who was a cousin of Charles Darwin –
performed a non-comprehensive examination of an English dictionary and
reported finding some 1000 terms potentially relevant to the measurement of
character. A little later, Partridge (1910) had collected approximately 750 English
terms for 'mental traits'. Then Webb (1915; see Chapter 1) went beyond compilation of a list and actually administered a list of mental qualities for ratings (by
prefects, i.e., higher-level students) of a substantial group of 194 male college
students in England after months of raters' tracking the assigned students in pri-
vate diary entries. This might qualify as the first statistical study of personality
differences using trait-names derived from the natural language. Webb found a
general factor generally corresponding to self-regulation (see Deary (1996) for
a re-analysis isolating six factors). Although Webb's study predates Cattell's better-
known studies of this sort from three decades later (see Chapter 3), it took account
of only 39 qualities so is in fact of a different research genre than the study of
Allport and Odbert (1936).

There were also attempts at a lexical-study compilation in Germany, in the last
years of that country's dominance in the field of psychology prior to World War II.
A study by Klages (1926/1932) of natural-language German descriptors led to an
estimate of some 4000 relevant words. Apparently emphasizing mainly terms in
frequent use, Baumgarten (1933) compiled a list of trait-names in German, with
941 adjectives and 688 nouns.

Given these earlier studies as background, the study by Allport and Odbert
(1936) was not entirely groundbreaking. But it was an entire paradigm-leap forward in terms of comprehensiveness and differentiation. That is, no one had
exhaustively cataloged all the potentially personality-relevant words in a language, nor systematically separated out the most from the least personality-relevant.
In the seriousness and thoroughness of the effort it stands out, by comparison, as
extremely remarkable.

DETAILED DESCRIPTION OF THE STUDY

Allport and Odbert turned to Webster's *New International Dictionary* (1925),
a compendium of approximately 400,000 separate terms. To their consideration they added 'a very few' (p. 24) slang terms in common use (actually well
over 100). Combining judgments of three investigators (themselves plus a person designated only as 'AL', who may have been Allport's wife, the former Ada
Lufkin Gould), they built a list of 17,953 trait-names in the English language that
drew on the following criterion for inclusion: 'the capacity of any term to
distinguish the behavior of one human being from that of another' (p. 24).

This criterion excluded terms referring to common, non-distinctive human behavior (e.g., digesting, walking). Adjectives (e.g., irritable) and participial forms (e.g., irritating) were favored, nouns (e.g., curmudgeon) being included only if there was no corresponding adjective or participle or if the meaning of the noun was judged distinctive from those other two forms (e.g., conformist as well as conforming was included). To deal with adjective-variants of the same word, they listed only the most common variant.

Beyond simply indicating a trait-name's inclusion, Allport and Odbert went further and differentiated terms into four categories or columns. The 4504 terms in Column I were 'neutral terms designating possible personal traits' (p. 38), more specifically defined as 'generalized and personalized determining tendencies – consistent and stable modes of an individual's adjustment' to his/her environment (p. 26). The 4541 terms in Column II were 'terms primarily descriptive of temporary moods or activities'; many were adjectives denoting emotional and other states, but a majority of these were participles (e.g., salivating, gambling). Some hesitation was expressed in the separation of Column II from I, since state descriptors are fairly readily adapted into descriptions of more permanent tendencies (e.g., from anxiety to anxiety-neurosis, p. 28).

The authors were less hesitant about separating out the other two categories. The 5226 terms in Column III were 'weighted terms conveying social and characterial judgments of personal conduct, or designated influence on others' (p. 27), later abbreviated as 'social evaluations' to distinguish them from personal dispositions. As examples, whereas *absent-minded* was placed in Column I (personal dispositions), *addle-brained* went into Column III; *self-indulgent* went into I, but *self-involved* into III; *trustful* into I, but *trustworthy* into III. The other 3682 terms fell into the miscellaneous category in Column IV, labeled as 'metaphorical and doubtful terms' (p. 38). This last grab-bag category included terms describing physical characteristics and various abilities (provided these were not decidedly evaluative in nature).

Figure 2.1 provides examples of those judged to be the most frequently used English terms falling into the four columns, above 7.00 on a 0-to-9 rating scale, ranked top to bottom by their estimated frequency. The terms and their frequency ratings in the figure come from a study by Saucier (1997). As part of Saucier's study, 3446 personality adjectives (drawn particularly from work by Norman (1967) that followed up on Allport and Odbert; see Chapter 5), had their relative frequency judged in two successive rounds of ratings by American college students and community members, with all results reflecting aggregated high (.90 and higher) inter-rater reliability.

Allport and Odbert report in some detail indicants of agreement among the three judges making the classification, which serve to indicate a certain degree of arbitrariness in the classification. For example, only 39% of Allport's Column I assignments agreed with both the other raters, and only 39% of Odbert's Column III assignments did so. Overall, complete agreement on classification appeared to be present for about 50% of terms, although any pairing of the judges appeared to have 60–65% agreement on classifications, which would lead to kappa (agreement) coefficients in the moderate range, around .50 (Cohen, 1960) for a coefficient that runs from .00 to 1.00. One source of disagreement would be that the proportions of assignments to the four columns differed across judges, with Allport assigning the largest numbers to Column I, Odbert to Column II and III, and the third judge ('AL') to Column IV.

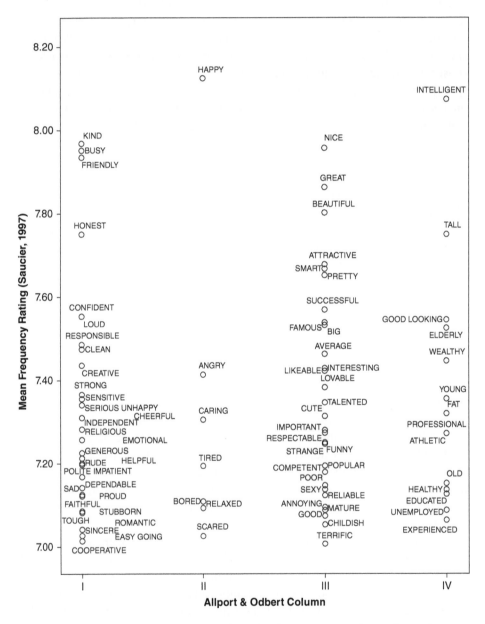

Figure 2.1 Adjectives with highest frequency of use, as assigned to columns by Allport and Odbert

IMPACT OF THE STUDY

The impact of Allport and Odbert's piece on subsequent work on taxonomies of personality was large, and has been detailed elsewhere (e.g., Angleitner, Ostendorf, & John, 1990). Notably, Column I, the personal trait-terms, was the main basis for Cattell's (1943, 1946; see Chapter 3) word-classification work that led to a smaller set of (160 or 171, depending on the source) word categories and eventually a set of 35 variables used as well by other investigators who identified the Big Five (Norman, 1963; Tupes & Christal, 1961/1992; see Chapter 5). And just as notably, Norman (1967) repeated the Allport and Odbert procedure using a newer edition of the same dictionary, arriving at a similar number of terms (18,125) and at a classification that led downstream to variable selections associated with the Big Five (Goldberg, 1990) and related six-factor structures (Ashton, Lee, & Goldberg, 2004; Saucier, 1997). The Big Five has become, and remained for at least a quarter century, the most standard model of personality variation in psychological science. Accordingly, the study of Allport and Odbert has been very influential, and to a degree far beyond its citation count, since it in turn influenced and was cited by enormously high-citation articles (e.g., Digman, 1990; Goldberg, 1990) crucial to generating the impact of the Big Five.

This is, however, merely a historical criterion of importance: the article was popular, and influenced what is popular today, so it is important. That alone merits a place in a history-of-psychology text, but in itself little more. In what follows, rather than a re-hash of downstream citation impact, I would like to gain more altitude and provide an original evaluation to highlight the continuing relevance of the monograph.

The manner in which I lay out this evaluation will essentially illustrate the principle that science is not religion. Science's mode of operation is not to generate infallible texts on which one might rely completely and forever. Rather, science's greatest works are openly susceptible to critique, and are crucial junctures in an evolving process. The value of a great work of science is partly what it demonstrates or accomplishes, and partly what it stimulates – based on what it leaves out, and how it can be critiqued. I will identify seven contributions made by this classic piece, as well as seven lines of critique each based on a problematic, questionable assumption adopted by Allport and Odbert. In a sense, these are a set of theses, each of which would contribute to Allport and Odbert's monograph being considered canonical for personality science (based on potential as well as previous applications), followed by a set of antitheses, each of which would undercut any canonical status. The reader is reminded that science ultimately goes against the canonical, so the existence of antithetical points of view does not invalidate the greatness of a scientific work. I will follow the thesis and antithesis sections with a short synthesis section arriving at conclusions going forward.

Contribution 1. Allport and Odbert cogently argue that, *basically, normal human life cannot proceed without some reference to personality dispositions.* Quite aside from the prefiguring of, setting the stage for, empirical work on personality structure, Allport and Odbert make an important point about the fundamental value of personality concepts. The naïve realism of commonsense personality description has a certain plausibility. There is no better argument than their trenchant words from the monograph:

> Even the psychologist who inveighs against traits, and denies that their symbolic existence conforms to 'real existence' will nevertheless write a convincing letter of recommendation to prove that one of his favorite students is '*trustworthy, self-reliant,* and keenly *critical.*' (pp. 4–5)

Indeed, it has not been observed that behaviorist and antidispositional advocates of the power of situations do either of two things: (a) entirely refrain from attributing dispositions in crucial contexts, or (b) apologetically admit that favorite students merely benefited from the situation afforded by engagement with their own eminent laboratories. And of course they do not. As Vazire and Doris (2009, p. 274) comment, 'capitulation to the "situationist" perspective (Ross & Nisbett, 1991) appears to compel us "beyond freedom and dignity".'

Contribution 2. Enduring words that describe attributes give some evidence of the reality of the attributes. Allport and Odbert indicate that the dispositions to which trait-names refer are more than conversational artifact, a form of everyday error (though in part they may be that). They are to some degree useful for understanding and prediction, as confirmed by later research (Roberts et al., 2007). There is, then, partial validation for a 'realist' view (cf. Funder, 1991) by which 'trait-names indicate corresponding realities' (p. 8). Allport and Odbert see a 'portion of plausibility' in the realist argument:

> Linguistic symbols have demonstrated utility; they have been tested through the ages for their power of representing stable facts of experience. If many human beings were not in fact *egotistic, aggressive,* or *timid,* the epithets would not have found a permanent place in language. (p. 19)

This principle – along with the follow-on assertion that 'the more often a disposition ... is encountered in the population the more chance it has of being christened' (p. 19) – became fundamental to the lexical rationale or 'hypothesis' that has been integral to discovery of and arguments for the importance of the Big Five personality factors (Saucier & Goldberg, 2001). This is the lexical principle referenced near the beginning of this chapter, that the degree of representation of an attribute in language has some correspondence with the general importance of the attribute in real-world transactions.

Contribution 3. Moreover, Allport and Odbert took it to the next step, recognizing that particularly with respect to patterns of personality, science can lean on and build on the body of commonsense concepts in language. Rather than relying exclusively on the top-down gambits of theorists, there is opportunity for a generative bottom-up approach. *A useful head-start on understanding personality is gained by collecting and codifying the commonsense concepts in trait-names.*

Admittedly, Allport and Odbert did not take this principle out to the full extent taken by modern lexical-study researchers (De Raad & Hendriks, 1997; Goldberg,

1981; Saucier & Goldberg, 2001). These researchers further reasoned that the covariation patterns among trait-names might lead to fundamentals of personality, in terms of factors. Allport and Odbert, in contrast, believed that factors were largely artifacts, and that little could be gained from studying patterns or average tendencies across a population. For them, it was enough that a compendium of trait-names would give resources for identifying the entirely 'personalized dispositions of single people' (p. 16).

Contribution 4. To their credit, Allport and Odbert recognized a difficulty inherent in personality language: *trait-names mean different things to different people.* To a degree, these meanings are contingent on one's 'habits of thought' (p. 4). One reason builds on the polysemy (multiple distinct meanings) that many words have. For me, the prime meaning of Curious may be 'inquisitive', but for you it might be 'strange'. But even if we agreed on one or the other meaning, we might still not agree on the degree to which 'to be curious' connotes something desirable or undesirable. This form of linguistic relativity between individuals might seem disturbing, or fuel for the nominalism that Allport and Odbert discuss and ultimately leave aside.

Disturbing perhaps, but since that time, the account provided by anthropology's 'distributive model of culture' (e.g., Schwartz, 1978) has yielded a useful analogy. By this model, culture is a complex pool of knowledge that is distributed variably across individual mind-sets, with some elements shared more widely, others less widely (Rodseth, 1998). Some individuals are better representatives than others of the central tendency in their cultural group. The model indicates a *cultural* relativity analogous to linguistic relativity, but also constraints on the degree of variation. It implies there is utility in aggregating understandings of meaning and relying particularly on the average. At least to some degree, this resolves the difficulty.

Contribution 5. Within science, the difficulty might be even further resolved by explicit communication and consensus. For Allport and Odbert, this meant *naming traits in a careful and logical way, and not merely codifying but also 'purifying' natural-language terminology* (p. vi). For example, the originally scientific neologism of 'extraversion' was popularized by Carl G. Jung, who attached to it an intended scientific meaning. It happens that Jung's intended meaning has not stuck, at least not in academic psychology where the consensual definition relies on various but highly intercorrelated measurement scales. A reasonable consensual definition is provided by Benet-Martinez and John (1998, p. 730): 'traits related to activity and energy, dominance, sociability, expressiveness, and positive emotions' – i.e., what such traits converge upon. This consensual definition is closer to the common-use meaning of extraversion than Jung's, but still purifies and standardizes natural-language terminology. There can be important difference between the 'purified' (measurement-tethered, so potentially enduring over time) way scientists use the concept, and laypersons' casual use of the term. The purification inherent in scientific terminology is likewise evident in the adoption of originally obscure natural-language phrasings like 'behavioral activation' or 'reward-dependence' into concepts with precise, measureable meaning. The purification operates even more so for refinements of natural language. Science can reduce the problematic linguistic relativity in trait-names.

Contribution 6. Allport and Odbert's monograph serves also to introduce two enduring foci for the science of personality. For them then, and for the field now, *personality psychology has a particular interest in (i) enduring attributes and in (ii) the 'biophysical' (biological) bases of attributes.* Allport and Odbert's prime interest was in tendencies that are 'consistent and stable modes of an individual's adjustment to his environment' rather than 'merely temporary and specific behavior' (p. 26). Moreover, they sought 'objective, neuropsychic dispositions' (p. 4), at least to the degree these could be inferred from the laboratories and armchairs of the 1930s! These twin emphases, however, remain hallmarks of the field, as reflected in various influential models (Cloninger, Svrakic, & Przybeck, 1993; Corr, 2004; Eysenck, 1970; McCrae & Costa, 2008).

Contribution 7. But Allport and Odbert were observant enough to not sink into a biophysical reductionism. The monograph contains an insightful perception, that *trait-names reflect a combination of the biophysical influences and something more cultural* (perhaps historically varying). Though they considered it 'unfortunate for scientific psychology' (p. 2), characterizations of human qualities are determined partly by 'standards and interests peculiar to the times' (p. 2) in a particular social epoch. Examples they provide include the Galenic humors, astrological superstition (e.g., jovial, lunatic), Church-endorsed Christian virtues (e.g., pity, patience), the subjective influences of 18th-century literature (e.g., enthusiastic, depressed), and recent contributions of psychological jargon (e.g., neurotic, schizoid). Rather than corresponding to 'fixed varieties of human dispositions' arising from the reality of neuropsychic dispositions, and found throughout the ages and regardless of culture, trait-names are partly 'invented in accordance with cultural demands' (p. 3). Implicit here, then, is a kind of dual-process, biocultural theory for the origin of trait-names, a theory that seems enduringly sensible.

A summary of contributions, beyond mere historical importance, identified in the foregoing section would then include the following. Allport and Odbert make a cogent case for the importance of personality dispositions, and suggest that those words/concepts that endure imply at least some reference to reality; therefore scientists can get a head-start on understanding personality by understanding the stock of natural-language concept-representing traits. On the other hand, they are able to recognize some interpersonal relativity in the meaning of trait-names, which reinforces a responsibility for scientists to improve on and standardize such terminology. And although they (Allport and Odbert) would prefer that scientific personality concepts refer to those enduring tendencies that have a 'biophysical' basis, in fact the sources of trait-names also involve historically and culturally specific factors.

CRITIQUE OF THE STUDY

This last point makes for an easy transition to the first of the questionable assumptions, which introduce some limitations on the absoluteness of the contribution. I will identify these next, labeled more briefly as a series of 'caveats'.

Caveat 1. Allport and Odbert deserve credit for recognizing the cultural imprints on content in trait-names. But they do not go far in this direction, perhaps characteristic of their time, when there was no (cross-)cultural psychology. Specifically, *they ignore and give short-shrift to culture, both with regard to issues of cross-cultural generalizability and of how traits themselves may reflect culture-relevant contents.* Let me explain both points.

The monograph never recommends that a scientist consult any compendium of trait-names other than one composed of English terms. Rather than lingering in a kind of ethnocentric bias, Allport and Odbert *could* have applied a cross-cultural generalizability criterion, by which important traits are indicated not merely by trait-names enduring within one language, but by having corresponding versions in many languages. Indeed, such cross-cultural generalizability could well strengthen the case for a given trait having a biophysical basis, since neuropsychic dispositions would presumably not differ greatly between populations. As an example, a study by Saucier, Thalmayer and Bel-Bahar (2014) found evidence that concepts like *jealous, disobedient, wise* and *foolish* are more cross-culturally ubiquitous than concepts like *disciplined, organized, assertive* and *introspective*. If we expect viable neuropsychic dispositions to be noticeable anywhere, in any societal context, then wouldn't the difficulty of translating the English word 'assertive' into many languages (which has been the author's own experience) suggest this disposition is not a good candidate for being called neuropsychic? Allport and Odbert apparently tend to assume that culture is always transient and local.

Moreover, certain traits appear to be very much 'about' culture – or rather the specific norms, standards, values and beliefs of a society. To stick to examples from the monograph's Column I (personal traits), *polite* and *rude* refer to whether one does or does not adhere to certain social norms, whereas *conventional* and *unconventional* apply analogously to less binding descriptive norms specific to a culture. To be *religious* is in good part to adhere to a particular subculture and its belief-system. And the social evaluations in the monograph's Column III (e.g., *mature, respectable, strange*) frequently seem to involve comparison to cultural standards for behavior. As in these examples, might there not be 'real' traits that are driven and determined by dynamics of culture, even perhaps in a rather ubiquitous way? And to the extent these dynamics recur across cultures, the associated trait tendencies might also recur.

Caveat 2. To linger on the theme of culture for a moment, consider the very individualistic nature of Allport and Odbert's formulations about traits. According to their distinctive 'trait hypothesis' (p. 12), no two persons 'possess precisely the same trait' (p. 14) and each 'individual differs in every one of his traits from every other individual' (p. 18). These are very idiothetic conceptions, that is, they emphasize unique, situational, subjective, or cultural phenomena rather than generalizing or proposing laws that would always or usually apply. According to such idiothetic conceptions, traits are not 'measurable excepting in a remote and approximate sense' (p. 16), and must be discovered 'in each individual life separately through the use of more direct clinical and experimental methods' (p. 13). This reflects the emphasis of what Triandis and Gelfand (1998) labeled 'horizontal individualism' – the importance of a person's distinctness, uniqueness and characteristics independent of others, a cultural value prominent in America and the West. The problem is not that individualism is wrong; rather, *it may be ethnocentric to impose an individualistic filter throughout personality psychology, and in fact such idiothetic approaches are outside the mainstream of current and recent personality psychology.*

This is not, of course, the only idiothetic-oriented theory or model ever to arise in the field of personality science. James Lamiell, who like Allport was much influenced by William Stern, has carried forward an unapologetically idiothetic 'critical personalism' based on Stern (Lamiell & Laux, 2010). George Kelly's signature Role Construct Repertory Test (Bell, 2005) reflected a fundamentally idiothetic organization of personal constructs. Narrative approaches, such as those that emphasize the integrative and causal impact of life-stories or dominant themes that emerge from narratives (e.g., McAdams, 1993), have a rather idiothetic cast. And because of its phenomenological presuppositions, humanistic psychology tends rather toward the idiothetic. However, none of these have ever taken over the mainstream of personality psychology, as Allport himself tragically lamented in his last comment on the matter (Allport, 1966). Scientific unpopularity (at least for a time) is not itself a problem, but sometimes the failure to catch on reflects a lack of compelling evidence. It appears that personality psychology has gained much from attention to average (i.e., nomothetic) tendencies in the population. Here, Allport and Odbert seem in retrospect to be out of step.

It might seem odd to the psychological sensibility of this current time to couple a devotion to idiothetic individuality with a priority for neuropsychic dispositions. But the two are not necessarily incompatible. For instance, if genomic and neurological tendencies manifested themselves coherently at the individual level in a highly *emergent* and nonadditive manner contingent crucially on subtle variations at a global level, this would direct attention to the unique genome or the unique brain, rather than resemblances among close biological kin. In that case, an idiothetic approach might indeed be the most fruitful.

Caveat 3. Another aspect of the thinking in Allport and Odbert's monograph that might appear odd, in retrospect, is the notion of a single, cardinal trait that provides determining tendencies in an individual life. It is not just that the monograph argues for 'personalized dispositions of single people' (p. 16), but that these unique patterns are portrayed as 'generalized determining tendencies' (p. 13). On this view, a particular attribute becomes so pervasive in a person that it becomes a distinct focus of organization. Then, it is not just a discernible or observable trait in the person, but a dominant or cardinal trait. Seventy years later, *there seems still to be a lack of evidence for cardinal traits that perform a more or less hostile takeover, coming to determine and structure the remainder of the personality system.*

The cardinal-trait idea, of course, is attractive to the human mind. It is not so far from the 'one underlying disease model' prominent in medical diagnosis. There, given a set of symptoms, the impetus is on identifying the single underlying disease that drives all the symptoms simultaneously. In the field of medicine, it would not be radical to suggest that a typical patient suffers from some cardinal disease or disorder-condition that would serve to make sense of many diverse symptoms.

But applied to the complexity of human psychology, the notion seems romantic, an oversimplifying narrative assuming that, in the course of development, an individual mind and behavior typically arrives at a high degree of consistency that is simultaneously a quite unique kind of consistency. In my view, better fitting the data would be a contrasting model, a more dynamic perspective under which there is tension within the personality between conflicting motives and trends, and thus some ambivalence and oscillation and unsettledness. Such a model would help make sense of the heterogeneity of personality tendencies that lays out well into dimensional constructs, with bipolar ends of the continua that help reveal the nature of the most important conflicts between motives and trends.

Caveat 4. Allport and Odbert argue for the desirability of neutral terminology in science. This certainly is not a radical view. Unfortunately, it appears that *they extend the desire for unweighted emotion-free vocabulary into the very attribute-contents evident in the trait-names in language, with confusing consequences.* On this view, the trait-names in language that are judgmental and 'emotionally toned' (p. v), having affective polarity, are suspect and less worthy of study than the neutral ones. This is sensible from the standpoint of their adoption directly into scientific discourse. But affectively toned concepts like evil and virtue are particularly worthy of study particularly because of their extreme affective tone, in that this extremity underlines their importance to human observers. It would seem odd for psychologists to refuse to study evil or its manifestations because the whole concept is too judgmental, although this is where the monograph's relegation of such concepts to an exclusion category would leave us. In line with the desirability of more neutral terminology in science, of course, we might expect the psychologist to frame the studies as being directed toward sadism or violence or coercion or abuse (terms discernibly more neutral). The point is that one can achieve neutral scientific terminology while studying affectively charged subjects; the desire for the former should not prevent the latter. Of course, the monograph may merely reflect a particular zeitgeist – its historical period within the development of psychology: Allport and Odbert inhabited the era of behaviorism with its hands-off attitude toward emotions, and of philosophers like A. J. Ayer (1936) and C. L. Stevenson (1944) who are called emotivists, because they suggested that moral judgments could be essentially reduced to being mere emotional outbursts.

The attitude toward emotion and affect in contemporary psychology is much different. Modern understandings of personality structure (since Eysenck) fully integrate emotional tendencies. In fact, many of the largest factors can be related to affect: neuroticism to a predisposition toward negative emotions of an internalizing nature, low agreeableness to negative emotions of an externalizing nature, and extraversion to positive emotions. From this perspective, the relegation of trait-names like *angry, happy* and *scared* to an exclusion category (as in the 1936 monograph) seems unwise.

It is also the case that locating 'unweighted vocabulary' is not so easy in the realm of natural language. Adjectives referring to personality – and probably adjectives descriptive of persons in general – have a distinctly bimodal distribution with respect to their levels of desirability or favorability (Cruse, 1965). The result is that research projects seeking distinctly neutral descriptions of person-ality (e.g., Saucier, 1994) are challenging; neutral personality adjectives tend to be relatively unfamiliar adjectives. In this light, taking Allport and Odbert's impera-tive for neutral description to an extreme would be a merely heroic (perhaps quixotic) quest, unless done with considerable precision as in the careful test-development procedures of Jackson (1970). Still, the gain in apparent objectivity from constraining oneself to neutral description may be offset by the loss in real-world importance from excluding what is consensually judged to be especially desirable or undesirable.

Caveat 5. An empirical result of Allport and Odbert's study was that the numer-ically largest category of trait-names was social evaluation. However, *they offer no account for why the third column – reflecting social judgments likely unconnected with biophysical traits – would be the biggest component in person perception.* To be fair, scrutiny of a table (p. 35) indicates it was only the biggest category for Odbert, and merely the second biggest for Allport and the third judge ('AL'); but it is the more reliable aggregate (combined data) that counts here.

The salience of highly evaluative social judgments appears to be no fluke. The earlier-presented figure (Figure 2.1) plots 86 person-descriptive adjectives having the highest level of frequency-of-use according to pooled reliable ratings based on 112 judges (as collected in the studies of Saucier, 1997). For high level of recurrent use, the social-evaluation concepts clearly give the personal dispositions (in Column I) a run for their money; it is columns II and IV that have less salience than their numbers in the 1936 monograph would suggest. And the sort of evaluative concepts empha-sized in column III – competence and morality – were found in studies of diverse, mutually isolated languages to be among the most ubiquitous, more so than most dispositional concepts that would be found in column I (Saucier et al., 2014). There is something fundamental about social evaluations for personality psychology to take account of, and Allport and Odbert don't take us there. After all, these authors counse-led that such 'evaluative (characterial) terms … should be avoided by psychologists' (p. vii) unless actually studying social judgment or mere subjective impressions, evalu-ative terms argued to be more appropriate for educators or moralists.

What might such an account be? The most evaluative personality language (evi-dent in English most extremely in the type-noun vocabulary with its references to jerks, sleazeballs and fully expletive descriptions; Saucier, 2003) concerns violation of or adherence to moral norms. This is consistent with the principles that (a) culture centers on social and moral norms, and (b) moral character (empirically a central dimension arising out of personality lexicons) is primarily about norm-oriented self-regulation (Saucier, 2017). Comparing individual behavioral tendencies to cultural standards and norms is so greatly important in social cognition that language bears the residue in a surprisingly oversized social-evaluation vocabulary, not to mention the difficulty one encounters in trying to describe someone's dispositions in a way that completely lacks a social-evaluative connotation.

Caveat 6. Another problem follows closely on the aforementioned problem of lacking an account for the large size of the purportedly non-useful social evaluations category. On several fronts, *the notion that censorial and moral terms – and virtues, vices, whatever is associated with blame or praise, not to mention social effects – have no use for a psychologist seems now obsolete.* Allport and Odbert placed in the Column III exclusion category terms like *agreeable, amicable, amoral, beneficient, ethical, fair, honorable, immoral, innocent, moral, noble, proper, trustworthy, unethical* and *upright.* But interest in prosocial (and antisocial) behavior has grown within psychology. Personality dimensions relevant to such behavior (e.g., agreeableness, honesty) have been incorporated increasingly into research over the last three decades. Allport and Odbert cite (p. 11) the Hartshorne and May (1928) study that ostensibly found little consistency in manifestations of dishonesty across situations, but a re-analysis of those data (Burton, 1963) indicates plenty of evidence for a moral trait-dimension. Reading the Allport/Odbert monograph, one might pick up the implication that moral and evaluative standards vary across historical and cultural contexts in a highly relativistic way, but there is evidence that cultures do not differ greatly on value priorities or on levels of moral traits (at least in self-report data) (Saucier et al., 2015). The vigor and utility of contemporary moral psychology, nonexistent in Allport's day, also tends to undercut the monograph's advocacy for excising moral terms from personality psychology. And finally, also included in Column III were 'social effect' terms indicative of an individual's social stimulus value (e.g., *annoying, charming, entertaining*), but recent studies indicate an interesting psychology behind them, reflective of basic variations in human motivation (Saucier, 2010). In sum, scientific developments seem to have overtaken Allport and Odbert's tendency to derogate their large (Column III) category of social evaluations. It no longer appears realistic to ignore morality and ethics.

Caveat 7. This problem is presented last for a reason: its outlines are sharpened by having the previously described problems in the background. In concluding their preface, Allport and Odbert state that the 'usefulness of our classification, we feel, is not in the slightest degree dependent upon the acceptance of any particular theory of the nature of human traits' (p. viii). Instead, they aver, they are simply providing data others may use in producing 'new and better theories of personality' (p. viii). They do imply that exclusive reliance on Column I (personal dispositions) might be to embrace their own 'special theory of traits' (p. viii). I argue that, here, the authors had an exaggerated estimate of their own objectivity, and we have here something of a theory-infused wolf dressed in the objective innocence of a sheep. *To accept at face value the particular Allport and Odbert classification of trait-names into four categories is to take on the assumptions of a specialized theory of traits*, whose main propositions can be construed based on the classification itself. Under this theory, attention to emotions and morality would distract us from the central aspects of personality which reflect enduring consistencies operating intrinsically in the person, and outside the influence of society (the standards of society being in constant flux).

One might construct alternative specialized theories that put the priority on other columns. For example, a Column-II, temporary-state-based theory might state that traits are mainly more or less enduring residues of temporary states (perhaps rather like those 'density distributions of states' in the proposals of Fleeson, 2001). A Column-III-based theory might propose that trait-concepts first and foremost evaluate, with a side-helping of some descriptive element to add specificity and context to the judgment; in other words, by this alternative theory, personality primarily concerns good vs. bad reputation, good vs. bad consequences), and good vs. bad effects on others (cf., Hogan, 1983). It should also be noted that later classifications of personality terms that followed on Allport and Odbert (Angleitner et al., 1990; Saucier, 1997) used more than four categories (adding, for example, abilities, attitudes and worldview, and descriptions of physique and appearance), which give even more possibilities for theoretical variation by prioritizing one or another category.

CONCLUSIONS

Allport and Odbert made a crucial empirical contribution in their classification of English trait-names, and added to that a realistic and nuanced dispositionalism that takes account of the importance of 'biophysical' bases. But in the process they bring along some questionable assumptions that, I would argue, should at least subjected to continuing debate. These involve the existence of cardinal traits, an over-insistence on neutral concepts, the supposed irrelevance of morality to psychology, and an insensitivity to matters of culture.

As argued earlier, science is not religion, and a crucial scientific text is rarely infallible. In fact, identifying limitations and caveats on influential works is a constructive operation in science. And there is much that is prescient. Although personality psychology has moved on since the time of Allport and Odbert (1936), there is still much that we can take from their monograph, moving forward, in the way of gem-like insight.

FURTHER READING

De Raad, B., & Hendriks, A. A. J. (1997). A psycholexical route to content coverage in personality assessment. *European Journal of Psychological Assessment, 13*, 85–98.

Goldberg, L. R. (1981). Language and individual differences: The search for universals in personality lexicons. In L. W. Wheeler (Ed.), *Review of personality and social psychology*. Beverly Hills, CA: Sage.

Saucier, G., & Goldberg, L. R. (2001). Lexical studies of indigenous personality factors: Premises, products, and prospects. *Journal of Personality, 69*, 847–879.

REFERENCES

Allport, G. W. (1966). Traits revisited. *American Psychologist, 21*, 1–10.

Allport, G. W., & Odbert, H. S. (1936). Trait-names: A psycho-lexical study. *Psychological Monographs, 47* (1, Whole No. 211).

Angleitner, A., Ostendorf, F., & John, O. P. (1990). Towards a taxonomy of personality descriptors in German: A psycho-lexical study. *European Journal of Personality*, *4*, 89–118.

Ashton, M. C., Lee, K., & Goldberg, L. R. (2004). A hierarchical analysis of 1,710 English personality-descriptive adjectives. *Journal of Personality and Social Psychology*, *87*, 707–721.

Ayer, A. J. (1936). *Language, truth, and logic*. London: Gollancz.

Baumgarten, F. (1933). Die Charaktereigenschaften [The character traits]. In *Beitraege zur Charakter- und Persoenlichkeitsforschung* (Whole No. 1). Bern: A. Francke.

Bell, R. C. (2005). The repertory grid technique. In F. Fransella (Ed.), *The essential practitioner's handbook of personal construct psychology*. New York: Wiley.

Benet-Martinez, V., & John, O. P. (1998). Los Cinco Grandes across cultures and ethnic groups: Multitrait multimethod analyses of the Big Five in Spanish and English. *Journal of Personality and Social Psychology*, *75*, 729–750.

Burton, R. V. (1963). Generality of honesty reconsidered. *Psychological Review*, *70*, 481–499.

Cattell, R. B. (1943). The description of personality: Basic traits resolved into clusters. *Journal of Abnormal and Social Psychology*, *38*, 476–506.

Cattell, R. B. (1946). *Description and measurement of personality*. New York: World Book.

Cloninger, C. R., Svrakic, D. M., & Przybeck, T. R. (1993). A psychobiological model of temperament and character. *Archives of General Psychiatry*, *50*, 975–990.

Cohen, J. (1960). A coefficient of agreement for nominal scales. *Educational and Psychological Measurement*, *20*, 37–46.

Corr, P. J. (2004). Reinforcement sensitivity theory and personality. *Neuroscience and Biobehavioral Reviews*, *28*, 317–332.

Cruse, D. B. (1965). Social desirability scale values of personal concepts. *Journal of Applied Psychology*, *49*, 342–344.

De Raad, B., & Hendriks, A. A. J. (1997). A psycholexical route to content coverage in personality assessment. *European Journal of Psychological Assessment*, *13*, 85–98.

Deary, I. J. (1996). A (latent) big five personality model in 1915? A reanalysis of Webb's data. *Journal of Personality and Social Psychology*, *71*, 992–1005.

Digman, J. M. (1990). Personality structure: Emergence of the five-factor model. In M. R. Rosenzweig & L. W. Porter (Eds.), *Annual review of psychology*, *41*, 417–440. Palo Alto, CA: Annual Reviews.

Eysenck, H. J. (1970). *The structure of human personality* (3rd ed.). London: Methuen.

Fleeson, W. (2001). Towards a structure- and process-integrated view of personality: Traits as density distributions of states. *Journal of Personality and Social Psychology*, *80*, 1011–1027.

Funder, D. C. (1991). Global traits: A neo-Allportian approach to personality. *Psychological Science*, *2*, 31–39.

Galton, F. (1884). The measurement of character. *Fortnightly Review*, *42*, 179–185.

Goldberg, L. R. (1981). Language and individual differences: The search for universals in personality lexicons. In L. W. Wheeler (Ed.), *Review of personality and social psychology*. Beverly Hills, CA: Sage.

Goldberg, L. R. (1990). An alternative 'Description of personality': The Big-Five factor structure. *Journal of Personality and Social Psychology, 59*, 1216–1229.

Goldberg, L. R., & Saucier, G. (1995). So what do you propose we use instead? A reply to Block. *Psychological Bulletin, 117*, 221–225.

Hartshorne, H., & May, M. A. (1928). *Studies in deceit*. New York: Macmillan.

Hogan, R. (1983). A socioanalytic theory of personality. In M. M. Page (Ed.), *Nebraska symposium on motivation*. Lincoln: University of Nebraska Press.

Jackson, D. N. (1970). A sequential system for personality scale development. In C. D. Spielberger (Ed.), *Current topics in clinical and community psychology, 2*. New York: Academic Press.

Klages, L. (1926/1932). *The science of character*. London: George Allen & Unwin.

Lamiell, J. T., & Laux, L. (2010). Reintroducing critical personalism: An introduction to the special issue. *New Ideas in Psychology, 28*, 105–109.

McAdams, D. P. (1993). *The stories we live by: Personal myths and the making of self*. New York: William Morrow.

McCrae, R. R., & Costa, P. T. (2008). The Five-Factor Theory of personality. In: O. P. John, R. W. Robins, & L. A. Pervin (Eds.), *Handbook of personality: Theory and research* (3rd ed.). New York: Guilford Press.

Norman, W. T. (1963). Toward an adequate taxonomy of personality attributes: Replicated factor structure in peer nomination personality ratings. *Journal of Abnormal and Social Psychology, 66*, 574–583.

Norman, W. T. (1967). *2800 personality trait descriptors: Normative operating characteristics for a university population*. Ann Arbor, MI: Department of Psychology, University of Michigan.

Partridge, G. E. (1910). *An outline of individual study*. New York: Sturgis and Walton.

Roberts, B. W., Kuncel, N. R., Shiner, R., Caspi, A., & Goldberg, L. R. (2007). The power of personality: The comparative validity of personality traits, socioeconomic status, and cognitive ability for predicting important life outcomes. *Perspectives on Psychological Science, 2*, 313–345.

Rodseth, L. (1998). Distributive models of culture: A Sapirian alternative to essentialism. *American Anthropologist, 100*, 55–69.

Ross, L., & Nisbett, R. (1991). *The person and the situation: Perspectives of social psychology*. New York: McGraw–Hill.

Saucier, G. (1994). Separating description and evaluation in the structure of personality attributes. *Journal of Personality and Social Psychology, 66*, 141–154.

Saucier, G. (1997). Effects of variable selection on the factor structure of person descriptors. *Journal of Personality and Social Psychology, 73*, 1296–1312.

Saucier, G. (2003). Factor structure of English-language personality type-nouns. *Journal of Personality and Social Psychology, 85*, 695–708.

Saucier, G. (2010). The structure of social effects: Personality as impact on others. *European Journal of Personality, 24*, 222–240.

Saucier, G. (2017). Personality, character, and cultural differences: Distinguishing enduring-order versus evolving-order cultures. In A. T. Church (Ed.), *The Praeger handbook of personality across cultures: Vol. 3*. Santa Barbara, CA: Praeger.

Saucier, G., & Goldberg, L. R. (2001). Lexical studies of indigenous personality factors: Premises, products, and prospects. *Journal of Personality, 69*, 847–879.

Saucier, G., Kenner, J., Iurino, K., Bou Malham, P., Chen, Z., Thalmayer, A. G., ..., Altschul, C. (2015). Cross-cultural differences in a global 'Survey of World Views'. *Journal of Cross-Cultural Psychology*, *46*, 53–70.

Saucier, G., Thalmayer, A. G., & Bel-Bahar, T. (2014). Human attribute concepts: Relative ubiquity across twelve mutually isolated languages. *Journal of Personality and Social Psychology*, *107*, 199–216.

Schwartz, T. (1978). Where is the culture? Personality as the distributive locus of culture. In G. D. Spindler (Ed.), *The making of psychological anthropology*. Berkeley, CA: University of California Press.

Stevenson, C. (1944). *Ethics and language*. New Haven, CT: Yale University Press.

Tellegen, A. (1985). Structures of mood and personality and their relevance to assessing anxiety with an emphasis on self-report. In A. H. Tuma & J. D. Maser (Eds.), *Anxiety and the anxiety disorders*. Hillsdale, NJ: Erlbaum.

Triandis, H. C., & Gelfand, M. J. (1998). Converging measurement of horizontal and vertical individualism and collectivism. *Journal of Personality and Social Psychology*, *74*, 118–128.

Tupes, E. C., & Christal, R. E. (1961/1992). *Recurrent personality factors based on trait ratings (USAF ASD Technical Report No. 61–97)*. Aeronautical Systems Division, Personnel Laboratory: Lackland Air Force Base, TX. (Reprinted as Tupes, E. C., & Christal, R. E. (1992). Recurrent personality factors based on trait ratings. *Journal of Personality*, *60*, 225–251.)

Vazire, S., & Doris, J. M. (2009). Personality and personal control. *Journal of Research in Personality*, *43*, 274–275.

Webb, E. (1915). Character and intelligence. *British Journal of Psychology*, *1*, 99.

Webster's new international dictionary of the English language (1925). Springfield, MA: Merriam.

3

Factor Analysis of Trait-Names

Revisiting Cattell (1943)

John S. Gillis and Gregory J. Boyle

BACKGROUND TO THE STUDY

Raymond B. Cattell was the seventh most highly cited psychologist of the 20th century – based on citations of the scientific peer-reviewed journal literature (Haggbloom et al., 2002). Upon completing a BSc (Hons) degree (with first-class honours in both chemistry and physics), Cattell switched to the newly emerging field of psychology where he perceived the need to undertake a comprehensive research programme into the basic description and measurement of psychological constructs. Thus, soon after accepting Gordon Allport's invitation to an academic position at Harvard University in 1941, Cattell began planning a grand project that he had been thinking about ever since commencing his PhD research in psychology at King's College London under the supervision of Francis Aveling (Cattell, 1941; and influenced also by Charles Spearman at nearby University College London). Cattell received his doctorate at only 23 years of age (Sheehy, 2004). Cattell set out to comprehensively map the human personality trait domain (both normal and abnormal traits) using the newly developed statistical method of multiple factor analysis (Thurstone, 1947) and designed a programmatic series of empirical factor-analytic studies in order to elucidate a taxonomy of personality and psychological constructs and a corresponding model of human personality structure (e.g., Cattell, 1934, 1946, 1965, 1973; Cattell & Kline, 1977; see also Boyle, 2008b; Boyle & Barton, 2008; Miller, 1998). In recognition of his already prodigious work, in 1939 the University of London honoured Cattell by conferring upon him its most prestigious doctorate (DSc).

Cattell (1946) had observed perceptively that the study of psychology had, to that point in time at least, tried to bypass the necessary stages of systematic description and measurement, critical to the development of other evidence-based scientific disciplines. He believed that advances could not have been made as rapidly without, for example, the framework of the periodic table in chemistry, contributed by Dmitri Mendeleev, as well as other pioneering efforts including the taxonomic classification schemes developed by biologists such as Carl Linnaeus.

Cattell's favourite example was from physics, where like many other young students, he had been drawn into science through his avid interest in astronomy. Consequently, he was well aware of how the careful measurements of Tycho Brahe were utilized by Johannes Kepler to develop laws of interplanetary motion that were essential for both Isaac Newton's and Albert Einstein's over-arching theories and contributions to modern physics. Parenthetically, Hans Eysenck also tried to take a physics approach to personality description and explanation (Eysenck, 1944 – see Chapter 4 in this book).

According to Cattell, what was needed in psychology was the overall plan he outlined in a series of three articles about the description of personality. In the first paper (written at Harvard University) he focused upon the foundations of the measurement of trait constructs (Cattell, 1943a). In the second, he described his views about how basic personality traits could be resolved into clusters (Cattell, 1943b). The third article presented principles and empirical factor analytic findings (Cattell, 1945a). All three articles have been highly cited over the years, but the second article (1943b), which is the focus of the present chapter, has been particularly influential.

DETAILED DESCRIPTION OF THE STUDY

Cattell's (1943b, 1945b) articles on trait clusters fit within an overall framework that is central to understanding his empirical taxonomic work. He proposed that the description and measurement of personality constructs should be undertaken via three basic media of observation (three different types of data). Firstly, *L*-data refers to information that is collected about individuals in real *Life* situations, either by recording a person's actual behaviour, or obtaining an observer's ratings of a given individual's behaviour. Secondly, *Q*-data provides measurements of humans' self-assessments of their own behaviour via self-report *Questionnaires. T*-data is obtained from objective *Tests* designed to measure actual behaviour (often within a laboratory setting – see Cattell, 1984; Cattell & Schuerger, 1978; Cattell & Warburton, 1967; Schuerger, 2008).

THEORY

Lewis Goldberg (1968) characterized Cattell as *Psychology's Master Strategist.* Nowhere is there a better example of Cattell's skill as a strategist than in his paper proposing to use *L*-data as an initial guide for undertaking an investigation into what he coined *the personality sphere.* The concept of the personality sphere (including both normal and abnormal personality domains) may be regarded as the cornerstone of Cattell's scientific approach to understanding personality. Cattell's demonstration of the use of the words in the English language as a means to systematically analyse personality constructs, has become widely known as the *lexical hypothesis* (and the corresponding *trait lexicon* – cf. Boyle, Helmes, Matthews, & Izard, 2015). According to Cattell (1943b, p. 483):

> The position we shall adopt is a very direct one, verging on a pragmatic philosophy, and making only the one assumption that all aspects of human personality which are or have been of importance, interest, or utility have already been recorded in the substance of language.

After outlining this conceptual foundation centred upon language, Cattell turned his attention to specific tactics to implement his strategy. In one of those serendipitous moments that often result in major scientific advances, it happened that his teaching duties at Harvard involved delivering a course on personality that he co-taught with the eminent personologist Gordon Allport (see Allport, 1937). While Cattell and Allport certainly had many theoretical differences, one common denominator between the two instructors was their emphasis upon the importance of personality trait constructs (Piekkola, 2011).

METHODOLOGY

Allport and one of his graduate students had carefully combed Webster's *New Unabridged International Dictionary* to compile a comprehensive list of 17,953 terms from the English language that related to human affects and personality (Allport & Odbert, 1936 – see Chapter 2 in this book). The authors classified these terms into four groups, labelled: personal traits, temporary states, social evaluations, and metaphorical or doubtful terms. From the first group they chose 4504 terms, constituting approximately 1% of all the words in the English dictionary – considered to be indicators of 'traits of personality'.

Cattell might well have discovered the Allport–Odbert list of trait-words without ever having co-taught with Allport. But it seems likely that this coincidence played a decisive role in Cattell subsequently using the (1936) dictionary-based compilation as a starting point for his empirical taxonomic personality research programme. Cattell proceeded by first reducing the list by grouping all synonymous terms together and then designating each synonym group under a key term. Cattell employed the term 'synonym' somewhat narrowly by classifying together only words which in the opinion of the 'average educated person' would be taken as approximately interchangeable in describing human personality (Cattell, 1947, 1957, 1973; Cattell & Kline, 1977).

With the assistance of a literature student, Cattell spent several months parsing the list to a more manageable number of 171 synonym terms, beginning without any preconceived idea as to the number of separate categories needed. Because raters had been shown not to completely agree in assigning terms to Allport and Odbert's four categories, Cattell and his student assistant did not confine themselves to the personal trait section. Hundreds of additional trait terms from the other groups were added, although many terms were rejected because they were considered too vague, figurative, metaphorical, or too rare and esoteric.

The next step was to organize most of the trait synonyms into a bipolar format by including opposites whenever possible. The following is a sample of the final list (the complete list may be found beginning on page 219 of Cattell's (1946) book *The Description and Measurement of Personality*):

ALERT -- ABSENT-MINDED

CHEERFUL -- GLOOMY

FRIENDLY --- HOSTILE

HONEST --- DISHONEST

IRRITABLE -- GOOD-TEMPERED

OPTIMISTIC -- PESSIMISTIC

RELIABLE --- UNDEPENDABLE

SENSITIVE -- TOUGH

TRUSTFUL -- SUSPICIOUS

WISE -- FOOLISH

Cattell then recruited a sample of 100 individuals, specifically selected to be as representative as possible of the general adult population. The sample included people such as domestic servants, janitors, artisans, a lumberjack, and a Nova Scotia fisherman. Members of the group were rated by a close (but not emotionally involved) acquaintance on each of the 171 trait terms. The raters estimated whether a person was high or low on each of the respective trait terms. Research assistants then calculated all 14,535 separate tetrachoric correlation coefficients between all of the 171 trait terms. Cattell employed the statistical technique of cluster analysis to create a list of 67 fundamental clusters representing *surface traits* of the normal personality sphere. He then reduced these cluster-based trait terms to a more practical number of 35 bipolar dimensions, which trained raters used in the format illustrated below to assess the everyday behaviour of 208 men in an empirical investigation into human personality structure (Cattell, 1945a):

POSITIVE POLE	NEGATIVE POLE
1. *Self-assertive*	*Self-submissive*
Boastful	Modest
Assertive	Submissive
Conceited	Self-critical, Dissatisfied
...	
31. *Sociable, Hearty*	*Seclusive, Shy*
Sociable (Forward, Gregarious)	Shy (Seclusive)
Responsive	Aloof
Hearty	Quiet

Cattell made every effort with the resources available to him at the time to avoid the trap of relying exclusively upon samples of undergraduate students. He intentionally sought as diverse a sample as possible because of his aim to create a universal multidimensional personality instrument derived from a comprehensive sampling of the normal personality trait domain that would serve as a common measurement standard in many areas of psychological research and practice (see Birkett-Cattell, 1989; Birkett-Cattell & Cattell, H. E. P., 1997; Cattell, 1973; Cattell, Eber, & Tatsuoka, 1970; Cattell, H. E. P., & Mead, 2008).

Similarly, with the clear intention to conduct a highly valid programmatic series of taxonomic studies, Cattell adopted stringent factor analytic methods (Cattell, 1978). Before the era of high-speed computing, the achievement of maximum simple-structure solutions often required months of topological rotations, typically via Cattell's analytical Maxplane programme (Cattell & Muerle, 1960) and then 'polished' by successive visual Rotoplot rotations (Cattell & Foster, 1963; cf. Boyle & Stanley, 1986). For example, in his (1945a) factor analysis, Cattell insisted upon rigorous standards for two critically important decision points: determining the number of factors to extract and rotating the factors to the most valid, maximum simple-structure position possible. During the next 40 years Cattell repeatedly advocated an approach typified by his statement (Cattell & Vogelmann, 1977, p. 289) that:

> A factor analytic research can be ruined at each of more than half a dozen stages ... but the two points at which a wrong decision produces misinformation most dangerous for subsequent theory is an arbitrary, inadequate rotation or when a wrong estimate is made of the number of factors.

Cattell backed up this position in great detail in numerous other publications, including two influential textbooks on advances in factor analytic methodology (Cattell, 1952, 1978), two major handbooks on multivariate experimental psychology (Cattell, 1966a; Nesselroade & Cattell, 1988) as well as many research articles in a plethora of high-impact scientific journals (e.g., Cattell, 1958, 1966b; Cattell & Krug, 1986; Hakstian, Rogers, & Cattell, 1982).

FINDINGS

In his (1945a) study, Cattell proceeded to extract factors one at a time from the Pearson product-moment correlation matrix until two independent statistical tests indicated there was no significant variance remaining to be extracted. Then he undertook blind (identities of variables not revealed) visual rotations over a period of several months. At the conclusion of these simple-structure factor rotations, Cattell (1944, 1946, 1973) concluded that there were at least 12–16 primary *source traits* underlying the *normal* human personality sphere alone (subsequently, Cattell also identified an additional 12 abnormal personality trait factors measured in the Clinical Analysis Questionnaire or CAQ – see Krug [1980, 2008], giving at least 28 primary personality trait dimensions [Cattell, 1973, p. 127]). At the second-stratum level in the normal personality sphere, Cattell reported 5–8 broad factors (Cattell & Nichols, 1972; Cattell, 1973; Gillis & Cattell, 1979; cf. Boyle & Robertson, 1989; Gillis & Lee, 1978; Krug & Johns, 1986). As expected, a similar number of second-stratum factors have been found in the psychopathological trait domain (abnormal personality sphere – see Krug, 2008).

IMPACT OF THE STUDY

The empirical finding of so many primary (first-stratum) factors resulted in a great deal of interest in the question of whether the 12–16 primary factors could be replicated (Cattell, 1979, 1980; Cattell & Krug, 1986; Chernyshenko, Stark, & Chan, 2001; Eysenck, 1985; McKenzie, Tindell, & French, 1997; Wiggins, 1984).

However, it was not until several years later, when Cattell had settled into a research professorship at the University of Illinois, that he was able carry out an integrated set of programmatic studies to check on the accuracy of his earlier findings. First, he published an investigation with 133 male undergraduate students, who had lived in the same residence for several months, which led him to conclude that he had replicated 9 or 10 factors from the earlier research (Cattell, 1947). In this research, he used essentially (some were altered slightly) the same group of 35 bipolar trait clusters that he had employed in the Cattell (1945a) study, as follows:

1.	Readiness to Cooperate	vs.	Obstructiveness
2.	Emotionally Stable	vs.	Changeable
3.	Attention-getting	vs.	Self-sufficient
4.	Assertive, Self-assured	vs.	Submissive
5.	Depressed, Solemn	vs.	Cheerful
6.	Frivolous	vs.	Responsible
7.	Attentive to People	vs.	Cool, Aloof
8.	Easily Upset	vs.	Unshakeable Poise, Tough
9.	Languid, Slow	vs.	Energetic, Alert
10.	Boorish	vs.	Intellectual, Cultured
11.	Suspicious	vs.	Trustful
12.	Good-natured, Easygoing	vs.	Spiteful, Grasping, Critical

13.	Calm, Phlegmatic	vs.	Emotional
14.	Hypochondriacal	vs.	Not So
15.	Mild, Self-effacing	vs.	Self-willed, Egotistic
16.	Silent, Introspective	vs.	Talkative
17.	Persevering, Determined	vs.	Quitting, Fickle
18.	Cautious, Retiring, Timid	vs.	Adventurous, Bold
19.	Hard, Stern	vs.	Kindly, Soft-hearted
20.	Insistently Orderly	vs.	Relaxed, Indolent
21.	Polished	vs.	Clumsy, Awkward
22.	Prone to Jealousy	vs.	Not Prone to Jealousy
23.	Rigid	vs.	Adaptable
24.	Demanding, Impatient	vs.	Emotionally Mature
25.	Unconventional, Eccentric	vs.	Conventional
26.	Placid	vs.	Worrying, Anxious
27.	Conscientious	vs.	Somewhat Unscrupulous
28.	Composed	vs.	Shy, Bashful
29.	Sensitively Imaginative	vs.	Practical, Logical
30.	Neurotic Fatigue	vs.	Absence of Neurotic Fatigue
31.	Aesthetically Fastidious	vs.	Lacking Artistic Feeling
32.	Marked Interest in Opposite Sex	vs.	Slight Interest in Opposite Sex
33.	Frank, Expressive	vs.	Secretive, Reserved
34.	Gregarious, Sociable	vs.	Self-contained
35.	Dependent, Immature	vs.	Independent-minded

Each item in the above list is a condensed version of the behavioural descriptions actually presented to raters in *L*-data research studies, such as:

Attentive to People	vs.	*Cool, Aloof*
Interested in people, their		Tends to be indifferent to, and
troubles, their personalities.		to ignore, people. Gives the
Makes friends with people and		impression of brooding on his
remembers their personal		own thoughts or of being cold
interests. Spends much time		and indifferent.
in dealing with people.		
Silent, Introspective	vs.	*Talkative*
Says very little; gives the		Talks a lot, to everybody.
impression of being intro-		
spective and occupied with		
thoughts.		

In Cattell's (1947) study, he modified the format to include more concrete examples from real-life situations with the goal of increasing inter-rater reliability. As in his (1945a) study, Cattell utilized Ledyard Tucker's statistical test for determining the appropriate number of factors to extract by calculating estimates of when the residual variance in the factor matrix had been minimized. Interestingly, Cattell's (1947) results can be checked with his widely employed *scree* test for determining the appropriate number of factors to extract (Cattell, 1966b). This test consists of plotting the eigenvalues of the unreduced (unities in the diagonal) correlation matrix. It is assumed that factors to the right of the break in the scree plot, analogous to rock debris at the bottom of a mountain slope, correspond to error variance (cf. Child, 1990, p. 38). Reanalysis of the data from Cattell (1947) reveals clear evidence of a gap in the scree plot indicating up to 14 factors in this particular sample showing that Cattell's original decision to extract 12 primary factors was rather conservative.

Shortly after completing his (1947) study with males, Cattell reported a follow-up investigation with 240 female undergraduates living together in sororities and independent houses (Cattell, 1948). The data from this study was obtained not only from a larger sample, but also the inter-rater reliabilities (16 raters for each participant) were considerably higher than with the previous group of male students. Results suggested that no fewer than 10 of the 11 factors were the same as those found in the first two studies. Re-analysis of Cattell's (1948) data using modern factor analytic methods together with oblique simple-structure rotation supports Cattell's pioneering research findings of 11–16 primary trait dimensions (e.g., Cattell & Krug, 1985; Chernyshenko et al., 2001; Gerbing & Tuley, 1991; McKenzie et al., 1997; Prieto, Gouveia, & Fernandez, 1996; Schneewind, & Graf, 1998) with the following 11 factors corresponding closely to Cattell's original factors:

Factor			Most salient loadings
A	Good-natured, Easygoing	vs.	Spiteful, Grasping, Critical
	Kindly, Soft-hearted	vs.	Hard, Stern
	Readiness to Co-operate	vs.	Obstructiveness
	Attentive to People	vs.	Cool, Aloof
B	Intelligent	vs.	Deficient in Intelligence
C	Not Hypochondriacal	vs.	Hypochondriaca
	Absence of Neurotic Fatigue	vs.	Neurotic Fatigue
	Placid	vs.	Worrying, Anxious
	Calm, Phlegmatic	vs.	Emotional
F	Frank, Expressive	vs.	Secretive, Reserved
	Talkative	vs.	Silent, Introspective
	Energetic, Alert	vs.	Languid, Slow
G	Persevering, Determined	vs.	Quitting, Fickle
	Insistently Orderly	vs.	Relaxed, Indolent
	Responsible	vs.	Frivolous
H	Marked Interest in Opposite Sex	vs.	Slight Interest in Opposite Sex
	Gregarious, Sociable	vs.	Self-contained
	Composed	vs.	Shy, Bashful
I	Sensitively Imaginative	vs.	Practical, Logical
K	Intellectual, Cultured	vs.	Boorish
	Polished	vs.	Clumsy, Awkward
L	Suspicious	vs.	Trustful
	Prone to Jealousy	vs.	Not Prone to Jealousy
M	Unconventional, Eccentric	vs.	Conventional
N	Polished	vs.	Clumsy, Awkward
	Aesthetically Fastidious	vs.	Lacking Artistic Feeling

During the 1950s Cattell improved methods of data collection and utilized new computer resources, as he extended his *L*-data work to different age levels. For example, Cattell and Gruen (1953) studied a group of 178 children in a residential school with 30 variables chosen to represent the normal personality trait sphere that had already been demarcated with adult samples. Since *L*-data was regarded as the foundation for keeping everything in perspective, the same essential rating scale used in Cattell's (1943b) study was modified for use with 11–12-year-olds, who rated the behaviour of their peers. The altered instrument had the form illustrated below:

1. *Cooperative*   vs.   *Does Not Cooperate*
   (A person who joins group activities and helps others vs. a person who refuses to help and is a spoilsport.)

2. *Gets Excited*   vs.   *Keeps Calm*
   (An excitable person with wild mood swings and extreme emotions vs. a quiet person who underreacts, even in extreme situations.)

The authors uncovered evidence of six factors, resembling some of the personality trait factors regularly seen in adults. They concluded that the smaller than previously encountered number of factors might have stemmed from either a diminished power of discrimination of behaviours among the child raters, or, that childhood personality structure is intrinsically more simple. Within a few years the former explanation appeared to be more plausible. Cattell and Coan (1957) used the basic clusters discovered in 1943 as a model to create a scale for teachers to rate their 6–8-year-old students. The modified list consisted of items such as:

1. Cooperative, compliant, courteous with children and adults vs. negativistic, stubborn, disobedient, discourteous, argumentative, 'poor sport'.

2. Outgoing, mixes freely with other children vs. shy, bashful, seclusive, aloof, remains fairly isolated from other children.

When teachers rated 198 children in the 6–8-year-old range, the analysis indicated at least 12 factors that matched adult patterns with considerable confidence. A few years later Cattell examined additional data produced with this personality-sphere-inspired rating scale for 6–8-year-olds. Cattell (1963) re-analysed a correlation matrix based on teacher ratings of students' behaviours collected by Digman (1963) that again demonstrated 'clear continuity' with the trait factors found in the earlier research.

CRITIQUE OF THE STUDY

Some other researchers, however, have tended to be less convinced than Cattell about the validity of his *L*-data results. For example, Donald Fiske (1949) reported a study with 128 males, who were applying for first-year positions in a Veteran's Administration graduate training programme in clinical psychology. Fiske employed only 22 items from Cattell's basic 35-item list of trait terms.

Fiske states that he was looking for 'surface' behaviours (p. 343) and that is exactly what he found with so few markers. More importantly, Fiske used raters who had known each other for *only a week*. This is a clear violation of the *minimum principles for adequate behaviour rating research* that Cattell diligently insisted upon throughout his years of research into *L*-data. Listed below are some of Cattell's rating guidelines (also see Cattell, 1973, p. 256):

1. Raters need to know the person whom they are rating *really well*. Ideally they should live together so that they can observe each other in many different situations over a significant period of time. Raters' situational contacts with ratees should be as broad as possible – for example, not restricted to one narrow role segment in daily life. Furthermore, it is desirable that raters not be asked to rate more than 16 other people, because typically it is difficult to know more than that number very well.

2. Researchers should utilize a procedure of ranking all persons on *one trait at a time*, not all traits on one person at a time. This helps minimize extraneous factors such as the infamous *halo effect* where positive attitudes about known characteristics carry over to less well-known traits.

3. Raters should *not* be asked to make greater than a five-point rating. Too many categories to choose from may reduce reliability.

4. Raters need to be well trained in the behavioural definition and illustration of the traits. In other words, they should not make their ratings based on single words, but on definitions with *concrete behavioural illustrations*, to ensure that terms mean the same for all judges and are anchored in actual observations.

5. Researchers should use *at least eight raters* whose ratings are pooled in order to cancel out the impact of each rater's own idiosyncratic personality biases, thus avoiding distortions from the potentially biased perceptions of a single rater.

In addition to the fact that Fiske's (1949) raters knew each other only for a week, there was clear evidence of distortion in the form of an overall general factor, which suggested the impact of a *halo effect* due to raters making all of their ratings on each person at the same time. The inter-rater reliability coefficient of 0.52 reported by Fiske was lower than the 0.60 found by Cattell (1947), and considerably lower than the 0.84 average reliability reported by Cattell (1948). Fiske also made the common mistake of criticizing Cattell for his interpretation of low factor loadings. Careful examination of Cattell (1947) reveals that he did not present a *factor loading* matrix but rather a matrix of *reference vector correlations*, which tend to run 20–30% lower for purely mathematical reasons (Cattell, 1978, p. 133). Since reference vector correlations are directly proportional to factor loadings, reference vectors are theoretically equivalent to factors.

Cattell used the reference vector system for practical reasons. In the 1940s, prior to modern high-speed computing, obtaining factor pattern matrices required hand-calculating the inverses of large matrices – an expensive and time-consuming procedure.

Fiske was not the only researcher who experienced difficulty in duplicating Cattell's early factor analytic results. Several years later, Tupes and Christal (1961) undertook an extensive programme of research with US Air Force personnel. This study is the subject of scrutiny in a separate chapter of the current book (see Chapter 5), so will be touched upon only briefly here. Tupes and Christal analysed three new datasets of their own, together with Fiske's (1949) data, and Cattell's (1947) and (1948) studies with male and female undergraduates. When they re-factored Cattell's data, Tupes and Christal were unable to reproduce his factors. As Boyle, Stankov and Cattell (1995, p. 432) pointed out, Tupes and Christal not only used rather crude factor analytic procedures, but also severely restricted their analysis to only 20 of Cattell's original 35 trait clusters, thereby ensuring that no more than five second-order personality factors would emerge. Moreover, as Hammond (1977) as well as Digman and Takemoto-Chock (1981) pointed out, the matrices that Tupes and Christal re-analysed contained clerical and computational errors, which also adversely impacted their results. Nonetheless, this research is often cited as support for the popular 'Big Five' and related Five-Factor Model (FFM) static descriptions of human personality structure (Cattell, 1983, 1995; Cattell, Boyle, & Chant, 2002) that are included in countless undergraduate psychology courses throughout the Western world (cf. Saucier & Goldberg, 1998; Paunonen & Jackson, 2000). Recognizing the deficiencies in Tupes and Christal's work, Norman (1963, p. 582) had specifically warned that:

> It is time to return to the total pool of trait-names in the natural language ... to search for additional personality indicators not so easily subsumed under one or another of these five recurrent factors.

Cattell's early *L*-data results also came under fire from Edgar Howarth (1976) in an article, 'Were Cattell's "personality sphere" factors correctly identified in the first instance?' Howarth limited his attention to Cattell (1947). But when this data is analysed appropriately with modern methods, there is unequivocal evidence of at least 12 primary factors, not merely the six that Howarth claimed based on his crude 'Little Jiffy' factor analysis. Also, if Cattell's (1948) data, which Howarth inexplicably ignored, is analysed with modern factor analytic methods, at least 12 primary factors are indicated.

At the same time as Howarth (1976) was preparing his critique of Cattell's work – from nearly 30 years earlier – Cattell, Pierson and Finkbeiner (1976) were collecting new data in order to build on past results. They used a rating scale based on the (1943b) study and followed all of Cattell's (1973) rating guidelines assiduously to obtain *L*-data markers for 16 previously identified factors. Then they administered *Q*-data markers for the same factors. After carefully estimating the number of factors with a scree test, Cattell et al. (1976) employed the latest computer programs available at the time to extract and meticulously rotate the factors to maximum simple structure. In doing so, they found evidence of an overlap between *L*-data and *Q*-data.

As had been made clear in 1943, Cattell was adopting an overall strategy based upon Charles Spearman's original postulate about the *indifference of indicators*. This hypothesizes that if a factor is 'real' it should be possible to find evidence for its existence using different scientific methods of investigation and different media of measurement. Cattell's plan was to use *L*-data, guided by the perspective gained from his personality sphere concept based upon language. Behaviour ratings were intended as scaffolding upon which to build a bridge to *Q*-data, and then ultimately connect with the most desirable form of scientific data – that was provided by objective tests (*T*-data).

In 1950 Cattell published the outcome of a major investigation, in which his 1947 and 1948 *L*-data studies were important components (Cattell & Saunders, 1950). The same students, who had participated in the behaviour rating research, had also completed a personality questionnaire aimed at measuring the behaviour rating source traits. These students also had undergone a gruelling 14 hours of testing with a wide variety of objective personality tests (see Cattell & Schuerger, 1978; Schuerger, 2008; Stankov, Boyle, & Cattell, 1995).

These preliminary results with regard to linking *L*-data and *T*-data factors were less convincing than Cattell had anticipated. However, the *L*-data and *Q*-data connections showed enough promise that he began to develop a theory about why it appeared to be so difficult to match factors identified using different data collection methods. Cattell postulated that the main reasons for problems in the cross-identification of factors across separate media were *perturbations* or disturbing factors inherent in the measurement processes. Thus, he published a series of theoretical papers in which he proposed what he called *Trait View* theory (Cattell, 1963, 1967, 1973; Cattell & Digman, 1964; Krug & Cattell, 1971). In essence, Cattell developed a sophisticated mathematical model to explain how apparent inconsistencies, like the discrepancies observed in astronomical observations about behaviour of the planet Mercury, could lead to improved understanding about human behaviour. The Cattell, Pierson and Finkbeiner study in 1976 demonstrated that it was possible to compensate for the perturbing instrument factors he had theorized about for many years. Cattell suggested that a key factor in the success of his 1976 study was the improvement made in the purity with which *Q*-data factors were being measured. The improved accuracy in measuring factors came from the fact that Cattell had shifted the main focus of his research activity. Originally, he had regarded questionnaires as being convenient stepping-stones on the way from *L*-data to *T*-data. But during the 1950s and 1960s, Cattell focused more of his scientific attention onto *Q*-data.

In literally dozens of studies, involving the creation of thousands of questionnaire items, targeted to measure previous *L*-data factors (and new *Q*-data factors) the *Sixteen Personality Factors Questionnaire* (16PF) underwent a process that

Cattell called *progressive rectification*. He replaced the 1949 edition with an updated 1956 edition, which was subsequently improved again in 1962 and 1967 editions. These were not superficial cosmetic changes. Each of these investigations involved a plethora of fresh factor analyses employing new more highly refined methods (Cattell & Kline, 1977) – many of which were developed in Cattell's highly productive multivariate research laboratory at the University of Illinois (Cattell, 1966a, 1973, 1984, 1990; Nesselroade & Cattell, 1988).

However, during the 1980s there was substantial controversy about the success of his overall *Q*-data enterprise. Other well-conducted studies could not replicate all of the primary *Q*-data factors that had been indicated in Cattell's cornerstone 1943[b] article (see Barrett & Kline, 1982; Matthews, 1989; McKenzie, 1988; Saville & Blinkhorn, 1981).

As a result, since about 1990 Five-Factor Models (FFMs) have steadily become more popular than Cattell's multiple primary-factor approach (overlooking Cattell's 5–8 broader second-stratum 16PF dimensions – see Cattell & Nichols, 1972; Gillis & Cattell, 1978; Krug & Johns, 1986; cf. Boyle, 1989; Gillis & Lee, 1978). During this time there has been an explosion of research about models focused upon just five broad factors (see Block, 1995; Boyle, 1989, 2008a; Boyle et al., 1995; Cattell, 1995; Cattell & Krug, 1986; Digman, 1990; Eysenck, 1992; Goldberg, 1993; McCrae, 2009; McCrae & Costa, 2008). Moreover, it should be noted that Cattell and H. E. P. Cattell (1995) had published evidence supportive of the primary and secondary factors measured in the 5th edition of the 16PF (16PF5) (Cattell, Cattell, A. K., & Cattell, H. E. P., 1993; Conn, & Rieke, 1994). Despite evidence that the latest revision of the 16PF exhibited satisfactory reliability and validity (Cattell & Cattell, H. E. P., 1995; Cattell, H. E. P., & Mead, 2008), this restructuring with only five second-stratum factors (in line with the popular Big Five notion) raises some concern since five factors do not provide comprehensive coverage of the trait domain. Moreover, despite the construction and publication of the 16PF5, Cattell (1995) himself had specifically repudiated any suggestion of there being *only* five second-stratum 16PF factors (Cattell, 1995). However, because of the vast array of research in recent years dealing with FFMs, many current-day psychologists and psychology students have remained unaware of the steady progress supporting the existence of the numerous primary trait factors originally elucidated factor analytically by Cattell in the 1940s.

Another major investigation, upholding the existence of 16 basic factors, originating in Cattell's classic 1943[b] study, was published by Chernyshenko et al. (2001). These authors analysed the responses of 11,846 participants and found a hierarchical solution in which 16 first-order factors and at least 5 second-order factors clearly corresponded with those from previous 16PF studies. More recently, Irwing, Booth and Batey (2014) published an impressive analysis with the 16PF5 in which they employed highly sophisticated, confirmatory factor analytic techniques based on a large calibration sample (N = 5130) and a corresponding validation sample (N = 5131). They reported (p. 38) 'all primary factors displayed good to excellent model fit' and that 'overall the analyses generally supported the proposed structure of the 16PF5.'

CONCLUSIONS

C learly, there is considerable evidence supporting the notion of at least 16 high-definition primary constructs within the normal personality trait domain alone, as well as *at least* five broad secondary trait constructs as postulated by Cattell in his taxonomic research into the normal personality sphere that began in the 1940s (e.g., Schuerger, 1995). In addition, as indicated above, there is also evidence of a further 12 abnormal primary trait constructs, and corresponding broader (higher-stratum) abnormal dimensions, as has been elucidated factor analytically within the *Cattellian School* (e.g., see Boyle, 1987, 2006; Krug, 1980, 2008).

Physics developed a quantum theory, in which both particle and wave models of light have become widely supported. Psychology needs to move forward as well. Instead of continuing to seek evidence about whether one or the other model exists, research effort would seem to be more profitably expended upon delineating the circumstances under which better criterion predictions may be obtained by either broad personality models with relatively few factors or, more highly focused many-factor conceptualizations (Anglim & Grant, 2104; Ashton, Paunomen, & Lee, 2014). In this regard, it is instructive to note that Mershon and Gorsuch (1988) have demonstrated empirically that broad higher-order factors (such as the various FFMs) can account for only a small fraction of the predictive variance as compared with the variance measured using multiple primary source-trait factors.

Similarly, as advances have been made in methods for investigating the biological basis of individual differences (Eysenck, 1982), it has become increasingly apparent that personality traits are highly polygenic in nature. Hence, future progress may depend upon a willingness to embrace and investigate within a poly-theoretical framework. Furthermore, it has been shown recently how empirical findings provide confirmation for both, Hans Eysenck's pragmatic three-factor model and Raymond Cattell's approach based upon a much larger number of factors.

Thus, it seems reasonable to conclude that the use of methodologically sound factor analyses of the English-language trait lexicon, as advocated by Cattell and his colleagues for more than 70 years, has proven to have been a valuable approach in investigating human personality structure.

FURTHER READING

Boyle, G. J. (2008). Simplifying the Cattellian psychometric model. In G. J. Boyle, G. Matthews, & D. H. Saklofske (Eds.), *The Sage handbook of personality theory and assessment: Vol. 1 – Personality theories and models*. Los Angeles, CA: Sage.

Boyle, G. J., Stankov, L., Martin, N. G., Petrides, K. V., Eysenck, M. W., & Ortet, G. (2016). Hans J. Eysenck and Raymond B. Cattell on intelligence and personality. *Personality and Individual Differences, 103*, 40–47.

Gillis, J. S. (2018). *Psychology's secret genius: The lives and works of Raymond B. Cattell*. Woodstock: Maxwell. Amazon Kindle Edition.

REFERENCES

Allport, G. W. (1937). *Personality: A psychological interpretation*. New York: Holt.

Allport, G. W., & Odbert, H. S. (1936). Trait-names: A psycho-lexical study. *Psychological Monographs, 47*, (211).

Anglim, J., & Grant, S. (2014). Incremental criterion prediction of personality facets over factors: Obtaining unbiased estimates and confidence intervals. *Journal of Research in Personality, 53*, 148–157.

Ashton, M. C., Paunomen, S. V., & Lee, K. (2014). On the validity of narrow and broad personality traits: A response to Salgado, Moscoso, and Berges (2013). *Personality and Individual Differences, 56*, 24–28.

Barrett, P., & Kline, P. (1982). An item and parcel factor analysis of the 16PF question-naire. *Personality and Individual Differences, 3*, 259–270.

Birkett-Cattell, H. (1989). *The 16PF: Personality in depth*. Champaign, IL: Institute for Personality and Ability Testing.

Birkett-Cattell, H., & Cattell, H. E. P. (1997). *16PF Cattell comprehensive personality interpretation manual*. Champaign, IL: Institute for Personality and Ability Testing.

Block, J. (1995). A contrarian view of the five-factor approach to personality descrip-tion. *Psychological Bulletin, 117*, 187–215.

Boyle, G. J. (1987). Psychopathological depression superfactors in the Clinical Analysis Questionnaire. *Personality and Individual Differences, 8*, 609–614.

Boyle, G. J. (1989). Re-examination of the major personality factors in the Cattell, Comrey and Eysenck scales: Were the factor solutions of Noller et al. optimal? *Personality and Individual Differences, 10*, 1289–1299.

Boyle, G. J. (2006). *Scientific analysis of personality and individual differences*. DSc Thesis, University of Queensland, St Lucia, Queensland.

Boyle, G. J. (2008a). Critique of the five-factor model of personality. In G. J. Boyle, G. Matthews, & D. H. Saklofske (Eds.), *The Sage handbook of personality theory and assessment: Vol. 1 – Personality theories and models*. Los Angeles, CA: Sage.

Boyle, G. J. (2008b). Simplifying the Cattellian psychometric model. In G. J. Boyle, G. Matthews, & D. H. Saklofske (Eds.), *The Sage handbook of personality theory and assessment: Vol. 1 – Personality theories and models*. Los Angeles, CA: Sage.

Boyle, G. J., & Barton, K. (2008). Contribution of Cattellian personality instruments. In G. J. Boyle, G. Matthews, & D. H. Saklofske (Eds.), *The Sage handbook of personality theory and assessment: Vol. 2 – Personality measurement and testing*. Los Angeles, CA: Sage.

Boyle, G. J., Helmes, E., Matthews, G., & Izard, C. E. (2015). Measures of affect dimen-sions. In G. J. Boyle, D. H. Saklofske, & G. Matthews (Eds.), *Measures of personality and social psychological constructs* (pp. 190–224). San Diego, CA: Elsevier/Academic Press.

Boyle, G. J., & Robertson, J. M. (1989). Anomaly in equation for calculating 16PF second order factor QIII. *Personality and Individual Differences, 10*, 1007–1008.

Boyle, G. J., Stankov, L., & Cattell, R. B. (1995). Measurement and statistical models in the study of personality and intelligence. In D. H. Saklofske & M. Zeidner (Eds.), *International handbook of personality and intelligence*. New York: Plenum.

Boyle, G. J., & Stanley, G. V. (1986). Application of factor analysis in psychological research: Improvement of simple structure by computer assisted graphic oblique transformation: A brief note. *Multivariate Experimental Clinical Research, 8*, 175–182.

Cattell, H. E. P., & Mead, A. D. (2008). The Sixteen Personality Factor Questionnaire (16PF). In G. J. Boyle, G. Matthews, & D. H. Saklofske (Eds.), *The Sage handbook of personality theory and assessment: Vol. 2 – Personality measurement and testing*. Los Angeles, CA: Sage.

Cattell, R. B. (1934). Friends and enemies: A psychological study of character and temperament. *Character and Personality*, *3*, 54–63.

Cattell, R. B. (1941). 'Francis Aveling: 1875–1941'. *American Journal of Psychology*, *54*, 608–610.

Cattell, R. B. (1943a). The description of personality: I. Foundations of trait measurement. *Psychological Review*, *50*, 559–594.

Cattell, R. B. (1943b). The description of personality: Basic traits resolved into clusters. *Journal of Abnormal and Social Psychology*, *38*, 476–506.

Cattell, R. B. (1944). Interpretation of the twelve primary personality factors. *Character and Personality*, *13*, 55–91.

Cattell, R. B. (1945a). The description of personality: Principles and findings in a factor analysis. *American Journal of Psychology*, *58*, 69–90.

Cattell, R. B. (1945b). The principle trait clusters for describing personality. *Psychological Bulletin*, *42*, 129–161.

Cattell, R. B. (1946). *The description and measurement of personality*. New York: World Book.

Cattell, R. B. (1947). Confirmation and clarification of primary personality factors. *Psychometrika*, *12*, 197–220.

Cattell, R. B. (1948). The primary personality factors in women compared with those in men. *British Journal of Mathematical and Statistical Psychology*, *1*, 114–130.

Cattell, R. B. (1952). *Factor analysis*. New York: Harper.

Cattell, R. B. (1956). Validation and intensification of the Sixteen Personality Factor Questionnaire. *Journal of Clinical Psychology*, *12*, 205–214.

Cattell, R. B. (1957). *Personality and motivation structure and measurement*. New York: World Book.

Cattell, R. B. (1958). Extracting the correct number of factors in factor analysis. *Educational and Psychological Measurement*, *18*, 791–838.

Cattell, R. B. (1963). Personality, role, mood, and situation-perception: A unifying theory of modulators. *Psychological Review*, *70*, 1–18.

Cattell, R. B. (1965). *The scientific analysis of personality*. Baltimore, MD: Penguin.

Cattell, R. B. (Ed.) (1966a). *Handbook of multivariate experimental psychology*. Chicago, IL: Rand McNally.

Cattell, R. B. (1966b). The scree test for the number of factors. *Multivariate Behavioral Research*, *1*, 245–276.

Cattell, R. B. (1967). Trait-view theory of perturbations in ratings and self ratings (L(BR)- and Q-data): Its application to obtaining pure trait score estimates in questionnaires. *Psychological Review*, *75*, 96–113.

Cattell, R. B. (1973). *Personality and mood by questionnaire*. San Francisco, CA: Jossey–Bass.

Cattell, R. B. (1978). *The scientific use of factor analysis in behavioral and life sciences*. New York: Plenum.

Cattell, R. B. (1979, 1980). *Personality and learning theory, Vols. 1 & 2*. New York: Springer.

Cattell, R. B. (1983). *Structured personality-learning theory: A wholistic multivariate approach*. New York: Praeger.

Cattell, R. B. (1984). The voyage of a laboratory, 1928–1984. *Multivariate Behavioral Research, 19*, 121–174.

Cattell, R. B. (1990). The birth of the society of multivariate experimental psychology. *Journal of the History of the Behavioral Sciences, 26*, 48–57.

Cattell, R. B. (1995). The fallacy of five factors in the personality sphere. *The Psychologist, May*, 207–208.

Cattell, R. B., Boyle, G. J., & Chant, D. (2002). The enriched behavioral prediction equation and its impact on structured learning and the dynamic calculus. *Psychological Review, 109*, 202–205.

Cattell, R. B., & Cattell, H. E. P. (1995). Personality structure and the new fifth edition of the 16PF. *Educational and Psychological Measurement, 55*, 926–937.

Cattell, R. B., Cattell, A. K., & Cattell, H. E. P. (1993). *16PF Fifth Edition: Questionnaire*. Champaign, IL: Institute for Personality and Ability Testing.

Cattell, R. B., & Coan, R. (1957). Child personality structure. *Journal of Clinical Psychology, 13*, 315–327.

Cattell, R. B., & Digman, J. M. (1964). A theory of the structure of perturbations in observer ratings and questionnaire data in personality research. *Behavioral Science, 9*, 341–358.

Cattell, R. B., Eber, H. W., & Tatsuoka, M. M. (1970). *Handbook for the Sixteen Personality Factor Questionnaire (16PF)*. New York: Plenum.

Cattell, R. B., & Foster, M. J. (1963). The rotoplot program for multiple, single-plane, visually-guided rotation. *Behavioral Science, 8*, 156–165.

Cattell, R. B., & Gruen, W. (1953). The personality factor structure of 11-year-old children in terms of behavior rating data. *Journal of Clinical Psychology, 9*, 256–266.

Cattell, R. B., & Kline, P. (1977). *The scientific analysis of personality and motivation*. New York: Academic.

Cattell, R. B., & Krug, S. E. (1986). The number of factors in the 16PF: A review of the evidence with special emphasis on methodological problems. *Educational and Psychological Measurement, 46*, 509–522.

Cattell, R. B., & Muerle, J. L. (1960). The 'maxplane' program for factor rotation to oblique simple structure. *Educational and Psychological Measurement, 20*, 569–590.

Cattell, R. B., & Nichols, K. E. (1972). An improved definition, from 10 researches, of second order personality factors in Q-data (with cross-cultural checks). *Journal of Social Psychology, 86*, 187–203.

Cattell, R. B., Pierson, G., & Finkbeiner, C. (1976). Alignment of personality source traits factors from questionnaires and observer ratings: The theory of instrument-free patterns. *Multivariate Experimental Clinical Research, 2*, 63–88.

Cattell, R. B., & Saunders, D. R. (1950). Inter-relation and matching of personality factors from behavior rating, questionnaire and objective test data. *Journal of Social Psychology, 31*, 243–260.

Cattell, R. B., & Schuerger, J. M. (1978). *Personality theory in action: Handbook for the Objective-Analytic (O-A) Test Kit*. Champaign, IL: Institute for Personality and Ability Testing.

Cattell, R. B., & Vogelmann, S. (1977). A comprehensive trial of the scree and K.G. criteria for determining the number of factors. *Multivariate Behavioral Research*, *12*, 289–325.

Cattell, R. B., & Warburton, F. W. (1967). *Objective personality and motivation tests: A theoretical introduction and practical compendium*. Champaign, IL: University of Illinois Press.

Chernyshenko, O. S., Stark, S., & Chan, K. Y. (2001). Investigating the hierarchical structure of the fifth edition of the 16PF: An application of the Schmid–Leiman orthogonalization procedure. *Educational and Psychological Measurement*, *61*, 290–302.

Child, D. (1990). *The essentials of factor analysis* (2nd ed.). London: Cassell.

Conn, S. R., & Rieke, M. L. (1994). *The 16PF fifth edition technical manual*. Champaign, IL: Institute for Personality and Ability Testing.

Digman, J. M. (1963). Principal dimensions of child personality as inferred from teachers' judgments. *Child Development*, *34*, 43–60.

Digman, J. M. (1990). Personality structure: Emergence of the five-factor model. *Annual Review of Psychology*, *41*, 417–440.

Digman, J. M., & Takemoto-Chock, N. K. (1981). Factors in the natural language of personality: Re-analysis, comparison, and interpretation of six major studies. *Multivariate Behavioral Research*, *16*, 149–170.

Eysenck, H. J. (1944). Types of personality: A factorial study of 200 neurotic soldiers. *Journal of Mental Science*, *90*, 851–861.

Eysenck, H. J. (1982). *Personality, genetics and behaviour*. New York: Praeger.

Eysenck, H. J. (1985). Review of Raymond B. Cattell's (1983). *Structured personality-learning theory: A wholistic multivariate research approach*. New York: Praeger.

Eysenck, H. J. (1992). Four ways five factors are not basic. *Personality and Individual Differences*, *13*, 667–673.

Fiske, D. W. (1949). Consistency of the factorial structures of personality ratings from different sources. *Journal of Abnormal and Social Psychology*, *44*, 329–344.

Gillis, J. S., & Cattell, R. B. (1979). Comparison of second order personality structures with later patterns. *Multivariate Experimental Clinical Research*, *4*, 92–99.

Gillis, J. S., & Lee, D. C. (1978). Second-order relations between different modalities of personality trait organization. *Multivariate Experimental Clinical Research*, *3*, 241–248.

Goldberg, L. R. (1968). Explorer on the run. (A review of R. B. Cattell, & F. W. Warburton, Objective personality and motivation tests: A theoretical introduction and practical compendium.) *Contemporary Psychology*, *13*, 617–619.

Goldberg, L. R. (1993). The structure of phenotypic personality traits. *American Psychologist*, *48*, 26–34.

Haggbloom, S. J., Warnick, R., Warnick, J. E., Jones, V. K., Yarbrough, G. L., Russell, T. M., Borecky, C. M., McGahhey, R., Powell, J. L., Beavers, J., & Monte, E. (2002). The 100 most eminent psychologists of the 20th century. *Review of General Psychology*, *6*, 139–152.

Hakstian, R. A., Rogers, W. T., & Cattell, R. B. (1982). The behavior of numbers-of-factors rules with simulated data. *Multivariate Behavioral Research*, *17*, 193–219.

Hammond, S. B. (1977). Personality studies by the method of rating in the life situation. In R. B. Cattell & R. M. Dreger (Eds.), *Handbook of modern personality theory*. New York: Wiley.

Howarth, E. (1976). Were Cattell's 'personality sphere' factors correctly identified in the first instance? *British Journal of Psychology*, *67*, 213–230.

Irwing, P., Booth, T., & Batey, M. (2014). An investigation of the factor structure of the 16PF, version 5: A confirmatory factor and invariance analysis. *Journal of Individual Differences*, *35*, 38–46.

Krug, S. E. (1980). *Clinical Analysis Questionnaire Manual*. Champaign, IL: Institute for Personality and Ability Testing.

Krug, S. E. (2008). The assessment of clinical disorders within Raymond Cattell's personality model. In G. J. Boyle, G. Matthews, & D. H. Saklofske (Eds.), *The Sage handbook of personality theory and assessment: Vol. 2 – Personality measurement and testing*. Los Angeles, CA: Sage.

Krug, S. E., & Cattell, R. B. (1971). A test of the trait-view theory of distortion in measurement of personality by questionnaire. *Educational and Psychological Measurement*, *31*, 721–734.

Krug, S. E., & Johns, E. F. (1986). A large scale cross-validation of second-order personality structure defined by the 16PF. *Psychological Reports*, *59*, 683–693.

Matthews, G. (1989). The factor structure of the 16PF: Twelve primary and three secondary factors. *Personality and Individual Differences*, *10*, 931–940.

McCrae, R. R. (2009). The five-factor model of personality traits: Consensus and controversy. In P. J. Corr & G. Matthews (Eds.). *The Cambridge handbook of personality psychology*. Cambridge: Cambridge University Press.

McCrae, R. R., & Costa, P. T. (2008). Empirical and theoretical status of the Five-Factor Model of personality traits. In G. J. Boyle, G. Matthews, & D. H. Saklofske (Eds.), *The Sage handbook of personality theory and assessment: Vol. 1 – Personality theories and models*. Los Angeles, CA: Sage.

McKenzie, J. (1988). Three superfactors in the 16PF and their relation to Eysenck's P, E and N. *Personality and Individual Differences*, *9*, 843–850.

McKenzie, J., Tindell, G., & French, J. (1997). The great triumvirate: Agreement between lexically and psycho-physiologically based models of personality. *Personality and Individual Differences*, *22*, 269–277.

Mershon, B., & Gorsuch, R. L. (1988). Number of factors in the personality sphere: Does increase in factors increase predictability of real life criteria? *Journal of Personality & Social Psychology*, *55*, 675–680.

Miller, K. M. (1998). *Festschrift for Raymond B. Cattell (1988). The analysis of personality in research and assessment: In tribute to Raymond B. Cattell*. (2 April & 17 June, 1986). University College London: Independent Assessment and Research Centre.

Nesselroade, J. R., & Cattell, R. B. (1988). *Handbook of multivariate experimental psychology* (2nd ed.). New York: Plenum.

Norman, W. T. (1963). Toward an adequate taxonomy of personality attributes: Replicated factor structure in peer nomination personality ratings. *Journal of Abnormal and Social Psychology*, *66*, 574–583.

Paunonen, S. V., & Jackson, D. N. (2000). What is beyond the big five? Plenty! *Journal of Personality*, *68*, 821–835.

Piekkola, B. (2011). Traits across cultures: A neo-Allportian perspective. *Journal of Theoretical and Philosophical Psychology*, *31*, 2–24.

Saucier, G., & Goldberg, L. R. (1998). What is beyond the big five? *Journal of Personality*, *66*, 495–524.

Saville, P., & Blinkhorn, S. (1981). Reliability, homogeneity and the construct validity of Cattell's 16PF. *Personality and Individual Differences, 2*, 325–333.

Schuerger, J. M. (1995). Career assessment and the Sixteen Personality Factor Questionnaire. *Journal of Career Assessment, 3*, 157–175.

Schuerger, J. M. (2008). The Objective–Analytic Test Battery. In G. J. Boyle, G. Matthews, & D. H. Saklofske (Eds.), *The Sage handbook of personality theory and assessment: Vol. 2 – Personality measurement and testing*. Los Angeles, CA: Sage.

Sheehy, N. (2004). *Fifty key thinkers in psychology*. London: Routledge.

Stankov, L., Boyle, G. J., & Cattell, R. B. (1995). Models and paradigms in personality and intelligence research. In D. H. Saklofske & M. Zeidner (Eds.), *International handbook of personality and intelligence*. New York: Plenum.

Tellegen, A. (1993). Folk concepts and psychological concepts of personality and personality disorder. *Psychological Inquiry, 4*, 122–130.

Thurstone, L. L. (1947) *Multiple factor analysis: A development and expansion of vectors of the mind*. Chicago, IL: University of Chicago Press.

Tupes, E. C., & Christal, R. E. (1961/1992). *Recurrent personality factors based on trait ratings (USAF ASD Technical Report No. 61–97)*. Aeronautical Systems Division, Personnel Laboratory: Lackland Air Force Base, TX. (Reprinted as Tupes, E. C., & Christal, R. E. (1992). Recurrent personality factors based on trait ratings. *Journal of Personality, 60*, 225–251.)

Wiggins, J. S. (1984). Cattell's system from the perspective of mainstream personality theory. *Multivariate Behavioral Research, 19*, 176–190.

4

The Dimensional Model of Personality and Psychopathology

Revisiting Eysenck (1944)

Kieron P. O'Connor and Philip J. Corr

BACKGROUND TO THE STUDY

Personality researchers had long been troubled by the sheer complexity of the field. This is seen in the proliferation of concepts, constructs and measurement scales to describe the many ways in which people differ from one another. This state of affairs has made difficult the task of relating normal variations in personality with related abnormal, clinical conditions. Such is the extent of the problem, it has even been argued that not only is personality complex but it is too nebulous a concept to be measured in any sensible fashion; and most certainly not readily, or sensibly, reduced to only a small number of factors or dimensions – Hans Eysenck was not one to share this view. Eysenck's 1944 classic study led the charge to make a number of significant advances that changed our notions of the fundamental nature of personality, especially how it relates the pattern of normal variations in the general population to clinical conditions ('psychopathology', more generally). Looking back over the past seven decades, his work is seen to be transformative and is now to be found in current scientific models of personality and psychopathology (O'Connor, 2008).

What stands out in Eysenck's 1944 work are four key tipping points in psychological thinking. First, the main aspects of personality can be reduced to a small number of dimensions, as identified and described by statistical analysis. Secondly, the (apparent) complexity of personality can be understood with reference to how people stand on these dimensions – even with only a few dimensions, there are a very large number of possible personality configurations that define the individual (in a similar fashion, we perceive a wide variety of colours, yet we have only three types of colour receptors in the eye – it is the complex information that comes from their *joint* activation that is of importance). Thirdly, personality dimensions are probabilistic functions that predict clinical disorders; and personal attributes link to specific clinical behaviours in a systematic fashion – in other words, why does *this* person react with these symptoms to the same event (discussed further below). Fourthly, experimental research as well as psychometrics, especially entailing biological variables, is needed to explain both personality and clinical disorder.

Around the time of the work in the early 1940s that went into Eysenck's 1944 classic study, other notable researchers were attempting to impose statistical order on the numerous descriptive approaches to personality. Preeminent here was Raymond B. Cattell, who made seminal and lasting contributions to personality psychology (see Chapter 3), although unlike Eysenck, Cattell preferred many more factors of personality, as shown by his Sixteen Personality Factor (16PF) model. But unlike Cattell, Eysenck's approach was always inspired by and focused on clinical disorder – for this reason, it is a mistake to mischaracterize Eysenck's personality work as purely statistical in nature (statistics was a means to an end and not the end in itself).

As we see in Chapters 1 and 2 of this volume, during the early years of the 20th century attempts were made to identify the main factors of personality and impose some order. This work eventually led to the development of various (statistically derived) trait models of personality, the most prominent today being the Big Five (see Chapter 5). But, none of these *descriptive* approaches addressed what Eysenck uniquely identified as missing in the field: over the next 50 years of his life, he advanced our understanding of the *underlying* psychological and physiological *causal* basis of personality, and extended the implications of these causes to all areas of psychological life (e.g., crime, sex, marriage, work, health, and even parapsychology; see Corr, 2016a).

But in the early 1940s, Eysenck's tipping points were, indeed, novel and bold. Whilst he was trying to put the study of behaviour on a scientific footing, we should remember that Medical Psychiatry was still touting a number of quack treatments with no proven scientific basis – and little theoretical rationale. These were largely derived from personal hunches and serendipitous observations, some of which would not be out of place in a chamber of horrors. Yet Psychiatry was happy to endorse them up until the 1960s. Amongst others that could be mentioned, these included insulin-induced coma therapy (discovered as a result of a chance dosing error) and seizure-induced therapy (inspired by watching pig stunning in an abattoir). In the 1940s, Walter Freeman was touring America with his 'lobomobile' offering onsite frontal lobotomies (for which Egon Moniz earned the Nobel prize in 1949) disabling frontal lobes with a hand-held ice pick. A more psychologically informed perspective in psychiatry was badly needed, and Eysenck set his mind to this task.

EYSENCK AND 'THE LONDON SCHOOL'

The intellectual background to Eysenck's early work may easily be traced to his education at University College London (UCL), in the mid-to-late 1930s (after he left Germany in 1934 at the age of 18 because he detested Hitler and all he stood for). At that time, UCL was renowned for its individual differences research, especially intelligence (many of the ideas and statistical techniques Eysenck extended to personality psychology had their roots in this very work).

As detailed by Corr (2016a), by the time Eysenck entered UCL in 1935, Sir Francis Galton and Charles Spearman were the ghosts of science past but their work lived on in Cyril Burt – he was later to be knighted in 1946 for his services to educational psychology – who greatly influenced Eysenck. In a short space of time, the young and eager Eysenck was to become the most prominent member of 'The London School' (Eysenck, 1997), so-called to differentiate it from 'The Cambridge School' which focussed on experimental psychology and had relatively little time for correlational psychology of the kind favoured by Galton, Spearman, Burt and Eysenck.

Starting in these early war-torn days, throughout his long and highly productive life, Eysenck set himself two principal objectives: first, to provide an adequate statistical description of *how* people differ from one other on basic dimensions of affect, thinking and behaviour (i.e., 'personality'); and secondly, to search for a causal explanation of *why* these differences existed in the first place and, by so doing it was hoped, explain the vulnerability of certain personality types to clinical (both neurotic and psychotic) disorder – indeed, Eysenck wanted to explain all forms of behaviour (e.g., sexual and marital satisfaction), especially criminal behaviour (something he called *sociopsychiatric* behaviour).

It would be useful to know something of the circumstances of Eysenck's life during the conduct of the research that went into his 1944 classic study. Following the award of his PhD, during the early 1940s, and after a short stint in the Air Raid Precautions (ARP) in Islington, North London, Eysenck served as an assistant psychologist at the Mill Hill Emergency Hospital, north of London, where he had access to patients and their clinical records (due to his status as an enemy 'alien' during World War II he was ineligible for military service). He saw the chance of making a significant contribution to psychology and he took it – freed of important, if tedious, war work, fortunately for Eysenck, he was one of the few bright young psychologists who had such a splendid personal opportunity of so doing at that time.

As part of his much wider psychological perspective, Eysenck saw personality as being fundamental in a number of ways. He believed that people have innate predispositions that determine how they react to the *same* environmental stimulus (or complex configuration of stimuli; i.e., the 'situation', or more loosely the 'event'). Secondly, traits are not static in their effects: they are predispositions to react to stimuli in certain, often complex, ways and they do not simply predict specific behaviours in all situations. Eysenck assumed that these features lead some people to be especially vulnerable to clinical disorder, while others are more prone to criminal behaviours. To his mind, personality was central to psychiatry. This view was endorsed by the words of the most foremost psychiatrist at that time, Sir Aubrey Lewis, who wrote in his Foreword to Eysenck's (1947) first book, *Dimensions of Personality*:

> Personality is so cardinal a matter in psychiatry, that any ambiguity in the concept or uncertainty about how to describe and measure the qualities it stands for, must weaken the whole structure of psychiatry, theoretical and clinical.

DETAILED DESCRIPTION OF THE STUDY

E ysenck's 1944 classic study was published in the *Journal of Mental Science*. Out of this study came the widespread acceptance of the personality dimensions of Extraversion (E) and Neuroticism (N) – in 1952, he added a third dimension, Psychoticism (P), which opposed the Freudian notion that neuroticism is on the same dimension as psychosis, with the hinterland between the two occupied by the 'borderline personality'.

THEORY

Starting off his 1944 paper, somewhat tongue-in-cheek, Eysenck noted that few psychologists and psychiatrists would dissent from the view that the field of personality is in a 'state of acute conflict and dissociation', and this was true also of the psychiatric field of classification and diagnosis of mental disorders. At the beginning of his paper and instructive of his whole approach which is evident so early on, Eysenck informed the reader that his theoretical basis is that neurosis is a failure of adaptation, which is the result of two components: 'constitution' and the 'environmental set-up of the moment'. Coupled with the idea that normality and abnormality are merely different points on the same dimension, according to Eysenck, it follows that the study of the symptoms of neurotic patients should reveal the structure of traits found in the general population: they are *writ large* in clinical (maladaptive) samples.

Eysenck was very familiar with the statistical technique of factor analysis, which had been pioneered by Charles Spearman at UCL specifically for the purpose of uncovering the structure of intelligence (divided into its general, *g*, and specific, *s*, components, such a performance, verbal, numerical, and so on). Although a complex statistical technique, factor analysis has a simple aim: to take a large set of intercorrelations – in this case, between 39 items on a medical checklist – and to reduce them to the minimum number of axes (or 'factors' – mathematical descriptions) that account for the shared 'common' variance between the items (all items have their own 'specific' variance and as this is not related to the variance of other items, this is ignored in 'common' factor analysis). Factor analysis aims for statistical parsimony with the hope of resulting theoretical elegance.

In his 1944 paper, and showcasing his distinctive approach, Eysenck highlighted several merits of his dataset over previous studies, which he said suffered from: small numbers of subjects; the biased method of selection of subjects; the small number of items which were not sufficiently large to allow the identification of factors with any confidence; raters untrained in the administration of test items; failure to consider such confounding factors as 'halo' effects (i.e., over-generalizing from one positive feature; and other forms of response bias, including confirming biases); and, all of this was made worse by the lack of care in providing a psychological interpretation of factors despite the sometimes great care taken over the mathematical aspects of these studies.

METHODOLOGY

Eysenck was truly fortunate to have landed the opportunity to access the records of some 1000 patients – who, it should be noted, mentally broke down during initial military training and not on operational duties or in battle. From this pool, he selected 700 patients (excluded are those with various form of organic brain injury, disease of the central nervous system, physical issues, epilepsy and 'cases in whose illness psychological causes were unimportant'). The final sample comprised neurotic male soldiers referred to the Mill Hill Emergency Hospital (North London), assumed to have a 'reactive' type of neurosis – that is, a 'failure of adaptation', as Eysenck saw it. The final sample was a rather mixed bunch, and specifically not equated on diagnosis, for example depression, anxiety, or psychopathy. One pleasing feature of the medical checklist is that it was completed by several psychiatrists which enhanced its reliability; as Eysenck noted: 'the ratings were made, not by one psychiatrist, but by over a dozen all different in their theoretical leanings' – this was made possible because the patients in his sample had 'successive admissions', which suggests that they had a chronic inability to adapt to the environment.

Eysenck took 39 items from 'some' 200 items recorded for each patient (some of these 39 items are shown below). They are scored on a variety of ordinal level scales (as shown below in italics).

Q. 4   'Work history degraded, or unduly frequent changes of occupation vs. study work history'

Q. 9   'Hobbies and interests' – *narrow vs. broad*

Q.13   'Weak, dependent, timorous personality' – *somewhat or very vs. not*

Q.14   'Drive and energy' – *inert, without initiative vs. average go or conspicuous energy*

Q. 20   'Fatigue, lassitude, effort intolerance' – *yes or no*

Q. 22   'Fainting fits' – *yes or no*

Q. 23   'Pain – not of demonstrable organic origin and excluding headaches' – *yes or no*

Q. 25   'Sexual anomalies (impotence, ejac. praecox, masturbation worries. Homo-sexuality, others)' – *yes or no*

Q. 31   'Anxiety, anxiety dreams, battle dreams' – *moderate or severe vs. none or mild*

Q. 32   'Depression' – *moderate or severe vs. none or mild*

Q. 34 'Hysterical conversion symptoms (motor, sensory, special senses, visceral or other)' – *any vs. none*

Q. 38 'Intelligence' – *below average vs. average or above*

Eysenck based his selection of items on two criteria. First, they had psychological meaning (at least in terms of adaptation to the environment). Secondly, they were found in more than 10%, but less than 90%, of patients – otherwise there would have been the statistical problem of 'range restriction' of the items. It is obvious that many of these items are objective, for example intelligence test scores, work histories, marital status, and so on. This meant that they were not contaminated by pre-existing psychiatric notions regarding clinical conditions – as Eysenck put it: 'Diagnoses, being of little objective value, were not included in the analysis'. Ratings by psychiatrists were informed by a number of sources, including relatives of the patients and nurses so Eysenck could have confidence in the accuracy of them. The binary nature of the response format helped Eysenck to reduce the biases inherent in the assessment of more subjective symptoms by psychiatrists; however, it also served to complicate the factor analysis and this led to criticisms, which we discuss below.

FINDINGS

Following a very laborious manual factor analysis, Eysenck reported finding four factors in the data, but he decided to focus on only two of them. Factor one was defined by 'badly organized personality', identified by him as 'Quite clearly, the factor is one of neuroticism' or 'lack of personality integration'. The second, bipolar, factor dichotomized anxiety/depression/obsessions and hysterical attitude (which people have referred to as 'acting out'). Quoting Jung, Eysenck concluded: 'The hysteric belongs to the type of Extraversion, the psychasthenic to the type of Introversion' and 'we consider this bipolar "type" factor to be identical with the introvert–extravert dichotomy.'

The respective Neuroticism and Extraversion factors Eysenck identified in this analysis were interpreted in line with previous theoretical speculation, especially Jung's work which related Extraversion (and its opposite pole, Introversion) to clusters of major neurotic disorders (Extraversion: externalizing, 'acting-out', disorders; Introversion: internalizing disorders, e.g., fear/anxiety). It is noteworthy that during these very early days, Eysenck wrote: 'we consider this bipolar "type" factor to be identical with the introvert–extravert dichotomy with ... Pavlov's concept of "inhibition"'. Eysenck was to make great use of Pavlov's notions of inhibition and excitation in his first, 1957, biological model of personality, *The Dynamics of Anxiety and Hysteria: An Experimental Application of Modern Learning Theory to Psychiatry.* (The title of this book captures well Eysenck's theoretical orientation – and the 'dynamics' may well hark back to Eysenck's first scientific love, physics.)

The lesser, third, factor Eysenck called 'Hypochondriasis', which he considered, for reasons not given, of little general theoretical interest. Regarding the fourth and last factor, in a rather forthright manner characteristic of the times, Eysenck noted it 'distinguishes between the stupid, drunken, shiftless social misfit on the one hand and the "psychological conflict" group on the other' – this factor might bear some resemblance to Eysenck's 'Psychoticism' factor that he identified in 1952, but in 1944 he did not pay it any further attention.

In interpreting the first two factors, Eysenck was at pains to acknowledge past research which provided him with much of the theoretical basis for their interpretation, which included the ideas of Freud, Jung and Pavlov. In this way, Eysenck was not left to interpret the statistical factors in a theoretical vacuum – this point is often overlooked when assessing his work.

IMPACT OF THE STUDY

At this point, it is important to note that Eysenck did not invent or discover extraversion or neuroticism – in different guises, they were known well before his time. But what his classic study did was to bring them to the forefront of research psychiatry and offered a way to understand the underlying psychological 'dynamics' by reference to experimental means of personality and psychopathology in the normal population. His approach was important, too, for inspiring other psychologists to pursue similar lines of research (see Chapter 7). It may be said with little fear of contradiction that as a direct result of Eysenck's thinking, theorizing, researching and popularizing, today we have a neuroscience of personality which not too many years ago was seen as something of an oxymoron, and a laughable one at that (especially when it was suggested that non-human animals have personalities too!). Times change, and in personality psychology they most certainly have. In all of these developments, Eysenck was highly influential in arguing for the need to relate normal variations in personality dimensions to clinical disorder, especially as it had long been suspected that personality and psychopathology are cut from much the same scientific cloth. Eysenck's 1944 study was the start of a revolution in this field, and it is rightly regarded as a classic.

Eysenck's 1944 classic study had an immediate impact and it was followed up in book form in 1947 with *Dimensions of Personality*, in which Extraversion and Neuroticism are sharpened up as statistical factors and, importantly, related to experimental variables that started to get closer to the causal underpinnings of them. This study and those that followed allowed Eysenck to press home the advantage of advocating a dimensional approach over a purely categorical one favoured by psychiatry – Eysenck long argued that this 'medical model' is not only an inaccurate depiction of the nature of psychological disorder, but a harmful one that impeded the development of a truly scientific clinical psychiatry.

METHODOLOGY

It is remarkable how many of the themes that characterize scientific Clinical Psychology today were either present or hinted at in Eysenck's 1944 classic study. Aside from the general aim of giving order and coherence to diverse personal attributes through the use of the advanced statistical technique of factor analysis, in his scientific rigour Eysenck foresaw practically all of the psychometric considerations required for constructing valid measurement instruments: test–retest reliability, internal consistency and external validity – ensuring that instruments (e.g., personality questionnaires or psychiatric rating) are consistent in measurement and related to the construct they purport to measure. Eysenck also foresaw the importance of eliminating subjective bias in ratings, which he did by estimating inter-rater reliability – which he did not publish because this reliability was so low – and he recognized such important issues as sample selection bias and observer bias (see MacCoun, 1998). Of no small importance, Eysenck also used intelligence tests as a way of controlling for cognitive ability as a confounding factor in personality assessment.

The overall implication of Eysenck's 1944 classic study is that clinical work can be linked with rigorous and reliable observation and, furthermore, statistics is a way of resolving clinical ambiguities – not all were in agreement with him at that time, but now most are. In his conclusions, Eysenck emphasized the importance of using objective tests to continue the process of construct validation: what is the test truly measuring? Important here were experimental measures, which can start to get at the causal basis of personality (e.g., ease of classical conditioning). These scientific checks and balances are now the gold standard in psychological assessment and *de rigueur* in any quality scientific paper – they were borne out of Eysenck's incisive research, which sometimes was met with opposition and, even outright hostility (see Corr, 2016a, 2016b, 2016c).

Another concern throughout Eysenck's 1944 classic study, which was embedded in its rationale, is the importance of applying rigorous methods to real life 'messy' problems. At the time, Eysenck was writing against a backdrop of increased interest and experimental activity in the evolving discipline of clinical behaviourism – such theories were bearing fruit on the importance of conditioned learned associations and reinforcement schedules in guiding behaviour. But much of the evidence came from laboratory studies on experimental animals (rats and pigeons) and the extent of their implications for humans were, at best, unclear and, often, contested. Eysenck was, of course, very aware of these developments and was edging towards the foundations of Behaviour Therapy, but one based on the direct study of the human animal. But, seemingly unlike other behaviourally inclined research psychologists, Eysenck was in the real world and so saw how important it was to measure human personality traits, especially those useful in identifying individual differences in the psychological processes behind clinical behaviour. He was quick to locate the organism (the person) between the stimulus (S) and the response (R) within the well-known sequence: S–O–R instead of S–R; in the 'O' resided individual differences in personality, broadly defined. Much of Eysenck's later work would focus exactly on such individual differences mediating learned behaviour. Elsewhere Joseph Wolpe, in fact, attributes the later promulgation and acceptance of behaviour therapy largely to Eysenck (Wolpe, 1973, pp. xi) – Eysenck's role in the establishment of behaviour therapy, and clinical psychology more generally, cannot be seriously questioned (see Corr, 2016a).

BEHAVIOUR AS A DIMENSION, NOT A CATEGORY

It is important to place Eysenck's dimensional approach in the context of the common psychiatric approach, at the time and still enduring, of classifying by exclusive categories. Such categories are usually the result of consensus and committees, and are not based on actual empirical (experimental or clinical) evidence; consequently they have little, except superficial face, validity. As is well documented, diagnostic categories often change with the political climate rather than facts: dogma over data. In contrast, Eysenck's dimensional approach achieves the following:

(a) It systematizes variations and renders traits measurable as quantifiable data – after all, natural traits (e.g., height) vary along a dimension, so why should not psychological ones?

(b) The diversity contained in dimensions can always later be systematically and empirically converted into categories (e.g., personality 'types'), but the reverse is not the case – importantly, the cut-off for clinical categories is empirically based and not arrived at arbitrarily by committee consensus.

(c) There is no contradiction where quantitative extremes on the same dimension, as calculated through statistical cut-offs, may subsequently differ qualitatively – an example here is hoarding disorder where a dimension of accumulation at extremes may be motivated by distinct processes (e.g., hoarders for whom hoarding is a clinically significant problem tend to vary from non-hoarders in terms of other dimensions as attachment issues, organisational strategies and self-ambivalence; Frost & Hartl, 1996; Koszegi, O'Connor, & Brodryzlova, 2017).

(d) A dimensional approach allows portrayal of an individual as complex and multidimensional and some dimensions may be more important than others at different times and occasions – this is a fundamental point of Eysenck's work, because a small number of dimensions allows for many individual configurations. People have profiles and are not one-dimensional and profiles may better predict pathology than single components.

(e) The dimensional approach allows us systematically to go beyond individual symptoms and signs which in themselves may not reliably appear but form rather part of a pattern (Polman, O'Connor, & Huisman, 2011). Knowing this personal pattern may permit prediction of further less obvious symptoms. For example, knowing how a person scores on dimensions of Impulsivity, Extraversion and Neuroticism allows us to predict wide-ranging behaviours such as leisure activities, lifestyle habits and physiological reactions to stimulation (Eysenck, 1967).

(f) Putting psychopathology on a dimension allows aberrant behaviour to be identified on one end of a continuum with normal behaviour. This allows for the understanding of patient behaviour as a *progression* (O'Connor, 2016). It also somewhat normalizes the behaviour since extreme anxiety, for example, can be related to a normal anxiety that everyone experiences – we are all somewhere along the dimension! (Abramowitz et al., 2014).

(g) Finally, a dimensional approach has a destigmatizing influence. Psychiatric patients do not come from another planet; their symptoms are cut from the same psychological cloth that the rest of us wear. We all exist on the same plane, but at different points with some people at the extremes. In addition, measuring symptoms dimensionally can sometimes indicate the normality of some symptoms, such as phobias, intrusions and even voice hearing, and this in itself can provide comfort (O'Connor, 2009; O'Connor, St-Pierre Delorme, Leclerc, Lavoie, & Blais, 2014).

There is something else of importance about the dimensional approach that has not been highlighted enough. Behavioural or psychological dimensions yield explanatory power greater than diagnostic category by treating the individual as a multidimensional being that cuts across diagnostic boundaries. This is seen in the case of neuroticism which, indeed, cuts across diagnostic boundaries and accounts for distress and adaptation more reliably than psychiatric classification (Hengartner, Tyrer, Ajdacic-Gross, Angst, & Rossler, 2017). Other related research confirms this general finding; for example, O'Connor et al. (2004) found that neuroticism better predicts withdrawal distress than psychiatric diagnoses. Eysenck's 1944 classic study was the first to say that this was the case, but it took many years to confirm, as it did in relation to his other theories (e.g., heritability is common in all psychological traits, including intelligence; Hagenaars et al., 2016).

An experimental approach to personality and clinical psychology

In his 1944 paper, Eysenck was at pains to offer suggestions as to the theoretical bases of the dimensions he thought he had isolated. He noted that the formation of a reflex to strong stimulus is a 'kind of sign of the "boldness" of the animal'. In relation to psychiatric disorder and following Pavlov's inspiring lead, Eysenck proposed that as people high on Neuroticism have a 'weak' nervous system, and their ability to form conditioned reflexes breaks down under conditions of strong stimulation and this predisposes them to a range of neurotic conditions, defined in terms of failures of adaptation. In relation to the Introversion–Extraversion dimension, Eysenck related this to the *balance* (as opposed to strength) of inhibitory and excitatory processes, which gave him further explanatory licence to relate both personality dimensions to mental illness – as the balance of nervous system weakness is in the direction of introversion, those most liable to neurotic breakdown are assumed to be neurotic introverts – in the opposite stable-extravert quadrant are found content and happy individuals.

As we can see, from this 1944 classic study came a flowering of new scientific ideas and explanatory models of personality. We have already seen something of the 1957 inhibition/excitation theory above – for further description, see

Corr (2016a). The 1967 theory extended this causal thinking in the direction of known neurophysiological systems. It postulated that variations along the Introversion–Extraversion dimension relate to variations in the sensitivity of an arousal system in the brainstem, known as the *Ascending Reticular Activating System* (ARAS). Activation of the ARAS has diffuse arousal effects on cortical areas of the brain, and higher cognition (thinking, reasoning, etc.). The ARAS can be likened to a volume dial, or sensory filter: the lower it is, the less arousal is sent to the higher brain areas and, thus, the lower a person's level of cortical (and cognitive) arousal.

According to this arousal theory, compared to extraverts, introverts have lower response thresholds of the ARAS (higher volume control) and, thus, more easily generate a higher level of cortical arousal. In consequence, they are easier to arouse and tend to be in a chronic state of high arousal throughout the day. In contrast, the ARAS of the extravert is sluggish (lower volume control) and it takes more stimulation to get them going to the same extent as the introvert. *For this reason*, introverts seek environments that do not over-stimulate them (therefore they are retiring and reserved in character); whereas extraverts behave in ways to increase their stimulation in order to reach an 'optimal' level of arousal defined in hedonic terms. In this way, introversion and extraversion themselves are reflections of behavioural strategies designed to modulate level of stimulation and, thus, level of arousal.

One demonstration of the greater arousability of introverts is seen in the lemon juice test, which attracts the attention of the media when they want a simple demonstration of Eysenck's personality theory (e.g., the BBC: www.bbc.co.uk/science/humanbody/mind/articles/personalityandindividuality/lemons.shtml). The test consists of four drops of lemon juice dripped on to the tongue and then the use of a dental swab to collect the resulting saliva – to establish a baseline, saliva is collected before the administration of the lemon drops. This beautifully simple experimental procedure leads to significantly more saliva generated in introverts than extraverts, and this happens even *before* the lemon drops are administrated, suggesting that placing the dental swab in the mouth is enough to stimulate the salivary glands. However, significantly more saliva is produced in introverts in response to the lemon drops as shown by the differences score in swab weight before and after lemon juice administration. Of interest here, the correlations, which are large in magnitude ($\sim$ −0.70) and statistically significant are with Introversion–Extraversion, not Neuroticism, suggesting that the Introversion–Extraversion dimension, and not the Neuroticism one, is the relevant personality dimension in relation to arousal.

In relation to his second dimension, Neuroticism, Eysenck relates this to *activation* of the limbic visceral system and emotional instability, although it must be said that he failed to elaborate this part of his theory to the same extent as Introversion–Extraversion and arousal (for further discussion of Eysenck's arousal/activation theory, see Chapter 7).

The arousal/activation theory has a high degree of relevance for clinical psychology, especially behavioural therapy. Eysenck assumed that, by virtue of their personality, people who develop neurosis have a predisposition to condition more easily to all stimuli, including aversive ones. Hence, they are more likely to become fearful and anxious than people low on this predisposition. For this reason, people who suffer neurosis tend to be introverted (i.e., highly arousable and chronically aroused), and this is especially true if they are also highly emotionally driven by virtue of their higher level of neuroticism. In contrast, lowly aroused extraverts show a variety of 'hysterical' behaviours – in modern day parlance, externalizing disorders. They are said to be more difficult to condition (socialize to societal mores), and in an attempt to modulate their arousal to reach an optimal level, more prone to 'act out', take more arousing drugs (e.g., amphetamine), and engage in a host of behaviours that often get them into trouble with the law – whether by direct behaviour (sensation-seeking) or as an indirect consequence (e.g., criminal behaviour to fund their drug addiction).

CRITIQUE OF THE STUDY

As should come as no surprise when the work of such a 'controversial' psychologist is discussed, there have been criticisms of Eysenck's 1944 classic study, which set a pattern of acrimonious debate that attended his entire professional life for the next 50 years (Corr, 2016a, b, c) – yet, as we will see, this is another example of, when scrutinized closely, Eysenck's work stands up very well.

The perceived problems with this 1944 classic study were highlighted in Buchanan's (2010, p. 158) biography of Eysenck, in which he states:

> Other researchers published inconsistent results. The most notable of these was a 1973 study by another former colleague, Edgar Howarth.

Howarth reported finding a very different structure to the one contained in Eysenck's 1944 own data. Howarth's first factor seemed to be cognitive ability, and Extraversion was poorly defined in the whole analysis. This outcome seems to undermine the very foundations of Eysenck's entire work in the field of personality psychology! It is, therefore, important to consider this matter in some detail, especially as few people have inspected Howarth's paper, and even fewer (if any) have reanalysed the actual data to arrive at their own conclusions.

Howarth started by acknowledging the importance of Eysenck's early work: 'In this foundation study he evoked, for the first time, the concepts of "neuroticism" and "extraversion" which have since played such a prominent part in his system' (p. 81) – although, as we have already seen, these constructs were already established in the psychology/psychiatry literature. Howarth then presented 'unrotated' and 'rotated' factor solutions – these are technical terms concerning how best to 'picture' in geometric and mathematical terms how items load on factors. The major thing to know about Howarth's two-factor *unrotated* solution is just how well it replicates Eysenck's own first two factors. There are, indeed, differences in the factor loadings, but the general pattern bears out Eysenck's interpretation in all essential respects. However, it is generally accepted that a *rotated* solution is best – factors are rotated in the first place to achieve psychological interpretability (e.g., a 'simple solution' in which items load on only one factor and are not confusingly spread over different factors).

In both Howarth's and Eysenck's analyses, factor one is defined by the following items: 'abnormality before illness', 'dependent', 'little energy', and in both analyses the highest loading is 'badly organized personality'. Both analyses indicate this factor is, most probably, Neuroticism. Howarth (p. 83) concluded: 'While the writer would prefer not to even attempt to interpret this unrotated factor there is an indication that this is a very broad kind of adjustment-emotionality factor.'

Concerning the second factor in the unrotated solution, both Howarth and Eysenck agree that this is a bipolar factor that contrasts anxiety/depression and hysteria. This outcome may be seen to support Eysenck labelling of this factor as Introversion–Extraversion (or for simplicity, Extraversion). However, Howarth (p. 83) preferred a different conclusion, saying: 'Thus our second factor is, possibly, a better candidate for "neuroticism" than the first. We would certainly not view this second factor as simply "hysteria–dysthymia" on the basis of only four variables among 39.' This is a fair point to make, but it is an *interpretation* of these data (no better or worse than Eysenck's alternate interpretation).

Concerning the third factor, which Eysenck identifies as Hypochondriasis, Howarth (p. 83) stated: 'Regarding the third factor, we find a similar grouping of salients [factor loadings] to that reported by Eysenck and have no quarrel with his interpretation.'

Turning to the two-factor *rotated* solution by Howarth, but not Eysenck, things are very different. Howarth used Principal Axis Factoring followed by Varimax rotation (the details are not of importance to the non-specialist aside from knowing that this procedure imposes statistical independence on the factors – i.e., they are not correlated). In Howarth's rotated solution, Factor 1 is defined by low intelligence, being unskilled, narrow interests and having little energy. Factor 2 seemed to Howarth to be an adjustment-emotionality factor reflecting a predisposition to either neurosis or psychosis – Howarth (p. 85) stated: 'The second factor cannot, in our opinion, be labelled "neuroticism"', although this interpretation would not be inconsistent with such a label.

Well, what about the hysteria–dysthymia factor (which forms the basis of Eysenck's later Extraversion)? Something similar to this is found in Factor 3, which contrasts 'obsessional' with 'hysteria'. Howarth (p. 85) noted: 'It would be unwise to name the factor "hysteria–dysthymia" solely on the basis of a restricted number of variables'. But an Eysenck-favourable interpretation is not inconsistent with the nature of this factor.

Therefore, what we seem to have is a rotated factor structure that lends itself to various interpretations, one of which is consistent with Eysenck's claim for his unrotated solution of two factors of maladjustment (Neuroticism) and dysthymia–hysteria (Introversion–Extraversion).

But, things did not stop there. Howarth went on to conduct another analysis based on an 'oblique' rotation – which allows factors to be correlated with one another. Howarth reported finding 16 such 'primary' factors, and his oblique rota-tion extracted the first factor which seemed to resemble Neuroticism and the second factor hysteria–dysthymia (Extraversion–Introversion). Although Howarth chose not to apply these labels to these two factors, the first two factors of the three-factor second-order solution do not contradict Eysenck's original unrotated two-factor solution and interpretation.

To reconsider this whole debate, Adam Perkins and Philip Corr asked one of the leading factor analysts in personality psychology, Professor William Revelle of Northwestern University in the USA, to reanalyse Eysenck's 1944 dataset. This is what Revelle reported: the analysis showed 'when the first four factors are extracted, the first 3 agree with the Eysenck solution – but the fourth factor does not resemble Eysenck's at all.' This reanalysis also showed that there were some aspects of the data, such as their ordinal nature, that render certain forms of factor analysis unreliable – this probably accounts for the aberrant findings of Howarth which have received so much attention by those who would want to criticize Eysenck's 1944 classic study.

What all of the above draws to our attention is that there are often tricky techni-cal issues that need to be considered when evaluating Eysenck's 1944 classic study. With the benefit of hindsight, no one would chose to rely upon the type of data presented to Eysenck in the early 1940s, and it really is not surprising that they lend themselves to very different interpretations. It is clear from this 1944 study that Eysenck was using the outcome of this statistical analysis to *inform* his theories; he was not using these data as the only means to arrive at a theory of the underlying factors of mental disorders. His 1944 data were a starting, not an end point. As the years rolled forward, Eysenck went on to confirm the existence of Introversion–Extraversion and Neuroticism in the normal population, and he spent the coming years refining their measurement and elucidating their biosocial natures. In recognition of their value, factors of Extraversion and Neuroticism are found in virtually all other descriptive measures of personality.

The fact that Eysenck wanted to develop a personality system that would be of practical use by psychiatrists and clinical psychologists has fared less well. Despite the many remarkable achievements during his lifetime (he died in 1997), Eysenck's personality questionnaires were never widely used by clinicians – they just seemed too distant from the patient's presenting symptoms. Whilst this was true, what they offered the research psychiatrist and clinical psychologist was a way of thinking, as well as measuring, the relationships between clinical condi-tions and broad dimensions of personality, the latter of which have considerable experimental evidence attached – this approach was more fully formed in the work of Jeffrey Gray and others who followed in his foot steps (see Chapter 7).

Despite the slow progress, there have been moves even within psychiatry to attempt to link human behaviour with psychopathology dimensionally and psychia-try is moving more towards dimensional assessment (Rosario-Campos et al., 2006). Normalization is now a common technique used in psychoeducation where, for example, normal curves of thoughts are shown to the patient to emphasize normal-ity. Also, research of traits on large numbers has become feasible exactly because concepts of dimensionality encourage the use of analogue samples to understand a problem (Abramowitz et al., 2014). However, the downside of the dimensional approach is in developing a dimension that is too abstract or too large and is not clinically precise enough. It may not relate satisfactorily to clinical significance.

So we have built on Eysenck in the refinement of personal constructs to make the constructs at the same time more clinically relevant but also more specific to the individual differences. One of the criticisms of Eysenck's personality theory was that the constructs such as extraversion, or arousability are simply too large to be relevant to specific clinical behaviour. For example, there are several activation systems of arousal and specific activation, such as: motor arousal, behavioural arousal, sensory arousal, which may often be discordant with each other. Does this mean we need to throw out the concept of general arousal? Absolutely not, since at a macro-level it still makes sense to describe a person along an aroused – not aroused dimension. Eysenck foresaw that many general notions may need operationalizing in specific ways as our knowledge becomes refined. The trick is to conserve both levels to predict both specific and general, as in recent attempts to characterize dimensions of motor arousability (O'Connor et al., 2015).

Eysenck's legacy from this 1944 paper lies perhaps not just in the applications of personality theory to clinical patients, but also in the refining of personal expressions and detecting subtle self-variables and measuring them and discovering new dimensions of clinically relevant behaviour which can be measured and linked to experimental constructs.

CONCLUSIONS

Already in 1944, Eysenck was speculating how his findings may translate into brain mechanisms and genetics. He clearly foresaw the necessity of cross-validation between psychometric and experimental methods. It may be time to recast Eysenck as a unifier in several respects. Apart from his concern to combine the two psychologies – normative (between individuals) and ipsative (within individual) – he was open to embracing a wide range of potential concepts if they could be operationalized and tested and he was at pains in his 1944 paper to integrate previous theories from a variety of theoretical sources.

It is appropriate to include the summary of Eysenck's work from one of his most severe critics (Lykken, 1982):

> He was perhaps the first experimental psychologist to realize the importance of individual differences, the first differential psychologist to exploit the causal theories and measurement techniques of the experimentalists, the first (only?) major psychologist to bridge the gulf between Cronbach's two disciplines of scientific psychology.

We owe it to Eysenck for enabling a whole new scientific field, personality neuroscience, to be developed which is bound to continue to make profound insights into individual variation seen in the general population and clinic – there is now even a journal, *Personality Neuroscience* (published by Cambridge University Press; founded and edited by one of the authors of this chapter), which in many ways is the culmination of Eysenck's 1944 classic study. Of considerable significance, Eysenck's idea that general dimensions of personality may determine vulnerability to clinical disorder is gaining scientific traction – this is seen in the remarkable finding that the general personality factor of Neuroticism cuts across a very broad range of psychiatric conditions (Hengartner et al., 2017), and now that we are gaining insight into the molecular genetics of Neuroticism (Luciano et al., 2018). Exciting times lie ahead for linking personality and psychopathology: it is what Eysenck promised us way back in 1944.

FURTHER READING

Corr, P. J. (2016). *Hans Eysenck: A contradictory psychology*. London: Palgrave.

Eysenck, H. J. (1967). *The biological basis of personality*. Springfield, IL: Charles C. Thomas.

Krueger, R. F., & Markon, K. E. (2014). The role of the DSM-5 personality trait model in moving toward a quantitative and empirically based approach to classifying personality and psychopathology. *Annual Review of Clinical Psychology, 10*, 477–501.

O'Connor, K., & Brodryzlova, Y. (2018). Patient oriented research in clinical and behavioral psychology. *Sage Research Methods Cases*. London: Sage.

REFERENCES

Abramowitz, J. S., Fabricant, L. E., Taylor, S., Deacon B. J., McKay, D. A., & Storch, E. A. (2014). The relevance of analogue studies for understanding obsessions and compulsions. *Clinical Psychology Review, 34*, 206–217.

Buchanan, R. D. (2010). *Playing with fire. The controversial career of Hans J. Eysenck*. Oxford: Oxford University Press.

Corr, P. J. (2016a). *Hans Eysenck: A contradictory psychology*. London: Palgrave.

Corr, P. J. (2016b). Hans J. Eysenck: Introduction to Centennial Special Issue. *Personality and Individual Differences, 103*, 1–7.

Corr, P. J. (2016c). The centenary of a maverick: Philip J. Corr on the life and work of Hans J. Eysenck. *The Psychologist, 29* (March), 234–238.

Eysenck, H. J. (1944). Types of personality. *Journal of Mental Science, 90*, 851–861.

Eysenck, H. J. (1947). *Dimensions of personality*. London: Kegan Paul.

Eysenck, H. J. (1952). *Scientific study of personality*. London: Routledge & Kegan Paul.

Eysenck, H. J. (1957). *The dynamics of anxiety and hysteria*. London: Routledge & Kegan Paul.

Eysenck, H. J. (1967). *The biological basis of personality*. Springfield, IL: Charles C. Thomas.

Eysenck, H. J. (1997). *Rebel with a cause: The autobiography of Hans Eysenck* (2nd ed.). Piscataway, NJ: Transaction Publishers.

Frost, R., & Hartl, T. L. (1996). A cognitive behavioral model of compulsive hoarding. *Behaviour Research and Therapy*, *34*, 341–350.

Hagenaars, S. P., & 18 others (2016). Shared genetic aetiology between cognitive functions and physical and mental health in UK Biobank (*N* = 112 151) and 24 GWAS consortia. *Molecular Psychiatry*, *21*, 1624–1632.

Hengartner, M. P., Tyrer, P., Ajdacic-Gross, V., Angst, J., & Rossler, W. (2017). Articulation and testing of a personality-centred model of psychopathology: Evidence from a longitudinal community study over 30 years. *European Archives of Psychiatry and Clinical Neuroscience*, 1–12.

Howarth, E. (1973). An hierarchical oblique factor analysis of Eysenck's study of 700 neurotics. *Social Behaviour and Personality*, *1*, 81–87.

Koszegi, N., O'Connor, K., & Brodryzlova, Y. (2017). Etiological models of hoarding disorder. *Journal of Psychology & Clinical Psychiatry*, *7*, 00453.

Luciano, M., Hagenaars, S. P., Davies, G., Hill, W. D., Clarke, T.-K., Shirlai, M., ... Deary, I. J. (2018). 116 independent genetic variants influence the neuroticism personality trait in over 329,000 UK Biobank individuals. *Nature Genetics*, *50*, 6–11.

Lykken, D. T. (1982). Book review of 'Personality, genetics, and behavior' by H. J. Eysenck. *Journal of Psychological Assessment*, *46*, 437–439.

MacCoun, R. J. (1998). Biases in the interpretation and use of research results. *Annual Review of Psychology*, *49*, 259–287.

O'Connor, K. P. (2008). Eysenck's model of individual differences. In G. J. Boyle, G. Matthews, & D. H. Saklofske (Eds.). *The Sage handbook of personality theory and assessment: Vol. 1 – Personality theories and models*. London: Sage.

O'Connor, K. P. (2009). Cognitive and meta-cognitive dimensions of psychoses. *Canadian Journal of Psychiatry*, *54*, 152–159.

O'Connor, K. (2016). Hans Eysenck and the individual differences paradigm in the clinical setting. *Personality and Individual Differences*, *103*, 99–104.

O'Connor, K. Audet, J. S., Julien, D., Aardema, F., Laverdure, A., & Lavoie, M. (2015). The style of planning action (STOP) questionnaire in OCD spectrum disorders. *Personality and Individual Differences*, *86*, 25–32.

O'Connor, K. P., Marchand, A., Bélanger, L., Mainguy, N., Landry, P., Savard, P., Turcotte, J., Dupuis, G., Harel, F., & Lachance, L. (2004). Psychological distress and adaptational problems associated with benzodiazepine withdrawal and outcome: A replication. *Addictive Behaviors*, *29*, 583–593.

O'Connor, K., St-Pierre Delorme, M.-E., Leclerc, J., Lavoie, M., & Blais, M. (2014) Meta-cognitions in Tourette syndrome, tic disorder, and body-focused repetitive disorder. *Canadian Journal of Psychiatry*, *59*, 417–425.

Polman, A., O'Connor, K. P., & Huisman M. (2011). Dysfunctional belief-based sub-groups and inferential confusion in obsessive–compulsive disorder. *Personality and Individual Differences*, *50*, 153–158.

Rosario-Campos, M. C., Miguel, E. C., Quatrano, S., Chacon, P., Ferrao, Y., Findley, D., Katsovich, L., Scahill, L., King, R. A., Woody, S. R., Tolin, D., Hollander, E., Kano, Y., & Leckman, J. F. (2006). The dimensional Yale–Brown Obsessive–Compulsive Scale (DY-BOCS): An instrument for assessing obsessive compulsive symptom dimensions. *Molecular Psychiatry*, *11*, 495–504.

Wolpe, J. (1973). *The practice of behavior therapy* (2nd ed.). New York: Pergamon Press.

5

Five Strong and Recurrent Personality Factors

Revisiting Tupes and Christal (1961)

John A. Johnson

BACKGROUND TO THE STUDY

After Allport and Odbert (1936; see Chapter 2 of this volume) found 17,953 words for human traits in Webster's unabridged *New International Dictionary*, an important question arose: how can we reduce this list to a more manageable number of traits? Allport and Odbert suggested reducing the list by using only words that referred to objectively real, stable behavioural tendencies such as *aggressive, introverted* and *sociable*, and setting aside words that referred to temporary states (e.g., *frantic*), value judgements (e.g., *worthy*), or characteristics only remotely related to personality (e.g., *lean*). This procedure narrowed the list to 4504 terms that Allport and Odbert considered to be suitable for a scientific description of personality.

Still, trying to measure 4504 personality traits would have been impractical, so personality researchers looked for additional ways to shorten the list of traits. Raymond Cattell (see Chapter 3 of this volume) reduced the list by grouping trait-words into 160 clusters, where each cluster contained words that were very similar in meaning. Cattell next had 100 people rate each other's personalities with these clusters, and, based upon patterns in these ratings, further reduced the number of trait-word clusters to 67. He compared his clusters to trait clusters described in a dozen published rating studies and retained only 35 personality trait clusters that were confirmed by other investigators.

Finally, Cattell reduced his set of 35 personality variables one more time with a statistical procedure called *factor analysis*. Factor analysis can identify a relatively small number of general themes, or *common factors*, within a larger set of personality measurements. His factor analyses indicated 11 personality factors in one study and 12 personality factors in a second study (Cattell, 1945, 1947).

All might have been well, except that another set of factor analyses published by Donald Fiske (1949; see Chapter 3 of this volume) repeatedly showed five rather than the 11 or 12 factors discovered by Cattell. The Tupes and Christal (1961/1992)[1] study was designed to explain the difference between Cattell's and Fiske's results.

Tupes and Christal note in the introduction to their paper that the difference between Cattell's and Fiske's results could have been due to Fiske's using only 22 of the 35 rating scales employed by Cattell. Or, the differences could have been a result of differences in the type of people being rated or the type of raters in each study. Yet another possible reason for the differences could have been the different forms of factor analysis used in each study. By reanalysing Fiske's and Cattell's data along with data they collected from U.S. Air Force personnel, Tupes and Christal hoped to clarify whether the universe of personality traits was better represented by five or 12 factors.

In addition to determining whether there were five or 12 broad factors in personality ratings, Tupes and Christal also hoped to convince readers that ratings of personality traits could predict important life outcomes, such as job performance. During the 1960s, some psychologists seriously doubted whether personality could be accurately measured by either self-report or ratings from acquaintances. Some even doubted whether there was enough consistency in people to say that they *have* personalities. Most of the introduction to the Tupes and Christal paper is actually devoted to reviewing and responding to those doubts and criticisms. In their introduction Tupes and Christal showed that if you measure personality properly, these measurements *will* predict important life outcomes. If Walter Mischel (see Chapter 6 of this volume) had read the introduction to the Tupes and Christal report, he might have never written his criticisms of personality.

DETAILED DESCRIPTION OF THE STUDY

THEORY

The word 'theory' does not appear in the Tupes and Christal (1961/1992) report because their research was not based on any particular psychological theory. They did list some hypotheses about the possible reasons why the Fiske and Cattell studies produced different results. First, Fiske (1949) used only 22 of the 35 rating variables that Cattell (1947) used. Furthermore, Fiske edited the wording of some of Cattell's rating scales. For example, whereas one of Cattell's rating scales was defined by 'sophisticated, intelligent, assertive' vs. 'simple, stupid, submissive', Fiske (1949) used only two trait-words for this scale: 'assertive vs. submissive' (John, Angleitner, & Ostendorf, 1988, p. 182). Tupes and Christal (1961/1992) also hypothesized that the differences in the number of factors could have been due to the different raters and persons rated across studies.

However, Tupes and Christal suspected that none of the possible reasons just listed were the real causes for the different results from the Cattell and Fiske studies. Rather, Tupes and Christal believed that the most likely reason for the different results was that Cattell used what is called *oblique rotation* of factors in his statistical analyses, while Fiske used what is called *orthogonal rotation* of factors. The difference between the two rotation strategies is that oblique factors are allowed to overlap with each other, whilst orthogonal factors are independent of each other – they do not overlap. Tupes and Christal (1961/1992) set up their study to test whether using the same (orthogonal) rotation method would produce the same factors across different sets of personality rating data, despite differences in the types of raters, types of persons being rated, and specific wording of the rating instruments.

METHODOLOGY

To see whether the same factors would emerge from different samples when the same form of factor analysis was employed, there was no need for Tupes and Christal to gather new data. Rather, they simply reanalysed eight existing datasets. In all of the samples, subjects had been rated with 22 or more of Cattell's (1947) 35 rating scales. Two data samples were from Fiske (1949), one from Cattell (1947), one from Cattell (1948), and four from one of their previous studies (Tupes & Christal, 1958). Tupes and Christal described the diversity of raters, the persons rated, and the nature of the relationship between raters and persons rated as follows:

> Briefly, they differ in length of acquaintanceship from 3 days to a year or more; in kind of acquaintanceship from assessment programs to a military training course to a fraternity house situation; in type of subject from airmen with only a high-school education to male and female undergraduate students to first-year graduate students; and in type of rater from very naïve persons to clinical psychologists or psychiatrists with years of experience in the evaluation of personality. (Tupes & Christal, 1992, p. 228)

Tupes and Christal's method was motivated by the observation that differences in the number of personality factors found in previous studies could have been due to either the differences in the participants and rating scales or to differences in the method of factor analysis (especially the type of rotation) used. By reanalysing data from these diverse samples with the same form of factor analysis, they reasoned that if similar factors are found across the samples, these factors might be 'universal enough to appear in a variety of samples, and [...] are not unduly sensitive to the rating conditions or situations' (p. 227). 'It would appear that any factors common to all of these groups would have a wide range of generality both in terms of type of subject and type of rating situation' (p. 228).

Today, desktop computers can perform a factor analysis in less than a second. Such computational power was not available to researchers who did factor analyses before 1950. Researchers like Cattell and Fiske had to manipulate large tables of data by hand, employing linear algebra with only the aid of mechanical adding machines. Short-cuts and estimations were used to save time and labour. Tupes and Christal (1961/1992) did have access to an IBM 650 computer, which was about 5 ft × 3 ft × 6 ft in size and weighed between 2000 and 3000 pounds. However, computer time was very expensive, so they used the computer to perform the orthogonal rotation of the factors in only one of their eight samples.

All of their other computations, which involved between 22 and 35 variables for the eight samples, were computed by hand with a desk calculator.

FINDINGS

Tupes and Christal (1992) summarized their findings in the following sentence: 'In every sample except one there appeared to be five relatively strong and recurrent personality factors and nothing more of any consequence' (p. 245). What Tupes and Christal meant by 'five strong and recurrent personality factors' is that, regardless of the total number of factors found in any sample, in every sample each of the first five factors was clearly defined by the same unique set of trait-words. Tupes and Christal labelled the common theme among the trait-words that defined each of the five factors with a term from previous factor-analytic studies. In particular, they often chose the labels used by John French (1953), a scientist at the Educational Testing Service who had published a thorough review of previous personality factor analyses. The traits that defined each factor and the labels chosen by Tupes and Christal are described below.

Tupes and Christal's first factor was defined by the following traits in all eight samples: *Silent vs. Talkative*; *Secretive vs. Frank*; *Cautious vs. Adventurous*; *Submissive vs. Assertive*; and *Languid, Slow vs. Energetic*. Additionally, *Self-Contained vs. Sociable* helped to define the first factor in six of the eight samples. (Keep in mind that some ratings cannot show high loading in all eight samples because some samples used only 22 or 30 of Cattell's 35 rating scales.) Together, according to Tupes and Christal, these traits described a recurrent factor labelled by French (1953) as *Surgency* and by others as *Extroversion*.[2]

Traits defining the second factor in all eight samples were *Spiteful vs. Good-Natured*; *Obstructive vs. Cooperative*; *Suspicious vs. Trustful*; *Rigid vs. Adaptable*; and *Cool, Aloof vs. Attentive to People*. In six of the eight samples, *Jealous vs. Not So*; *Demanding vs. Emotionally Mature*; *Self-Willed vs. Mild*; and *Hard, Stern vs. Kindly* helped to define the second factor. Tupes and Christal noted that this second factor corresponded closely to the *Agreeableness* factor described by French (1953).

Traits that defined the third factor in all eight samples were *Frivolous vs. Responsible* and *Unscrupulous vs. Conscientious*. In addition, *Relaxed, Indolent* vs. *Insistently Orderly*; *Quitting vs. Persevering*; and *Unconventional vs. Conventional* defined the third factor in six of the eight samples. Tupes and Christal, following French (1953), labelled this factor *Dependability*.

Traits defining the fourth factor in all eight samples were *Worrying, Anxious, vs. Placid*; *Easily Upset vs. Poised, Tough*; and *Changeable vs. Emotionally Stable*. Additional traits that defined this factor in six of the eight samples were *Neurotic vs. Not So*; *Hypochondriacal vs. Not So*; and *Emotional vs. Calm*. Tupes and Christal chose their own label, *Emotional Stability*, for this factor.

The fifth factor was less clearly defined than the first four. For one, the personality traits that defined this factor in the seven male samples split into two different factors in the female sample, which we might call 5A and 5B. Overall, only the following three traits defined the fifth factor in all eight samples: *Boorish vs. Intellectual,*

Cultured; *Clumsy, Awkward vs. Polished*; and *Immature vs. Independent-Minded*. In four of the male samples, *Lacking Artistic Feelings vs. Esthetically Fastidious* helped to define the fifth factor. *Lacking Artistic Feelings vs. Esthetically Fastidious* also helped to define factor 5B in the female sample. And, *Practical, Logical vs. Imaginative* helped to define the factor in four of the male samples, but was barely related to either factor 5A or 5B in the female sample. Following French (1953), Tupes and Christal labelled the fifth factor *Culture*.

The first paragraph of the Discussion section and the last two sentences of the Tupes and Christal (1992) article summarize well the major findings of their research:

> The results of these analyses clearly indicate that differences in samples, situations, raters, and lengths and kinds of acquaintanceship have little effect on the factor structure underlying ratings of personality traits. Statistical tests are not needed to indicate the similarity of corresponding factors from one analysis to another. There can be no doubt that the five factors found throughout all eight analyses are recurrent. (p. 244)

And,

> The five recurrent factors were labelled as (*a*) Surgency, (*b*) Agreeableness, (*c*) Dependability, (*d*) Emotional Stability, and (*e*) Culture. While no claim is made by the authors that the five factors identified are the only personality dimensions, reasons are given in support of their fundamental nature and probable invariance.

IMPACT OF THE STUDY

Historical reviews of the five major personality factors (e.g., Digman, 1990; Goldberg, 1993, 1995; Johnson, 2017; McCrae, 1992) agree that the Tupes and Christal (1961/1992) study would have had zero impact on the field of personality because it appeared as an obscure Air Force technical report, but for the fact that Warren Norman, a professor at the University of Michigan, became aware of the report when he was contracted by the Air Force to develop a self-report version of the peer-rating instrument used by Tupes and Christal. Eventually Norman (1963) published in a mainstream academic journal a peer-rating study similar to Tupes and Christal's. Using four rating scales that he thought best represented each of the five factors identified by Tupes and Christal, Norman (1963) found exactly the same five factors as Tupes and Christal, although he chose slightly different names for some of the factors. Norman used the following Roman numerals and labels for the factors. *I. Extroversion or Surgency*; *II. Agreeableness*; *III. Conscientiousness*; *IV. Emotional Stability*; and *V. Culture*. Identifying the five factors in this order with Roman numerals became standard in subsequent research (e.g., Hofstee, de Raad, & Goldberg, 1992).

Research published by Jack Digman and Lewis R. Goldberg led to increased acceptance of the five personality factors (Goldberg, 1993). Also, in the realm of self-report personality questionnaires, Hogan (1986) published a new personality inventory based explicitly on the Tupes and Christal factors. Johnson (2017) reported that Hogan invited Paul T. Costa, Jr and Robert R. McCrae to Johns Hopkins in the late 1970s to convince them to add Agreeableness and Conscientiousness scales to their NEO personality inventory (which had been designed around three clusters they found in Cattell's 16PF questionnaire), but Costa and McCrae were not convinced. At least not until Goldberg showed them how he and Digman kept finding the Tupes and Christal factors in every dataset they analysed. After a meeting with Goldberg, Costa and McCrae revised their inventory so that its five major domain scales paralleled the five factors identified by Tupes and Christal (McCrae & Costa, 1985). By comparing scores on their new inventory (NEO PI; Costa & McCrae, 1985, 1992) to nearly every other major personality inventory, Costa and McCrae were able to demonstrate that all of these other inventories assessed at least some of the Tupes and Christal factors and nothing significant beyond them (Johnson, 2017).

The combined efforts of trait-word analysts Norman, Digman and Goldberg with NEO PI authors Costa and McCrae finally led to a broad acceptance of the Big Five or Five-Factor Model (FFM) as the dominant view of the basic factors of personality from the 1990s to the present (Johnson, 2017). The Big Five or Five-Factor Model (FFM) has had a strong influence on research undertaken during this time. Researchers who submitted for publication manuscripts on narrow personality traits without mentioning the Big Five were often asked by reviewers and editors to explain how their work related to the five major personality factors. Researchers who wanted to perform personality meta-analyses (studies that reanalysed and compared results of research that had already been completed) now had a framework for comparing results from studies that used different personality measures. All that had to be done was to translate the measures of each study into Big-Five terms, and studies that previously could not have been compared could now be compared. One of the most important examples of such a meta-analysis was a study by Barrick and Mount (1991).

Prior to the Barrick and Mount (1991) study, psychologists were largely sceptical about the ability of personality measures to predict job performance. Part of this scepticism arose from the general criticism of personality traits in the 1960s. But the absence of positive consensus about applying personality assessment to personnel selection was also due to the fact that dozens of different personality measures had been used in research on this topic and there was no way of comparing and combining research findings. By classifying personality measures with the Big Five, Barrick and Mount (1991) were able to reach solid conclusions about the personality traits that influenced and various aspects of job performance. The Barrick and Mount article became a citation classic; it has been cited 9392 times (via Google Scholar [April 24, 2018]).

Another landmark meta-analysis of the impact of the Big Five on important life outcomes was published by Roberts, Kuncel, Shiner, Caspi and Goldberg (2007). In this study they compared the impact of the Big Five personality traits to cognitive ability and socioeconomic status on mortality, divorce and occupational attainment.

They concluded that the amount of personality influence was similar to the influence of cognitive abilities and socioeconomic status.

When many meta-analyses of a particular topic have been completed, it is possible to do a meta-analysis of the meta-analyses, which is called a *metasynthesis study*. Strickhouser, Zell and Krizan (2017) did a metasynthesis study of 36 meta-analyses of the impact of personality on physical and mental health. They found a significant impact of personality on overall health, with a multiple correlation of .35 with the Big Five traits. The impact of personality on mental health was found to be stronger than the impact on physical health, and the effects were stronger for Agreeableness, Conscientiousness and Neuroticism than for Extraversion and Openness to Experience.

Another major influence of the Big Five model has been its impact on how we think about personality disorders. Prior to the Big Five model, personality disorders were seen as categories – you were either in a personality disorder category or not. When the *Diagnostic and Statistical Manual* (DSM) was revised from Version IV-TR to Version V, the personality disorder category system was not abandoned completely, but was revised to include a five-dimensional diagnosis system highly similar to the Big Five (Widiger, Gore, Crego, Rojas, & Oltmanns, 2017). In this new way of thinking, the line between normal and disordered personality is blurred. Personality disorder is now considered a matter of degree, where extremely high or low scores on the Big Five can indicate disorder.

The integrating framework of the Big Five also made it possible to better understand the heritability of personality. Genetic effects account for about half of the differences in each Big Five personality factor, while the remaining differences are due to environmental influences that make family members different from one another (Kandler, Bleidorn, Riemann, Angleitner, & Spinath, 2011).

The Big Five model has also been found useful for studying different kinds of personality change and stability over the lifespan. A meta-analysis of 152 longitudinal studies (Roberts & DelVecchio, 2000) examined what is called *rank-order stability versus change* in personality traits (e.g., whether the most extraverted young adults continue to be the most extraverted individuals during middle age and late adulthood). They found an increase in rank-order stability across the decades of life, rising from average correlations in the .40s during the first decade of life to about .74 in the 50s. Because the rank-order of stability of .74 is close to the reliability of personality measurement, one can conclude that rank-order of personality traits is extremely stable by age 50.

Another meta-analysis of 92 longitudinal studies by Brent Roberts and his colleagues (Roberts, Walton, & Viechtbauer, 2006) examined changes in the *average level* of the Big Five personality traits. The study found that people generally increased in Social Dominance (one aspect of Extraversion), Agreeableness, Conscientiousness and Emotional Stability over the lifespan. In contrast, while initially increasing in Openness to Experience and Social Vitality (a second aspect of Extraversion) during the first two decades of life, people decreased thereafter.

In summary, Tupes and Christal's five-factor view of personality has had an enormous impact on personality research since 1990. By providing an organizing framework, the Five-Factor Model has allowed meta-analyses of the impact of personality on important life outcomes such as divorce, health and mortality, and occupational behaviour and job performance, as well as meta-analyses of genetic and environmental influences on personality and change and stability of personality over the lifespan. These demonstrations of the ability of personality assessments to predict significant life outcomes was exactly what Tupes and Christal (1961/1992) hoped that personality research could achieve.

CRITIQUE OF THE STUDY

Although strong and solid in many respects, the Tupes and Christal (1961/1992) study is not without weaknesses. One of the first questions one should ask about any study is, 'How representative is the subject sample?' Unlike so many published studies that employed one group of undergraduate students as subjects, Tupes and Christal used eight groups, and only two of them were undergraduates. However, two of the samples were psychology graduate students (a rather exclusive group), and the other four were students or graduates of Officer Candidate School for the US Air Force (again, a rather specialized group). Worst of all, only one of the eight samples was female, and in this sample the ratings that defined the Culture factor in the seven male samples split into two factors. This should immediately raise the question of whether personality factor structure is actually the same for males and females.

Tupes and Christal (1961/1992) do not report the nationality and ethnicity of subjects in the eight samples. Neither do the original reports from which they drew their data, but we can be fairly confident that nearly all of them were native-English-speaking, Caucasian Americans. Subsequent research has revealed consistent sex differences on some of the Big Five traits, with women expressing higher levels of Agreeableness and Neuroticism than men (e.g., Costa, Terracciano, & McCrae, 2001), but no studies have presented evidence that there are different basic personality factors for men and women. Costa et al. (2001) also report that the sex differences they obtained were greater in modern, egalitarian societies than in more traditional societies. This finding, which was confirmed in a later study by Schmitt, Realo, Voracek and Allik (2008), is important for understanding the biological and cultural basis for the Big Five traits.

The cultural and national factors that Tupes and Christal ignored have been the focus of intense, cross-cultural research on language and personality. The Allport–Odbert strategy of compiling a comprehensive list of personality trait-words from the dictionary has now been repeated in many languages other than English. Saucier and Goldberg (2001) provided one of the first reviews of non-English-language personality studies. They noted that factor analyses of German personality traits ratings produced nearly exactly the same Big Five factors found in English and therefore referred to these personality factors as the Anglo-Germanic Big Five or AGBF. Factor solutions highly similar to the AGBF have also been reported in Dutch, Polish, Czech and Turkish language studies. Italian,

Hungarian and Korean studies also produced the Big Five, but with two separate Agreeableness factors: one emphasizing a peaceful, quiet versus irritable disposition and the other, sincerity or integrity versus selfishness. Finally, two similar seven-factor solutions were reported – one for Hebrew and the other for Filipino. Analyses of these languages produced the Big Five with two Agreeableness factors similar to the Italian, Hungarian and Korean studies, but also produced a factor called Negative Valence, consisting of a mixture of undesirable traits from the Big Five. Saucier and Goldberg (2001) concluded that that AGBF can be found in many languages, but that the personality factors most likely to be found across most languages were Extraversion, Agreeableness and Conscientiousness.

A second major review of cross-language personality studies was done by de Raad, Barelds, Timmerman, de Roover, Mlačić and Church (2014). In addition to the studies cited by Saucier and Goldberg (2001), de Raad et al. noted studies of Albanian, Arabic, Bulgarian, Chinese, Croatian, French, Greek, Indian, Japanese, Maa, Malay, Norwegian, Persian, Portuguese, Russian, Slovak, South African, Spanish and Supyire-Senufo. A majority of these studies produced five or six interpretable factors. If there is a sixth major factor beyond the Big Five, the best candidate appears to be what has been called *Sincerity, Integrity*, or *Honesty-Humility* (Ashton, Lee, & Son, 2000).

Even with a good deal of consensus about the presence of the Big Five across languages and cultures, there are still critics who question the use of ordinary language for scientific purposes. The reasoning behind this criticism is that concepts in other, much more-developed sciences such as physics, biology and astronomy have evolved far beyond the concepts that in ordinary language describe everyday experiences. Everyday experience told us for thousands of years that the sun moves across a bowl-shaped sky above the earth, that whales and dolphins are fish, that bats are a type of bird, and that mass and time are not affected by velocity. However, modern astronomy tells us that the earth revolves around the sun, modern biology tells us that whales, dolphins and bats are mammals like us, not fish or birds, and modern physics tells us that mass increases and time slows as velocity increases.

A related objection to the Big Five factors from ordinary language is that there is no theory that explains the factors. In contrast to modern astronomy, biology and physics, which explain visible appearance in terms of unseen, theoretical entities, factor analyses of trait ratings merely describes how some personality judgements are related to other personality judgements, with no theory to explain why personality ratings cluster into five factors and what these factors really represent (Block, 1995; McCrae, 1990; McCrae, Costa, & Piedmont, 1993).

Authors of many personality *questionnaires*, on the other hand, have designed their questionnaires to assess supposedly scientific, theoretical concepts (McCrae & John, 1992). Hans Eysenck, for example, created a theory of personality based on theoretical differences in genes, behaviouristic learning and physiology. He viewed the psychiatric patients he saw at Maudsley Hospital and criminals as exhibiting extreme forms of traits found in the normal population. He concluded after a review of the literature on questionnaires, ratings and other assessment methods that three recurrent personality dimensions underlay normal and extreme varia-tions in personality: extraversion, neuroticism and psychoticism, and his factor analyses (with orthogonal rotation) of items on existing questionnaires confirmed his conclusions (Jensen, 1958).

Two major responses can be made to the criticism that the Big Five model is unscientific because a scientific model of personality should employ theoretical concepts that go beyond ordinary language. One is to distinguish between two scientific questions: (a) what is the nature of qualities inside of persons that give rise to personality? versus (b) how do people's perceptions of personality in oth-ers in everyday life influence their behaviour? Without considering the answer to (a), one can still do scientific research on (b) how ordinary persons' perceptions of personality (described in everyday language) influence their behaviour toward the persons they perceive. The perception of others' personalities is a topic that lies at the intersection between personality and social psychology and is used to help explain phenomena such as aggression, altruism, coalition formation, coop-eration and prejudice.

Another response to the criticism that the Big Five model has no theory behind it is to admit that the model _is_ atheoretical, but to point out that sciences often begin with observations and descriptions of patterns, followed by alternative theories of these patterns, which then direct future research. Even a psychologist as theoretically inclined as Eysenck declared that 'description, classification, and measurement must be worked out in the personality field before worthwhile attempts can be made to explain the underlying causes of differences in personal-ity' (Jensen, 1958). After the Big Five model was widely accepted, various theories have been proposed to explain the five factors. A number of these theories have been published in a book edited by Wiggins (1996).

CONCLUSIONS

Tupes and Christal (1961/1992) not only helped to initiate the enormously successful Big Five or Five-Factor Model, they also contributed to our under-standing of how sound personality assessment can predict significant life outcomes. Their research was not perfect. Despite an unusually large subject sample with a variety of raters and persons rated, females were underrepre-sented, as were non-Caucasian, non-English-speaking participants. Science advances by correcting for weaknesses in any research study, and research building on the Tupes and Christal study affirmed that the Five Factors are found in women as well as people of various ages, educational levels and ethnicities living in different cultures.

An irony of the Tupes and Christal study is that they developed their peer rating scales to overcome a concern that self-report measures of personality would be biased by self-enhancement, but the peer rating project was dropped because of a similar concern from the officer candidates that their peers were giving them biased, low ratings in order to improve their own chances (Christal, 1992).

'In Christal's words, "some applicants would stab their mother to be a pilot"' (Kyllonen, 2013). Personality researchers are still concerned today about how to obtain accurate, unbiased self-reports and acquaintance judgements of personality (Funder, 1995; Johnson & Hogan, 2006). Again, science advances by noting methodological problems and devising solutions for them.

A history of any subject always has to simplify reality by ignoring the countless, messy details in order to create an understandable story. Many details of the research leading up to the Tupes and Christal classic study could not be included in this chapter. Likewise, only a small sampling of current controversies and developments of the Big Five after Tupes and Christal has been presented here. The reader is encouraged to read any of the references in the reference list for more details on past and present Big Five research. In particular, the John, Angleitner and Ostendorf (1988) article gives a detailed, interesting history of personality assessment through trait-words. If you read the portion of this article that describes Cattell's research programme, you will be amazed by the number of inconsistencies and uncertainties in his reports and will probably see the emergence of the reliable Big Five as a miracle. Goldberg (1981, 1990, 1993, 1995), a central figure in promoting the Tupes and Christal model, is a genuine wordsmith; his articles are as enjoyable as they are informative. Finally, for understanding the place of Tupes and Christal within the overall history of Big-Five research, there is Johnson (2017).

NOTES

1. 'Recurrent personality factors based on trait ratings' was originally submitted as a US Air Force technical report by Ernest C. Tupes and Raymond E. Christal in 1961. The report is unclassified and lies in the public domain because it was written for and funded by the federal government. A PDF copy can be obtained from the Defense Technical Information Center at the following URL: www.dtic.mil/dtic/tr/fulltext/u2/267778.pdf. In 1992, Robert R. McCrae edited a special issue of the *Journal of Personality* on the Five-Factor Model (FFM). Because the Tupes and Christal (1961) report was considered to be a pivotal step toward the development of the FFM, McCrae approached Christal about reprinting the report in the special issue. Christal agreed. McCrae described the editing for the 1992 reprint version as follows: 'In preparing it for publication, the front matter and appendices have been omitted, the entries in the tables have been given to two decimal places where possible, and the format of tables and references has been updated. Except for minor corrections, approved by Dr. Christal, the text has been given verbatim; occasional editorial clarifications are given in brackets' (p. 218). The only significant information missing in the 1992 reprint are the complete matrices of correlations and factor loadings that appear in the appendix of the 1961 report. In accordance with APA citation style, the Tupes and Christal report is cited in this chapter as (1961/1992), unless the citation includes a direct quotation, in which case a reference is made to the more legible 1992 *Journal of Personality* reprint.

2. Although the spelling *extroversion* is very common today, *extraversion* is actually the original spelling used by the originator of the term, C. G. Jung. Kaufman (2015) has reviewed the history of the spelling of this word, arguing that *extraversion* is the preferred spelling.

FURTHER READING

Goldberg, L. R. (1993). The structure of phenotypic personality traits. *American Psychologist, 48*, 26–34.

John, O. P., Angleitner, A., & Ostendorf, F. (1988). The lexical approach to personality: A historical view of trait taxonomic research. *European Journal of Personality, 2*, 171–203.

Johnson, J. A. (2017). Big-Five Model. In V. Ziegler-Hill & T. K. Shackelford (Eds.), *Encyclopedia of personality and individual differences*. New York: Springer.

REFERENCES

Allport, G. W., & Odbert, H. S. (1936). Trait-names: A psycho-lexical study. *Psychological Monographs, 47* (Whole No. 211).

Ashton, M. C., Lee, K., & Son, C. (2000). Honesty as the sixth factor of personality: Correlations with Machiavellianism, primary psychopathy, and social adroitness. *European Journal of Personality, 14*, 359–368.

Barrick, M. R., & Mount, M. K. (1991). The Big-Five personality dimensions and job performance: A meta-analysis. *Personnel Psychology, 44*, 1–26.

Block, J. (1995). A contrarian view of the five-factor approach to personality description. *Psychological Bulletin, 117*, 187–215.

Cattell, R. B. (1945). The description of personality: Principles and findings in a factor analysis. *American Journal of Psychology, 58*, 69–90.

Cattell, R. B. (1947). Confirmation and clarification of primary personality factors. *Psychometrika, 12*, 197–220.

Cattell, R. B. (1948). The primary personality factors in women compared with those in men. *British Journal of Psychology, 1*, 114–130.

Christal, R. E. (1992). Author's note on 'Recurrent Personality Factors Based on Trait Ratings'. *Journal of Personality, 60*, 221–224.

Costa, P. T., Jr., & McCrae, R. R. (1985). *The NEO Personality Inventory manual*. Odessa, FL: Psychological Assessment Resources.

Costa, P. T., Jr., & McCrae, R. R. (1992). *Revised NEO Personality Inventory (NEO PI-R) and NEO Five-Factor Inventory (NEO-FFI): Professional manual*. Psychological Assessment Resources, Odessa, FL.

Costa, P. T., Terracciano, A., & McCrae, R. R. (2001). Gender differences in personality traits across cultures: Robust and surprising findings. *Journal of Personality and Social Psychology, 81*, 322–331.

de Raad, B., Barelds, D. P. H., Timmerman, M. E., de Roover, K., Mlačić, B., & Church, A. T. (2014). Towards a pan-cultural personality structure: Input from 11 psycholexical studies. *European Journal of Personality, 28*, 497–510.

Digman, J. M. (1990). Personality structure: Emergence of the Five-Factor Model. *Annual Review of Psychology, 41*, 417–440.

Fiske, D. W. (1949). Consistency of the factorial structures of personality ratings from different sources. *Journal of Abnormal and Social Psychology, 44*, 329–344.

French, J. W. (1953). *The description of personality measurements in terms of rotated factors*. Princeton, NJ: Educational Testing Service.

Funder, D. C. (1995). On the accuracy of personality judgment: A realistic approach. *Psychological Review, 102*, 652–670.

Goldberg, L. R. (1981). Language and individual differences: The search for universals in personality lexicons. In L. Wheeler (Ed.), *Review of personality and social psychology: Vol. 2*. Beverly Hills, CA: Sage.

Goldberg, L. R. (1990). An alternative 'description of personality': The Big-Five factor structure. *Journal of Personality and Social Psychology, 59*, 1216–1229.

Goldberg, L. R. (1993). The structure of phenotypic personality traits. *American Psychologist, 48*, 26–34.

Goldberg, L. R. (1995). What the hell took so long? Donald W. Fiske and the big-five factor structure. In P. E. Shrout & S. T. Fiske (Eds.), *Personality research, methods, and theory: A Festschrift honoring Donald W. Fiske*. Hillsdale, NJ: Lawrence Erlbaum.

Hofstee, W. K. B., de Raad, B., & Goldberg, L. R. (1992). Integration of the Big Five and circumplex approaches to trait structure. *Journal of Personality and Social Psychology, 63*, 146–163.

Hogan, R. (1986). *Hogan Personality Inventory manual*. Minneapolis, MN: National Computer Systems.

Jensen, A. R. (1958). The Maudsley personality inventory. *Acta Psychologia, 14*, 314–325.

John, O. P., Angleitner, A., & Ostendorf, F. (1988). The lexical approach to personality: A historical view of trait taxonomic research. *European Journal of Personality, 2*, 171–203.

Johnson, J. A. (2017). Big-Five Model. In V. Ziegler-Hill & T. K. Shackelford (Eds.), *Encyclopedia of personality and individual differences*. New York: Springer.

Johnson, J. A., & Hogan, R. (2006). A socioanalytic view of faking. In R. Griffith (Ed.), *A closer examination of applicant faking behavior*. Greenwich, CT: Information Age Publishing.

Kandler, C., Bleidorn, W., Riemann, R., Angleitner, A., & Spinath, F. M. (2011). The genetic links between the Big Five personality traits and general interest domains. *Personality and Social Psychology Bulletin, 37*, 1633–1643.

Kaufman, S. B. (2015). *The difference between ExtrAversion and ExtrOversion* [Blog post, 31 August]. Retrieved from https://blogs.scientificamerican.com/beautiful-minds/the-difference-between-extraversion-and-extroversion/# (accessed 19 July 2018).

Kyllonen, P. C. (2013). Profiles in military psychology: Raymond E. Christal. *The Military Psychologist, October*. Retrieved from www.apadivisions.org/division-19/publications/newsletters/military/2013/10/raymond-christal.aspx (accessed 19 July 2018).

McCrae, R. R. (1990). Traits and trait names: How well is Openness represented in natural languages? *European Journal of Personality, 4*, 119–229.

McCrae, R. R. (1992). Editor's introduction to Tupes and Christal. *Journal of Personality, 60*, 217–219.

McCrae, R. R., & Costa, P. T., Jr. (1985). Updating Norman's 'adequate taxonomy': Intelligence and personality dimensions in natural language and in questionnaires. *Journal of Personality and Social Psychology, 49*, 710–721.

McCrae, R. R., Costa, P. T., Jr., & Piedmont, R. (1993). Folk concepts, natural language, and psychological constructs: The California Psychological Inventory and the five-factor model. *Journal of Personality, 61*, 1–26.

McCrae, R. R., & John, O. P. (1992). An introduction to the five-factor model and its applications. *Journal of Personality, 60*, 175–215.

Norman, W. T. (1963). Toward an adequate taxonomy of personality attributes: Replicated factor structure in peer nomination personality ratings. *Journal of Abnormal & Social Psychology, 66*, 574–583.

Roberts, B. W., & DelVecchio, W. F. (2000). The rank-order consistency of personality traits from childhood to old age: A quantitative review of longitudinal studies. *Psychological Bulletin, 126*, 3–25.

Roberts, B. W., Kuncel, N. R., Shiner, R., Caspi, A., & Goldberg, L. R. (2007). The power of personality: The comparative validity of personality traits, socioeconomic status, and cognitive ability for predicting important life outcomes. *Perspectives on Psychological Science, 2*, 313–345.

Roberts, B. W., Walton, K. E., & Viechtbauer, W. (2006). Patterns of mean-level change in personality traits across the life course: A meta-analysis of longitudinal studies. *Psychological Bulletin, 132*, 1–25.

Saucier, G., & Goldberg, L. R. (2001). Lexical studies of indigenous personality factors: Premises, products, and prospects. *Journal of Personality, 69*, 847–879.

Schmitt, D. P., Realo, A., Voracek, M., & Allik, J. (2008). Why can't a man be more like a woman? Sex differences in Big Five personality traits across 55 cultures. *Journal of Personality and Social Psychology, 94*, 168–182.

Strickhouser, J. E., Zell, E., & Krizan, Z. (2017). Does personality predict health and well-being? A metasynthesis. *Health Psychology, 36*, 797–810.

Tupes, E. C., & Christal, R. E. (1958). *Stability of personality trait rating factors obtained under diverse conditions. (Technical Note WADC-TN-58-61.)* Personnel Laboratory, Wright Air Development Center: Lackland Air Force Base, TX.

Tupes, E. C., & Christal, R. E. (1961/1992). *Recurrent personality factors based on trait ratings (USAF ASD Technical Report No. 61–97).* Aeronautical Systems Division, Personnel Laboratory: Lackland Air Force Base, TX. (Reprinted as Tupes, E. C., & Christal, R. E. (1992). Recurrent personality factors based on trait ratings. *Journal of Personality, 60*, 225–251.)

Widiger, T. A., Gore, W. L., Crego C., Rojas, S. L., & Oltmanns, J. R. (2017). Five-Factor Model and personality disorder. In T. A. Widiger (Ed.), *The Oxford handbook of the Five Factor Model of personality*. New York: Oxford University Press.

Wiggins, J. S. (Ed.) (1996). *The Five-Factor Model of personality: Theoretical perspectives*. New York: Guilford Press.

6

The Challenge to Trait Theory

Revisiting Mischel (1968)

Michael W. Eysenck

BACKGROUND TO THE STUDY

Non-psychologists sometimes mistakenly believe that psychologists focus mostly on individual differences in intelligence and personality. In fact, that has never been the case. As Murphy and Kovach (1972, p. 138) pointed out in their history of psychology, 'Individual differences had not been seriously treated before [the publication of Galton's book *Hereditary Genius* in 1869] as part of the subject matter of psychology. Perhaps their neglect had been the most extraordinary blind spot in previous formal psychology.'

During the first half of the twentieth century, numerous psychologists made use of self-report questionnaires and/or personality ratings in the attempt to uncover the major personality traits (see H. J. Eysenck & M. W. Eysenck, 1985, for a review). It was typically assumed that the optimal approach to capturing most of the complexity of individual differences in personality was to focus on identifying a relatively large number of primary or correlated personality traits. For example, consider this quotation from Guilford (1939, p. 331): 'The number of primary traits that exist in personality is probably very large, although those of greatest social importance may not exceed a score in number.' In practice, he identified 11 such personality traits.

Cattell also focused on primary or correlated personality traits. This led him to develop the Sixteen Personality Factor Questionnaire (16PF), which was first published in 1949 and revised several times thereafter (see Cattell & Cattell, 1995, for a review). The 16 primary traits he identified overlapped only partially with the 11 traits previously identified by Guilford. Matters were further confused when H. J. Eysenck (1944) identified only two secondary personality factors that were independent of each other (i.e., orthogonal) (see Chapter 4).

We have seen so far that part of the background to Mischel's (1968) book *Personality and Assessment* was the existence of heterogeneous views concerning the number and nature of personality traits. There were also profound disagreements about the optimal method for assessing personality. While many psychologists relied on self-report questionnaires or ratings, others made use of projective tests (e.g., the Rorschach Inkblot Test; the Thematic Apperception Test). These tests provided individuals with considerable scope in terms of how they responded to ambiguous stimuli and were designed to reveal their hidden emotions and motivations.

As is perhaps apparent from what has been said so far, all was not well with personality research and theory in the years leading up to Mischel's (1968) book. Of particular importance was a book by Vernon (1964). He was an expert in personality research and he was very unimpressed by it. As Jones (1965, p. 341) pointed out in a review of the book, '[The approach used by Eysenck and Cattell] is shown to have grave weaknesses and very limited application ... despite a vast amount of research into personality, psychology has failed to provide any satisfactory system of assessment ... any adequate system must allow for the interactions between inner dispositions, ... external stimulation, and a person's behaviour.'

DETAILED DESCRIPTION OF THE STUDY

M ischel (1968) provided a lengthy (and very discursive) account of the approach taken by personality theorists and researchers. Much of his focus was on the concept of the trait, which is central to many theories of personality. Personality traits can be defined as stable aspects of a person that are moderately stable or consistent over time and that exhibit individual differences. Examples of major personality traits are openness, conscientiousness, extraversion, agreeableness and neuroticism (Costa & McCrae, 1992). As Mischel (1968, p. 42) pointed out, 'The intuitive conviction that persons do have consistent and widely generalised personality traits seems very compelling.'

Mischel (1968, 1969) was totally unconvinced of the importance of personality traits. In essence, he argued that there were major problems with their conceptualization. He also argued that the empirical evidence available in the research literature failed to provide more than modest support for the existence of personality traits. Below we consider his arguments in more detail.

First, he was concerned that personality traits lack explanatory power. According to him, what happens very often in personality research and theorizing is as follows: 'To invoke trait names as explanatory entities ... confuses constructions about behaviour with the causes of behaviour. Traits are used first simply as adverbs describing behaviour (e.g., "he behaves anxiously") and then abstracted to "he has anxiety"... We quickly emerge with the tautology, "He behaves anxiously because he has a trait of anxiety"' (p. 42). In other words, 'The trait serves essentially as a summary term for the behaviours that have been integrated by the observer' (Mischel, 1973, p. 262). In other words, Mischel is alleging that the entire trait approach is based on a circular argument and so lacks explanatory power – he was neither the first nor the last to make this claim.

Second, Mischel (1968) was sceptical of the value of inferring personality traits on the basis of observers' ratings of other individuals: 'The conviction that highly

generalised traits do exist may reflect in part (but not entirely) behavioural consistencies that are *constructed* by observers, rather than actual consistency in the
subject's behaviour ... [trait ratings] often may be more relevant to the rater's
categories than to the ratee's behaviour' (p. 43). He adduced various lines of argument and research to support this position (discussed below).

Norman (1963) found that five relatively orthogonal personality traits (extraversion, agreeableness, conscientiousness, emotional stability and culture) based
on rating data were reliably found in several diverse samples (see Chapter 5).
These findings suggest that personality has a reliable five-factor structure.
However, subsequent research by Passini and Norman (1966) revealed that a very
similar five-factor structure emerged when complete strangers were rated! Passini
and Norman also found that these personality ratings by complete strangers correlated very poorly with the ratees' own assessment of their personality. These
findings suggested to Passini and Norman that the most important information
available to the raters was 'whatever they carried in their heads'.

Further problems for the validity of observers' ratings were reported by Mulaik
(1964). He collected ratings from 76 trait scales under three conditions: (1) judges
rated actual individuals (e.g., family members; close acquaintances); (2) they rated
stereotyped hypothetical individuals (e.g., suburban housewife; mental patient);
or (3) they rated the meanings of selected trait-words on the scales without any
reference to individuals (actual or hypothetical). Mulaik's key finding was that
there was reasonably high overlap in the factors that emerged from these three
very different approaches. He concluded that, 'These results suggested that "personality factors" based upon trait ratings of persons can be interpreted as distinct
concepts implied by trait-words rather than internal structural features of
persons' (p. 506).

Mischel (1968, p. 71) concluded his evaluation of the rating approach to assessing personality as follows: '[Personality ratings] are easily and quickly generated
from minimal information; readily and often erroneously generalised to events
which they actually do not fit well; highly influenced by the details of the eliciting
situation; and often firmly maintained in the face of contradictory evidence.'

Third, Mischel (1968) considered the relationship between individuals' self-
reports of their own personality and the personality ratings provided by others.
We saw in the previous paragraph some of the reasons why Mischel was sceptical
of the value of personality ratings. He was also sceptical of the value of self-reports,
arguing that they can be inaccurate because of 'a variety of distorting motivational
forces, including deliberate faking, lack of insight and unconscious defensive reactions' (p. 69). In view of his dismissive attitude towards self-reports and ratings, it
is unsurprising that Mischel claimed that the correspondence between them was
unacceptably low.

The fourth major criticism made by Mischel (1968, pp. 9–10) was based on the
argument that support for the value of the trait-based approach 'would require
demonstrating that people do behave consistently across many diverse situations ...
Such evidence ... would be essential to sustain the belief in the broad personality
dispositions which the [trait] theories posit. It would also be necessary to show

that inferences about an individual's traits and states permit important predictions about his behaviour.'

Mischel (1968) discussed much research that appeared to belie the notion that individuals exhibit strong consistency of behaviour across different situations. Here I will discuss only a small fraction of this research starting with the extensive research of Hartshorne and May (1928) and Hartshorne, May and Shuttleworth (1930). They assessed character (moral conduct) by putting thousands of children in situations (e.g., the home, the classroom and athletic contexts) in which they had the opportunity to lie, steal, or cheat. The main conclusion from this research was as follows: 'As we progressively change the situation we progressively lower the correlations between the tests' (Hartshorne & May, 1928, p. 384). For example, cheating by copying from an answer key on one test correlated +.70 with copying from an answer key on a different test and cheating by adding on scores for one speed test correlated +.44 with adding on scores on a different test. Of most importance, cheating by copying from an answer key on one test correlated only +.29 with adding on scores on another test.

Mischel (1968) also considered the research of Mann (1959), who carried out a thorough review of research on the relationships between various personality measures (e.g., extraversion and dominance, masculinity) and leadership perception in groups. For most personality traits, the median correlation with leadership perception was only approximately +.15. In passing, note that Lord, De Vader and Alliger (1986) reanalysed the findings on which Mann's review was based using more sophisticated statistical techniques and including subsequent studies. They reported somewhat higher correlations (e.g., adjustment correlated +.24 with leadership perception and extraversion correlated +.26). However, these correlations also suggest a modest relationship between personality and leadership perception.

Mischel (1968, p. 77) concluded that, 'The phrase "personality coefficient" might be coined to describe the correlation between .20 and .30 which is found persistently when virtually any personality dimension inferred from a questionnaire is related to almost any conceivable external criterion involving responses sampled in a different medium – that is, not by another questionnaire.'

Mischel believed the implication of research on personality–behaviour correlations was clear-cut. According to Mischel (1969, p. 1014), 'I am more and more convinced, however, hopefully by data as well on theoretical grounds, that the observed inconsistency so regularly found in studies of non-cognitive personality dimensions often reflects the state of nature and not merely the noise of measurement.'

The fifth major criticism that Mischel (1968) made of the trait approach was an extension of his fourth criticism (i.e., that individuals behave inconsistently across situations). More specifically, he argued that this strongly implies that their behaviour is determined primarily by the specific nature of each situation. Mischel can thus be identified as an advocate of situationism, an approach that 'emphasises the importance of the situational determinants of behaviour while minimising the importance of dispositional or intrapsychic determinants' (Bowers, 1973, p. 307). Mischel's (1968) situationist approach has been extremely influential even though some aspects of his approach had been proposed much earlier by Skinner (1938), who similarly focused on situational influences on behaviour while ignoring individual differences in personality.

In spite of the fact that Mischel's (1968) book seems unequivocally to endorse the situationist approach, Mischel has always been strangely reluctant to agree with that assessment. For example, here is a quotation from Mischel (1973, p. 255): 'Is information about individuals more important than information about situations? The author has persistently refrained from posing this question because posed that way it is unanswerable and can serve only to stimulate futile polemics.' This seems ironic to me given that Mischel himself is clearly a strident polemicist!

As we will see, there are persuasive counterarguments with respect to all the indictments of the trait-based personality approach put forward by Mischel (1968). In my opinion, however, Mischel had surprisingly little to say about one of the greatest weaknesses in the trait approach at that time (mentioned earlier). By 1968, the number of different personality traits that had been proposed and assessed by self-report questionnaires and/or ratings ran into the hundreds. As we have seen, there were major disagreements on the number (as well as the nature) of personality traits. For example, Cattell argued that there were 16 major personality traits or factors and produced several revisions of the 16PF test (e.g., Cattell, Eber, & Tatsouka, 1970) to assess those traits. In contrast, H. J. Eysenck (1944) identified only two major personality factors or traits (extraversion and neuroticism) before subsequently increasing the number to three with the addition of psychoticism (see Chapter 4).

IMPACT OF THE STUDY

It is indisputable that Mischel's (1968) book has had a huge impact within the field of personality research. Early in 2017, this book had attracted over 6200 citations on Google Scholar, which is an exceptional number for publications within psychology. Below I consider some of the main reasons why Mischel's book has proved so influential. The overarching reason for its massive influence is that it led personality psychologists to respond to the limitations in personality research prior to 1968 by developing new research designed to address directly those limitations. Note that much of the next section of this chapter is concerned with research influenced at least to some extent by Mischel's book.

First, Mischel (1968) emphasized that the research base supporting the personality traits identified by various groups of researchers was generally rather narrow. Typically, individual differences in a personality trait were correlated with one or more behavioural measures. Such a narrow approach has the limitation that it often involves a circular argument: the trait is inferred from behavioural observations and is then used to 'explain' the behavioural observations.

More generally, significant positive correlations between personality traits and behavioural observations cannot in and of themselves shed any light on causality. Mischel's arguments led many personality theorists and researchers to devote more attention to identifying potential causal factors accounting for the existence of individual differences in personality traits. The most fruitful approach involves the use of twin studies: individual differences in a personality trait depend in part on genetic influences if monozygotic twins are more similar in personality than dizygotic twins. In a recent meta-analytic review, Vukasović and Bratko (2015) discussed 45 twin studies, virtually all of which indicated that genetic factors are moderately important in accounting for individual differences in personality.

Second, another beneficial effect of Mischel's (1968) book was that it led personality psychologists to focus in more detail on the concept of 'consistency'. Fleeson and Noftle (2008) argued that we can potentially identify 36 concepts of consistency. For example, we can assess behavioural consistency across time, situation content, or behaviour content. Measures of consistency can involve correlating two single behaviours or aggregates of behaviour. In addition, we can distinguish between absolute consistency (i.e., the extent to which each individual's behaviour is the same across situations) and relative consistency (i.e., the extent to which each individual's behaviour *relative* to other individuals remains the same across situations). Fleeson and Noftle gave the following example of relative consistency: we would expect nearly everyone to be more talkative when at a party than at a funeral. However, it could still be the case that individuals who talk more than most other people at a party will also talk more than others at a funeral. As we will see in the next section, the extent of behavioural consistency can vary dramatically dependent on the precise approach taken to assessing it.

Third, Mischel's dismissive views on the validity of self-report data led personality researchers to consider more carefully ways of addressing the limitations of such data. For example, as Mischel had indicated, individuals may be tempted to 'fake good' when completing self-report questionnaires. This typically takes the form of social desirability bias with individuals responding in ways that are socially desirable but inaccurate (e.g., Ferrando, 2008). One approach to assessing the impact of social desirability bias is to include questionnaire items on which the socially desirable response is very unlikely to be true. Examples include, 'I do not dislike anyone I know', and 'All my habits are desirable ones.' Still another way to avoid social desirability bias is to use the ipsative method where a choice is forced between two equally socially undesirable items.

Fourth, Mischel's (1968) dismissive views concerning the validity of both self-report and rating data and his consequent pessimism concerning correlations between the two types of data eventually triggered relevant research. I use the word 'eventually' because it was a long time after 1968 before there was much research comparing self-reports and ratings. For example, McCrae (1994) considered the period between January 1987 and September 1992. During that time, he located 3921 articles focusing on self-reports and 720 articles focusing on ratings. However, there were only 184 articles that considered self-reports and ratings, and only 55 of them considered normal adult personality. Since then, there has been some increase in such articles.

Fifth, before the publication of Mischel's (1968) book, practically no researchers had ever directly compared the influence of individual differences in personality and of the situation on behaviour. In addition, there was a lack of a common metric. More specifically, personality researchers often assessed the influence of personality by calculating correlations between a personality trait and some aspect of behaviour, whereas the impact of situations on behaviour was typically assessed in terms of significance level on a statistical test. Mischel was probably more instrumental than any other psychologist in encouraging research-ers to compare the impact on behaviour of personality and of the situation.

Sixth, Mischel's critique indicated that there should be increased research on the impact of the situation on individuals' behaviour. Mischel (1973) identified some of the relevant factors that needed to be considered in his cognitive social learning approach. His starting point was that there is an important distinction between the *objective* situation and our *subjective* interpretation of it. We have an impressive 'discriminative facility' that allows us to attach different meanings to apparently similar situations.

What processes are involved in our 'discriminative facility'? According to Mischel (1973), individuals differ in their encoding strategies (e.g., how the situa-tion is categorized), in the expected outcomes associated with specific responses or stimuli in a given situation, and in the subjective values of those outcomes. In other words, individual differences in behaviour in a given situation depend in part on differences in cognitive appraisal of that situation. These cognitive differ-ences in turn depend upon individuals' previous experience.

In sum, Mischel's (1968) book played a key role in the development of personal-ity research. As we will see in the next section, personality researchers in the years since 1968 have successfully addressed nearly all of Mischel's swingeing attacks on the inchoate state of personality research in the late 1960s.

CRITIQUE OF THE STUDY

We start with the first major criticism (see above) that Mischel (1968) made of the personality approach, namely, that it is often tautological and thus lacks explanatory power. Inexplicably, Mischel does not consider at all the possibility that individual differences in major personality traits or factors might be determined at least in part by genetic factors. There is compelling evidence that this is, indeed, the case. Vukasović and Bratko (2015) recently discussed comprehensive meta-analytic evidence based on twin, family and adoption studies of personality. Overall, 39% of individual differences in extraversion were due to genetic factors, as were 42% of individual differences in neuroticism and 30% of those in psychoticism. While most of these studies were carried out after Mischel's (1968) book was published, five were published beforehand and all showed strong evidence for the importance of genetic factors. Such evidence totally undermines Mischel's notion that personality traits are tautological and lack explanatory power.

Other kinds of research also indicated that personality traits are not tauto-logical. For example, consider theory and research on the physiological bases of individual differences in extraversion and neuroticism (see M. W. Eysenck, 2016, for a review). In the years prior to the publication of Mischel's book in 1968, attempts had been made to relate extraversion to cortical arousal. More specifically, Corcoran (1965) and then later H. J. Eysenck (1967) accounted for numerous behavioural differences between extraverts and introverts by assuming the latter generally have higher arousal than the former. Such theorizing moved far beyond simply using the trait term 'extraversion' to describe observed patterns of behaviour.

Gray (1981) developed the physiological approach substantially. He argued that aspects of extraversion are related to susceptibility to reward and a reward system in the brain whereas aspects of neuroticism and trait anxiety are related to susceptibility to punishment and is related to the brain's behavioural inhibition system. By providing the physiological underpinnings of extraversion and neuroticism/trait anxiety, Gray's approach is clearly exempt from Mischel's claim that personality traits are based on tautology and circular processing.

Mischel's (1968) second and third major criticisms of the trait-based approach to personality both related to the alleged inadequacies of trait ratings of personality. In essence, Mischel argued that ratings can provide an illusion of consistency because raters construct simplistic interpretations of others' personalities based on their preconceptions about human personality. As a result of these supposed deficiencies and the different deficiencies of self-report measures of personality (e.g., deliberate faking stemming from various motivational forces), it is clear that Mischel (1968) expected little correspondence between self-report and rating data. Below we consider some of the relevant evidence.

Costa and McCrae (1988) carried out a study on married couples which included comparing self-reports and spouse ratings for three factors assessed by the NEO Personality Inventory: Neuroticism, Extraversion and Openness. Self-reports and ratings for neuroticism correlated +.54, and the correlations were +.60 and +.52 for extraversion and openness, respectively. In a study on married couples, Smith and Williams (2016) correlated self-reports and spouse ratings using the orthogonal dimensions of dominance–submissiveness and warmth–hostility based on items taken from the extraversion and agreeableness scales of the NEO Personality Inventory. On average, the correlation was +.54 for dominance, +.54 for submissiveness, +.43 for warmth and +.37 for hostility.

Watson, Hubbard and Wiese (2000) used the NEO Personality Inventory to assess self–other agreement in personality in three different samples: friends; dating couples; and married couples. Of the 15 correlations (5 factors × three samples), 100% exceeded +.30, 73% exceeded +.40, and 40% exceeded +.50. The mean correlation between self-reports and ratings across the Big Five factors assessed by the NEO Personality Inventory was +.41 with friends and increased to +.47 with dating couples and +.56 with married couples. These findings are most plausibly explained on the basis that the validity of raters' judgements tends to increase with increased length of knowledge of the other person.

In sum, the level of self–other agreement in personality assessment is much higher than the ceiling of approximately +.30 that Mischel (1968) would have predicted. The findings are especially impressive given that self-reports and ratings are both susceptible to distortion. As we have seen, self-reports are often influenced by social desirability bias, which is the tendency to provide socially desirable responses rather than accurate ones when there is a conflict between them. In contrast, ratings are often limited in that raters have typically observed the individual being rated in a relatively small range of situations and so the behaviour they have observed may well not be representative of his/her behaviour generally. All in all, the take-home message is that the level of self–other agreement is sufficiently high to provide strong support for the validity of both self-reports and ratings.

We now consider Mischel's (1968) fifth criticism discussed above by looking briefly at research that has compared the predictive power of individual differences in personality with situational differences. Sarason, Smith and Diener (1975) calculated the percentage of the variance (differences in behaviour among individuals) accounted for by personality and by the situation across 138 experiments. On average, the situation accounted for 10.3% of the variance whereas personality accounted for 8.7% of the variance. Thus, behaviour was *not* determined substantially more by situational factors than by personality. In addition, the interaction of personality and situation accounted for a further 4.6% of the variance. If we followed Mischel in disregarding any factors not accounting for far more than 9% of the variance in behaviour, we would be in danger of finding nothing is worth studying!

In similar fashion, Bowers (1973) carried out a meta-analytic review of studies in which the percentage of the variance in behaviour due to persons and to situations was calculated. Persons accounted for an average of 11.27%, situations accounted for 10.17%, and the interaction between persons and situations accounted of 20.77%. These findings clearly provide no support at all for situationism as proposed by Mischel (1968).

It could be argued that situational factors might be much more important if we considered some of the most dramatic findings in social psychology. Funder and Ozer (1983) addressed this issue by reanalysing findings from studies such as those on obedience to authority by Milgram (1974) and Darley and Latané's (1968) research on bystander intervention. The mean correlation between the major situational factors manipulated in these studies and behaviour was approximately +.38 or 14% of the variance, which is only modestly greater than numerous correlations between behaviour assessed across situations.

Next, I turn to the central criticism that Mischel (1968) made of the entire trait-based approach to personality: the extensive evidence that individuals typically exhibit far less behavioural consistency across situations than would be predicted from the trait approach. More specifically, Mischel's review of the literature suggested that personality rarely accounts for more than approximately 9% of individual differences in any given aspect of behaviour and so has very little predictive power. Several rebuttals of this central criticism have been put forward and I will discuss them one by one.

First, his rationale for deciding that any factor should account for considerably more than 9% of the variance in order to be of importance is obscure. Whatever his reasons, Mischel's viewpoint is clearly oversimplified. In the field of medicine, there was a large trial in the 1980s to see whether aspirin would reduce the number of heart attacks. The trial was successful and led to the widespread administration of aspirin to those at risk of a heart attack. The correlation between taking or not aspirin and having or not having a heart attack was +.034, accounting for 0.1% of the variance (see Rosnow & Rosenthal, 1989). Here is an example where thousands of lives have been saved on the basis of a factor accounting for considerably less than 1% of the variance!

Second, Mischel (1968) failed to consider consistency findings in the personality literature in the context of psychology generally. Meyer et al. (2001) considered numerous findings across many areas within psychology. The typical finding was that the modal effect size expressed as a correlation was between +.10 and +.40 for psychology as a whole. Related problems were identified in a recent attempt to replicate 100 findings in various areas (cognitive psychology; social psychology) (Open Science Collaboration, 2015). Only 61% of these findings were replicated. Thus, there is compelling evidence that relatively small correlations and problems with reliability of findings are prevalent throughout psychology. If there is a 'problem', it is one that applies to the whole of psychology and is not specific to personality research as was implied by Mischel.

Third, Mischel (1968) exaggerated the value of high consistency between, say, a measure of personality and some behavioural measure but minimized the nature of the behavioural outcome being predicted. Suppose I designed a personality test that assessed only the level of interest the individual had in numerous different sports and the behavioural measure was the number of hours every month spent watching live sports or sports programmes on television. The personality test would probably prove very successful at predicting the outcome of hours watching sports programmes. However, this demonstration of high consistency would be relatively trivial and have little practical significance.

In contrast, major personality traits have been shown to have a wide range of applicability to important real-world outcomes even though there was only moderate consistency or predictability. For example, Roberts, Kuncel, Shiner, Caspi and Goldberg (2007) considered the relationship between personality (the Big Five personality factors) and three important life outcomes (mortality, divorce and occupational achievement). Mortality was best predicted by conscientiousness, divorce by neuroticism and low conscientiousness, and occupational achievement by a combination of personality factors. For example, Judge, Higgins, Thoresen and Barrick (1999) found that adolescent ratings of neuroticism, extraversion, agreeableness and conscientiousness predicted occupational achievement 46 years later. Of importance, the magnitude of the effects of personality traits on mortality, divorce and occupational achievement was comparable to that of socioeconomic status and IQ.

Similar findings were reported by Gutiérrez, Gárriz, Peri, Vall and Torrubia (2016) in a study of a sample of individuals, most of whom had personality disorders. The personality trait of persistence accounted for 24% of the variance with respect to career success, with self-directedness explaining 21% of the variance in social functioning and harm avoidance explaining 34% of the variance in clinical problems.

Fourth, Mischel argued that individuals display very limited cross-situational consistency on the basis of studies that had mostly assessed consistency by correlating *single* behaviours in different situations. This approach has the disadvantage that there can be substantial errors of measurement when the focus is on single behaviours (Epstein, 1977). By analogy, it would be absurd to argue that intelligence does not exist because IQ assessed by an intelligence test poorly predicted performance on a single crossword puzzle!

As was discussed earlier, there are many other ways in which behavioural consistency can be assessed (Fleeson & Noftle, 2008). Epstein (1977) assessed consistency by using aggregated measures. More specifically, he asked students to record their most positive and negative emotional experience every day for two weeks. When the mean intensities of positive or negative experiences were aggregated separately for all the odd days and all the even days, the mean correlation for positive emotional experiences was +.88 and was only slightly lower than that for negative experiences. In contrast, when either positive or negative experiences were compared on only two days, the mean correlation was under +.20. Thus, there was a massive difference in consistency depending on whether correlations were calculated between two aggregated sets of behaviour or two single behaviours.

Finally, there are criticisms to be made of Mischel's (1968) predominant emphasis on personality and situational factors as independent factors that influence behaviour. Admittedly, Mischel discusses briefly the notion that personality and situation may interact to determine behaviour, but his approach is nevertheless much oversimplified. We can see this by considering Bandura's (1999) triadic reciprocal model. Bandura argued that the influences of personal factors (e.g., personality) and of the situation on behaviour are merely two out of six influences that need to be considered. The four influences largely or totally ignored by Mischel are as follows: (1) influence of personal factors (e.g., personality) on the situation; (2) influence of behaviour on personal factors (e.g., personality; (3) influence of behaviour on the situation; and (4) influence of the situation on personal factors (e.g., personality).

Of most relevance here is the notion that the situations individuals choose to be in are determined in part by their personality. Research supporting this notion was reviewed by Ickes, Snyder and Garcia (1997). For example, extraverts are more likely than introverts to engage in activities that are stimulating and involve other people whereas introverts tend to prefer leisure activities involving a sense of order and planning.

What are the implications of the above research? In most research, the experimenter determines the situations in which participants find themselves and they are unable to change or control the situation. Wachtel (1973, p. 330) used the term 'implacable experimenter' to describe this state of affairs. With such research, it is impossible to demonstrate the impact of personality on situational choice.

CONCLUSIONS

Mischel's (1968) book was timely in that theory and research in personality were at a low ebb in the late 1960s. Most of the major criticisms he made of the personality trait approach possessed some validity, although he often exaggerated the limitations of that approach.

As we have seen, impressive progress has been made in the area of personality in the 50 years since Mischel's (1968) book. Indeed, I would argue that none of Mischel's main criticisms is applicable to contemporary personality research and theory.

To what extent is progress in personality research over the past half-century directly attributable to Mischel's critique? That is an interesting (but ultimately an unanswerable) question. It is important not to be unduly influenced by the notion of *post hoc ergo propter hoc* (after this and therefore caused by this). Nevertheless, my personal opinion is that, while there are numerous reasons for progress in personality research, Mischel's (1968) book can reasonably be identified as the single most important one.

FURTHER READING

Eysenck, H. J., & Eysenck, M. W. (1985). *Personality and individual differences: A natural science approach.* London: Plenum.

Eysenck, M. W., & Eysenck, H. J. (1980). Mischel and the concept of personality. *British Journal of Psychology, 71,* 191–204.

Mischel, W. (1968). *Personality and assessment.* London: Wiley.

REFERENCES

Bandura, A. (1999). Social cognitive theory of personality. In L. A. Pervin & O. P. John (Eds.), *Handbook of personality: Theory and research* (2nd ed.). New York: Guilford Press.

Bowers, K. S. (1973). Situationism in psychology: An analysis and a critique. *Psychological Review, 80,* 307–336.

Cattell, R. B., & Cattell, H. E. P. (1995). Personality structure and the new fifth edition of the 16PF. *Educational and Psychological Measurement, 55,* 926–937.

Cattell, R. B., Eber, H. W., & Tatsouka, M. M. (1970). *Handbook for the Sixteen Personality Factor Questionnaire (16 PF).* Champaign, IL: Institute for Personality and Ability Testing.

Corcoran, D. W. J. (1965). Personality and the inverted-U relation. *British Journal of Psychology, 56,* 267–273.

Costa, P. T., & McCrae, R. R. (1988). Personality in adulthood: A six-year longitudinal study of self-reports and spouse ratings on the NEO Personality Inventory. *Journal of Personality and Social Psychology, 54,* 853–863.

Costa, P. T., & McCrae, R. R. (1992). *NEO-PI-R, Professional manual.* Odessa, FL: Psychological Resources.

Darley, J. M., & Latané, B. (1968). Bystander intervention in emergencies: Diffusion of responsibility. *Journal of Personality and Social Psychology, 38*, 115–134.

Epstein, S. (1977). Traits are alive and well. In D. Magnusson & N. S. Endler (Eds.), *Personality at the crossroads: Current issues in interactional psychology*. Hillsdale, NJ: Erlbaum.

Eysenck, H. J. (1944). Types of personality – a factorial study of 700 neurotics. *Journal of Mental Science, 90*, 851–861.

Eysenck, H. J. (1967). *The biological basis of personality*. Springfield, IL: Charles C. Thomas.

Eysenck, H. J., & Eysenck, M. W. (1985). *Personality and individual differences: A natural science approach*. London: Plenum.

Eysenck, M. W. (2016). Hans Eysenck: A research evaluation. *Personality and Individual Differences, 103*, 209–219.

Ferrando, P. J. (2008). The impact of social desirability bias on the EPQ-R item scores: An item response theory analysis. *Personality and Individual Differences, 44*, 1784–1794.

Fleeson, W., & Gallagher, P. (2009). The implications of Big Five standing for the distribution of trait manifestation in behaviour: Fifteen experience-sampling studies and a meta-analysis. *Journal of Personality and Social Psychology, 97*, 1097–1114.

Fleeson, W., & Noftle, E. E. (2008). Where does personality have its influence? A supermatrix of consistency concepts. *Journal of Personality, 76*, 1355–1385.

Funder, D. C., & Ozer, D. J. (1983). Behaviour as a function of the situation. *Journal of Personality and Social Psychology, 44*, 107–112.

Galton, F. (1869). *Hereditary genius*. London: Macmillan.

Gray, J. A. (1981). A critique of Eysenck's theory of personality. In H. J. Eysenck (Ed.), *A model for personality*. Berlin: Springer-Verlag.

Guilford, J. P. (1939). *General psychology*. New York, NY: Van Nostrand.

Gutiérrez, F., Gárriz, M., Peri, J. M., Vall, G., & Torrubia, R. (2016). How temperament and character affect our career, relationships, and mental health. *Comprehensive Psychiatry, 70*, 181–189.

Hartshorne, H., & May, M. A. (1928). *Studies in the nature of character: Vol. 1 – Studies in deceit*. New York: Macmillan.

Hartshorne, H., May, M. A., & Shuttleworth, F. K. (1930). *Studies in the nature of character: Vol. 3 – Studies in the organization of character*. New York: Macmillan.

Ickes, W., Snyder, M., & Garcia, S. (1997). Personality influences in the choices of situations. In R. Hogan, J. A. Johnson, & S. R. Briggs (Eds.), *Handbook of personality psychology*. New York: Academic Press.

Jones, H. G. (1965). Review of assessment: A critical survey by Philip E. Vernon. *British Journal of Criminology, 5*, 341.

Judge, T. A., Higgins, C. A., Thoresen, C. J., & Barrick, M. R. (1999). The big five personality traits, general mental ability, and career success across the life span. *Personnel Psychology, 52*, 621–652.

Lord, R. G., De Vader, C. L., & Alliger, G. M. (1986). A meta-analysis of the relation between personality traits and leadership perceptions: An application of validity generalisation procedures. *Journal of Applied Psychology, 71*, 402–410.

Mann, R. D. (1959). A review of the relationships between personality and performance in small groups. *Psychological Bulletin, 56*, 241–270.

McCrae, R. R. (1994). The counterpoint of personality assessment: Self-reports and observer ratings. *Assessment, 1*, 159–172.

Meyer, G. J., Finn, S. E., Eyde, L. D., Kay, G. G., Moreland, K. L., Dies, R. R., et al. (2001). Psychological testing and psychological assessment. *American Psychologist, 56*, 128–165.

Milgram, S. (1974). *Obedience to authority*. New York: Doubleday.

Mischel, W. (1968). *Personality and assessment*. London: Wiley.

Mischel, W. (1969). Continuity and change in personality. *American Psychologist, 24*, 1012–1018.

Mischel, W. (1973). Toward a cognitive social learning reconceptualisation of personality. *Psychological Review, 80*, 252–283.

Mulaik, S. A. (1964). Are personality factors raters' conceptual factors? *Journal of Consulting Psychology, 28*, 506–511.

Murphy, G., & Kovach, J. K. (1972). *Historical introduction to modern psychology*. London: Routledge & Kegan Paul.

Norman, W. T. (1963). Toward an adequate taxonomy of personality attributes: Replicated factor structures in peer nomination personality ratings. *Journal of Abnormal and Social Psychology, 66*, 574–583.

Open Science Collaboration (2015). Estimating the reproducibility of psychological science. *Science, 349* (6251), aac4716.

Passini, F. T., & Norman, W. T. (1966). A universal conception of personality structure? *Journal of Personality and Social Psychology, 4*, 44–49.

Roberts, B. W., Kuncel, N. R., Shiner, R., Caspi, A., & Goldberg, L. R. (2007). The power of personality: The comparative validity of personality traits, socioeconomic status, and cognitive ability for predicting important life outcomes. *Perspectives on Psychological Science, 2*, 313–345.

Rosnow, R. L., & Rosenthal, R. (1989). Statistical procedures and the justification of knowledge in psychological science. *American Psychologist, 44*, 1276–1284.

Sarason, I. G., Smith, R. E., & Diener, E. (1975). Personality research: Components of variance attributable to person and situation. *Journal of Personality and Social Psychology, 32*, 199–204.

Skinner, B. F. (1938). *The behaviour of organisms*. New York: Appleton–Century–Crofts.

Smith, T. W., & Williams, P. G. (2016). Assessment of social traits in married couples: Self-reports versus spouse ratings and the interpersonal circumplex. *Psychological Assessment, 28*, 726–736.

Vernon, P. E. (1964). *Personality assessment: A critical survey*. New York: Wiley.

Vukasović, T., & Bratko, D. (2015). Heritability of personality: A meta-analysis of behaviour genetic studies. *Psychological Bulletin, 141*, 769–785.

Wachtel, P. L. (1973). Psychodynamics, behaviour therapy and the implacable experimenter: An inquiry into the consistency of personality. *Journal of Abnormal Psychology, 82*, 324–334.

Watson, D., Hubbard, B., & Wiese, D. (2000). Self–other agreement in personality and affectivity: The role of acquaintanceship, trait visibility, and assumed similarity. *Journal of Personality and Social Psychology, 78*, 546–558.

7

Sensitivity to Punishment and Reward

Revisiting Gray (1970)

Neil McNaughton and Philip J. Corr

BACKGROUND TO THE STUDY

R esearch on personality is notoriously fragmented. Can we make it a coherent whole? In particular, can low-level (brain/body) processes explain high-level stable *patterns* of affect, behaviour and cognition, expressed in traits? Neuroscience has had a major impact on state psychology – can it help personality psychology too?

Here, we will take you 'Back to the Future'. We look at Jeffrey Gray's early sketch[1] of a neuroscientific theory of personality (Gray, 1970a), which used the concepts and experimental tools of *learning theory* (Gray, 1975) to explain the effects of extraverting drugs. Even early learning theory used mathematical models (Hull, 1943, 1952) of the *control* of behaviour. Lower-level learning constructs (habit strength, drive, goal gradients, generalization and reinforcement) mapped, implicitly, to physiological systems. Before this, Ivan Pavlov's (1927) book on 'Conditioned Reflexes' was explicitly subtitled 'an investigation of the physiological activity of the cerebral cortex'; and he viewed physiology as absolutely fundamental to an understanding of learning (Pavlov, 1932). One can, and Gray in particular did, map in both directions: between a 'conceptual nervous system' (cns) of the type inferred by Hebb (1955) from the careful observation of experimentally constrained behaviour and the real 'central nervous system' (CNS) studied by neuroanatomy and neurophysiology. Gray's unique step was to use drugs as a conceptual dissection tool – assuming that a drug changes synaptic activity (CNS) and so behaviour (cns) in parallel. Suppose a drug affects behaviour A but *not* behaviour B. We can be sure that A depends on a process not shared by B. Critically, this means we exclude from consideration all cognitive and neural processes that are not drug-sensitive. Drugs, thus, dissect *both* the cns *and* CNS in a highly replicable, *theory-independent*, way. Intracranial injections even allow microdissection of process. As we will see, we can use brain lesions similarly, whether controlled (in experimental animals) or naturally occurring (in human patients). Gray used drug dissection in a particularly powerful way: using drugs (and their parallels with specific lesions) to tie together specific behaviours, neural systems, personality systems and clinical disorders.

Gray's (1970a) cns–CNS approach has had an enormous, still increasing,[2] influence on current-day thinking – promoting the conceptual anchoring of personality traits to well-delineated brain systems. There is now even a journal, *Personality Neuroscience*, published by Cambridge University Press, dedicated to this field. But, despite this apparent progress, when you go back to Gray's classic paper you will uncover fundamental bedrock, obscured by the later rush to develop personality scales statistically. With modern neuroscience we can now incorporate fundamental principles of learning and of the real neural systems that are the substrates for all traits measured by personality questionnaires. As we shall see, Gray's overall vision in 1970 encompassed a surprising number of the types of fact that a modern neuroscientific theory of personality must accommodate but that few do. But, before visiting the past in the hope of illuminating the future, we should look at our present.

Personality research has certainly moved on from when relief was expressed that 'at least it can be said of personality that there are *now* facts and ways of gathering facts that we *can* argue about' (Claridge, 1967, p. ix, our emphasis); and it no longer has a 'Babel of concepts and scales' in which one name (e.g., 'anxiety') could include another quite different concept (e.g., 'fear'); and different names (e.g., 'emotional resilience' and 'emotional stability'), based on different scales, could refer to essentially the same trait (now, inversely, named 'neuroticism').

Indeed, 20 years ago, John and Srivastava (1995)[3] could present the 'Big Five' dimensional approach to personality traits as an emergent consensus allowing translation of the previous Babel. The Big Five dimensional axes are based on a taxonomy of patterns in natural language usage (see Chapter 5). These axes imposed order on the chaos of potential factors linked to innumerable scales; seeming to provide 'a starting place for vigorous research and theorizing that can eventually lead to an explication ... in causal and dynamic terms' (John & Srivastava, 1995, p. 103).

Two decades later, we may be closer to the causal/dynamic Nirvana that they desired. For example, Cybernetic Big Five Theory (DeYoung, 2015, p. 33), based on 'the study of goal-directed, adaptive systems', provides a foundation from which the theory 'attempts to provide a comprehensive, synthetic and mechanistic explanatory model' of personality. DeYoung's approach has the potential to progress to a general-purpose model. His appeal to mechanism encourages mapping between descriptive personality traits and underlying biological causes. This echoes Gray's own theory development (Gray, 1982; Gray & Smith, 1969), which employed cybernetic principles: inputs, outputs, feedback, regulators and, particularly, comparators.

Despite these advances, the present still lacks a genuinely biological general theory of personality. Even Cybernetic Big Five Theory 'does not depend on complete or immediate translation into biological mechanisms for its utility' (DeYoung, 2015, p. 33); and so the Big Five system remains fundamentally taxonomic (i.e., it is simply a description of apparent structure and order in superficial observations).

In particular, the Big Five defines the structure of personality top-down via surface-level labels (i.e., personality traits – typically defined by self-reported patterns of affect, behaviour and cognition). But, 'taxonomy is always a contentious issue because the world does not come to us in neat little packages' (Gould, 1981, cited by John & Srivastava, 1995, p. 102). Importantly, a taxonomy based on language use – however correct in the linguistic domain – may not map to the taxonomy that ultimately emerges from lower-level causal analysis of brain processes.

We believe that the entire field of personality psychology suffers from overuse of top-down descriptions and a lack of bottom-up mechanisms. We should heed the lesson of zoology. The older top-down classification of species relationships via their superficial morphological characteristics had to be modified considerably in response to modern bottom-up genomic molecular biology (Dawkins, 2005).

A second problem all psychologists must face is inherent to any use of everyday language: the conventional meanings of our words may not map to scientific reality. In physics, an electron is a particle or a wave or neither or (paradoxically) both, depending on context and on what aspect of reality we are forcing into words. Personality may match our everyday words no better; after all, the lexicon derives from society's changing usage not biological science.

Our time travel takes us back to an important early attempt at a quite different approach to personality: where personality traits emerge, bottom-up, from the sensitivities of biological systems. Most importantly, Gray (1970a) used neural and drug data ('a reconsideration of what is known about the physiological basis of introversion', p. 257) to generate what was, in essence, a new theory of personality and almost a new approach to the entire field, albeit borrowing from early 20th-century giants such as Pavlov.[4]

The novelty of Gray's approach may not be immediately obvious since he reviews existing personality theory and learning theory before presenting the physiological conceptual bedrock that provided 'the strongest support for the present hypothesis' (p. 257). His subsequent publications and theory development were also strongly focused on pharmacology and neurophysiology (Gray, 1982; Gray & McNaughton, 2000). For Gray, descriptive personality structure (traits) always had to adjust to biological findings. Current personality science is increasingly seeking a foundation in Gray's fundamental neural, particularly pharmacological, bedrock.

Gray's (1970a) paper on 'the psychophysiological basis of introversion–extraversion' included the equally important trait of neuroticism–stability. Both traits are still very much with us as two of the current major Big Five 'domains'.[5]

Gray was inspired by the audacity of Hans Eysenck's (1967), then dominant, top-down theory of personality (see Chapter 4). Eysenck started with a medical checklist; statistically extracted a surface-level taxonomic structure of introversion–extraversion and neuroticism–stability; and, only then, searched for biological correlates (individual differences in arousability and conditionability, discussed further below). Finally, he derived a lower-level (biological) explanation of the traits from their correlates:

1. introverts have high arousal and so high *general* conditionability (i.e., a greater ease of learning, whether driven by reward or punishment), which enhances social learning and gives them an over-socialized conscience;

2. conversely, extraverts are chronically under-aroused, so learn only with difficulty, are under-socialized and prone to break societal rules.

Importantly, Eysenck's biology attempted a *causal* explanation of the differences between two types of psychiatric disorder that are both more likely in people with high levels of neuroticism. The group of what we would now call 'internalizing disorders' (e.g., anxiety and depression) generally occur in people who also score high on introversion, while the group of externalizing disorders (e.g., aggression and substance misuse but particularly for Eysenck, psychopathy) generally occur in people who also score high on extraversion.

Eysenck thus explained both types of psychiatric disorder in terms of the combination of extremes of two distinct personality traits: (a) neuroticism + introversion → internalizing; and (b) neuroticism + extraversion → externalizing. Here, neuroticism amplifies (and stability suppresses) the effects of both introversion and extraversion on behaviour, while introversion–extraversion determines the particular type of disorder that results from neuroticism.

Note that Eysenck saw the trait extremes themselves as risk factors more than disorders. Eysenck's explanation depended on a causal neuropsychological hypothesis that made the theory scientific in the sense of eminently falsifiable. We can test each step from his postulated fundamental arousal process to cognitive and social levels of explanation, particularly via his learning theory assumptions. That is, according to Gray (1970a, p. 251), Eysenck supposed the fundamental introvert property to be high general arousability, located in the brain areas controlling arousal.

People saw Eysenck's theory as problematic because it required two personality factors (introversion–extraversion *and* neuroticism) to account for both of two sets of disorders (internalizing and externalizing). One trait per set would have been neater and so Gray suggested that internalizing and externalizing could have quite separate causes: sensitivity to punishment and reward, respectively.

Gray's theory differed from Eysenck's primarily in its biology. He accepted the overall architecture and psychological/social superstructure of Eysenck's theory but used a different type of learning theory,[6] different crucial aspects of learning, and invoked different neural systems to explain introversion–extraversion. Gray's review of the literature on trait variation in arousal and sensitivity to punishment concluded that introverts condition better than extraverts *only when* there is aversive stimulation: 'High degrees of introversion represent high levels of sensitivity to punishment' (p. 259). As we discuss below, he bundled the fundamental learning theory concept of punishment together with the more esoteric one of 'frustrative nonreward'.

An important support to Gray's argument was pharmacological: non-sedative doses of alcohol and barbiturates lead to extraverted behaviour in humans but also, as is particularly well demonstrated in animal studies, only affect responses controlled by punishing stimuli and do not change responses controlled by rewarding stimuli. This *lack of effect* of extraverting drugs on rewarded learning drove Gray to conclude that extraversion does not depend on generally poorer learning and that introversion depends on a *specific* 'susceptibility to punishment', connected to a fear system. He claimed: 'The hypothesis that introversion involves a heightened susceptibility to fear (or to express the same point differently, a heightened sensitivity to punishment and warnings of punishment) has a great deal of face validity' (p. 255).

However, susceptibility to fear/punishment carried within it, like a Trojan Horse, a change in the structure of Eysenck's two dimensions of introversion–extraversion and neuroticism–stability. In particular, Gray proposed, as a corollary of his arguments about introversion, 'a new conception of neuroticism as reflecting a degree of sensitivity to both reward and punishment'. This seems not too far off Eysenck's claim of neuroticism as a general emotional *activation* factor, linked to the notion of general drive as a single process (Hull, 1943, 1952). However, Gray had split reward and punishment following the distinct two-process learning theory tradition.

Gray's (1975, p. 176) view of learning is stated as:

> essentially the same as that proposed by Mowrer in 1960 which supposes that observed learning and behaviour is the outcome of an interaction between two underlying processes: one (a classical conditioning component) responsible for the acquisition by initially neutral stimuli of reinforcing and motivational properties, the other (the instrumental component proper) responsible for the guidance of behaviour in such a way as to maximize positive reinforcement and minimize negative reinforcement.

This second step in two-process theory requires that rewarding and punishing stimuli activate distinct systems that increase or decrease, respectively, the occurrence of the behaviour that results in the stimulus. It follows that there must be two personality factors: one to reflect individual differences in reward sensitivity and one punishment sensitivity (with high neuroticism being measured when both are high). For Gray, it was important that these processes had different sensitivities to drugs and brain lesions (e.g., some drugs/lesions reduce punishment-related behaviours without decreasing reward-related behaviours, while other drugs/lesions show the opposite pattern of behavioural effects).

DETAILED DESCRIPTION OF THE STUDY

As we have noted, Gray's intellectual starting point is the biological component of Hans Eysenck's theory of introversion–extraversion and neuroticism–stability. Gray's focus on this theory and his learning theoretical approach to it are not surprising as he undertook his PhD at the Institute of Psychiatry in London, which was headed by Eysenck – who wrote an introduction to Gray's (1964c) book *Pavlov's Typology*. This 'edited' book included two chapters by Gray that were nothing short of a brilliant literal and conceptual translation of Russian psychology into Western concepts based on learning theory and arousal. There is a twist to this history: this earlier work by Gray inspired Eysenck's own 1967 arousal theory by suggesting that the 'Strength of the Nervous System' – according to Eysenck, low in introverts and high in extraverts – resulted from individual differences in cortical arousability. As another example of the strong links between Eysenck and Gray, the 1970 paper appeared in a journal, *Behaviour Research and Therapy*, founded and edited by Eysenck in 'the belief that behavioural disorders ... are essentially *learned responses*, and that modern learning theory ... has much to teach us' (Eysenck, 1963, p. 1). Eysenck hoped 'that this new Journal will be of interest to those who wish to apply more scientific rigour to the various fields of psychology'; and took as a motto (borrowed from the famous behaviourist John B. Watson) that 'psychology as the behaviourist views it is a purely objective, experimental branch of natural science. Its theoretical goal is the prediction and control of behaviour' (Eysenck, 1963, p. 2).

Let us briefly compare each of the levels of the distinct explanations Eysenck and Gray provide of introversion–extraversion (Figure 7.1). The primary points of difference are in the earlier levels of explanation. Eysenck saw introverts and extraverts as differing primarily in *general conditionability* (whether with reward or punishment as the reinforcer) resulting from *arousability* (shaded in Figure 7.1). In contrast, Gray suggested that they differ, instead, in *specific conditionability* (shaded in Figure 7.1), related to sensitivity to punishment (sometimes he said fear) *but not reward*. Gray's change appears very simple, but it has profound consequences for the lower levels of explanation that take us to neural systems. It also has some impact on explanations of disordered social behaviour – although, for both theories, the most important consequence of introversion for psychiatry is high conditioning of fear. (Eysenck focused on the general conditioning aspect, and Gray focused on the specific fear aspect.) For both theories, high/low fear conditioning results in high/low socialization, respectively. Both theories presumed that these introversion-/extraversion-based differences in socialization would lead to psychiatric disorder when combined with high levels of neuroticism, which acts like an amplification factor. Despite this similarity in primary social and psychiatric predictions (based on conditioning via punishment), the two theories differ in their predictions about conditioning via reward. However, Gray's approach provides a much more nuanced account of the types of behaviour, derived from learning theory, to characterize internalizing and externalizing disorders.

The theory presented in Gray's paper as a whole links arguments between these various levels of explanation. It also involves novel suggestions at each level. We will look at the elements of Gray's argument using his original section headings.

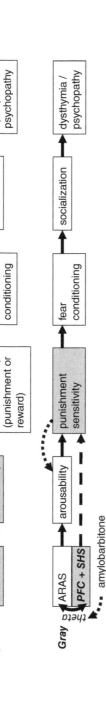

Figure 7.1 Eysenck's theory of introversion–extraversion compared with Gray's as shown in Figure 2 and Figure 6 of Gray (1970a) with additions based on his text. Both theories presume that conditioning of fear is high in introverts and low in extraverts and so, at the social and then psychiatric level, introverts with internalizing disorders (dysthymia) are over-socialized and extraverts with externalizing disorders (psychopathy) are under-socialized. Gray's key modification (shaded) is to attribute variations in fear conditioning to differing sensitivities to punishment, whereas Eysenck attributes it to variations in general arousability (in the ascending reticular activating system, ARAS) and so, as a consequence, conditionability in general. Gray located punishment sensitivity (in the sense of susceptibility to fear; see Gray, 1970a, p. 255) in the prefrontal cortex (PFC) and the septo-hippocampal system (SHS), as shown by the dashed arrow. He connected PFC, SHS and ARAS in a feedback loop, controlled by 'theta' rhythm, and impaired by extraverting (anti-anxiety) drugs such as amylobarbitone. High arousal could generate punishment (with effects similar to those proposed by Eysenck). Conversely, high punishment sensitivity would generate high arousal in punishing situations (dotted arrow) due to interaction of PFC + SHS with ARAS.

Conditionability

Much of the debate on personality in the human conditioning literature revolved around a particular type of conditioning, namely that of the eyeblink. Gray's first data-oriented section focuses on eyeblink conditioning in both introverts and those high on 'Manifest Anxiety' (Taylor, 1956), who he argues (via his Figure 3) are neurotic introverts. The eyeblink conditioning data, and arguments, are complicated (particularly where partial reinforcement schedules are used) but best fit the idea that introverts learn better than extraverts *only* under conditions where they are more highly aroused; with those high on trait anxiety (i.e., neurotic introverts) showing better conditioning when exposed to threat. In passing, Gray suggested that this trait arousability is equivalent to Pavlov's 'Strength of the Nervous System',[7] which we have already come across above derived from analysis of individual differences in conditioning (Gray, 1964a). While working through the arguments Gray presented in this section, you should bear in mind that eyeblink conditioning is aversive (see below) and that, in any case, arguments about conditioning in general would be better if based on more than one paradigm.

To understand the eyeblink conditioning paradigm, imagine yourself in Eysenck's laboratory at the Institute of Psychiatry in London. You seat yourself in a comfortable chair in a small room some 6 by 10 ft (you have time-travelled prior to metrication). White metal plates cover the walls and have holes in them to dampen reflected sound (the same as in sound recording studios of that era). On the wall directly in front of you, a small spot of red light appears. Shortly after, a device attached to your eye delivers a puff of air, which makes you blink. After a number of such trials, you will blink when the light occurs and before the air puff.

In learning theory terms, this is a classical conditioning procedure in which a (to be) *conditioned stimulus*[8] (CS; the light) is reliably and swiftly followed by the *unconditioned stimulus* (US; air puff), which elicits the *unconditioned response* (UR; eyeblink). A sensor over the eye carefully records the response producing a trace automatically recorded on paper in an adjoining room. After enough CS:US pairings, the CS *alone* is enough to trigger the eyeblink, which in the absence of the US we call the *conditioned response* (CR). Importantly, the traces of the UR and CR are somewhat different. We can score learning as the strength of the CR after a fixed number of trials, or the number of conditioning trials needed to reach some criterion strength. During 'extinction', when the CS occurs alone (i.e., it is not reinforced by the US), we can measure the number of trials needed to reach some criterion of non-response.

Neurotic introverts usually condition eyeblinks faster and extinguish them slower than other people. If we can generalize from this to all learning (particularly social), we can then account for their introverted symptoms in the same way as Eysenck. As you might well imagine, eyeblink conditioning is (mildly) unpleasant. If we assume that introversion, especially with high neuroticism, amplifies the unpleasantness we can account for the eyeblink results in the same way as Gray.

SENSITIVITY TO PUNISHMENT AND NONREWARD

If high conditioned fear, as shown by the eyeblink-conditioning paradigm, is not due to *better conditioning* in general, Gray suggested, it could be due to *susceptibility to fear* and particularly its induction by punishment. Susceptibility to *fear* (although not always due to conditioning, see below) fitted well with a number of facts (p. 255). We can easily see internalizing disorders ('dysthymias', e.g., phobia, anxiety and obsession) as excessive fear of one form or another. As we noted, eye-blink conditioning is aversive; furthermore, trait-anxious people (neurotic introverts) condition better only if there is threat. At the other end of the scale, we can view externalizing disorders (e.g., psychopathy) as insufficient sensitivity to punishment. Of course, for proof that good conditioning is selective to fear/punishment 'the crucial test would be [of] introverts and extraverts using non-aversive reinforcement in a definitely unthreatening environment; but ... no such experiment [had] yet been carried out' (Gray, 1970a, p. 255) – but this experiment did follow (e.g., Corr, Pickering, & Gray, 1995).

Depression seems to stand apart from fear, anxiety, punishment and conditioning; but, like 'other dysthymic neuroses (i.e., phobias, anxiety state and obsessive compulsive neurosis'; p. 256), it is related to introversion and high neuroticism. Gray accommodated depression, perhaps surprisingly given its nature, via his first detailed application of learning theory. His immediate problem was reactive depression resulting from loss of reward (e.g., death of a spouse), not punishment. In his solution, we can see the power of a properly formulated learning theory perspective of the kind urged by Eysenck (1963, p. 1). To understand Gray's argument, we need to take a step back. Gray's primary hypothesis concerned punishment. So, he obviously needed to equate loss of reward with punishment. Serendipitously, he had previously proposed the 'fear = frustration hypothesis' to explain emotional reactions (Gray, 1967). All Gray said in 1970 was that 'the evidence for this hypothesis is rather strong' (1970a, p. 256); but you can check this evidence in his 1967 paper and in his later book *The Psychology of Fear and Stress* (Gray, 1971, 1987). Briefly, when an animal *fails to* receive an *expected* reward its immediate reactions (increased arousal, escape, attack if a conspecific is present) are 'functionally and physiologically very similar, and perhaps identical' (1970a, p. 256) to when it receives a shock (or other punisher). The reactions show that failure of expected reward generates an emotional state, usually called 'frustration', and this has received extensive analysis (Amsel, 1992). Gray's conclusion is that introverts, who are more sensitive to fear, will also be more sensitive to frustration in the extreme form generated by severe loss, and so are more likely to become depressed.

THE PHYSIOLOGICAL BASIS OF INTROVERSION – DRUGS

The core of Gray's argument is a new proposal for the neural substrate of introversion, which he based on a learning-theory-driven overview of the effects of extraverting drugs. He thus linked behaviour to neural systems by using extraverting drugs as a kind of tracer.

The extraverting drugs had made a major contribution to his previous paper on the 'fear = frustration hypothesis' (Gray, 1967). Crucially, their pattern of effects on conditioned and unconditioned responses is the same with frustration as it is with fear. His 1967 paper focused on ethanol and barbiturates,[9] particularly amylobarbitone – but its conclusions have proved true for modern anti-anxiety agents. 'Anxiolytic' drugs, both classical and novel, reduce *response suppression* and partial schedule effects similarly, whether we omit expected food or present shock (Gray, 1977; Gray & McNaughton, 2000, Appendix 1). *In that limited sense*, as Gray claimed, they do 'reduce the effects of punishment and of frustrative nonreward' (1970a, p. 257).

Equally important for Gray's argument was the complementary 'hope = relief hypothesis' (Gray, 1971, 1972),[10] derived from his concept of relieving nonpunishment (a mirror image of frustrative nonreward). Extraverting drugs *do not impair avoidance* unless some form of conflict is present (i.e., avoidance is passive, not active – a subtle but fundamental distinction). *Provided we are dealing with learning*, we can see an active avoidance response as one rewarded by stimuli that signal safety and generate the positive emotion of relief; and so we can explain the lack of effect of anti-punishment drugs. (Escape and related forms of active avoidance represent withdrawal from fear not approach to relief.) Results in 'the Miller–Mowrer shuttle-box' are particularly interesting (1970a, p. 257). This apparatus was popular because it automated instrumental conditioning; but you will need a bit of thought to understand the effects of extraverting drugs in it. The shuttle-box has two adjacent compartments; and we train the animal to shuttle between them through a door. The animal starts in one compartment. We present a tone followed by a shock and the animal escapes to the next compartment. After a pause, we present the tone and then shock – this time in the second compartment – and the animal shuttles back. After several repetitions, the animal will shuttle at the tone and so not get shock – this is learned avoidance. Perhaps unexpectedly, extraverting drugs *improve* shuttle-box ('2-way active') avoidance. Why? First, note that early on the animal has to escape into a compartment in which it received a shock on the immediately previous trial. The expected punishment will produce a tendency to passive avoidance that will slow escape and active avoidance. Gray explained amylobarbitone's improvement of 2-way avoidance as a reduction in conflict[11] between primary, correct, active avoidance (known to be unaffected by the drug) and secondary, interfering, passive avoidance (known to be reduced by the drug). This pattern of effects across the three avoidance paradigms will be particularly important when we compare drug and lesion effects below.

THE PHYSIOLOGICAL BASIS OF INTROVERSION – BRAIN

Eysenck identifies the Ascending Reticular Activating System (ARAS in Figure 7.1) as the substrate for arousal at the state level and arousability (hence introversion) at the trait level. At the neural level, Gray retained a contribution from the ARAS but restricted its importance by embedding it within an important feedback loop involving the prefrontal cortex and hippocampus (PFC and SHS in Figure 7.1). A key element of his neural argument was evidence that extraverting drugs (barbiturates and alcohol) impair slow rhythmical activity 'theta' that functions to coordinate both hippocampal and orbital frontal cortex function. Gray's basic argument, here, is that these drugs reduce introversion (and move the individual in the direction of extraversion) and reduce theta; and so systems that depend on theta are likely to be the substrate of introversion.

The key neural component for Gray is the septo-hippocampal system. The hippocampus is renowned for its theta rhythm – one of the strongest sine wave-like rhythms recorded from the brain. Critically, Gray had shown that amylobarbitone (the main drug of his behavioural review) impaired the control of hippocampal theta by its pacemaker in the medial septum particularly at a frequency that he had shown occurred when the animal experienced frustrative nonreward (Gray, 1970b; Gray & Ball, 1970).[12] Crucial for Gray's proposal of the septo-hippocampal system as the functional site of anxiolytic action was that septal and hippocampal lesions are like amylobarbitone in that they 'impair passive avoidance and extinction of once-rewarded behaviour, but enhance two-way active avoidance' (Gray, 1970b, p. 466). This drug–lesion parallel has held up and been massively extended over the years (Gray, 1982; Gray & McNaughton, 1983, 2000).

Gray (1970a) added two extra ingredients to this primary septo-hippocampal hypothesis of amylobarbitone action:

(a) 'the similarity between the effects of this drug in Man and the effects of damage to the frontal cortex in Man' (p. 259); and

(b) that 'lesions to the frontal cortex ... produce the same pattern [of behavioural effects as] lesions to the septal area and lesions to the hippocampus' (p. 259).

It is important to note that 'pattern' here refers not only to the dysfunctions produced by the drugs on some measures but, equally importantly, to the *lack* of dysfunction on others (which dissect away some processes) on a battery of tests. Gray scatters the parallels through his paper and so we summarize them in Table 7.1. Comparing the rows, we can conclude that the treatments have essentially the same effects as each other across the battery of paradigms. Comparing the columns, we can conclude that learning to produce an active response is unimpaired (contrary to Eysenck's theory if we believe the treatments are extraverting) while learning to suppress responding is impaired. This specificity to suppression later became the foundation for Gray's most influential suggestion: that the brain contains a distinct Behavioural Inhibition System (Gray, 1975, p. 250; 1976; see particularly Gray, 1977). From all this work, Gray concludes 'that *it is activity in this frontal cortex-medial septal area-hippocampal system which determines the degree of introversion*: the more sensitive or the more active this system is, the more introverted will the individual be' (1970a, p. 260).

Table 7.1 Summary of the effects of Gray's treatments of interest across a range of learning paradigms

Treatment	Rewarded learning	Rewarded extinction	One-way avoidance	Passive avoidance	Two-way avoidance
Anxiolytic drug	0	–	0	–	+
Septal lesion	0	–	0	–	+
Hippocampal lesion	0	–	0	–	+
Frontal lesion	0	–	0	–	+

The important point to note is that not only are the deficits the same across treatments but so are the failures to have an effect. Critically in contrasting rewarded learning with extinction and one-way active avoidance with passive avoidance we can conclude that the treatments are reducing response suppression but not response learning (which is actually improved in the case of two-way avoidance). You can view rewarded extinction as a form of passive avoidance resulting from frustrative nonreward.

AROUSABILITY AND SENSITIVITY TO PUNISHMENT

Gray wanted his new approach to accommodate Eysenck's existing theory as far as possible. He says, 'it would be in the interests of parsimony if we could now relate differences in susceptibility to punishment to differences in arousability *in the same way that Eysenck* relates conditionability to arousability' (1970a, p. 26, our italics). According to Gray, arousability is a general concept that should apply to both reward and punishment. To explain activity in a 'system whose chief function appears to be that of inhibiting maladaptive behaviour' (p. 260), general arousability needs explanation. For Gray, if we invert the causal order, it seems perfectly reasonable that higher susceptibility to the threats that abound in everyday life would lead to higher levels of arousal. But what about the effects of arousal highlighted by Eysenck? Gray noted that 'any stimulus, if it is made sufficiently intense, may act as a punishment'. High enough arousal will be punishing and so its performance-impairing effects are punishment-mediated – neatly explaining Eysenck's U-shape arousal-performance effects. For Gray, arousal, however it is produced, serves to invigorate behaviour (his Figure 5), unless it is so intense it becomes punishing. This can give rise to paradoxical effects: for example, mild punishment will induce arousal and may invigorate reward-mediated reactions – so long as the punishment-inducing effects are smaller than the reward-inducing effects.

Nevertheless, Gray, rather surprisingly, tries to retain Eysenck's suggestion that the ARAS is the key neural structure. He does this by saying that high ARAS activity would feed, via the medial septum, into changes in the hippocampal theta rhythm, and so changes in the hippocampus and frontal cortex. The whole point about the reticular (net-like) aspect of the ARAS is that it sends neural tentacles everywhere. As with his treatment of arousability, then, Gray ignores the general impact that the ARAS has on the brain, focusing on the frontal cortex-medial septal area-hippocampal system (and so deriving at the neural level punishment-specificity). As mentioned above, we can expect ARAS-induced arousal to augment reward-related reactions too, although at low levels of arousal we should expect this effect to be mild and, as we have already seen, with increasing intensity of arousal, punishment-mediated processes are most likely to dominate. In later work Gray focused almost entirely on the septo-hippocampal system.

THE NATURE OF NEUROTICISM AND ANXIETY

This final section is where the Trojan Horse of punishment sensitivity unleashes unexpected effects on the relationship of Gray's theory to Eysenck's. So far (especially in his attempt to include arousal), Gray could be seen to simply provide a slight modification to the neural elements of Eysenck's theory without much altering its superstructure (right-hand side of Figure 7.1). Moreover, in this section on neuroticism and anxiety, Gray first accepts, apparently wholeheartedly, the idea that neurotics have more intense emotional reactions both positive and negative. Neuroticism, here, is akin to emotionality. Then a twist appears.

Taking an explicitly two-process learning approach, Gray first recasts the combination of neuroticism with introversion. If reward and punishment sensitivities are distinct, and we employ only two factors for our explanations, then high neuroticism/emotionality as normally measured must represent a *combination* of high reward and high punishment sensitivity. Gray's initial equation of introversion with punishment sensitivity means that the *neurotic introvert* will be particularly sensitive to punishment. From this position, we would expect that those high on the Manifest Anxiety Scale (or suffering from any internalizing disorder) would be neurotic introverts, as his Figure 3 shows. Gray also simply asserts as a corollary ('which we now offer as a more precise statement of the present hypothesis'; 1970a, p. 262) that those with externalizing disorders would be neurotic extraverts: particularly sensitive to reward.

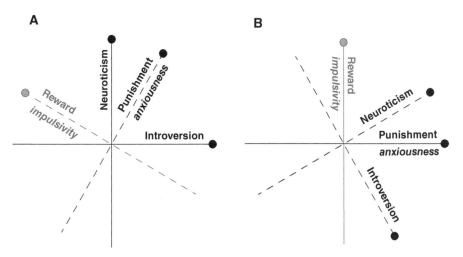

Figure 7.2 Relationship of Gray's factor axes of trait reward sensitivity (impulsivity) and trait punishment sensitivity (anxiousness) to Eysenck's factor axes of neuroticism and introversion (see also Pickering et al., 1999). (A) Treating Eysenck's factors as primary, note that the top right quadrant matches Gray's Figure 3. (B) With the space rotated to treat Gray's factors as primary.

Gray then presents in his Figure 7 a translation between susceptibility to punishment/reward and the combination of introversion and neuroticism. Here he said only that 'the most rapid increase in absolute sensitivity to punishment' (in which he included frustrative nonreward) should match the position of Taylor's Manifest Anxiety (Taylor, 1956). His footnote makes clear that this punishment sensitivity/anxiousness axis is equivalent to a mix of one-third introversion and two-thirds neuroticism as plotted in his Figure 3 (redrawn as the upper right quadrant of our Figure 7.2A). However, he also implied a second independent axis of trait sensitivity to reward (i.e., trait impulsivity; added in grey in Figure 7.2A.). In taking the two most basic concepts of learning theory (reward and punishment) as the basis of key independent traits, Gray rotated Eysenck's parameter space (Figure 7.2B) in a functionally important way (made quite explicit in Pickering et al., 1999). This rotation triggered a minor revolution, which was to go beyond Eysenck's biological theory of introversion–extraversion, and neuroticism–stability and became a completely new field. Note, here, that there are some subtle problems with Figure 7.[13] The first is that, as drawn, it implies an interaction between neuroticism and introversion, with higher neuroticism increasing values disproportionately (see Gray & McNaughton, 2000, p. 336). The second, mentioned in his footnote, is that its reward and punishment effects are symmetrical (i.e., an axis rotation of 45° not the 30° shown in Figure 7.2).

IMPACT OF THE STUDY

Gray's 1970[a] classic study had an enormous influence on the field of personality psychology. Maybe its most important achievement was to provide a different way of thinking about personality factors and their biological basis. Although Gray took his lead from Eysenck (and Pavlov) – informed by a rich literature of brain-behavioural psychology – he went further than anyone else at the time to show how a sophisticated approach to learning theory and neurophysiology, especially the use of drugs as an experimental tool, can contribute to understanding the causal dynamics of personality. This came at a price, which it still pays today: Gray's approach is complex; can be difficult to understand; and requires a breadth of not only disciplines but also technical approaches that can make it difficult to implement in personality psychology.

In consequence of Gray's work, today there is a large and growing family of approach–avoidance personality theories,[14] which include the differing approaches of Elliot and Thrash (2002, 2010), Cloninger (Cloninger, 1986; Cloninger, Svrakic, & Przybecky, 1993; Gardini, Cloninger, & Venneri, 2009), Depue (Depue & Collins, 1999; Zald & Depue, 2001), Davidson (Davidson, Ekman, Saron, Senulis, & Friesen, 1990; Davidson, Shackman, & Maxwell, 2004) and Carver (Carver, 2005; Carver & Harmon-Jones, 2009; Carver & White, 1994).

Gray's own fuller development of his ideas (Gray, 1982) has been further extended by students and former colleagues, including us (Corr & McNaughton, 2008, 2012; Gray & McNaughton, 2000; McNaughton & Corr, 2004, 2014) in what is now called the Reinforcement Sensitivity Theory (RST) of personality (Corr, 2008). RST is now a complex neuropsychological theory of personality and clinical disorder (e.g., Corr & McNaughton, 2016; McNaughton & Corr, 2016) with known links to neuroimaging data (McNaughton, DeYoung, & Corr, 2016). Other research-ers around the globe have also made significant contributions to these empirical advances.

CRITIQUE OF THE STUDY

G ray's 1970[a] synthesis was unprecedented and fundamentally changed per-sonality psychology. However, his approach had several problems, some of which linger to this day. Most obviously, its theoretical elegance is fraught with complexity. His neural and psychological *state* theory has now been greatly extended; but even this updated theory has not been easy to translate into human personality psychology; although there have been major recent moves in this direction.

The paper's complexity may seem a trivial issue – something one expects scien-tists to deal with. However, even half a century later, readers (including us) struggle with it. The biggest problem is that the theory spans multiple disciplines – with each integral to the whole. It is a major strength for a theory to explain more of the data: less complete theories fall before Occam's razor.[15] However, the range and depth of Gray's multidisciplinary arguments make them impenetrable for those who normally work within only one of the contributing disciplines.

Gray's detailed exposition also has some specific problems that we discuss here. At the theoretical level, his use of the terms 'punishment' and 'fear' were ambigu-ous: blurring key points when he shifted between one and the other conceptually. At the measurement level, while proposing a rotation of Eysenck's axes, he did not tell us how to assess his proposed reward and punishment sensitivities – a psycho-metric issue that troubles us to this day.

'Punishment' (or its alter ego 'frustrative nonreward') can suppress ongoing responding (passive avoidance); generate approach to safety; or elicit escape/withdrawal. Extraverting drugs reduce only the effects of the first of these three effects. For the second case, Gray argued that, for example, shuttle-box avoidance is unimpaired by the drugs because *relief* rewards avoidance rather than fear pun-ishing non-avoidance. His paper focused on 'reward' and 'punishment' in the context of conditioning. He, therefore, did not discuss the third case of escape/withdrawal in any detail. At this time, he distinguished between a learning-related 'punishment mechanism for passive avoidance [and] a separate punishment mechanism for organizing the unconditioned response to a punishment. We shall call this the "fight/flight" system' (Gray, 1971, p. 194; note that 'punishment' means three different things within this one quote). However, it is via fight/flight that he included obsessive–compulsive disorder, with its compulsive rituals and obsessive rumination, within the dysthymic disorders. Gray says the 'symptoms bear all the marks of an *active* avoidance response' (p. 255, our italics) equating this with *fear* (see also Rapoport, 1989). However, we cannot link this (active avoidance) 'fear' to (passive avoidance) 'punishment' behaviourally; nor do extraverting drugs (like amylobarbitone) treat obsessions or compulsions. Other, similar, mismatches occur in the clinic. Neuroticism appears to be a quite general risk factor for a wide array of dysthymic disorders (Andrews, Stewart, Morris-Yates, Holt, & Henderson, 1990; Hengartner, Tyrer, Ajdacic-Gross, Angst, & Rossler, 2017). However, many of these disorders do not involve passive avoidance (not just obsessive–compulsive disorder, but also simple phobia, panic, depression) and do not respond to Gray's key pharmacological tool: the extraverting drugs[16] that reduce behavioural inhibition in animal tests and reduce generalized anxiety in humans. In explaining reactive depression, Gray notes that Maudsley Reactive rats, taken as a model of introversion, 'show a bigger frustration effect in the Amsel and Rousell (1952) double runway' (1970a, p. 256) but he does not note that he had already shown that amylobarbitone does *not reduce* the frustration effect (Gray, 1967, p. 601). Gray's 'punishment sensitivity' as defined by the drugs, even at the time, was more restricted than neurotic introversion or dysthymia.

Gray set out to replace Eysenck's theory of introversion and neuroticism with his own; but as RST has evolved, he appears more to have provided an explanation of how neuroticism and introversion give rise to the psychiatric disorders that were Eysenck's primary starting point. Given his bottom-up biological approach, it may seem surprising that Gray retained Eysenck's two-dimensional personality space, simply rotating the introversion–extraversion and neuroticism axes to form punishment and reward sensitivity factors (Figure 7.2). He retained this structure even in the substantial revision of the state theory by Gray and McNaughton (2000).

Many personality researchers have sought specific scales for Gray's biological factors (see Corr, 2016b). But even Gray's own attempt, the Gray–Wilson Personality Questionnaire (Wilson, Barrett, & Gray, 1989; Wilson, Gray, & Barrett, 1990), does not have the predicted factor structure. The most recent attempt of this kind, the Reinforcement Sensitivity Theory Personality Questionnaire (Corr & Cooper, 2016), is the most elaborate and professes to have been developed exclusively on the basis of the most recent state version of RST.

However, none of these attempts (including Gray's own) has used biological anchors as a starting point and all have assumed that the experimenter's use of language will map to the underlying biology. One reason for this is that many personality researchers prefer the persuasive mono-disciplinary simplicity of language, as reflected in the Big Five and, so, do not anchor their personality constructs in well-delineated biological systems (McNaughton & Corr, 2014). This is a preference Gray warned us against all those years ago in 1970, but the lesson has still to be learned. This warning may well be Gray's truly lasting legacy to personality psychology. A second reason is that development of Gray's state theory did not offer, until recently, an obvious anchor that personality theorists could use. However, based on the fundamental ideas in Gray's (1970b) paper on conflict and drug-sensitive theta rhythm (and some decades of practical development) we now have a human biomarker for Gray's Behavioural Inhibition System that offers the first such (albeit weak) biological anchor for personality research (McNaughton, 2017). It will be interesting to see if personality researchers wish to take it up.

CONCLUSIONS

You have just seen how Gray's 1970[a] classic study contributed to personality psychology. His theoretical brilliance is not in doubt: he posed new and exciting questions for the 'student of personality'. The paper showed that we should anchor personality measures to known biological entities; and it anticipated the links research is now forging between personality and the psychobiology of the mental illnesses that still blight the lives of millions with high costs to society. Gray was right to not simply accept that statistically derived lexical factors reflect the true nature of personality. He did accept that we need them as a starting point for biological exploration – all science has to start with a superficial descriptive phase. But, his multidisciplinary sophistication is still not a feature of personality psychology, where most research workers are yet to grapple with the more fundamental biological reality that underlies systematic individual differences in patterns of affect, behaviour, cognition and desire: personality.

NOTES

1. N. McN. remembers him saying that, like Archimedes, the crucial ideas came to him during a bath and he wrote the paper straight out in a day or two.

2. Gray (1970a) has recently had steadily increasing citations, averaging about 10/ year around 2000, 20/year around 2005, 25/year around 2010, and well over 30/ year around 2015 according to Web of Knowledge.

3. They provide a broad coverage of the history and development of the Big Five.

4. See Pavlov (1927), Lecture XVII, p. 284 on 'The different types of nervous system' and their links to pathology and Gray's (1964c) overview of Pavlov's theory of types and its mapping to Western views of personality and arousal.

5. The other three are Conscientiousness, Agreeableness, and Openness to Experience.

6. In the history of learning theory, there have been two main traditions: single-process (used by Eysenck, following Hull) and two-process (which we will meet shortly). In Hull's theory, all learning depends on a single process, drive reduction (Hull, 1943, 1952) – reinforcement occurs when a stimulus (e.g., water, money, or verbal praise) reduces drive. Concurrent active drives summate, and the amount of conditioning (based on drive reduction) should increase with increases in general arousal (which reflects increased summated drive), except when drive/ arousal is too high. The idea of an inverted-U relationship between arousal and performance goes back at least to the time of the Yerkes–Dodson law (Yerkes & Dodson, 1908). Eysenck's insight was that introversion–extraversion could map to this arousal–performance relationship, with both extremes producing sub-optimal performance. (For a discussion of this literature, see Corr, 2016a, pp. 115–130).

7. Strictly (Gray, 1964b, p. 158) this is what Pavlov would have called the strength of the excitatory process (which would include transmarginal and external inhibition) and is distinct from his strength of the inhibitory process (involving

internal inhibition). However, like Gray (1970a), we can ignore these details in concluding that Eysenck's theory does not match the eyeblink data.

8. 'According to one story, the English versions of Pavlov's writings were first translated with the guidance of the German translation from the original Russian. The German word "bedingt" has two meanings that have different words in English: "conditioned" and "conditional". It was translated as the more common conditioned, but Conditional and Unconditional are more accurate translations of the Russian, and they fit the underlying idea of conditioning.' www.indiana.edu/~p1013447/dictionary/origcond.htm

9. A class of drug abused by, and one of the causes of death of, Marilyn Monroe.

10. Gray (1972) is the same chapter as that cited by Gray (1970a) as 'Gray, in press, b'. However, it appeared in a different book than that in the original reference, with Gray's contribution to Cattell's book being on a different topic.

11. As a cherry on this icing to his cake, Gray provided in his Figure 5a sketch of the Gray and Smith (1969) 'arousal-decision model for partial reinforcement and discrimination learning' (also reprinted in Gray, 1975). Your most important take-home message from the model is that Gray saw it as 'a model for conflict situations', by which he very much meant the kind of situations analysed behaviourally and pharmacologically by Neal Miller (Bailey & Miller, 1952; Barry & Miller, 1962, 1965; Kimble, 1961; Miller, 1944, 1959). In these situations, avoidance *opposes* approach and – depending on goal gradients and other factors – the animal may approach, avoid passively, explore, or dither. Whether approach occurs, or not, depends on the decision mechanism (the box [D.M.] in Figure 5). How fast the individual acts, and things like whether they explore (which we can view as risk assessment) or how much they dither depends on the arousal summation mechanism (the box [A] in Figure 5). Note that general effects of the functions of [A] are very similar to those of Hull's generalization of drive that we discussed earlier.

12. Gray (1970b) is nominally a review article but, unusually, contains original data. The key findings were reported in *Science* by Gray and Ball (1970), which is not cited by Gray (1970a). Gray produced all three papers during his visit to Neal Miller's laboratory.

13. In 1999, Gray acknowledged these facts in a *mea culpa* when Dr Alan Pickering pointed them out (Pickering et al., 1999).

14. For a review of influential theories in personality neuroscience, see DeYoung and Gray (2009).

15. 'Pluralitas non est ponenda sine necessitate' (keep assumptions to the minimum necessary to explain the available data) Guilelmus de Occam: Quodlibeta, V, Q.i.

16. For Gray (1970a) the key drugs were barbiturates, usually sodium amylobarbitone, and also alcohol. The same lack of effect on fear disorders has proved true of currently prescribed anxiolytic drugs, both 'classical' benzodiazepines and more novel 5HT1A agonists like buspirone and calcium channel agents such as pregabalin.

FURTHER READING

Elliot, A. J., & Thrash, T. M. (2002). Approach-avoidance motivation in personality: Approach and avoidance temperament and goals. *Journal of Personality and Social Psychology, 82*, 804–818.

Gray, J. A. (1981). A critique of Eysenck's theory of personality. In H. J. Eysenck (Ed.), *A model for personality*. New York: Springer.

Gray, J. A. (1987). *The psychology of fear and stress*. London: Cambridge University Press.

REFERENCES

Amsel, A. (1992). *Frustration theory: An analysis of dispositional learning and memory*. Cambridge: Cambridge University Press.

Andrews, G., Stewart, G., Morris-Yates, A., Holt, P., & Henderson, S. (1990). Evidence for a general neurotic syndrome. *British Journal of Psychiatry, 157*, 6–12.

Bailey, C. J., & Miller, N. E. (1952). The effect of sodium amytal on an approach–avoidance conflict in cats. *Journal of Comparative and Physiological Psychology, 45*, 205–208.

Barry, H., & Miller, N. E. (1962). Effects of drugs on approach–avoidance conflict tested repeatedly by means of a telescope alley. *Journal of Comparative and Physiological Psychology, 55*, 201–210.

Barry, H., & Miller, N. E. (1965). Comparison of drug effects on approach, avoidance and escape motivation. *Journal of Comparative and Physiological Psychology, 59*, 18–24.

Carver, C. S. (2005). Impulse and constraint: Perspectives from personality psychology, convergence with theory in other areas, and potential for integration. *Personality and Social Psychology Review, 9*, 312–333.

Carver, C. S., & Harmon-Jones, E. (2009). Anger is an approach-related affect: Evidence and implications. *Psychological Bulletin, 135*, 183–204.

Carver, C. S., & White, T. L. (1994). Behavioral inhibition, behavioral activation, and affective responses to impending reward and punishment: The BIS/BAS scales. *Journal of Personality and Social Psychology, 67*, 319–333.

Claridge, G. S. (1967). *Personality and arousal: A psychophysiological study of psychiatric disorder*. Oxford: Pergamon Press.

Cloninger, C. R. (1986). A unified biosocial theory of personality and its role in the development of anxiety states. *Psychiatric Developments, 3*, 167–226.

Cloninger, C. R., Svrakic, D. M., & Przybecky, T. R. (1993). A psychobiological model of temperament and character. *Archives of General Psychiatry, 50*, 975–990.

Corr, P. J. (2016a). *Hans Eysenck: A contradictory psychology*. London: Palgrave.

Corr, P. J. (2016b). Reinforcement sensitivity theory of personality questionnaires: Structural survey with recommendations. *Personality and Individual Differences, 89*, 60–64.

Corr, P. J. (Ed.) (2008). *The reinforcement sensitivity theory of personality*. Cambridge: Cambridge University Press.

Corr, P. J., & Cooper, A. B. (2016). The Reinforcement Sensitivity Theory of Personality Questionnaire (RST-PQ): Development and validation. *Psychological Assessment, 28*, 1427–1440.

Corr, P. J., & McNaughton, N. (2008). Reinforcement sensitivity theory and personality. In P. J. Corr (Ed.), *The reinforcement sensitivity theory of personality*. Cambridge: Cambridge University Press.

Corr, P. J., & McNaughton, N. (2012). Neuroscience and approach/avoidance personality traits: A two stage (valuation–motivation) approach. *Neuroscience and Biobehavioral Reviews, 36*, 2339–2354.

Corr, P. J., & McNaughton, N. (2016). Neural mechanisms of low trait anxiety and risk for externalizing behaviour. In T. P. Beauchaine & S. P. Hinshaw (Eds.), *The Oxford handbook of externalizing spectrum disorders*. Oxford Handbooks Online: Oxford University Press.

Corr, P. J., Pickering, A., & Gray, J. A. (1995). Personality and reinforcement in associative and instrumental learning. *Personality and Individual Differences, 19*, 47–71.

Davidson, R. J., Ekman, P., Saron, C. D., Senulis, J. A., & Friesen, W. V. (1990). Approach–withdrawal and cerebral asymmetry: Emotional expression and brain physiology I. *Journal of Personality and Social Psychology, 58*, 330–341.

Davidson, R. J., Shackman, A. J., & Maxwell, J. S. (2004). Asymmetries in face and brain related to emotion. *Trends in Cognitive Sciences, 8*, 389–391.

Dawkins, R. (2005). *The Ancestor's Tale: A pilgrimage to the dawn of life.* London: Phoenix (Orion Books Ltd).

Depue, R. A., & Collins, P. F. (1999). Neurobiology of the structure of personality: Dopamine, facilitation of incentive motivation and extraversion. *Behavioral and Brain Sciences, 22*, 491–569.

DeYoung, C. G. (2015). Cybernetic Big Five theory. *Journal of Research in Personality, 56*, 33–58.

DeYoung, C. G., & Gray, J. R. (2009). Personality neuroscience: Explaining individual differences in affect, behaviour and cognition. In P. J. Corr & G. Matthews (Eds.), *The Cambridge handbook of personality psychology.* Cambridge: Cambridge University Press.

Elliot, A. J., & Thrash, T. M. (2002). Approach–avoidance motivation in personality: Approach and avoidance temperament and goals. *Journal of Personality and Social Psychology, 82*, 804–818.

Elliot, A. J., & Thrash, T. M. (2010). Approach and avoidance temperament as basic dimensions of personality. *Journal of Personality, 78*, 865–906.

Eysenck, H. J. (1963). Editorial. *Behaviour Research and Therapy, 1*, 1–2.

Eysenck, H. J. (1967). *The biological basis of personality.* Springfield, IL: Charles C. Thomas.

Gardini, S., Cloninger, C. R., & Venneri, A. (2009). Individual differences in personality traits reflect structural variance in specific brain regions. *Brain Research Bulletin, 79*, 265–270.

Gray, J. A. (1964a). Strength of the nervous system and levels of arousal: A reinterpretation. In J. A. Gray (Ed.), *Pavlov's typology.* Oxford: Pergamon Press.

Gray, J. A. (1964b). Strength of the nervous system as a dimension of personality in man. In J. A. Gray (Ed.), *Pavlov's typology.* Oxford: Pergamon Press.

Gray, J. A. (Ed.) (1964c). *Pavlov's typology.* Oxford: Pergamon Press.

Gray, J. A. (1967). Disappointment and drugs in the rat. *Advancement of Science, 23*, 595–605.

Gray, J. A. (1970a). The psychophysiological basis of introversion–extraversion. *Behaviour Research and Therapy, 8*, 249–266.

Gray, J. A. (1970b). Sodium amobarbital, the hippocampal theta rhythm and the partial reinforcement extinction effect. *Psychological Review, 77*, 465–480.

Gray, J. A. (1971). *The psychology of fear and stress.* London: Weidenfeld and Nicolson.

Gray, J. A. (1972). Learning theory, the conceptual nervous system and personality. In V. D. Nebylitsyn & J. A. Gray (Eds.), *The biological bases of individual behaviour.* London, New York: Academic Press.

Gray, J. A. (1975). *Elements of a two-process theory of learning.* London: Academic Press.

Gray, J. A. (1976). The behavioural inhibition system: A possible substrate for anxiety. In M. P. Feldman & A. M. Broadhurst (Eds.), *Theoretical and experimental bases of behaviour modification*. London: Wiley.

Gray, J. A. (1977). Drug effects on fear and frustration: Possible limbic site of action of minor tranquilizers. In L. L. Iversen, S. D. Iversen, & S. H. Snyder (Eds.), *Handbook of psychopharmacology: Vol. 8 – Drugs, neurotransmitters and behaviour*. New York: Plenum Press.

Gray, J. A. (1982). *The neuropsychology of anxiety: An enquiry in to the functions of the septo-hippocampal system*. Oxford: Oxford University Press.

Gray, J. A. (1987). *The psychology of fear and stress*. London: Cambridge University Press.

Gray, J. A., & Ball, G. G. (1970). Frequency-specific relation between hippocampal theta rhythm, behavior and amobarbital action. *Science, 168*, 1246–1248.

Gray, J. A., & McNaughton, N. (1983). Comparison between the behavioural effect of septal and hippocampal lesions: A review. *Neuroscience and Biobehavioral Reviews, 7*, 119–188.

Gray, J. A., & McNaughton, N. (2000). *The neuropsychology of anxiety: An enquiry into the functions of the septo-hippocampal system* (2nd ed.). Oxford: Oxford University Press.

Gray, J. A., & Smith, P. T. (1969). An arousal-decision model for partial reinforcement and discrimination learning. In R. Gilbert & N. S. Sutherland (Eds.), *Animal discrimination learning*. London: Academic Press.

Hebb, D. O. (1955). Drives and the C.N.S. (conceptual nervous system). *Psychological Review, 62*, 243–254.

Hengartner, M. P., Tyrer, P., Ajdacic-Gross, V., Angst, J., & Rossler, W. (2017). Articulation and testing of a personality-centred model of psychopathology: Evidence from a longitudinal community study over 30 years. *European Archives of Psychiatry and Clinical Neuroscience*, 1–12.

Hull, C. L. (1943). *Principles of behaviour*. New York: Appleton–Century–Crofts, Inc.

Hull, C. L. (1952). *A behavior system*. New Haven, CT: Yale University Press.

John, O. P., & Srivastava, S. (1995). The Big Five trait taxonomy: History, measurement and theoretical perspectives. In L. A. Pervin & O. P. John (Eds.), *Handbook of personality: theory and research* (2nd ed.). London: Guilford Press.

Kimble, G. A. (1961). *Hilgard and Marquis' conditioning and learning*. New York: Appleton–Century–Crofts.

McNaughton, N. (2017). What do you mean 'anxiety'? Developing the first anxiety syndrome biomarker. *Journal of the Royal Society of New Zealand, 48*, 177–190.

McNaughton, N., & Corr, P. J. (2004). A two-dimensional neuropsychology of defense: Fear/anxiety and defensive distance. *Neuroscience and Biobehavioral Reviews, 28*, 285–305.

McNaughton, N., & Corr, P. J. (2014). Approach, avoidance, and their conflict: The problem of anchoring. *Frontiers in Systems Neuroscience, 8*.

McNaughton, N., & Corr, P. J. (2016). Mechanisms of comorbidity, continuity, and discontinuity in anxiety-related disorders. *Development and Psychopathology, 28*, 1053–1069.

McNaughton, N., DeYoung, C. G., & Corr, P. J. (2016). Approach/avoidance. In J. R. Absher & J. Cloutier (Eds.), *Neuroimaging personality, social cognition and character*. San Diego, CA: Elsevier.

Miller, N. E. (1944). Experimental studies of conflict. In J. M. Hunt (Ed.), *Personality and the behavioural disorders*. New York: Ronald Press.

Miller, N. E. (1959). Liberalization of basic S-R concepts: Extensions to conflict behaviour, motivation and social learning. In S. Koch (Ed.), *Psychology: A study of a science*. New York: Wiley.

Mowrer, O. H. (1960). *Learning theory and behavior*. New York: Wiley.

Pavlov, I. P. (1927). *Conditioned reflexes* (trans. G. V. Anrep). London: Constable & Co. Ltd, Dover edition, by special arrangement with Oxford University Press.

Pavlov, I. P. (1932). The reply of a physiologist to psychologists. *Psychological Review*, *39*, 91–127. (Reprinted in Kaplan, M. (1966) *Essential works of Pavlov*. London: Bantam Books.)

Pickering, A. D., Corr, P. J., & Gray, J. A. (1999). Interactions and reinforcement sensitivity theory: A theoretical analysis of Rusting & Larsen (1997). *Personality and Individual Differences*, *26*, 357–365.

Rapoport, J. L. (1989). The biology of obsessions and compulsions. *Scientific American*, *260* (March), 63–69.

Taylor, J. (1956). Drive theory and manifest anxiety. *Psychological Bulletin*, *53*, 303–320.

Wilson, G. D., Barrett, P. T., & Gray, J. A. (1989). Human reactions to reward and punishment: A questionnaire examination of Gray's personality theory. *British Journal of Psychology*, *80*, 509–515.

Wilson, G. D., Gray, J. A., & Barrett, P. T. (1990). A factor analysis of the Gray–Wilson personality questionnaire. *Personality and Individual Differences*, *11*, 1037–1045.

Yerkes, R. M., & Dodson, J. D. (1908). The relation of strength of stimulus to rapidity of habit-formation. *Journal of Comparative Neurology and Psychology*, *18*, 459–482.

Zald, D., & Depue, R. (2001). Serotonergic modulation of positive and negative affect in psychiatrically healthy males. *Personality and Individual Differences*, *30*, 71–86.

8

Effects of Rewards on Self-Determination and Intrinsic Motivation

Revisiting Deci (1971)

Richard M. Ryan, William S. Ryan and Stefano I. Di Domenico

BACKGROUND TO THE STUDY

In 1971 Edward Deci published a seminal paper that challenged dominant conceptions of motivation and laid the foundations for what would become *self-determination theory* (SDT; Deci & Ryan, 1985; Ryan & Deci, 2017). At the time the paper was published, behaviourism dominated the field of psychology. Behaviourism of that era was focused on the use of external reinforcers – contingent rewards and punishments – to control behaviour. The dominant view was that behaviour is a function of these external consequences, which make specific actions more or less probable. Drive theory (Hull, 1943; Spence, 1956) similarly focused on reinforcers, but additionally included an account of the types of events that would be reinforcing – those that support physiological needs (food, water, sex and freedom from pain). Behaviours that satisfy these physiological needs, and return the organism to equilibrium, will be reinforced. That is, the reduction in the drive serves as the reinforcer, strengthening the connection between behaviour and external stimuli. Although some recognized differential sensitivity to reinforcing properties in the environment (e.g., Gray, 1970), it was the rewarding and punishing properties external to the organism that were seen as shaping emitted responses.

Yet, behaviourist and drive theories were unable to account for the observation that behaviours such as play and exploration seemed to occur spontaneously, without external reinforcement. For curiosity-based and exploratory behaviours the reinforcement appeared to be inherent to the behaviour itself. The reward-contingent motivation documented by behaviourists is referred to as extrinsic motivation, whereas behaviours that are enacted out of interest, enjoyment, or curiosity are considered to be intrinsically motivated.

Intrinsic motivation would later become a core component of self-determination theory (Ryan & Deci, 2017), which is a theory of human motivation and personality that highlights the importance of internal resources and needs for personality development and self-regulation. SDT distinguishes between different types of motivation that fall along a continuum from fully externally controlled to fully intrinsically motivated (Ryan & Deci, 2000). Importantly, one might engage in the same activity (e.g., reading a book) for either extrinsic (e.g., in order to receive a reward) or intrinsic (e.g., because the content is interesting) reasons. Motivation is therefore defined as the cause of or reason for goal pursuit, the *why* of behaviour (Deci & Ryan, 2000).

Within the SDT framework, intrinsically motivated behaviours are viewed as exemplifying humans' (and other organisms') inherent propensities for growth and knowledge acquisition. According to SDT, humans are not merely passive objects pushed around by outside forces (though they can be), but are agents operating on the environment and within relational contexts with innate propensity toward growth, self-regulation and integration (Ryan & Deci, 2000). In order for these growth tendencies to be actualized, however, the organism must be provided with certain nutrients. These essential nutrients make up the *basic psychological needs* posited by self-determination theory: competence, autonomy and relatedness. Competence refers to the feeling that one is effective in one's social interactions and has opportunities to exercise and develop one's capacities. Autonomy refers to the perception that one is the source or origin of one's own behaviour or that one is act-ing in accord with one's personal values and beliefs (Deci & Ryan, 1985). The third need, relatedness, is defined as the feeling of being connected to other individuals and one's community; it is the sense of caring for others and having them care for you in return (Ryan, 1995). These three needs are *basic* in the sense that they are universal and essential to optimal functioning, growth, integration, social develop-ment and well-being (Ryan & Deci, 2001). When these needs are not met, the organism suffers. Autonomy, competence and relatedness are thus the psychological equivalents of the physical needs (e.g., food, water, sex) that arouse drive states (e.g., hunger, thirst, lust; Hull, 1943).

Today considerable evidence supports the view that the satisfaction of auton-omy, competence and relatedness affects the quality and persistence of behaviour. We also know that incentives (e.g., money), styles of feedback (e.g., praise, infor-mational feedback) and social support (e.g., instrumental and emotional support) differentially affect motivation and performance at work, school, sports and other domains as a function of how they impact these basic psychological needs. These basic psychological needs and their impact on the quality of motivation are, how-ever, relatively new developments in psychology. Here we look back almost 50 years ago to a humble set of experiments that, although being far from definitive, set the stage for a new motivational science focused not just on motivation due to external forces, but also on the motivation that comes from within people. These experiments emerged from a doctoral dissertation by Edward Deci, a social psy-chologist examining the impact of external rewards on intrinsic motivation.

The three experiments published by Deci in 1971 included two major contribu-tions to the study of motivation. First, they introduced a method to assess intrinsic motivation in humans by behavioural means. This operational definition helped bring the concept of intrinsic motivation into the world of experimental social psychology, where previously the emphasis was much more on how individuals are shaped by being part of a social group. Second, these experiments purported to demonstrate that external rewards, when experienced as causing or controlling one's behaviour, undermine intrinsic motivation (e.g., a person may feel that they are 'being bought' by money). Feeling controlled, even by positive rewards, eroded a psychological satisfaction essential to intrinsic motivation – a sense of initiative and volition. Although such notions were previously discussed in terms of cognitive dissonance (Festinger, 1957), and even the effects of expectations of reward and punishment from a purely learning approach (see Chapter 7), these theories failed to provide an explanation of observed behavioural effects in terms of basic psychological needs. These findings opened a new direction for studies in human motivation by focusing on intrinsic motivation and the psychological need satisfactions required to sustain it. In addition, these studies laid the foundation for understanding both the positive and negative effects of external rewards on volitional behaviour –the implications of which are vast.

BEHAVIOURISM

In the 1960s the predominant model of behavioural regulation in mainstream psychology was *radical behaviourism*, which as we noted focused on the control of behaviours through contingencies of reinforcement – human behaviour was modelled on that of the rat and pigeon. This was for good reason. Decades of experiments had reliably shown that, when carefully applied in controlled settings, external reinforcements could control (shape and sustain) specific behaviours (Skinner, 1953). The sophistication of this behavioural control technology appealed to many, not least of all the advertising industry.

Still there were rumblings of dissent within the field. Although behaviourists had clearly shown how behaviours *can* be controlled by external reinforcements, many researchers questioned whether *all* organized actions are, in natural environments, motivated by such contingencies – in addition, the most powerful demonstration of these effects were found in laboratory animals where psychological needs of any complexity are absent. In particular, there was the problem of *intrinsic motivation* – spontaneous behaviours that seem to occur out of interest, curiosity, or playfulness, and no previous conditioning/learning. Many activities, even in rats, as well as primates and humans (i.e., the primary species targeted in experiments), such as exploration, play and object manipulation, frequently occur without prior external (at least, explicit) reinforcements. Experiments even showed that animals would endure pain or forgo primary reinforcers, such as food and water, for opportunities to explore or exercise their capacities (e.g., Nissen, 1930). Furthermore, as Harlow (1950) and Gately (1950) observed in primate studies, such 'intrinsically motivated' activities could be disrupted rather than enhanced by the introduction of external rewards. It could always be asserted that, in some way, such behaviours were controlled by non-obvious prior exposure to reinforcement, but this approach fails to provide a satisfactory scientific explanation.

In a seminal paper, White (1959) famously summarized the failures of both drive theories (Hullian and psychoanalytic) and operant or 'radical' behavioural theories to explain intrinsically motivated behaviours. White argued that, rather than being dependent on reinforcement, such activities were innate adaptive propensities and that they were proximally motivated by psychological needs, especially the need to impact or effect one's environment, which he termed *effectance motivation*. White's focus was on psychological or intrinsic satisfactions (rather than either drive reductions or external rewards) as the motivational basis for activities, such as play, exploration, curious learning, and other activities that engage and elaborate human capacities.

Building on White's (1959) idea of effectance motivation, as well as Heider's (1958) attribution theory of perceived causality, de Charms (1968) argued that a key psychological satisfaction underlying intrinsic motivation is that of being an *origin* of one's actions, or experiencing a sense of initiative and autonomy. Following Heider's (1958) terminology, de Charms described this sense of behaviour originating from the self as having an *internal perceived locus of causality* (IPLOC). Opposite to perceiving oneself as the origin of one's behaviour is the feeling that one is a pawn whose actions are driven by forces outside of the self. Having an *external perceived locus of causality* (EPLOC) is thus the perception that factors external to the self are the cause of one's behaviour. De Charms (1968) further speculated that being extrinsically motivated (e.g., being motivated by grades or other rewards) should, by diminishing one's sense of being an origin and fostering an EPLOC, negatively impact intrinsic motivation.

As we shall see, Deci's (1971) experiments built on both of these theoretical foundations. In keeping with both White and de Charms, Deci suggested that whether rewards, feedback, and other events enhance or diminish intrinsic motivation will be a function of how they affect feelings of self-determination (being an origin) and competence (experiences of effectance). Financial rewards, because they readily foster an EPLOC, should diminish intrinsic motivation. Yet, when rewards support or encourage self-determination and competence, they should maintain or enhance intrinsic motivation. Verbal rewards and positive feedback were hypothesized to do just that.

Such proposals were at that time highly controversial. First, the consideration of any 'inner' forces within an organism 'causing' behaviours as implied by the construct of *intrinsic motivation* was, within at least some behaviourist circles, anathema. To many, this idea seemed reminiscent of the Cartesian 'ghost in the machine' of *vitalist* philosophy. Beyond that, another contentious issue was the notion that an effective reinforcement could *decrease* subsequent behaviour relative to no external reinforcement. Several decades of systematic research had clearly established the power of reinforcements to control and sustain behaviour, at least while contingencies remain in effect. It was recognized, of course, that any given stimulus might not function as an effective reinforcer and that withdrawal of reinforcement would lead to extinction of the previously reinforced behaviour. However, financial payments, or what Skinner described as that 'universal generalized reinforcer, money' (1953, p. 62), were posited to be an effective strategy for increasing or maintaining behaviours — of course, it may control immediate behaviour (receiving £10 each for each jump), but it would hardly lead to longer-term behaviour in the absence of such a reward (jumping would then become aversive). The idea that such a reinforcer might *undermine* subsequent motivation was for some scientifically problematic, if not downright heretical (e.g., see Scott, 1976).

Deci's 1971 and 1972 publications were important in part because they provided an empirical methodology for addressing an area of controversy within the field of behaviour regulation and motivation at the time. In these experiments, Deci specifically introduced an operational and behavioural definition for *intrinsic motivation* – the *free-choice behavioural paradigm*, an approach that became a standard in the field. Furthermore, these studies tested nascent ideas about the role of psychological needs in maintaining intrinsically motivated behaviours, as well as the varied effects of external factors such as rewards, praise, and evaluative feedback on intrinsic motivational processes.

DETAILED DESCRIPTION OF THE STUDY

DIFFERING PREDICTIONS

Deci (1971) began with this question: if a monetary reward is offered for performing an activity one already finds interesting, what effect will this reward have on subsequent intrinsic motivation? At the time, existing literature offered differing predictions as to what should occur.

Operant psychology maintained (albeit using different language) that intrinsic and extrinsic motivation would be additive. Behaviour would increase when effective reinforcers (in this case financial rewards) were applied, and would return over time to pre-reward baseline after the reinforcement was removed (extinction). Expectancy-valence theories of motivation, which were prominent at this time within organizational psychology, similarly assumed that intrinsic and extrinsic motivation would have an additive behavioural effect (e.g., see Porter & Lawler, 1968).

Counter to this, Deci (1971) anticipated that the motivational impact of rewards might depend on how they are experienced. Building on de Charms (1968), Deci reasoned that the application of contingent extrinsic rewards to an intrinsically motivated activity could prompt a change in the *perceived locus of causality* from internal (IPLOC) to external (EPLOC). Although participants would have initially been doing the activity because it was interesting and challenging (i.e., for internal reasons), those in reward conditions may come to view the activity as something done in order to obtain an externally controlled reward. In other words, offering rewards would shift participants' perceived locus of causality from internal to external, undermining their experience of being an origin, and thus their intrinsic motivation. In behavioural terms, Deci hypothesized that rewarding participants for engaging in interesting activities would cause performance of that behaviour to drop below baseline levels, rather than simply returning to baseline, once these incentives were removed. Alternatively, Deci reasoned that rewards that did not interfere with participants' experiences of 'self-determination and competence' should not produce this undermining effect on subsequent intrinsic motivation.

Deci's primary measure of intrinsic motivation was what he called the *free-choice behavioural paradigm*, a strategy upon which most subsequent experimental work on intrinsic motivation has been based. In this approach, intrinsic motivation is operationalized as the amount of time participants spend engaged with a target activity when they are alone, are not being observed, are free to choose what to do, have alternative activities available, and have no explicit incentives for continuing on the target task.

EXPERIMENT 1

Deci (1971) had two groups of participants work on interesting spatial puzzles over three sessions, each separated by at least one day. The task was called a SOMA puzzle, the goal of which is to assemble a set of three-dimensional shapes such that they match various depicted figures, with some figures more difficult to construct than others. In the initial experimental session, both groups worked on these puzzles without mention of incentive or reward. To assess baseline intrinsic motivation, Deci assessed free-choice behaviour during an 8-minute break in the middle of this initial session. After administering a few puzzles the experimenter left the room under the pretext of selecting additional materials. Participants were told they could continue to do puzzles, read magazines, or do whatever they chose while they waited for the experimenter to return. The room contained magazines and alternative activities, as well as more of the spatial puzzles. Participants were surreptitiously observed during this time and the number of seconds they spent on the target activity – that is, working on these spatial puzzles – was recorded.

In a second session, participants in the experimental group were offered rewards for completing these puzzles ($1 for each puzzle solved — remember it's 1970!), whereas the control group continued to work on these puzzles without knowledge or expectation of a reward. Finally, in a third session, participants in the experimental condition were told that unfortunately the budget was not enough to pay them for more than one session. Therefore, both groups participated in the final session without expecting any reward. As in the initial session, this third session included a free-choice period in the middle where participants could occupy themselves as they pleased, presumably unobserved.

The question of interest was what effect receiving rewards for performing the puzzle task in session 2 would have on intrinsic motivation for the task, operationalized as a change in the time spent working on the puzzle task during session 1 (baseline) and session 3's free-choice periods. If rewards undermined the IPLOC for doing the puzzle task, rewarded participants should show a greater decrease in this behaviour during the final free-choice period compared to those who had never received rewards for this activity.

By any modern view this initial study was quite statistically underpowered – and with only 24 participants, the effects of this first study were only marginally significant. Nonetheless these results were provocative in suggesting a potential negative effect of rewards on post-reward persistence, an outcome not previously observed in experiments with humans. Specifically, participants who had received extrinsic rewards for solving these interesting puzzles spent much less time working on the puzzles during the final free-choice period than they had in the initial one (before incentives were introduced). Those who never received rewards for completing these puzzles evidenced a smaller decrease in time spent working on the puzzles between the first and last free-choice periods. These results were interpreted by Deci to represent the undermining of intrinsic motivation by the financial rewards – participants who had been rewarded were now less interested in the task than those who had not been.

EXPERIMENT 2

Deci's second 1971 study was a field experiment conducted at a college newspaper office. The experiment utilized the newspaper's staffing structure, which had two four-person teams of headline writers whose schedules did not overlap. After four weeks of normal work (period 1, baseline), one of these teams was given $0.50 for each headline they wrote, a contingency that continued for three weeks (period 2). The other (control) group did not receive and did know about any rewards. After being paid for these three weeks, the experimental group was told that funds for payment had been exhausted and that they could no longer be paid. Both groups were then observed over the final three-week period (period 3), as well as during the first two weeks of the following semester (period 4, follow-up), which began five weeks later. During each of these periods the time taken to write each headline was surreptitiously recorded by the experimenter, whom both teams believed to be a supervisor. This was used to index intrinsic motivation based on the assumption that faster work (better performance) is indicative of higher intrinsic motivation. The number of times team members were absent was also assessed.

On the performance measure the primary hypothesis was supported. Whereas the unrewarded group continued to become more efficient (faster) in headline writing, the reward group showed little increase in efficiency after rewards were withdrawn. The experimental group also showed a trend toward increased absenteeism after the reward period relative to controls. Both findings were interpreted to indicate a relative decrease in intrinsic motivation in the reward group.

EXPERIMENT 3

Study 3 in this series was almost identical to the first in design. This time, however, Deci used 'verbal rewards' (praise and positive feedback) rather than financial rewards as the experimental manipulation. Verbal rewards can, of course, take many forms. For example, such rewards might involve telling people that they did well at a task, that they have shown great effort, or that they outperformed others. In study 3, participants in the verbal rewards condition received feedback such as: 'You did very well in completing the task; many participants did not complete it.' If they failed to complete a puzzle they were told: 'This was a very difficult one, and you were progressing very well with it.' These forms of verbal rewards were specifically chosen, as they are likely to support feelings of competence and efficacy. Deci hypothesized that verbal rewards like these would typically not be experienced as controlling, but rather as 'encouragement'. Therefore, unlike contingent financial rewards, this type of verbal reward would be unlikely to create an EPLOC or undermine intrinsic motivation.

As expected, results showed no undermining effect of these verbal rewards on intrinsic motivation. Whereas intrinsic motivation in the control group declined over sessions, that of the experimental group was maintained. Yet, as with the previous two experiments, small sample size, baseline differences in intrinsic motivation between groups and even some apparent subgroup differences (arts versus technical students) suggest that effects obtained may be readily moderated, if not unreliable. Nonetheless, the interpretation drawn from these three studies was that receiving an external reward for doing an activity can, under some circumstances, lead to a loss of intrinsic motivation. In contrast, positive feedback can maintain or increase intrinsic motivation.

It is important to note that the detrimental and facilitating effects of specific types of rewards in these early experiments concerned people's *subsequent* motivation – after rewards are removed. There was no argument from Deci as to whether rewards, when salient and potent, could motivate *immediate* behaviour. Thus, the scientific problem here was specifically the impact of rewards on the maintenance of intrinsically motivated behaviour, after rewards had been removed. What Deci purported to demonstrate was that a reward, when experienced as the external cause of one's behaviour, could undermine subsequent persistence by taking away some of the psychological satisfactions that had been there – specifically here the sense of being an origin, which de Charms had argued was essential to intrinsic motivation.

Deci's (1971) experiments were published nearly simultaneously with a set of related experiments intended to clarify these novel, yet somewhat shaky findings, as well as to resolve a few of the more obvious experimental limitations. Thus Deci (1972a, 1972b) altered the within-person free-choice paradigm. In the 1971 experiments participants came for three separate sessions, each a day apart, with the key comparison being session 1 versus session 3 free-choice behaviour. In the 1972 studies Deci employed a simpler approach that he called the *general one session paradigm* (Deci, 1975). In this procedure participants are randomly assigned to work under various conditions (e.g., contingent vs. non-contingent rewards, verbal vs. tangible rewards, etc.). Immediately following the experimental session they are assessed for intrinsic motivation using a free-choice behaviour period. Based on randomization assumptions, hypothesis testing then focuses on between-condition differences on this 'post-only' free-choice persistence measure. Using this simpler paradigm, the initial 1971 findings demonstrating the undermining effect were supported and extended. These studies again provided evidence that financial rewards could undermine free-choice behaviour relative to no rewards, and that, at least for males, verbal rewards seemed to enhance intrinsic motivation.

Deci also examined the effects of monetary rewards that were not contingent on specific engagement with the activity or successful completion of it. Thus, whereas in the initial 1971 experiments participants were given a financial reward for each task correctly completed, in this second series some were paid simply for showing up for the experiment. Here rewards were not expected to foster an EPLOC as they are not really controlling task activity. Indeed, results indicated that this type of financial reward did not decrease intrinsic motivation, highlighting the idea that the influence of rewards depends on how they impact people's perceptions of the source of their behaviour. Only rewards that foster an EPLOC undermine intrinsic motivation.

Based on these early experiments (Deci 1971, 1972a, 1972b), Deci introduced a tentative *cognitive evaluation theory* (CET) to account for his varied results. He argued that there are at least two aspects to any external reward: a 'controlling' aspect and an 'informational' aspect. The controlling aspect leads to a decrease in intrinsic motivation by changing the perceived locus of causality from internal to external. The informational aspect leads to an increase in intrinsic motivation by increasing the person's sense of 'competence and self-determination'. For example, whereas money given as an external reward for task completion is salient as a control and readily fosters an EPLOC, verbal rewards (positive competence feed-back) tend to be interpreted as informational, and support feelings of 'self-determination and competence' essential to intrinsic motivation.

IMPACT OF THE STUDY

Well beyond the specific issue of rewards, Deci's 1971 paper opened the door to what has become a vigorous field of experimentation on intrinsically moti-vated behaviours. By looking at the effects of external factors on free-choice behaviour as mediated by various psychological need satisfactions or frustrations, new under-standings of intrinsic motivation and strategies for catalysing or sustaining it have emerged. These models, and the interventions based on them, show reliable path-ways toward enhancing people's quality of engagement and performance.

Deci's (1971) work also suggested that rewards could shift people's perceived locus of causality, diminishing their sense of 'self-determination and competence'. The implications of these early CET findings turned out, however, to be even broader than just intrinsic motivation. Indeed, perceptions of autonomy and com-petence impact the quality of extrinsic as well as intrinsic motivation. In fact, the primary distinction within SDT, accounting for substantial variance in the out-comes of studies in occupational contexts, as well as across domains, is the distinction between *autonomous motivation* and *controlled motivation* (e.g., Deci & Ryan, 2000; Ryan & Deci, 2017), into which these early experiments had only begun to tap.

Deci's 1971 classic studies also planted the seed of what has become a broad and general organismic theory of human motivation, namely self-determination theory (Deci & Ryan, 1985; Ryan & Deci, 2017). CET is now but one of six mini-theories within the broader framework of SDT, which deals with the impact of psychological needs for autonomy, competence, and relatedness on motivation, development and well-being (Ryan & Deci, 2017). CET posits that experiences of autonomy and competence were essential to intrinsic motivation. Subsequent work has gone on to show how autonomy, competence and a third need for relatedness are all essential to the process of internalizing extrinsic motivation and becoming autonomous for behaviours that are not in themselves intrinsically motivating. Moreover, research has continuously shown that the very same need satisfactions that support intrinsic motivation and internalization are also critical factors in determining well-being across the lifespan. SDT research has taken these formulations into nearly every practical domain, including work, sports, healthcare, behaviour change, education and even virtual worlds. In each domain both growth and wellness have been shown to be largely a function of these psychological need dynamics, resulting in a strong evidence base for clinical trials and interventions.

CRITIQUE OF THE STUDY

Looking back on these early experiments one can find much to criticize from a methodological standpoint. Most outstanding is that all three of the 1971 studies are statistically underpowered – or carried out with very small samples. This meant it was difficult to detect an experimental effect where it existed (Type II error). Due in part to these small sample sizes, many findings do not reach an acceptable level of inferential statistical significance; several findings are trends or significant but with weak effects. In some of these studies, specific condition effects occur that are clearly not what was predicted. For example, in one study (Deci, 1972b) men's, but not women's, intrinsic motivation was enhanced by verbal rewards. There is considerable discussion in each article of post-hoc interpretations of these unanticipated effects. Another issue stems from the within-person design used in studies 1 and 3 of the 1971 paper, which took place over three separate sessions, and used a free-choice period collected in the middle of each session. That initial design entailed much statistical noise, such as differing means at baseline in intrinsic motivation, or unpredicted variations over time. It is also unclear the extent to which a free-choice period in the middle of an experiment is truly apt, as participants may still think they need to perform. Some of these problems were improved by developing the 'post-only' experimental design used in 1972a and 1972b. Finally, yet another weakness is one common to much research from this era in experimental social psychology – the research was exclusively based on a relatively homogeneous group of northeastern US university students.

Despite these many flaws, collectively these early behavioural studies of intrinsic motivation conveyed a strong and new message: the effect of external rewards on intrinsic motivation could vary as a function of how those rewards are interpreted by participants. Experiences of self-determination (IPLOC) and competence (effectiveness) were important predictors, indeed, they were mediators of these outcomes. All of these features would become core principles in later theorizing and empirical models, especially within self-determination theory

(SDT; Deci & Ryan, 1985; Ryan & Deci, 2017). Yet in 1972, these findings stood merely as initial evidence supporting a new approach to thinking about motivation.

REACTIONS AND SUBSEQUENT FINDINGS

Given both the controversial nature of these claims and the methodological issues of these studies, it is not surprising that in the short term a number of behaviourists made varied attempts to attribute these findings to methodological flaws or biases (e.g., see Calder & Staw, 1975; Scott, 1976). With time, however, other investigators began to replicate the undermining effect of rewards on intrinsic motivation using different tasks, different rewards and reward contingencies, and different age groups. For example, Lepper, Greene and Nisbett (1973) provided school children with materials to engage in a drawing task expected to be intrinsically motivating. Some were given an extra incentive: they were told that they would receive a 'good player award' if they did the drawing. Others did the same activity with no mention of an award. In a free-choice period held days later, children who had received the award spent significantly less time engaged with the drawing materials than children in the no-award group, replicating the undermining effect.

By 1980, there was substantial experimental evidence of the undermining effect stemming from the use of the free-choice behavioural paradigm. Deci and Ryan (1980) reviewed this literature and formalized *Cognitive Evaluation Theory* (CET; Deci & Ryan, 1980), which represented the first of what are now the six mini-theories of *self-determination theory* (Deci & Ryan, 2000; Ryan & Deci, 2017). CET argues that intrinsic motivation is supported and maintained by the satisfaction of basic psychological needs. These include the needs for autonomy and competence. The impact of rewards on intrinsic motivation depends upon how the reward affects these satisfactions. Rewards can have a negative impact on autonomy by creating an external perceived locus of causality for engaging in an activity. They can also impact competence, either supporting a sense of effectance (White, 1959), or contributing to a sense of incompetence. Thus, the effects of rewards and feedback are a function of their controlling (autonomy-relevant) or informational (competence-relevant) aspects.

FURTHER DEVELOPMENTS

These early experiments were important in opening up systematic research on the effects of different reward contingencies on intrinsic motivation. Ryan, Mims and Koestner (1983) developed a taxonomy of reward types based on CET, to specify which types of reward structures would undermine intrinsic motivation and which would maintain or even enhance it. The taxonomy was accompanied by experimental data using the free-choice behavioural paradigm, and post-only design introduced by Deci (1972b). Results demonstrated support for the central tenets of CET. Specifically, when external rewards were used to motivate either task engagement or performance they ran significantly greater risk of undermining free-choice behaviour than when non-contingent or no rewards were employed. These results also indicated that verbal rewards could be delivered in informational or controlling ways, with only the former enhancing intrinsic motivation. In line with Deci (1971), the more salient the controlling aspects of rewards are, the greater their undermining effect on intrinsic motivation will be.

The current status of research on the 'undermining effect'

Research on CET and the undermining effect continue, as does much research on the motivational effects of rewards from other theoretical perspectives. There have been a number of meta-analyses of this impressively large research field, all but one of which supported CET. However, in the mid-nineties, the *American Psychologist* published a heavily disputed meta-analysis (see Ryan & Deci, 1996) that claimed to show that the undermining effect of rewards on intrinsic motivation was a 'myth' (Eisenberger & Cameron, 1996). Given both the suspected problems with this meta-analysis, and the high profile of this venue, a reanalysis of these data, and an even more detailed meta-analysis, was presented by Deci, Koestner and Ryan (1999). This new meta-analysis specifically documented the mistaken numerical values and miscategorized entries that were the basis of Cameron and Eisenberger's finding of a 'null' effect for rewards on intrinsic motivation. Aggregating over a hundred experimental studies, results instead showed robust support for all the major predictions of CET, including those from Deci's 1971 and 1972 papers, as well SDT's reward taxonomy (Ryan et al., 1983). Meta-analytic results indicated that the effects of rewards varied systematically: contingencies likely to foster an EPLOC (e.g., task-contingent, tangible rewards) were more undermining of intrinsic motivation than non-controlling rewards (e.g., unexpected rewards; verbal rewards). Although invited, there were no significant challenges to the findings of this reanalysis (e.g., see Eisenberger, Pierce, & Cameron, 1999) leaving CET's organization of results the standard point of reference for understanding these effects.

Recent examples of the undermining effect

The undermining effect as studied by Deci (1971) was focused on intrinsic motivation for solving a puzzle – largely a cognitive challenge. But as understanding of intrinsic motivational processes has expanded so too have the domains in which CET principles have been applied. Here we provide a few examples illustrating the currency of this paradigm and its important predictions regarding a range of phenomena.

Prosocial behaviours

Developmental evolutionary researchers Warneken and Tomasello (2008) posit that some prosocial behaviours, such as the propensity to help others, might be intrinsically motivated. To show this, they first had to establish evidence of a strong and early spontaneous interest in helping, and second, that this seemingly natural propensity could be undermined, rather than enhanced, by external rewards.

In one study from their research programme, Warneken and Tomasello (2008) observed that toddlers (average age 20 months) in a laboratory setting attempted to help adults at a very high rate. Nearly 90% of the time when they saw something dropped, or something out of the adult's reach, they attempted to aid the adult. But was such helping intrinsically motivated?

To test this hypothesis, Warneken and Tomasello contrasted three conditions. In the first, when children helped, the adult simply did not respond. In a second, when the toddler helped, he or she was praised, but in a non-controlling way ('Thank you, that's really nice'). In a third condition, the child was given a reward for helping (a cube which operated a jingle toy), with the adult saying: 'For this, you get a cube'. The cube was pre-established to be desirable to the children, who knew how it operated. This third condition thus represents a type of reward contingency that, according to CET, should foster an EPLOC. Because this desirable, but contingent reward makes salient the external control it should therefore undermine intrinsic motivation for helping, if such intrinsic motivation exists.

Subsequently, children were invited to return to the laboratory for what was essentially a 'free-choice period,' in which they could spontaneously help, or not. Warneken and Tomasello's findings confirmed a pattern similar to that expected in Deci (1971), but this time for toddlers' helping behaviours. Children given rewards for helping were subsequently *less* likely to engage in helping behaviours than those in either of the other conditions. Contingent positive rewards had undermined the intrinsic motivation that otherwise was present for doing good (see also Weinstein & Ryan, 2010).

EAT YOUR VEGETABLES

Motivating children to eat healthy foods is not always an easy task. In an intriguing experiment Dominguez et al. (2013) applied CET to motivating 4- to 6-year-old children to eat vegetables. Recall that CET argues that an IPLOC, or sense of volition, enhances intrinsic motivation. Experiments within CET have shown in fact that having choice in one's activity can enhance an IPLOC, as it supports that sense of autonomy or volition (Patall, Cooper, & Robinson, 2008). Thus, Dominguez and her colleagues created conditions under which children had choice or no choice regarding which vegetable they consumed, using vegetables that had been similarly rated at pre-test. Results showed that children in the two conditions where choice was offered consumed more vegetables than those in the no choice condition. This finding was interpreted to indicate that the choice condition enhanced children's IPLOC, or autonomy, for the behaviour and that this, in turn, increased the children's intrinsic motivation for eating vegetables.

A NEUROSCIENCE ILLUSTRATION

Researchers have begun to examine how intrinsic motivation and its undermining by external rewards is manifested in neurophysiological processes (Di Domenico & Ryan, 2017). Among these new experiments we select and describe one that is close in spirit to the Deci (1971) studies.

Murayama, Matsumoto, Izuma and Matsumoto (2010) did an experiment in which Japanese participants worked on an interesting activity inside an fMRI scanner. If you have ever been inside an fMRI magnet, you might expect that it is not easy to find something fun to do in that setting! However, Murayama and colleagues introduced a reaction-time game using a virtual stopwatch that participants found enjoyable. Participants completed two experimental sessions each of which included task trials completed within the fMRI as well as a free-choice period outside of the scanner during which participants could choose to continue to play the stopwatch game. Participants received feedback about whether they succeeded or failed on each trial completed during the fMRI portion of each session. During session 1, half of the participants were randomly assigned to a reward condition in which they were told they could expect performance-contingent monetary rewards for successful responses. The other half of participants received instead a comparable, but unexpected, reward upon completing the fMRI trials. Such unexpected task-non-contingent rewards had previously been shown not to yield an undermining effect (Ryan et al., 1983; Deci et al., 1999). All participants then completed a free-choice period. In the second experimental session all participants were informed that no performance-based rewards would be offered and again completed the stopwatch task in the fMRI as well as a final free-choice period. Of interest, first, was whether participants who received performance-contingent rewards would show the undermining effect during the two free-choice periods that followed. Second, and most important to this study, was whether patterns of brain activity would differ for participants who received performance-contingent rewards (and evidenced an undermining effect on intrinsic motivation) compared to those did not receive performance-contingent rewards.

Results indicated that participants who received performance-contingent rewards evidenced significantly less time spent on the target activity during free-choice periods relative to those who received the unexpected, non-contingent reward. Findings further showed significant differences in brain activity for the participants receiving expected versus unexpected rewards. Targeted analyses focused on striatal activation and midbrain activity, as these areas are part of the neural 'reward network'. Notably, both groups showed greater bilateral anterior striatum and midbrain activity when they succeeded versus failed, regardless of reward condition, illustrating the internally rewarding effects of competence feedback. Further, in the first session, when one group of participants was working to get rewards and one was not, the reward group showed significantly greater bilateral striatum activation and midbrain activity than did the no-reward group, indicating that the reward was working to activate the reward network. Yet, it bears emphasis that both groups showed significant activation, indicating that this enjoyable and challenging task was 'rewarding' even for those not receiving external rewards.

Most important for our discussion, however, are findings from the second session, when expected rewards were removed. Results revealed significantly *less* reward-network activation in participants who had been in expected-reward condition compared with those in the unexpected-reward condition. Expected and contingent rewards resulted in decreased activity in the anterior striatum and midbrain once these rewards were no longer offered. Parallel results emerged for another region of interest – the right lateral prefrontal cortex. These findings suggested that the expected reward group was less cognitively engaged post-rewards than those who had received unexpected rewards. As well, levels of activity in the three regions (i.e., anterior striatum, midbrain and right prefrontal cortex) were correlated with each other, and participants who evidenced lower levels of activation in these three regions during this second session, spent less of the free-choice period engaging with the target activity.

Although a relatively new area of research, studies of the neural patterns associated with the motivational dynamics specified in CET are rapidly emerging. These studies highlight that the phenomenological distinctions made within SDT have reliable correspondence to activation in expected brain regions (Di Domenico & Ryan, 2017). Indeed, this interface holds great promise for deepening our understanding not only of the undermining effect of rewards, but also of other phenomena encompassed by SDT.

CONCLUSIONS

It is interesting to note that today this 'classic' 1971 paper from Deci, with its small samples and relatively shaky findings, would very likely not be published, and certainly not in the field's top journal. It was not the strength of its data that made this report noteworthy in its time, or explains why it remains such a highly cited classic today. Rather, the impact of this paper is due to its introduction of a new behavioural method of assessing intrinsic motivation, the free-choice period, along with new theoretical ideas about how that important type of human motivation can be understood. Instead of attempting to control behaviour using rewards, Deci was instead looking for facilitation or undermining effects on a form of motivation he assumed was already there. These early studies thus provided a new direction for motivation research and planted a seed that later became self-determination theory (Deci & Ryan, 1985; Ryan and Deci, 2017), an approach to learning, development, and wellness that has generated effective frameworks for research and practice that continue to go beyond reinforcement.

FURTHER READING

Deci, E. L. (2016). Intrinsic motivation: The inherent tendency to be active. In R. J. Sternberg, S. T. Fiske, & D. J. Foss (Eds.), *Scientists making a difference: One hundred eminent scientists talk about their most important contribution*. Cambridge: Cambridge University Press.

Deci, E. L., Koestner, R., & Ryan, R. M. (1999). A meta-analytic review of experiments examining the effects of extrinsic rewards on intrinsic motivation. *Psychological Bulletin, 125*, 627–668.

Di Domenico, S. I., & Ryan, R. M. (2017). The emerging neuroscience of intrinsic motivation: A new frontier in self-determination research. *Frontiers in Human Neuroscience, 11*, 145.

Ryan, R. M., & Deci, E. L. (2017). *Self-determination theory: Basic psychological needs in motivation, development, and wellness.* New York: Guilford Press.

Self-determination theory website: www.selfdeterminationtheory.org

REFERENCES

Calder, B. J., & Staw, B. M. (1975). Self-perception of intrinsic and extrinsic motivation. *Journal of Personality and Social Psychology, 31*, 599–605.

de Charms, R. (1968). *Personal causation: The internal affective determinants of behavior*. New York: Academic Press.

Deci, E. L. (1971). Effects of externally mediated rewards on intrinsic motivation. *Journal of Personality and Social Psychology, 18*, 105–115.

Deci, E. L. (1972a). The effects of contingent and non-contingent rewards and controls on intrinsic motivation. *Organizational Behavior and Human Performance, 8*, 217–229.

Deci, E. L. (1972b). Intrinsic motivation, extrinsic reinforcement, and inequity. *Journal of Personality and Social Psychology, 22*, 113–120.

Deci, E. L. (1975). *Intrinsic motivation*. New York: Plenum Press.

Deci, E. L., Koestner, R., & Ryan, R. M. (1999). A meta-analytic review of experiments examining the effects of extrinsic rewards on intrinsic motivation. *Psychological Bulletin, 125*, 627–668.

Deci, E. L., & Ryan, R. M. (1980). The empirical exploration of intrinsic motivational processes. In L. Berkowitz (Ed.), *Advances in experimental social psychology*. New York: Academic Press.

Deci, E. L., & Ryan, R. M. (1985). *Intrinsic motivation and self-determination in human behavior*. New York: Plenum Press.

Deci, E. L., & Ryan, R. M. (2000). The 'what' and 'why' of goal pursuits: Human needs and the self-determination of behavior. *Psychological Inquiry, 11*, 227–268.

Di Domenico, S. I., & Ryan, R. M. (2017). The emerging neuroscience of intrinsic motivation: A new frontier in self-determination research. *Frontiers in Human Neuroscience, 11*, 145.

Dominguez, P. R., Gámiz, F., Gil, M., Moreno, H., Zanmora, R. M., Gallo, M., et al. (2013). Providing choice increases children's vegetable intake. *Food Quality and Preference, 30*, 108–113.

Eisenberger, R., & Cameron, J. (1996). Detrimental effects of reward: Reality or myth? *American Psychologist, 51*, 1153–1166.

Eisenberger, R., Pierce, D. W., & Cameron, J. (1999). Effects of reward on intrinsic motivation – negative, neutral, and positive: Comment on Deci, Koestner, and Ryan. *Psychological Bulletin, 125*, 677–691.

Festinger, L. (1957). *A theory of cognitive dissonance*. Stanford, CA: Stanford University press.

Gately, M. J. (1950). *Manipulation drive in experimentally naive rhesus monkeys*. Unpublished manuscript, University of Wisconsin, Madison, WI.

Gray, J. A. (1970). The psychophysiological basis of introversion-extraversion. *Behaviour Research and Therapy, 8*, 249–266.

Harlow, H. F. (1950). Learning and satiation of response in intrinsically motivated complex puzzle performance by monkeys. *Journal of Comparative and Physiological Psychology, 43*, 289–294.

Heider, F. (1958). *The psychology of interpersonal relations*. New York: Wiley.

Hull, C. (1943). *Principles of behavior: An introduction to behaviour theory*. New York: Appleton–Century–Crofts.

Lepper, M. R., Greene, D., & Nisbett, R. E. (1973). Undermining children's intrinsic interest with extrinsic reward: A test of the 'overjustification' hypothesis. *Journal of Personality and Social Psychology, 28*, 129–137.

Murayama, K., Matsumoto, M., Izuma, K., & Matsumoto, K. (2010). Neural basis of the undermining effect of monetary reward on intrinsic motivation. *Proceedings of the National Academy of Sciences, 107*, 20911–20916.

Nissen, H. W. (1930). A study of exploratory behavior in the white rat by means of the obstruction method. *Pedagogical Seminary and Journal of Genetic Psychology, 37*, 361–376.

Patall, E. A., Cooper, H., & Robinson, J. C. (2008). The effects of choice on intrinsic motivation and related outcomes: A meta-analysis of research findings. *Psychological Bulletin, 134*, 270–300.

Porter, L. W., & Lawler, E. E. (1968). *Managerial attitudes and performance*. Homewood, IL: Irwin.

Ryan, R. M. (1995). Psychological needs and the facilitation of integrative processes. *Journal of Personality, 63*, 397–427.

Ryan, R. M., & Deci, E. L. (1996). When paradigms clash: Comments on Cameron and Pierce's (1994) claim that rewards don't affect intrinsic motivation. *Review of Educational Research, 66*, 33–38.

Ryan, R. M., & Deci, E. L. (2000). Self-determination theory and the facilitation of intrinsic motivation, social development, and well-being. *American Psychologist, 55*, 68–78.

Ryan, R. M., & Deci, E. L. (2001). On happiness and human potentials: A review of research on hedonic and eudaimonic well-being. *Annual Review of Psychology, 52*, 141–166.

Ryan, R. M., & Deci, E. L. (2017). *Self-determination theory: Basic psychological needs in motivation, development, and wellness*. New York: Guilford Press.

Ryan, R. M., Mims, V., & Koestner, R. (1983). Relation of reward contingency and interpersonal context to intrinsic motivation: A review and test using cognitive evaluation theory. *Journal of Personality and Social Psychology, 45*, 736–750.

Scott, W. E. (1976). The effects of extrinsic rewards on 'intrinsic motivation': A critique. *Organizational Behavior and Human Performance, 15*, 117–129.

Skinner, B. F. (1953). *Science and human behavior*. New York: Macmillan.

Spence, K. (1956). *Behavior theory and conditioning*. New Haven, CT: Yale University Press.

Warneken, F., & Tomasello, M. (2008). Extrinsic rewards undermine altruistic tendencies in 20-month-olds. *Developmental Psychology*, *44*, 1785–1788.

Weinstein, N., & Ryan, R. M. (2010). When helping helps: Autonomous motivation for prosocial behavior and its influence on well-being for the helper and recipient. *Journal of Personality and Social Psychology*, *98*, 222–244.

White, R. W. (1959). Motivation reconsidered: The concept of competence. *Psychological Review*, *66*, 297–333.

9 | Genetic Influences on Behaviour

Revisiting Bouchard et al. (1990)

Wendy Johnson

The proximal cause of most psychological variance probably involves learning through experience, just as radical environmentalists have always believed. The effective experiences, however, to an important extent are self-selected, and that selection is guided by the steady pressure of the genome (a more distal cause). .... The developmental experiences of MZ [monozygotic, born from a single fertilized egg that later splits to form two individuals] twins are more similar than those of DZ [dizygotic, born from two fertilized eggs that were released in one menstrual cycle] twins, again as environmentalist critics of twin research have contended. However, even MZA [monozygotic, reared apart] twins tend to elicit, select, seek out, or create very similar effective environments ... (Bouchard et al., 1990, pp. 227–228)

BACKGROUND TO THE STUDY

Today, genetic influences on behaviour and psychological characteristics are commonly accepted and public discussion of particular genetic variants potentially involved in specific characteristics is commonplace. Indeed, people often even only half-jokingly refer to genes for things like preferences for musical genres and colours. Until the latter third of the 20th century, however, most psychologists were quite firmly convinced that we become who we are solely through the experiences we have: the ways we are raised by our parents, the schools we attend, the cultures we live in, the 'slings and arrows of outrageous fortune' that befall us; these are known as *tabula rasae*. Psychologists tended to be especially committed to this view when thinking about intelligence, particularly as measured by IQ tests. To a steady minority, however, this assumption that our behaviour and psychology are independent of our genes seemed rather naïve. They knew that dogs and horses have long been bred very effectively to display behavioural as well as physical traits. They also had heard of the Russian experiment that 'created' what was effectively another breed of domestic dogs by selecting for tameness in wild foxes within just a few generations (Trut, 1999). Aware that humans are mammals too, they suspected that genes are also involved in human behaviour and psychological characteristics – it was hard for them to imagine that we could be completely 'blank slates' at birth or even conception when these other animals most clearly are not. But evidence of genetic influences on behaviour in other animals had been developed through human intentional selective breeding. Most of these psychologists had absolutely no interest in doing this in humans, and it would not have been allowed if they had. Yet they were extremely interested in understanding how and to what extent genes influence human behaviour, to understand better how we become who we are.

Their task of developing ways to test for genetic influences in humans was thus much more difficult than that in other animals. They were aided, however, by newly emerging understanding of twinning in humans. Twins have fascinated curious minds throughout history. They tend to be just common enough so that almost everyone encounters them along the way somewhere, but rare enough for the experience to be memorable. Among North Americans and Europeans, about 2% of births have been twins, with rates among Africans about double that, and rates among Asians and Latin Americans about half that. Since 1980, however, rates have almost doubled in Western countries, due to increasing use of in vitro fertilization. Twins' inherent 'pairness' and common ability to confuse others about their identities has often been exploited in literature, from Apollo and Artemis in Greek mythology to Shakespeare's *Twelfth Night* to Carroll's Tweedledum and Tweedledee and Rowling's Fred and George Weasley. Their tendency to develop similar diseases has attracted the attention of physicians going back at least as far as the 5th-century BCE. Hippocrates, and philosophers have used twins as metaphors for the many dualities of human nature that form the backdrops to many philosophical questions. Today, it is common knowledge that there are two kinds of twins, but scientific understanding that this is the case only emerged around the turn of the last century. It was the biological distinction between MZ (monozygotic, commonly called identical) and DZ (dizygotic, commonly called fraternal) twins that psychologists interested in understanding to what degree and how genes are involved in human behaviour began to exploit. The fact that MZ twinning occurs when a single fertilized egg divides to form two embryos means that the twins are effectively genetically identical. DZ twins, however, are like ordinary biological siblings, except that they share the gestational womb. They thus each independently inherit half their genes from the same mother and father. This means that, when parents mate randomly, DZ twins share, on average, half the genes on which humans tend to differ, or some 99.5% of all their genes rather than the 100% shared by MZs. When MZ twins are more similar than DZ twins for some characteristic, we can infer that genes influence that characteristic.

That nonshared 0.5% of the human genome may sound tiny, but it is sufficient to distinguish genetic and environmental variance and to distinguish variance that can be attributed to variation in environmental circumstances that also tends to make members of the same family similar for that characteristic (typically termed 'shared environment'), and variation in environmental circumstances that tends to make family members different – as long as several key assumptions hold.

First, twins must be 'ordinary folks' – aside from sharing a womb and birthdate, they must be no more or less likely to be any particular 'way' than singletons, as a whole, in either genetic background or the ranges of environments they experience. Moreover, the environments of MZ and DZ twins must not differ systematically. For example, in particular it cannot be the case that other people tend to treat MZ twins more similarly than they do DZ twins. The genetic and shared and non-shared environmental sources of influence must be independent, with no correlations or interactions, and degree to which parents have mated randomly must be specified, with random mating being the most common specification. Given these assumptions, the mathematics involved is easy, and studies of samples of twin pairs quickly and consistently began to reveal evidence of genetic influences on human psychological characteristics.

These assumptions, however, are strong, and their appropriateness drew ongoing question and critique from the majority of psychologists who believed human psychology to be shaped entirely environmentally. Most of these criticisms centred on the assumptions that twins can be considered ordinary folks, due to the unusual degree of sharing in twins' gestational and early-life experiences, and that MZ cannot experience more similar environments than do DZ twins. To their credit, twin researchers have invested considerable effort in testing the validities of their analytical assumptions as well as the impacts of potential violations. Fifty years ago, it appeared that twins may have lower average intelligence and be more subject to some medical problems, but studies of more recently born cohorts, done more carefully to match twins with singleton siblings, no longer show these patterns. A major factor is likely the ability of medical science to deal with the common obstetrical problems of twin pregnancies and births has improved. And they have generally observed that parents and others such as school officials treating MZ and DZ twins differently on such dimensions as dressing them alike, having them share bedrooms and placing them in the same classrooms or activities could not account for greater MZ similarity.

All analytical methods require assumptions, and the twin method of estimating genetic influences on human characteristics is certainly no exception, as noted above. One way to get around the inferential limitations relying on these assumptions imposes is to apply other methods that rely on different assumptions. Consistency in results among various methods requiring different assumptions improves those results' credence. Twin researchers have been particularly energetic in doing this. They have also estimated genetic influences in samples with family situations with features complementary to those of most twins, that thus rely on different assumptions than does the twin method. Similarities in most adoptive sibling pairs, for example, can be attributed entirely to shared environmental influences because such pairs generally have no genetic relationship either to their adoptive parents or to each other, and such families are common enough for samples to be accumulated relatively easily. These studies have generally shown little or no similarities after rather early childhood, but rather persistent similarities between the adopted-away offspring and their biological parents when such data were available. These tests did not satisfy the critics, however, and genetic influences on human behaviour and psychology tended to be resisted well into the 1980s. Yet today, even casual conversation is sprinkled with reference to genes 'for' this and that behavioural quirk.

Such paradigm shifts never have single causes, and this one was no exception. Many social forces, psychological studies and researchers, and breakthroughs in genetics and genome technology contributed, but one study arguably brought the gravitational centre of discussion 'around the corner' from general denial to general acceptance of the idea of genetic influences on behaviour and psychological characteristics. This was the Minnesota Study of Twins Reared Apart (MISTRA; Segal, 2012). Researchers had realized early on that twins who were separated early in infancy and reared in different homes could offer particularly strong tests of genetic influence because, at least in the most direct sense of 'environmental influence' (after birth), any similarity in such pairs has to be due to genetic influence. Such pairs are very rare, however, so the few studies conducted prior to MISTRA (Juel-Nielsen, 1965; Newman, Freeman, & Holzinger, 1937; Shields, 1962) had all been very small, and many of the twins studied had experienced ongoing contact despite growing up in separate homes, limiting their impact. Another study had been involved in a rather high-profile controversy over scientific legitimacy (Joynson, 1990), which certainly had not helped. MISTRA's impact was different.

DETAILED DESCRIPTION OF THE STUDY

As usual, there were several reasons for MISTRA's different impact. At 139 pairs, MISTRA was by far the largest study of reared-apart twins. It was also extremely thorough and well-designed. Study leader Tom Bouchard's interest in human individual differences is polymathic in scope and his commitment to scientific objectivity and psychometric rigour, absolute. Participants spent 50-hour weeks in Minnesota being assessed on everything from finger lengths and wrist breadths to leisure-time interests, sexual life histories, aesthetic sensibilities and activity-related things in their childhood homes, never mind characteristics more commonly assessed in psychological studies such as cognitive abilities, personality, occupational interests, psychopathologies, political attitudes and childhood (upbringing) environment and current demographics. Individual primary psychological characteristics such as cognitive abilities (42 different tests spanning three full test batteries), personality (four inventories, each assessing many different characteristics), and occupational interests (three inventories, each assessing multiple specific interest areas) were assessed using several different underlying models and response modes, to avoid distortions in results due to methodological factors. Twins completed all assessments under staff supervision, and with individually administered instruments. Co-twins were not assessed by the same examiner.

The sample was recruited beginning in 1979 over a period of 20 years, through many different sources ranging from members of the adoption movement and social work and other professionals to individuals who had recently learned they had a twin, heard of the project, and were seeking help in finding the co-twin.

All were vigorously recruited for participation to build as large a sample as possible and ensure that it was as representative of its population as possible. Bouchard was unable to recruit only six of the pairs encountered. MZ or DZ status was ascertained by comparing serological assessments, fingerprint ridge counts and anthropometric measurements (state of the art for the day), with a probability of misclassification of .001.

Impact was also high because the study attracted public attention from the beginning. The first pair was recruited when a then-PhD student who later became a MISTRA staff member, aware of Professor Bouchard's interests, noted a newspaper article about a pair of 39-year-old MZ twins who had recently been reunited over 38 years after their separate adoptions at the age of 4 months. Each set of adoptive parents had been told the co-twin had died at birth, but in finalizing adoption papers, a court official had made an off-handed remark to one of the mothers suggesting that was not true. Over the years, she had occasionally urged her son to find out more, which he had finally decided to do. Initially, Bouchard figured he would study this one pair and that would be the end of it, but both his results and the pair's experience of reunification attracted further media attention, and Bouchard began to receive reports of other separated pairs. He responded with characteristic enthusiasm and energy, and began active recruitment and search for needed funding to see how many pairs he could accumulate for study. The study continued to attract media attention as it grew, including interviews of Bouchard and even some of the participating twins on late-night American TV talk shows and articles in popular magazines. This both helped to locate more pairs and built interest in the study's results.

Because separating twins is rare, the circumstances of adoption in the sample varied considerably and were often informal. The adoptive parents were thus more representative of the overall population in educational attainment, income and social status than are most parents who participate in adoption studies. The twins themselves had also all been separated very young. All had been separated before age 5, and the average time together before separation was 5.1 months (standard deviation, SD, 8.5 months). The average time apart was 30 years (SD 14.3), and ranged from half a year to 64.7 years. At time of study, the pairs had been in contact for on average 112.5 weeks (with a considerable range from 1–1233 weeks [23.7 years]). The lengths of separation and contact of course also varied with age at study – older twins had more time either to be separated or in contact – which ranged from 19 to 68 years, with an average of 41.0 (SD 12.0). This degree of separation is probably especially hard to achieve in larger studies. For example, the Swedish Adoption/Twin Study of Aging, a long-running longitudinal study begun in 1984, has 328 pairs of reared-apart twins, but they experienced considerably more contact: all were separated by age 10, but 18% were separated after age 5, 36% after age 2, and 52% after age 1, with an average age at separation of 2.8 years (Pedersen, McClearn, Plomin, & Nesselrode, 1992).

When he began MISTRA, Bouchard fully expected that he would find that some individual characteristics would show genetic influences and others not. This was a major reason for the extensive nature of the MISTRA assessment. Bouchard also expected that reared-apart twins would be distinctly less similar than reared-together twins, again more so for some characteristics than others. Hard-headed scientist that he is, however, he knew this needed testing, and was also curious to see if there were systematic patterns in what characteristics showed genetic influence and did not, and greater and less difference in reared-apart and reared-together pair similarity. He was fortunate in having several colleagues with similar interests in his department. Along with Irving Gottesman, David Lykken and Auke Tellegen, they began the Minnesota Twin Registry (Krueger & Johnson, 2002), consisting of more than 8000 pairs born in Minnesota between 1936 and 1955, in 1983 to offer reared-together twin comparisons. Its sample is comparable in age to most of the MISTRA twins, representative of the Minnesota population, and has completed many of the same measures as the MISTRA twins, mostly via post.

MISTRA has generated almost 200 scientific papers due to its extremely extensive assessment and long-running nature. Many have been ground-breaking, both theoretically and empirically, but perhaps one stands out as having had particular impact on the field. This is also the one Bouchard considers the study's greatest accomplishment: 'Sources of human psychological differences: The Minnesota Study of Twins Reared Apart' (Bouchard, Lykken, McGue, Segal, & Tellegen, 1990), published in *Science* in 1990. It had particular impact for two reasons. First, it focused on genetic influences on IQ, a question that has long been particularly controversial and did so in an especially thorough manner, testing the assumptions of the models used to test for genetic influences more thoroughly than any prior study had been capable of. But second, though IQ was its focus, it explored and compared reared-apart and reared-together twin similarity in general particularly thoroughly, noting many puzzling features and offering possible explanations that are only now really being actively considered by the field in general.

DETAILED DESCRIPTION OF THE STUDY

The MISTRA assessment included three independent measures of IQ. The Wechsler Adult Intelligence Scale (WAIS) is one of the most reputable and often used. The specific form administered consisted of six verbal and five performance subtests administered individually, simultaneously and in separate rooms to each member of a pair by professional psychologists. Administration takes about 1.5 hours and generates age-adjusted estimates of full-scale IQ. This was supplemented by administration of the standard form of Raven's Progressive Matrices, considered one of the best measures of nonverbal reasoning, and the Mill–Hill Vocabulary Test, in which respondents select which of several options best defines target words. The two scores from these tests, which correlated .57, were age- and sex-adjusted, re-scaled to have means of 50 and standard deviations of 10, and summed to produce IQ-scaled scores. In addition, participants completed an expanded version of the cognitive battery used in the Hawaii Family Study of Cognition (Bennet, Fulker, & DeFries, 1985) and the Comprehensive

Ability Battery (Hakstian & Cattell, 1978), which involved a total of 31 subtests of a wide variety of specific abilities spanning verbal, reasoning, computational, memory, fluency and spatial domains. The first principal component scores of these tests, which captured the variance common to all of them, thus serving as measures of general intelligence, were age- and sex-adjusted and transformed to IQ scale to serve as its third measure.

The first study results were intra-class correlations of these three IQ scores in the MISTRA MZ twins. In reared-apart MZ (MZA) twins who directly/formally share effectively no environmental influences, these correlations are optimal because they are especially for data organized in groups – the twin pairs – rather than simply observations of different variables pertaining to the same sample member as are most correlations. They are direct estimates of the proportions of variance that can be attributed to genetic influence. Two were .78; the third was .69, with a mean of .75. Characteristically, these were presented along with those available from all prior studies of reared-apart twins, all of which fell within a range of .64 to .74. This kind of comparison of results from studies using different samples, conducted at different times in different countries using different specific measures, is important in placing any one observation in context and evaluating robustness of any conclusions. It is suggested here that, assuming appropriateness of the assumption of no environmental similarity, genetic influences account for about 70% of population variance in IQ in adulthood. This was not the only important comparison made. Bouchard et al. noted that this estimate was higher than other recently published summary estimates (.47 to .58) based on literature reviews of all kinship pairings (Bouchard & McGue, 1981; Loehlin, 1989). They also noted, however, that the vast majority of studies included in these reviews used samples of children and adolescents, and it had already been robustly observed that proportions of genetic influence on intelligence tend to increase with age (McCartney, Harris, & Bernieri, 1990), so the MZA summary estimate in adults was not inconsistent with these reviews.

The next study result presented addressed possibilities besides genetic influence that might explain the similarity in these reared-apart twins. Considering alternative explanations for any observation is essential in all scientific study, and is especially so in the social sciences, where alternative explanations tend to be plentiful and researchers often have ideological and/or idealistic investment in some over others. Sceptics of genetic influences on behaviour have often claimed, for example, that adoption agencies often try to match child characteristics with adoptive parent characteristics. They suggest that, when faced with placing twins in separate homes, they may also take considerable pains to place them in homes they consider similar, which could then induce similar behaviours and psychological characteristics in the twins. If so, the twins should be similar to the extent that home features were shared and those features affected the relevant behaviours or characteristics.

MISTRA's assessment included considerable details about the twins' rearing families. Each twin completed a checklist of resources in their childhood homes intended to index cultural and intellectual resources (things such as globes, books, power tools, musical instruments). Each also completed the Moos Family Environment Scale (Moos & Moos, 1986), which retrospectively surveys parental treatment and rearing in childhood and adolescence. Separate indices of similarity of twins' adoptive parent socioeconomic status; material, scientific/technical, and cultural possessions in the home, and parental encouragement of achievement and own intellectual orientation, coupled with the associations between these home features and IQ, indicated not just no significant impact of placement similarity on IQ, but also measured its impact at effectively 0. Again, the article compared this observation to other studies, noting that associations between rearing SES and IQ had been noted in adopted youth samples (e.g., Capron & Duyme, 1989), but adoptive samples assessed for IQ in adulthood had found no association (e.g., Scarr & Weinberg, 1978).

The twins of course shared their prenatal environments, but, as the article noted, there is little evidence that this causes similarity in IQ, at least in the absence of exposures that can cause overt brain damage, such as to alcohol, illegal drugs, and, unfortunately, some prescription medicines. Twin pregnancies are also especially prone to pre- and perinatal obstetrical complications that can have lasting fetal effects, but these tend to affect one twin more than the other, thus decreasing similarity. Twins who had been reared together and remained in closer contact in adulthood had been observed to be more similar in some ways than those maintaining less (Rose & Kaprio, 1988), but there was evidence in another reared-together sample that similarity did more to encourage contact than vice-versa (Lykken, Bouchard, McGue, & Tellegen, 1990). The MISTRA contact data indicated no greater similarity with greater time together before separation, time apart to first reunion, total time, or percentage of lifetime spent apart. Along with the tests of similarity of features of the twins' rearing environments, this was important in ruling out environmental explanations for the twins' similarity.

Given Bouchard's going-in expectation that some behaviours and psychological characteristics would show genetic influence and others not, and hope that he might be able to discern patterns in which did and did not, another key aspect of MISTRA investigations was comparing analogous estimates of genetic and environmental influences on the various areas assessed. The next section of the article summarized MISTRA's MZA correlations on its anthropometric and physiological measures, and its measures of personality and temperament, specific cognitive abilities and information processing capacities, leisure and occupational interests, and social attitudes, including religiosity, and compared them to correlations on the same measures from studies of MZT twins. Because the upper bounds of such correlations are always constrained by the test–retest reliabilities (correlations between scores of the same individuals tested on the same test twice) of the measures (Johnson, Penke, & Spinath, 2011), the summary included them, as well as ratios of MZA to MZT correlations. Most of the data presented had previously been published, but not summarized and compared in this manner, and doing so was important to this article's impact on the field.

The measures that are both most stable within individuals throughout adulthood and most reliably measured had the highest correlations, in both the reared-apart and reared-together twins. This similarity can be attributed to genetic influence alone in the MZA twins, some unknown combination of genetic and shared environmental influence in the reared-together MZ (MZT) twins, but also must be attributed to lifetime stability and test reliability, though the extent to which this is true is never completely clear. The most-correlated were primarily the anthropometric variables of fingerprint ridge count and height, but also WAIS Full-Scale IQ and other composite scores such as the Raven–Mill–Hill mean and the mean of the 11 Multi-dimensional Personality Questionnaire scores. Such composite scores always tend to be both more reliable over short-term retest and more lifetime-stable. It was plain that test-reliability and lifetime stability were relevant, as the pattern of higher correlation in the better-measured and more lifetime-stable measures was quite consistent. At the same time, all the measures were substantially correlated in the MZA twins, to degrees that constituted high proportions of the reliable variance, and nearly as highly as in the MZT twins, indicating substantial genetic variance on all the characteristics. Bouchard has often commented that, to him, this was the most surprising conclusion of the MISTRA study. It is also arguably the one that did the most to convince the field to accept genetic influence on behaviour and psychological characteristics – and shift debate from *whether* genes are involved to *how*.

But not only did the MISTRA data surprisingly indicate genetic, along with environmental, influence on everything. They also, perhaps even more surprisingly, very often indicated that MZA twins are almost as similar as MZT twins, sometimes even as similar as the same person assessed twice within some rather short time-span such as a month (too short to consider substantive trait-level change likely, making error of trait-level measurement, including short-term perturbations, the most likely source of any dissimilarity). This suggested that neither common upbringing nor ongoing contact between family members does much to make them similar, at least in adulthood. Other studies were also producing evidence that this is the case, particularly the rarer studies of unrelated adoptive siblings reared together that also had access to biological parent data. These showed little to no similarity in adulthood, but substantive similarity to their separate sets of biological parents. MISTRA's reared-apart perspective and data on extent of similarities in home features long believed relevant to children's personality and cognitive development and educational and occupational aspirations and attainments in the twins' separate rearing homes, however, brought the point home especially convincingly.

Returning to their initial focus on IQ, Bouchard et al. suggested several implications of their data. First, something over two-thirds of the variance in typical population-level IQ or general intelligence should be attributed to genetic influence. The word 'typical' here is important, as the article explained: very few of the MISTRA twins (or, more generally, participants in *any* psychological studies of individual differences, even samples used to norm IQ tests intended for general use, including diagnostic and forensic purposes) were raised by illiterate parents, in abject poverty, or subject to high levels of abuse, and none was intellectually disabled. This means that the two-thirds estimate should not be assumed to apply to groups who unfortunately experience these kinds of extreme environmental deprivation and hardship. This estimate also says nothing about what level of what we measure as intelligence could be achieved in that typical population if environments were ideal. Today, the fact that mean typical population-level IQ test scores have risen rather steadily ever since the tests were first developed over a century ago is well established (and known as the Flynn Effect, in recognition of the man who first extensively documented it; Flynn, 1987). This was still rather breaking news when the article called attention to it in support of this point, yet too many still tend to forget that even strong genetic influence says nothing about potential population mean levels. (Height shows a strong 'Flynn Effect' over the same time period, for example.) The two-thirds estimate, especially corroborated as it is by data from many other studies using various approaches, does indicate the state of affairs in the typical broadly construed 'middle-class' environments of current industrialized societies.

The second implication noted was that, within that broadly construed 'typical' environment, neither public institutions and much smaller and more personal social structures such as families nor their practices do much to constrain development of individual differences in psychological characteristics and behaviours. Bouchard et al. noted that, in general, relative levels of variance from genetic and environmental influences are not constants: when the environment is very uniform for everyone, most individual differences observed are genetic in origin. But when the environment matters and varies considerably within a population, more overall individual differences are observed, and substantial proportions of them are environmental in origin. Observing that Western societies tolerate and even encourage and nurture wide ranges of personality, interests, attitudes, abilities and activities yet these all show substantial genetic influence, they inferred that particular 'cultural agents' such as parents are less able and/or less inclined to mould children's development of these characteristics in specific ways – or at least in the same ways within families. That is, the environment may matter a lot in who we become, but the same environment does not seem to affect us all in the same way.

This led directly to the third implication Bouchard et al. saw: MZA twins must be so similar because their basically identical genomes lead them to experience more similar environments. This begins very early in life, with infant temperament affecting caretaking responses. As they grow mobile, caretaker response sensitivity to temperament is augmented by differences in what infants do themselves: active and adventurous toddlers encounter different experiences and learn different things than those rather sedentary or timid, as well as responding differently to the same experiences. The gene–environment correlations and interactions all this creates increase in power to influence development as toddlers grow into children and adolescents and move into adulthood. Thus, they inferred, the most directly relevant 'cause' of psychological characteristics and behaviours is learning through experience, as the field's dominant environmental paradigm has always taught. But the relevant learning experiences are self-selected to important degrees, as are the specific lessons learned from any experience. And the genome exerts 'steady pressure' on both. Thus, environmental options and the experiences and lessons they offer more often accentuate and deepen genetic influence than dampen it.

Importantly, Bouchard et al. recognized and pointed out that, if this is correct, the criticism of classical twin studies that MZ and DZ twins do not experience similar environments to the same degree as assumed is valid: MZ twins do experience more similar environments than do DZ twins. This is not, however, because they grow up together sharing the same environment imposed upon them. Instead, it is because, in 20th-century Western societies, pretty much everyone grows up with enough freedom to seek, select and elicit environments that foster the psychological characteristics and behaviours their genomes most readily express. They emphasized that this does not mean intervention to channel development in adaptive directions has no place. Rather, it means that interventions will be more effective when tailored to the receiving individuals' interests and inclinations.

The article concluded by putting research questions about the sources and persistence of individual differences and tentative answers from MISTRA in an evolutionary perspective. Today, thinking in these terms within psychology is common, even over-used and superficially applied. Evolutionary psychology was in its infancy in 1990, however, so this was an important contribution. Bouchard et al. noted the tension between trying to understand persistence of individual differences among humans associated with highly socially relevant variance in life trajectories and psychological well-being and trying to identify and understand species-typical behaviour patterns, especially when those patterns appear to be counter-productive to health and well-being in today's world. Because population-level genetic change is a slow process, pervasive presence of genetic influences on psychological characteristics and behaviours could be holdovers from the genetic divergence through which our species emerged from other archaic *homo sapiens* species. This is generally timed some 200,000 years ago and placed in Africa, though there is considerable recently-uncovered evidence that this 'modern' human species continued to admix with some of the others such as Neanderthals and Denisovans as it spread beyond Africa into their areas until they had all been either absorbed or wiped out, perhaps 25,000 years ago. Despite the vastness of this timespan relative to recorded human history, there is little question that the exigencies of daily life facing humans in those two times were more similar to each other than either was to those of most people in Western societies today. Yet whatever directly causative effects those genes that emerged as adaptive specifically for our species had then are very likely still affecting us now.

Some have suggested that the genes involved in individual differences in general and psychological characteristics and behaviours in particular are evolutionary 'junk' that had no impact on survival or reproductive fitness in prehistoric times, and perhaps were not even expressed in those environments. Others believe that, even back then, these differences were important and maintained through selection advantage in particular ecological and/or social niches. Bouchard et al. left resolving that debate to future research, instead highlighting that, whatever went on back then, modern societies, both within and across cultural groups, both act to accentuate expression of genetic influence on individual differences and permit (even encourage) this variability to influence cultural change.

IMPACT OF THE STUDY

B ouchard et al.'s (1990) article had been cited almost 700 times by May 2017 according to Web of Science (stricter in standards about what to count as a citation than Google Scholar), including 10 times in 2017, indicating ongoing recognition over 25 years later. This is far beyond the average paper, definitely indicative of impact on its field, but it pales in comparison to two more recent papers in this area: Caspi and colleagues' (Caspi, et al., 2002, 2003) studies of interactive effects of specific genetic variants and particular environmental experiences on violent behaviour and depression, respectively, had been cited 2182 and 4216 times. The comparison actually says more, however, about the foibles of citation counts as indicators of scientific impact than it does about the relative impacts of these three papers, all published in the premier-impact journal *Science.* First and foremost, as I have noted, MISTRA in general and the 1990 article in particular did much to foster the paradigm shift from assumption that psychological characteristics and behaviours emerge through environmental experiences to acknowledgement that they are pervasively genetically influenced as well. Without that paradigm shift, which can be dated pretty closely to the decade of the 1990s, Caspi's group would never have conducted those two much more frequently cited studies. It would not have occurred to them to do so; much of the genetic technology on which they relied may not have even been available; and no scientific funding body would have made them financially feasible.

Importantly as well, the care taken in Bouchard et al.'s paper to compare MISTRA results to those from similar studies as well as those investigating similar questions using different methods, to test potential alternative explanations for their results, and to place the evidence for genetic influence in a broader context of current gene–environment transaction and evolutionary history was typical of all the MISTRA-based papers. This kind of care characterizes this research area in general, but Bouchard has always been prominent among its leaders. MISTRA was thus important not just in making the idea of actively studying genetic influences on psychological characteristics and behaviours respectable and fundable, but also in getting serious scientists actively interested in understanding gene–environment interplay rather than simply producing evidence of presence and extent of genetic influence. No single study could have done this alone, however. All science is accumulative; no one study ever conclusively establishes any scientific principle or fact, but consistency of results across many, many studies using different approaches, specific measures and samples is especially important in any area such as individual differences in psychological characteristics and behaviours that cannot ethically manipulate its study participants in question-relevant ways.

A third factor is that, appropriately, the Caspi et al. (2002, 2003) gene–environment interaction studies spawned veritable 'cottage industries' of replication studies, and these account for many of the citations those papers garnered. Far from all have replicated the original results, and even the meta-analyses they in turn generated have not agreed. These interactions thus have to be considered at best fragile, subject to particular environmental circumstances, study procedures and measures, sampling techniques, populations, or some combination of these factors. Such single-genetic variant–environment interactions may in fact be pervasive in our world, but it is very hard to distinguish chance statistical results from real effects specific to particular populations or environments. Conclusions from MISTRA have not been at all fragile though. Replication of reared-apart twin studies is of course difficult because such twins are so rare, and replicating MISTRA would be especially difficult because its assessment was so broad – the IQ assessment alone was arguably the most comprehensive and thorough ever. So replications of evidence for genetic influences have been targeted at reared-together twin studies, complementary approaches requiring different assumptions such as adoption studies, extended-family studies, children-of-twins studies, and tests of alternative explanations for MISTRA's reared-apart twin results. The paradigm shifted as it did because of Bouchard's and many other researchers in the field's pugnaciousness in applying those complementary study methods and testing those alternative explanations, resulting in steady accumulation of consistent observations that the genes are always there.

This established the needed scientific evidence base. But the paradigm shift really took place much more broadly, at the public level, and here, MISTRA's impact was massive. As I noted earlier, the seed for the study was in the media spotlight from the beginning, when the recent reunion of the pair that became MISTRA's first recruit was featured in a newspaper article. Public attention built from there because the human interest in participants' unusual rearing situations and often dramatic reunion circumstances, and the many quirky characteristics individual pairs shared was high. Moreover, Bouchard proved to be a dynamic interview subject and excellent public lecturer, with an infectious enthusiasm for his work, a straight-shooting manner of speaking, and strong ability to make the substance of often-technical material clear to everyone. He clearly enjoyed the media attention, which made him popular with them too, and the fact that several of the twin pairs were also happy to engage with the media augmented media ability to feature the study. Nancy Segal, a post-doctoral research associate and then assistant director of MISTRA during its most intense years of recruitment and assessment, has kept the study in the public eye since 2000, as well. Herself a (reared-together, DZ) twin and now a researcher and blogger about all aspects of twinning and larger multiple births in her own right, she has authored two highly readable books featuring the study (2000, 2012). She also mentions it regularly in her blog posts and other media projects, such as the recent documentary film *Twinsters* (2015) about two young women's discovery of their separated twinship.

CRITIQUE OF THE STUDY

T hough the impact of MISTRA in general and the 1990 paper in particular was substantial in shifting the paradigm in psychology from denial to acceptance of genetic influence on psychological characteristics and behaviour, in many ways much of the profundity of the messages throughout particularly Bouchard's first-authored papers has been missed by the field. As in the 1990 paper, Bouchard has been consistent in pointing out that the similarities of MZ twins in adulthood, whether they have been raised together or apart, indicate that genetic proclivities figure importantly in how humans navigate among the large smorgasbord of environmental opportunities in modern Western societies. He has not generally pointed out directly, however, that this means that the assumptions on which his own and others' estimates of proportions of variance attributable to genetic influences are routinely violated, and that we know the directions, if not the absolute magnitudes, of the distortions various kind of violations introduce. It is hard to fault him much for this, however – for many years he was writing in an environment reluctant even to listen to evidence about genetic influence, never mind the much more subtle implications of these violations of statistical niceties portend. Moreover, the rapid advances in genomic technology over this same period worked strongly against anyone keeping these implications in focus.

Unfortunately for the field and perhaps especially for public understanding, however, the upshot has been that the paradigm shift got rather stalled. It is not unlike the lingering impressions that many retain that evolution took place a long time ago and was guided by a goal to achieve some kind of pinnacle of development, as finally realized in emergence of our species, and that human history has been one of continuous advancement since. That is, genetic influence on psychological characteristics and behaviour is widely acknowledged and considerable scientific resources are invested in identifying which genes are involved in what, but it is largely still assumed that identifying associations between genes and traits inevitably means that the genes unilaterally exert direct causal effects on the traits, albeit generally individually tiny. But the similarities of MZA and MZT twins, along with much other developmental genetic evidence from other species, indicates that the experiences we encounter, many of which we have had genetically influenced hands in selecting and shaping, are doing at least as much to shape how our genes are expressed as the genes are to shape what is expressed. Contrary to the assumptions underlying all the models currently in use, genes and environment are not independent.

As exemplified by the Caspi et al. (2002, 2003) studies noted above, the field has partially acknowledged this, by seeking to identify gene–environment interactions, or particular environmental circumstances that elicit expression of particular variants of particular alleles (specific locations on the genome) but not others. Not only are these perennially statistically fragile, but the models used to identify them retain the assumption that, if they are associated with some trait, the association is inevitably causal. This leads to interpretations that genes are destinies left to themselves, and that our greatest opportunities to interrupt their courses involve silencing them individually through genetic modification or deletion. Gene–environment correlation, a potentially much more potent source of individual differences in health and socioeconomic inequalities most societies consider troublesome and regrettable, remains largely ignored and its pathways unexplored. Finishing the needed paradigm shift is the major challenge facing the field today.

CONCLUSIONS

M ISTRA was likely a unique study, due to the (probably increasing) rarity of its participants' life circumstances and extensiveness and thoroughness of its assessment, and the hard-headed commitment to breadth of interests in all aspects of individual differences and commitment to scientific objectivity and rigour of its leader, Tom Bouchard. These established its scientific impact, but his ebullient enthusiasm for his work and willingness to share it with others in comprehensible terms cemented the study's public impact. The study's timing was perfect as well: evidence of genetic influences on psychological characteristics and behaviour was accumulating from many research quarters, and genomic technology was advancing rapidly. The most fundamental questions regarding *how* our genes transact with our environments so that we become who we are remain largely unanswered, but it is now generally accepted that, as the 1990 article noted, 'The genes sing a prehistoric song that today should sometimes be resisted but which it would be foolish to ignore' (p. 228). Still, 1990 was a long time ago now, and the field needs to build on the kind of thinking that went into the MISTRA study to tap into their tune.

FURTHER READING

Bouchard, T. J., Jr (2016). Experience-producing driving theory: Personality 'writ large'. *Personality and Individual Differences, 90*, 302–314.

Hayes, K. J. (1962). Genes, drives, and intellect. *Psychological Reports, 10*, 299–342.

Johnson, W. (2010). Extending and testing Tom Bouchard's Experience-Producing Drive Theory. *Personality and Individual Differences, 49*, 296–301.

Johnson, W. (2014). *Developing difference.* London: Palgrave Macmillan.

Segal, N. L. (2012). *Born together, reared apart: The landmark Minnesota twin study.* Cambridge, MA: Harvard University Press.

REFERENCES

Bennet, B., Fulker, D. W., & DeFries, J. C. (1985). Familial resemblance for general cognitive ability in the Hawaii Family Study of Cognition. *Behavior Genetics, 15*, 401–406.

Bouchard, T., Jr., Lykken, D. T., McGue, M., Segal, N. L., & Tellegen, A. (1990). Sources of human psychological differences: The Minnesota Study of Twins Reared Apart. *Science, 250*, 223–228.

Bouchard, T. J., Jr., & McGue, M. (1981). Familial studies of intelligence – A review. *Science, 250*, 223–228.

Capron, C., & Duyme, M. (1989). Assessment of effects of socio-economic status on IQ in a full cross-fostering study. *Nature, 340,* 552–554.

Caspi, A., McClay, J., Moffitt, T. E., Mill, J., Martin, J., Craig, I. W., ... Poulton, R. (2002). Role of genotype in the cycle of violence in maltreated children. *Science, 297,* 851–854.

Caspi, A., Sugden, K., Moffitt, T. E., Taylor, A., Craig, I. W., Harrington, H., ... Poulton, R. (2003). Influence of life stress on depression: Moderation by a polymorphism in the 5-HTT gene. *Science, 301,* 386–389.

Flynn, J. R. (1987). Massive IQ gains in 14 nations: What IQ tests really measure. *Psychological Bulletin, 101,* 171–191.

Hakstian, A. L., & Cattell, R. B. (1978). Higher-stratum ability structures on a basis of 20 primary abilities. *Journal of Educational Psychology, 70,* 657–669.

Johnson, W., Penke, L., & Spinath, F. M. (2011). Understanding heritability: What it is and what it is not. *European Journal of Personality, 25,* 254–266.

Joynson, R. B. (1990). *The Burt affair.* London: Routledge.

Juel-Nielsen, N. (1965). Previous investigations of monozygotic twins reared apart. *Acta Psychiatrica Neurology Scandinavia Supplement, 183,* 30–36.

Krueger, R. F., & Johnson, W. (2002). The Minnesota Twin Registry: Current status and future directions. *Twin Research, 5,* 488–492.

Loehlin, J. C. (1989). Partitioning environmental and genetic components to behavioral development. *American Psychologist, 44,* 1285–1292.

Lykken, D. T., Bouchard, T. J., Jr., McGue, M., & Tellegen, A. (1990). Does contact lead to similarity or similarity to contact. *Behavior Genetics, 20,* 547–561.

McCartney, K., Harris, J., & Bernieri, F. (1990). Growing up and growing apart – A developmental meta-analysis of twin studies. *Psychological Bulletin, 107,* 226–237.

Moos, R. H., & Moos, B. S. (1986). *Manual: Family Environment Scale.* Palo Alto, CA: Consulting Psychologists Press.

Newman, H. H., Freeman, F. N., & Holzinger, K. J. (1937). *Twins: A study of heredity and environment.* Chicago, IL: University of Chicago Press.

Pedersen, N. L., McClearn, G. E., Plomin, R., & Nesselroade, J. R. (1992). Effects of early rearing environment on twin similarity in the last half of the life-span. *British Journal of Developmental Psychology, 10,* 255–267.

Rose, R. J., & Kaprio, J. (1988). Frequency of social contact and intrapair resemblance of adult monozygotic co-twins – Or does shared experience influence personality after all? *Behavior Genetics, 18,* 309–328.

Scarr, S., & Weinberg, R. A. (1978). Influence of family background on intellectual attainment. *American Psychological Review, 43,* 674–692.

Segal, N. L. (2000). *Entwined lives: Twins and what they tell us about human behavior.* New York: Plume.

Segal, N. L. (2012). *Born together, reared apart: The landmark Minnesota twin study.* Cambridge, MA: Harvard University Press.

Shields, J. (1962). *Monozygotic twins: Brought up apart and brought up together.* London: Oxford University Press.

Trut, L. (1999). Early canid domestication: The farm-fox experiment. *American Scientist, 87,* 160.

10

The Evolution of Personality

Revisiting Buss (1991)

Aurelio J. Figueredo, Heitor B. F. Fernandes, Mateo Peñaherrera-Aguirre and Steven C. Hertler

BACKGROUND TO THE STUDY

It is worth recalling the state of personality as a psychological sub-discipline at the time that Buss asked rhetorically: '*Why does personality psychology need evolutionary theory?*' His immediate answer recalled all those intellectuals, from Comte to Wilson, who have variously insisted on the general need to ground psychology within biology. Buss (1991, p. 3) argued that personality psychology should be grounded in evolutionary theory so as to 'circumvent the plethora of seemingly arbitrary personality theories'. Evolution was successful in organizing and explaining many facts, so much so that Buss convincingly insisted that minds are biological products of that evolutionary process. Yet not much more than that could be said, as Evolutionary Psychology (EP) was then primarily concerned with human universals rather than individual differences. Questions of violence, sex, mate preference, jealousy and altruism were at once more pressing and more easily answered. EP was then a young sub-discipline distracted by other successes, and lacking sufficient theory and research on individual differences. In consequence, when it was not ignored, personality variation was dismissed as devoid of fitness consequences, as per the *selective neutrality theory* advanced by Tooby and Cosmides. Thus, EP did not stoop to notice personality. Only later would this lesson be learned: far from preserving the remaining variation through neglect, selection actively created and maintained personality variation.

Thirty years have passed since Buss's classic paper, and personality psychology's grounding in evolutionary theory has been established most powerfully by its ability to answer *why* questions. As summarized by Penke, Denissen and Miller (2007), an evolutionarily informed personality psychology has used *adaptive diversification, environmental heterogeneity* and *negative frequency dependent balancing selection* to explain why personality varies within and between populations. These theories are predicated on the idea that there are a variety of niches which persons may profitably inhabit. So whether this niche-based landscape be conceived of socially, as in the coral reef model, or ecologically, as in environmental heterogeneity models, it is sufficiently variegated to afford different personality traits and styles competitive advantages within each of their respective spheres. By way of analogy, we may envision a mass of people escaping a burning building by different exits: main exits, emergency exits, windows and service doors. Personality is similar. Just as everyone has to escape the burning building in the analogy, so there is the evolutionary imperative to reproduce before death; and just as there are many exits, one can foster successful reproduction by being gregarious and charming as with the social extravert, dogged and persevering like the exceedingly conscientious, or ingratiating and affiliative like the highly agreeable. Thus, different personality styles and strategies have evolved in competition with one another for the same goal of survival and reproduction, but with different ways and means of adaptation. This phenomenon is likely to have evolved in a complex social world.

Furthermore, evolutionary theory is now capable of explaining personality as bundles of strategically co-varying traits contributing to fitness relevant tradeoffs via *coherent behavioural packages, adaptive suites and behavioural syndromes*. Similar concepts have also originated in non-human animal research. These terms are variations on a theme, in that they all in some way denote nonrandom collections of traits. Whether speaking of packages, suites, or syndromes, these terms mark a growing awareness that traits strategically co-vary, and so are apt to cohere in reliably detectable patterns. The evolutionary logic of such *packages* centres on a particular trait being more or less adaptive in the context of other traits. By way of example, consider *psychopathy*, a collection of traits combining sensation-seeking, low anxiety, restricted altruism, a propensity to rove, callous indifference and glib superficial charm. Mealey (1995) proposed that this recurrently observed psychopathic pattern may well recur and perpetuate itself, as these traits combine to effectuate the exploitation of others.

Viewing psychopathy as a coherent behavioural package brings up yet another advance, namely evolutionary psychology's unique ability to parse between *true* and *pseudo* pathologies. Mealey viewed psychopathy, long considered a diagnosable pathology, through the evolutionary lens as *pseudopathology* because psychopathic behaviours, while they harm society at large, function to enhance the fitness of the psychopaths. Finally, *life history theory*, the biological theory governing an organism's pace of life, has placed personality within the context of an overarching adaptive strategy. These and some related constructs, defined and discussed hereinafter, have effectively transitioned EP to an active engine of explanation. It is now clear that personality psychology requires evolutionary theory to instil functional, adaptive explanations into what would otherwise be a purely descriptive science.

PERSONALITY COMPRISES PSYCHOLOGICAL MECHANISMS AND BEHAVIOURAL STRATEGIES

Description

In this section, Buss broadly declares EP *uniquely positioned* to comment on central questions of personality psychology:

1. The *state–trait* debate: social and personality psychologists have respectively emphasized situational determinants of behaviour and trait-based determinants of behaviour.

2. *Gene–environment interactions*: genes and environments dynamically and recursively influence one another's action rather than simply statically summate to account for individual variability.

3. Individual differences in *strategic choices*: personality differences evoke reliable behavioural differences that ultimately enhance fitness.

4. *Ultimate origins* of personality variation: individual differences are connected to the evolutionary dynamics by which they were created.

Buss divides the remaining 23 pages of his treatise among the following four parts: (I) a review of how personality is a reflection of evolutionarily relevant psychological mechanisms and behavioural strategies; (II) a description of the evolutionary foundations of personality; (III) commentaries on how core controversies in personality psychology are elucidated by evolutionary theory; and (IV) a summation with concluding remarks.

Part I might have been a rarefied metaphysical preamble to Buss's paper, but for focused discussion of the *sociobiological fallacy* (emphasis on adaptive outcomes, purportedly to the exclusion of mediating psychological thought), the *fundamental situational error* (the assumption that environmental stimuli can alone elicit behaviour with no reference to trait- or brain-based mechanisms), and the *fallacy of genetic determinism* (explanatory reliance on genetics, purportedly to the full exclusion of environmental determinants). These three themes follow a common thread, arguing for a science of human behaviour that, in Biblical language, renders unto evolution what is evolution's, and renders unto the environment what is the environment's. This balance between evolved mechanisms and environmental determinants is instantiated when Buss writes of creating the fundamental situational error – the organism and its genetically influenced features are lamentably ignored when considering the impact of environmental stimuli. He insists that evolution forges the 'physiological, anatomical and psychological mechanisms' that inform choice, inclination, aversion and attraction.

IMPACT

FUNDAMENTAL SITUATIONAL ERROR

Many studies have accumulated showing evidence that, while no psychological characteristic is fully heritable, all show substantial genetic influence. While the environment will bring behavioural changes, these changes will fluctuate around a baseline established by genetic influence.

More recently and perhaps more importantly, however, a more substantial amount of evidence has also indicated that most developmental *environments* show significant genetic influence, as organisms are not randomly assigned to natural conditions. More than 150 articles have been published after this classic where environmental measures were employed in *genetically sensitive designs*, meaning those research designs capable of delineating environmental and genetic inputs, and estimating the effects of each. Because organisms select, evoke and manipulate environments based on their genetic makeup, they at least partly shape the conditions to which they are exposed. Therefore, the apparent effect of environments upon psychological characteristics is not independent of genetic influences. Environments are instead mediators as well as moderators of genetic effects; thus, environments are an intermediate step in the causal sequence from genes to psychological characteristics.

PROBLEM-SPECIFICITY OF PSYCHOLOGICAL MECHANISMS

This research and several other classics have stimulated a plethora of research lines examining how domain-specific psychological mechanisms (those affecting a delimited psychological module) operate in humans and nonhuman animals, as well as how numerous they are with respect to the domain-general ones (those affecting brain and behaviour at large). While earlier discussions had taken place mostly based on theoretical arguments, since the 1990s empirical efforts have been undertaken.

This culminated in attempts to categorize data accumulated on domain-specific mechanisms into a compendium of human psychological modules, such as seen in PsychTable.org developed by Balachandran and Glass (2012). The categories include modules that appear to be shaped mainly by either natural selection, sexual selection, kin selection, or a combination, drawing evidence from psychological, medical, physiological, cross-cultural, genetic, phylogenetic and hunter–gatherer lines of research that may either support or falsify the idea that these particular mechanisms are domain-specific. Similarly, the accumulation of research on domain-specificity in the last decades has permitted comprehensive reviews of the neuropsychological literature (including information from neurophysiology, neuroanatomy and neuroimaging) to make a list of regionally specific psychological mechanisms (functions performed solely or mostly in one brain region) and functionally specific regions in the human brain (regions that perform only or mostly one psychological function).

As some authors recognize, and Buss indicated as a possibility, many psychological phenomena studied do not seem strictly to conform to the standard criteria defining domain-specificity. Some even appear to be far from that, and behave as very domain-general processes. General intelligence, a construct that was proposed and extensively examined through most of the 20th century, does not appear to be a by-product of measurement or culture-specific issues in humans, as it is both generalizable to individual differences in other species and to comparisons among species as reviewed by Burkart, Schubiger and van Schaik (2016). More specifically, across and within most animal species studied on intelligence, cognitive ability performance appears not to be domain-specific; these domains are instead affected similarly by a common factor, called general intelligence (or g factor). Such findings indicate that abilities are not independent, but interconnected and largely influenced by g. As discussed further below, similar methodological approaches have been applied to the study of personality traits, leading to similar conclusions.

CRITIQUE

TRAIT-BY-SITUATION INTERACTIONS

A more sophisticated conception of the theoretical matrix of *trait-by-situation interactions* (contingent influence of traits within different environments) can perhaps be better expressed in terms of the schematic diagram for the generalization of these complementary effects shown in Figure 10.1.

	Situation 1	Situation 2	Situation 3	Row means
Pearson A	A1	A2	A3	A
Pearson B	B1	B2	B3	B
Pearson C	C1	C2	C3	C
Column means	1	2	3	

Figure 10.1 Schematic diagram for generalization of effects of traits and situations.

To estimate the overall effect of an individual difference trait, its influence upon behaviour must generalize across alternative situations. The main effect of a trait's influence upon behaviour is the mean observed score for that trait's effect, averaged across a representative sample of alternative situations, as represented in the diagram by the 'Row Means' (T.1, T.2, T.3); the main effect of a situational influence upon behaviour is the mean observed score for that situational effect, averaged across a representative sample of alternative traits, as represented in the diagram by the 'Column Means' (S.1, S.2, S.3). A trait-by-situation interaction represents how each individual trait responds in each different situation, as represented by each individual cell in the cross-tabulation (A.1, A.2, A.3, B.1, B.2, B.3, C.1, C.2, C.3). This latter term serves as our measure of the variability in the effect of each trait across different situations. Thus, there is no fundamental contradiction between speaking of additive variance components of trait and situational influences in addition to the unique non-additive variance components contributed by the trait–situation interactions. To make overblown pronouncements such as the oft-repeated claim that either trait or situational influences have been rendered meaningless or obsolete by the discovery of trait–situation interactions is therefore mathematically illiterate.

HIGHER-ORDER REGULATORY FACTORS

Following the relabelling of *sociobiology* as *evolutionary psychology* in the late 1980s and thereafter, many theorists, Buss included, have emphasized the problem-specificity or 'modularity' of psychological mechanisms as one way of distinguishing the new thinking from the old. Sociobiology purportedly emphasized the ultimate adaptive functions of behaviours bearing on why individual differences exist; whereas EP now emphasized the mediating proximate mechanisms, relating to intermediate mechanics of how a behaviour is accomplished, rather than why it evolved. Among the 'fallacies' attributed to sociobiology was thus mistaking one for the other, in claiming that the behaviours emitted by organisms were explicitly directed towards maximizing their inclusive fitness. In this view, the new science of EP correctly represented emitted behaviours as the product of the interactions between evolved psychological mechanisms and specific stimulus inputs from the environment to which they were finely tuned. The inclusive fitness outcomes of these interactions were, of course, still subject to selection; and it is selection, whether acting on genes within an organism or within a lineage, which is the shaping force that finely tuned these mechanisms. The key difference attributed to the EP view was that the mechanisms themselves were not literally detecting or monitoring 'fitness' in any explicit manner.

Nevertheless, it is possible that much polemic might have been avoided had it been recognized that whereas the proximate mechanisms are indeed exerting the *direct* effects upon behavioural outputs (meaning those which are measurable in particular instances), the ultimate selective pressures are exerting the *indirect* effects upon behavioural dispositions (meaning evolved dispositions preparative to the behaviour; Figueredo, Garcia, Cabeza de Baca, Gable, & Weise, 2013). The ultimate-level selective pressures reconstructed by EP thus shape the more immediate proximate-level mechanisms that directly control behaviour.

An overly modularized view of behavioural mechanisms separates the brain and its behaviour into discrete components as would be seen among the various transistors, cables and processors of an electronic instrument. One problem, however, is that many behavioural tactics would benefit greatly by being coordinated with each other to be deployed in some kind of coherent master plan. Such coordination is by no means guaranteed by each mechanism being specifically fine-tuned to different environmental inputs, unless one could rely on the environment to provide correlated inputs. A premier example of this kind of problem is in the coordination of life history traits.

Life history *theory* is fundamentally an evolutionary-economic theory of *resource allocation* among different components of fitness, such as survival and reproduction. Life history *traits* are the basic *descriptive units* that comprise an organism's life history, including fundamental parameters such as: spacing of births, length of gestation, weight at birth, size of litters, length of lactation, length of juvenile dependency, postnatal growth rates, age at sexual maturity, adult body size and length of lifespan. Each different life history trait is presumably controlled throughout development by a somewhat distinct proximate mechanism, but having too much autonomy in the systems controlling each might produce a chimera of discrepant and mutually inconsistent behavioural outputs representing a functional mismatch of life history tradeoffs. Life history *tradeoffs* are the basic *tactical elements* within an organism's life history, including parental survival versus current reproduction, parental growth versus current reproduction current versus future reproduction, current versus future offspring quantity, current versus future offspring quality, and current offspring quantity versus quality.

Fortunately, Figueredo, Vásquez, Brumbach and Schneider (2004) have proposed explanatory solutions to this particular adaptive problem based on the results of behavioural genetic analyses. Both the separate *heritabilities* and *genetic correlations* among a wide array of life history traits were assessed, and found to be quite substantial. Heritabilities are the proportions in which traits are genetically influenced; genetic correlations are the heritable components of observed correlations among phenotypic traits. The genetic correlations among the measured life history traits accounted for the preponderance of observed phenotypic correlations. Nevertheless, the latent common factor underlying the genetic correlations among all the life history traits measured was not sufficient to account for all the heritable variations within each of the different traits. That means that some genes were evidently influencing each separate life history trait uniquely, whereas others were influencing them in common.

Although no direct evidence could be provided by such behavioural genetic analyses for the interpretation proposed, the special genes that were exerting common influences upon the array of life history traits were hypothesized to be regulatory genes, which are genes that moderate the action of other genes by either promoting or inhibiting their expression. It was proposed that the observed coordination among life history traits was centrally controlled by a set of such regulatory genes, having the function of directing the domain-specific psychological mechanisms to act in concert throughout development.

More recently, Garcia and colleagues (2017) applied Bronfenbrenner's *ecological systems theory* to construct and test structural path models comparing the performance of alternative developmental models for a series of life history traits. Ecological systems theory depicts the 'mutually shaping' relationships between organisms and their environments 'as a set of nested structures, each inside the next, like a set of Russian dolls' (Bronfenbrenner, 1979, p. 22): (1) the *microsystem*; (2) the *mesosystem*; (3) the *exosystem*; (4) and the *macrosystem*. Thus, various psychosocial life history traits were assessed and arrayed in a theoretically derived developmental sequence, based on Bronfenbrenner's concentric systems, as shown in Figure 10.2.

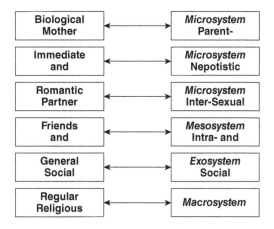

Figure 10.2 Domain-specific resource allocations: predominant linkages to social affordances.

Three alternative sets of causal pathways tested by Garcia and colleagues modelled scenarios in which: (1) the relations among several different life history traits were influencing each other sequentially without any central coordination; (2) the shared causal influence of a latent common factor was accounting for the correlations among each trait in the developmental sequence; and (3) the shared causal influence of a latent common factor was affecting every stage of behavioural development directly in addition to the direct effects among sequential pathways between successive stages. The structural path model that contained both the hypothesized developmental pathways and the pervasive common causal influence of the central latent variable performed the best, as shown in Figure 10.3.

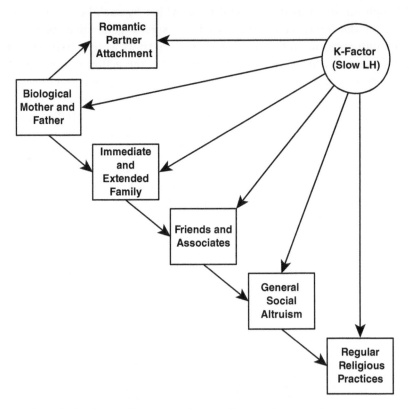

Figure 10.3 Hybrid model: common factor plus developmental sequence.

On the basis of these findings, these authors hypothesized regulatory genes to be guiding developmental pathways from one life history stage of development to the next, with the function of achieving a strategically coordinated set of life history traits in interaction with relevant inputs from the environment. Thus, this view of behavioural control is neither: (a) purely situation-based and environmentally deterministic, nor (b) trait-based and genetically deterministic. Instead, it represents a more inclusive synthesis of both perspectives. Furthermore, we have no reason to believe that all coordination among psychological mechanisms need be handled by a single central processor. Instead, we envision an entire hierarchy of behavioural control mechanisms, each operating at the requisite level for responsiveness to the adaptive problems posed by the environment.

EVOLUTIONARY FOUNDATIONS OF PERSONALITY

DESCRIPTION

This section again discusses human traits as understood within the context of adaptive problems. 'Food shortages, harsh climate, disease, parasites, [and] predators' (Buss, 1991, p.464), Buss writes, are among those 'hostile forces of nature' (Darwin, 1859, p. 63) with which humans are evolved to contend.

More specifically, Buss outlined eight exigencies of survival and reproduction in any adaptive landscape populated by concentrations of conspecifics: (1) successful intrasexual competition, (2) mate selection, (3) successful conception, (4) mate retention, (5) reciprocal dyadic alliance formation, (6) coalition-building and maintenance, (7) parental care and socialization and (8) extra-parental kin investment. There follows a continuation of Buss's claim that EP is an able arbiter of theory in its ability to impose a biologically informed kind of Occam's razor upon theoretical claims within personality psychology. In reviewing grand theories of personality populating the 19th-century intellectual landscape, Buss asserts that 'personality theories have typically been formulated in innocence of the processes that shaped personality'. What we discuss as personality are evaluative differences relevant to a series of questions Buss compiles:

> Who is high or low in the social hierarchy? Who is likely to rise in the future? Who will make a good member of my coalition? Who possesses the resources that I need? Who will share their resources with me? With whom should I share my resources? Who can I go to for advice? Whom can I depend on when in need? With whom should I mate? Who will be a good cooperator and reciprocator? Who might do me harm? Whom can I trust? Who will betray my trust? (Buss, 1991, p. 472)

These are the features of the social environment which persons have evolved to 'attend to and act upon' in competing with one another for reproductive advantage. Evolution, Buss intimated, would more and more precisely specify a species-typical nature around which heritable, strategic variation can be objectively observed. Buss more explicitly claims that evolution will synthesize personality psychology's myriad phenomena, just as plate tectonics synthesized volcanoes, earthquakes, continental drift and mountain formation.

IMPACT

ADAPTIVE PROBLEMS AND THEIR SOLUTIONS

For didactic purposes, researchers continue to divide adaptive problems and solutions into categories such as survival and reproduction (as when organizing chapters on a book on evolutionary psychology or ecology), but this has not translated into an attempt to assign them to personality characteristics. Neuroticism, for example, can influence survival as it involves threat-avoidance and the stress responses, but also impacts mate choices – those lower on this trait are generally preferred as partners.

Social selection was a largely untouched but important category of adaptive problems in Buss's classic. This concept refers to the differential success in the social realm – which involves, especially in human groups, cooperation, altruism, alliance formation and related enterprises. Organisms may thus not only be preferred differentially for reproduction, but also for social relations due to their partner value. Recent studies have examined the relation between personality and social effectiveness, identifying that a general factor of personality – the common factor of shared variance among specific personality traits – largely relates to success in navigating the social world, as recently demonstrated by van der Linden, Dunkel and Petrides (2016). It therefore appears that, even though it is difficult and perhaps unwise to pinpoint one adaptive domain for each personality trait, broadly human personality deals with the complexities of sociality.

SELECTION, PLASTICITY AND ROBUSTNESS

A common misconception regarding the evolution of personality, critiqued by Buss (2011), is that selection acts as a homogenizing force leading to single point of optimality in the phenotype distribution. In contrast, evolutionary theory predicts that the location of this point will vary depending upon the type of selective pressures active, in accordance to the relationship between a trait and its fitness. Thus, based on these criteria, selective pressures can be classified into *directional, disruptive, stabilizing*, or *correlational selection* (as defined below).

Sinervo and colleagues (2010) describe *directional* selection as a process through which values located in one of the extremes of trait distributions are favoured over more moderate variants. Hence, this type of selection is manifested as the migration of the optimality peak from one side of the distribution to the other. Alternatively, according to Dingemanse and Réale (2013), the curve representing the trait fitness distribution under *disruptive* selection instead evidences a higher frequency of values located at both extrema, displaying two peaks. Thus, disruptive selection is best understood as a process disfavouring organisms with moderate values and favouring those with extreme scores. Sinervo and colleagues (2010) view *stabilizing* selection as instead proliferating moderate values while removing extreme variants.

Dingemanse and Réale (2013) describe *correlational* selection as occurring when selective pressures are not exerted separately upon *each* trait, but operates upon the *association* between two or more traits. As personality is comprised of multiple correlated characteristics, evolutionary studies face the challenge of examining the effects of selection operating simultaneously over the association among personality traits. Nevertheless, correlational selection should not be confused with a correlated response to selection. According to Dingemanse and Réale (2013), a correlated response occurs when selection operates over the frequency of A which due to its genetic association with B, subsequently influences the prevalence of B in the population, whereas correlational selective pressures fall upon the correlation between traits A and B.

Personality evolution has also been hypothesized to depend on the commonality of one phenotype relative to frequency of other morphs in the population, a phenomenon also known as *frequency-dependent* selection. For example, Bergmüller and Taborsky (2010) suggested that diversification occurring within a species is inherently related to this type of selection, with organisms adopting alternative strategies destined to decrease the competition with other members of the same species. Therefore, variability in personality traits is hypothesized to be the outcome of organisms performing various strategies and specializing in different social niches, understanding a social niche as the interactive potential (*adaptive affordances*) between the organism and its social environment.

HUMAN NATURE

As Buss predicted, academic effort (and arguably, scientific progress) towards identifying the fundamental psychological mechanisms that comprise human nature has accelerated. The number of journals dedicated exclusively or substantially to this line of research has increased considerably, now including *Evolution and Human Behavior, Evolutionary Psychology, Human Nature, Evolutionary Behavioral Sciences, Evolutionary Psychological Science, Adaptive Human Behavior and Physiology, Journal of Evolutionary Psychology* and others. A recent review by Martins and colleagues (2012) has indicated that, across many other journals, academic books, theses and dissertations, EP has appeared prominently as the foundation on which attempts to identify the components of human nature are made, and has become applied with increasing frequency, especially starting in the 2000s.

However, while this is true of evolutionary psychology, it does not seem to apply to evolutionary personality psychology or the evolutionary study of other individual differences. Kennair (2014) correctly identified a large ratio of theory to data in evolutionary psychopathology; the study of individual differences in maladaptive psychological characteristics, the largest share of contributions made by evolutionary psychologists in the study of personality, has been restricted to theory. The 2011 volume entitled *The Evolution of Personality and Individual Differences*, edited by Buss and Hawley (2011), contains numerous chapters that intend to elucidate theoretically why personality variations exist, and what hypotheses could be tested to shed light on that issue by stimulating research. One might not have expected that, just as empirical research on domain-specific and universal aspects of human nature grew exponentially in EP in the last 25 years since the publication of Buss's classic, empirical research on evolutionary personality psychology should have remained comparatively stagnant.

Fortunately, there are exceptions to this general tendency. Sex differences in personality, relations between personality traits and mating strategies, and between personality traits and life history strategies have been the focus of a substantial number of studies. In these lines of research, several hypotheses are forwarded proposing that persons of different sexes, different mating strategies, or different life history speeds should exhibit personality traits that facilitate the implementation of whatever evolved behavioural strategies they have. Thus, personality characteristics should vary *in concert with* these fitness-relevant (having a bearing on the organism's ability to survive and reproduce) variables; personality is therefore fitness-relevant as well. For instance, organisms with a predominantly short-term mating strategy (preferring and investing more in casual relations of little or no exclusive commitment) would not benefit from having an introverted personality and little openness to experience, and these characteristics can hinder or prevent successful mate searching in short-term mating markets (Schmitt & Shackelford, 2008). Empirical tests such as these have contributed to the crystallization of evolutionary personality psychology and its integration with other subfields of evolutionary psychology.

DISPOSITIONS AS EVOLVED PROBLEM-SOLVING STRATEGIES

The alternative explanations summarized by Buss (1991) for the origins of partially heritable personality characteristics and the retention of individual differences remain as possibilities, but the list of alternatives has been expanded considering new developments in evolutionary genetics, as proposed by several different authors in the volume edited by Buss and Hawley (2011). For example, it has been argued as possible that selective sweeps within the past several thousand years – fast positive selection of gene variants, which also modify the frequency of their neighbouring regions in the genome – are behind the large variation among humans. Gene flow due to accelerated migration of individuals among human populations is also a contender hypothesis. *Balancing* selection, whereby multiple phenotypes are adaptive in a complementary way, each in a specific subset of the species niches, has remained as a focus of discussion. Unfortunately, even more than 20 years after the publication of Buss's classic, the field seems just as far or even farther from reaching any form of consensus on the matter. This situation is further complicated by the difficulty in reconstructing the history of behavioural traits, as compared to anatomic ones, and by the lack of agreement on what model of personality traits should be the initial focus of empirical study.

CRITIQUE

As described above, the bioenergetic tradeoffs among *Survival Problems* and *Reproductive Problems* are addressed by evolutionary life history theory. For example, this theory partitions the organism's resource allocations among two major categories: (1) *Somatic Effort*, which constitutes the bioenergetic and material resources devoted to the continued survival of the organism; and (2) *Reproductive Effort*, which constitutes the bioenergetic and material resources devoted to the production of new organisms as vehicles for survival of the organism's genes

Many seemingly 'Grand' theories within the Standard Social Science Model (SSSM) propose different fundamental motivations as paramount. One example is the pivotal role played by the concept of 'self-esteem' within most social psychological theories as the central motivating factor behind behaviour. More specific formulations, such as Social Identity Theory, reduce the individual's desire to belong and conform to a social group as driven by the need to derive one's 'self-esteem' from one's 'social identity', constructed as a consequence of one's group membership. EP theory, on the other hand, treats many of these putatively motivating factors as proximate mechanisms rather than ultimate goals. Sociometer Theory is an evolutionary theory that represents conventional 'self-esteem' as constituting a mechanism for monitoring one's value to others within certain social contexts that presumably determine the probability of one's inclusion and retention within a social group.

Thus, although it is often possible to achieve consilience among SSSM and EP theories, it may come at the cost of demoting their hypothesized behavioural objectives to specific adaptations rather than more fundamental principles of motivation. The key difference resides in the fact that ultimate EP 'goals' must be fitness-relevant and not intrapsychic. The term *intrapsychic* denotes processes contained purely within the mind, such as 'self-esteem', and not in external reality. For evolutionary Sociometer Theory to work, material consequences to either survival or reproduction must ensue from group inclusion or exclusion. Otherwise, 'self-esteem' would be fitness-irrelevant and thus immune from selection.

A useful way to highlight these differences is to emphasize the definitional distinctions between *strategies* and *tactics*, which are often mutually confounded and confused within EP. Within Military Science, which is whence these terms ultimately derive, *tactics* denote the elemental *means* employed to obtain an objective; *strategy* instead denotes the overall plan of the campaign that involves the coordinated deployment and execution of multiple tactical elements towards an overarching *end*. These two related concepts must be better distinguished to elucidate the dynamics of behavioural control systems. By this analogy, the *sociometer* would be a tactical control system subservient to an overall social strategy, which is itself subsidiary to the more ultimate objectives of survival and reproduction.

Similarly, many modern models of the latent structure of personality are hierarchical. This means that the 'Big Five' factors (Extraversion, Neuroticism, Agreeableness, Conscientiousness and Openness to Experience) may be modelled as indicators of two higher-order factors, often called 'Alpha' and 'Beta'. The Alpha factor loads positively on Agreeableness and Conscientiousness, but negatively on Neuroticism, and has been variously characterized as 'communion' and 'stability'. The Beta factor loads positively on both Extraversion and Openness to Experience, and has been variously characterized as 'agency' and 'plasticity'. Furthermore, both the Alpha and Beta factors may in turn be modelled as indicators of a single higher-order factor, often called the 'General Factor of Personality' or 'GFP'.

Although some view these hypothesized latent structures as attributable to various statistical or methodological artefacts, others view them as instead representing hierarchical systems of behavioural control and regulation, with the higher-order systems helping to coordinate the function of the lower-order systems into coherent behavioural strategies. For example, the GFP has been shown to be both phenotypically and genetically correlated with a higher-order factor of life history strategy, often called the 'K-Factor', representing the dimension of fast-to-slow life history speed. This implies that the optimal implementation of life history strategy entails some degree of coordination of the lower-order factors of personality, as tactical elements to be deployed in the service of a coherent and coordinated plan for survival and reproduction.

CORE CONTROVERSIES IN PERSONALITY PSYCHOLOGY

DESCRIPTION

This section again comments on how evolutionary psychology reconciles *demand characteristics*, as described within the social psychology literature, with the notion of *individual differences*, as described within the personality psychology literature. Pursuant to demonstrating the role of evolution in this *state–trait debate*, Buss outlines the following four contexts wherein personality differences will be reliably observed: (1) genetically inherited behavioural strategies and decision thresholds; (2) evolved developmental switches wherein different environmental cues evoke one or another developmental trajectory; (3) behavioural strategies deployed in response to selective contingencies; and (4) the adoption of behavioural strategies consonant with one's ability and morphology. Thus, the state–trait debate, like the nature–nurture debate, is settled, not by one side overpowering the other, but by replacing the adversarial, zero-sum dichotomy with 'evolution-based examples of person–environment interactions'.

Part III continues by commenting on sex differences, mate choice, emotion and motivation as they relate to individual differences in personality functioning from an evolutionary perspective. Lastly, Buss transitions from context to culture, describing personality research from a cross-cultural perspective that was just then burgeoning. To the credibility of an evolutionary perspective, kindness, emotional stability and dependability were found to vary among, and be valued by members within, more than 30 cultures studied. Though he does not discuss how personality and persons construct culture from the bottom up, Buss does insist that persons be understood as evolved organisms vying within the cultural milieu, using diverse strategies towards the common ends of survival and reproductive advantage.

IMPACT

EVOLUTIONARY RESOLUTIONS OF THE PERSONALITY CONSISTENCY DEBATE AND PERSPECTIVES ON INTERACTIONISM

As fitness is affected by the match between the organism's strategy and its environment, personality traits will be optimized by selection depending on the context. The expression of personality traits during ontogeny is an intricate process governed by both gene–environment (G–E) correlations and gene-by-environment (GxE) interactions. According to Buss (1987), three mechanisms produce G–E correlations such that: (1) the organism actively seeks and chooses an environment (habitat *selection*); (2) the organism generates predictable environmental responses (*evocation*); or (3) the organism significantly alters the ecology (*manipulation*). Figueredo and colleagues (Figueredo, Wolf, Gladden, Olderbak, Andrzejczak, & Jacobs, 2011) also reviewed various GxE interactions (as opposed to G–E correlations) and defined as either: (1) the organism's phenotypic expression is dependent on the exposure of its genotype to a specific environment; or (2) organisms respond to the environment differently depending on their genotype. In this view, the evolution of personality by means of frequency-dependent selection relies on the occurrence of G–E correlations, with organisms seeking a social microniche in which to specialize. Furthermore, evocative and manipulative mechanisms facilitate organisms' ability to modify their immediate ecology, thereby altering or creating a new social microniche. Besides reducing the level of intraspecific competition, Bergmüller and Taborsky (2010) suggested that selection will favour personality variation under circumstances where behavioural reliability is associated with a fitness payoff. Hence, organisms displaying temporal and spatial behavioural consistencies may attain benefits that are beyond the reach of organisms behaving erratically.

Any examination of the evolutionary correlates of personality requires an understanding of the degree of *plasticity* or *robustness* displayed by each trait. Bateson and Gluckman (2011) define plasticity as the degree of change occurring in a trait during development in response to environmental variations interacting with the organism's genotype. According to the type of variation, plasticity is further subdivided into continuous and discrete. Continuous plasticity is distinguished from its discrete counterpart due to the existing gradation between various morphs. The range of continuous variation between phenotypes is referred to as a *reaction norm*. For West-Eberhard (2003), despite this difference, both continuous and discrete plasticity occur as outcomes of environmental influences by means of developmental *switches*. Furthermore, certain environmental stimuli may have a greater effect during a restricted ontogenic stage (*sensitive period*), influencing the organism to adopt a developmental pathway instead of others. Stearns (1989) further distinguished plasticity from other indicators of developmental variability such as flexibility; whereas the former is characterized by its irreversible nature, the latter is characterized as reversible.

Although the facilitation of the expression of a particular phenotypic trait by the environment appears to portray the organism as a passive agent, contemporary models, such as those proposed by Bateson and Gluckman (2011), acknowledge this process to be a dynamic exchange between the organism and its ecology. In this view, organisms may actively assess various ecological cues and generate a reliable template of their current environment, and this information may also be used to forecast the future ecological conditions.

A trait is described as robust (as opposed to plastic) when it remains invariant to other genotypic and environmental influences. Whereas plasticity allows organisms to react to environmental changes with a diversity of responses, robustness exemplifies a restriction in the range of response. According to Bateson and Gluckman (2011), robustness is facilitated through a series of mechanisms such as: (1) insensitivity of the organism in detecting environmental cues associated with developmental changes; (2) morphological and physiological constraints; (3) redundancy of multiple systems exerting a similar function; (4) repair of a lesion to a tissue or organ, reconstructed to restore its original form; (5) regulation by physiological feedback loops generating stable internal conditions, or *homeostasis*; and (6) canalization of later stages of phenotypic expression, achieved regardless of the occurrence of environmental changes during development.

Despite the underlying differences between plasticity and robustness, both processes are generators of interindividual variability. For example, Sih and colleagues (2004) view behavioural consistency across spatial and temporal contexts as one of the main characteristics of personality. Thus, although at first glance plasticity may seem to run counter to this description, evolutionary studies of personality do not reject the role of plasticity. Nevertheless, robustness must be limited to some extent for personality to evolve plasticity.

EMOTIONS, DESIRES, PREFERENCES

Precisely because emotions – and related phenomena, such as moods and desires – are not stable, but rather volatile and context-specific, they have been studied in efforts to explain person–situation interactions. While personality traits are broad tendencies, problem-solving in a specific context may require the deployment of emotions.

It follows that emotions can be the connectors between personality *tactics* and *behaviours*. Broad strategies involve tactics that can be deployed through actual behaviour, when the context triggers a corresponding emotion in the organism. Several studies attempting to connect these hierarchically organized concepts have been conducted in EP since the publication of Buss's classic. The flagship example is the study of jealousy and monitoring manipulative and aggressive behaviour as consequences, and as components of sex-biased mating tactics as reviewed by Buss (2001); however, other examples have gone farther: Fernandes, Kennair, Natividade, Hutz and Kruger (2016), for example, examined how certain emotions are triggered in sexual relationships as not only as part of a mating tactic, but also as part of a broader life history strategy. As further examples, irritability, desire to be alone, and disgust for one's partner are commonly activated immediately after sexual intercourse by organisms who prioritize short-term mating (having preferences for casual, non-committed sexual relationships), and who exhibit faster life history strategies more broadly.

When attempting to make sense out of the many alternative propositions for the origin and maintenance in heritable individual differences of personality traits, considering emotions may help elucidate the problem. Balancing selection has been one of the most prominent candidate explanations, but relies on the assumption that different personality traits are needed for different subcomponents of the ecology of a species or a population. However, what emotions permit is precisely the ability to modulate one's behaviour in a flexible way rapidly to accommodate to the contours of each subcomponent of the ecology. Complementarity of traits among organisms in a population may not be as necessary if the complementarity is already contained within each organism through flexible deployment of emotions. Thus, the balancing selection hypothesis might be considered an unparsimonious explanation in comparison.

Nevertheless, organisms within a population may have the capacity for different *ranges* of emotions, or for the threshold for their activation, and therefore for the frequency with which emotions will be triggered. Balancing selection would thus not produce perfectly stable traits that are always active, such as permanent sadness, or a permanent desire to socialize.

CRITIQUE

Among the statements made in Buss's seminal article is the following: '"Organism" and "situation" do not independently affect personality or behaviour' (Buss, 1991, p. 481). Referring back to Figure 10.1 above, we can discern that this statement has some degree of truth, but that it might also become partially misleading if interpreted simplistically. In Figure 10.1, the main body of the table of elements is comprised of 'cells' containing tiny traits-by-situation interactions. These are the fundamental constituents of the crossbreak, with the row and column means being statistical aggregates that assess and estimate the averaged effects. Thus, to characterize the overall 'effect' of a situation is not completely meaningless, if one understands that such an estimate represents an aggregate. Similarly, when one casually remarks that another person is 'cheerful', one typically does not mean that the other person is in a literally constant and invariant state of cheerfulness, but instead that the other person is *generally* cheerful, as observed across a variety of different situations. This is what is understood by common sense in normal conversation. Nevertheless, Buss is being technically accurate when he states that traits and situations do not affect behaviour *independently* (Buss, 1991, p. 481).

Buss also remarks that: 'It makes no sense to create a "taxonomy of situations" independent of the psychological mechanisms within humans' (Buss, 1991, p. 481). Nevertheless, Figueredo and colleagues (Figueredo, Brumbach, Jones, Sefcek, Vásquez, & Jacobs, 2007) did just that, and Buss (2009) later endorsed and reinforced this exercise as valuable. Although one might acknowledge that the existence of evolutionarily recurrent classes of situations naturally select for the evolution of suitably responsive psychological mechanisms within humans and other animals, it is nonetheless reasonable to classify the potentially divergent demand characteristics of different social situations to attempt to understand the different selective pressures that they generate and evolutionary affordances that they provide.

Finally, one might exert some caution in responding to Buss' call for more cross-cultural research on personality. For example, there are problems inherent in the possibility of switching among locally variable frames of reference when doing cross-cultural personality comparisons. Arguably, self-reported levels of conscientiousness in Japan should not be uncritically compared to self-reported levels of conscientiousness outside Japan. Most Japanese respondents are likely comparing themselves to a population of other highly conscientious Japanese, whereas most non-Japanese respondents are likewise comparing themselves to a population of other possibly less conscientious non-Japanese (*gaijin*). In both cases, individuals are implicitly comparing themselves to the means of their local populations, but inasmuch as those means might differ, the raw self-ratings might not be directly comparable.

CONCLUSIONS

Part IV repeats the now familiar refrain that EP has a unique ability to reevaluate individual differences as goal-directed tactics and strategies relevant to reproductive success and reiterates Buss's views on states and traits, as well as on how personality relates to culture. At the end of this closing section, Buss ventures beyond summation to cautiously specify the productive application of evolutionary principles to personality psychology, warning that evolutionary theorizing must proceed from a mastery of biological principles. After cataloguing some early EP missteps, Buss then separates the endeavour from the execution, specifically recognizing confirmation biases, fallacies and genetic determinism as *misunderstandings* that can be corrected through future advances. Buss presciently prognosticates that EP will take its place as the *metatheory* that puts personality psychology into a *grand framework*, heretofore sorely absent from classical personality theories. Buss' few final sentences speak of evolution as providing 'tools for understanding the core of our human nature and the most important ways in which we differ from one another' (Buss, 1991, p. 486). This final statement consolidates his view that EP is much more than a product of theory construction: EP is a tool, a lens, a scientific process, with credible pretensions to the status of metatheory – pretensions that suggested the ability to articulate a universal human nature and to properly understand personality as strategic variation around that human norm.

FURTHER READING

Bateson, P., & Gluckman, P. (2011). *Plasticity, robustness, development and evolution*. Cambridge: Cambridge University Press.

Buss, D. M., & Hawley, P. H. (2011). *The evolution of personality and individual differences*. New York: Oxford University Press.

West-Eberhard, M. J. (2003). *Developmental plasticity and evolution*. New York: Oxford University Press.

REFERENCES

Balachandran, N., & Glass, D. J. (2012). PsychTable.org: The taxonomy of human evolved psychological adaptations. *Evolution: Education and Outreach*, *5*, 312–320.

Bateson, P., & Gluckman, P. (2011). *Plasticity, robustness, development and evolution*. Cambridge: Cambridge University Press.

Bergmüller, R., & Taborsky, M. (2010). Animal personality due to social niche specialization. *Trends in Ecology & Evolution*, *25*, 504–511.

Bronfenbrenner, U. (1979). *The ecology of human development*. Cambridge, MA: Harvard University Press.

Burkart, J. M., Schubiger, M. N., & van Schaik, C. P. (2016).The evolution of general intelligence. *Behavioral and Brain Sciences*, *1*, 1–65.

Buss, D. M. (1987). Selection, evocation, and manipulation. *Journal of Personality and Social Psychology*, *53*(6), 1214–1221.

Buss, D. M. (1991). Evolutionary personality psychology. *Annual Review of Psychology*, *42*, 459–491.

Buss, D. M. (2001). Are men really more "oriented' toward short-term mating than. *Psychology, Evolution & Gender*, *3*, 211–239.

Buss, D. M. (2009). How can evolutionary psychology successfully explain personality and individual differences? *Perspectives on Psychological Science*, *4*, 359–366.

Buss, D. (2011). *Evolutionary psychology: The new science of the mind* (4th ed.). Hove, UK: Psychology Press.

Buss, D. M., & Hawley, P. H. (2011). *The evolution of personality and individual differences*. New York: Oxford University Press.

Darwin, C. (1859). *On the origin of the species by means of natural selection*. London: John Murray.

Dingemanse, N. J., & Réale, D. (2013). What is the evidence for natural selection maintaining animal personality variation? In Carere, C., & Maestripieri, D. (Eds.), *Animal personalities: Behaviour, physiology, and evolution*. Chicago, IL: Chicago University Press.

Fernandes, H. B. F., Kennair, L. E. O., Hutz, C. S., Natividade, J. C., & Kruger, D. J. (2016). Are negative postcoital emotions a product of evolutionary adaptation? Multinational relationships with sexual strategies, reputation, and mate quality. *Evolutionary Behavioral Sciences*, *10*, 219–244.

Figueredo, A. J., Brumbach, B. H., Jones, D. N., Sefcek, J. A., Vásquez, G., & Jacobs, W. J. (2007). Ecological constraints on mating tactics. In Geher, G., & Miller, G. F. (Eds.), *Mating intelligence: Sex, relationships and the mind's reproductive system*. Mahwah, NJ: Lawrence Erlbaum.

Figueredo, A. J., Cabeza de Baca, T., Garcia, R. A., Gable, J. C., & Weise, D. (2013). Revisiting mediation in the social and behavioral sciences. *Journal of Methods and Measurement in the Social Sciences*, *4*, 1–19.

Figueredo, A. J., Vásquez, G., Brumbach, B. H., & Schneider, S. M. R. (2004). The heritability of life history strategy: The K-factor, covitality, and personality. *Social Biology*, *51*, 121–143.

Figueredo, A. J., Wolf, P. S., Gladden, P. R., Olderbak, S., Andrzejczak, D. J., & Jacobs, W. J. (2011). Ecological approaches to personality. In D. M. Buss & P. H. Hawley (2011), *The evolution of personality and individual differences*. New York: Oxford University Press.

Garcia, R. A., Cabeza de Baca, T., Black, C. J., Sotomayor-Peterson, M., Smith-Castro, V., & Figueredo, A. J. (2016). Measures of domain-specific resource allocations in life history strategy: Indicators of a latent common factor or ordered developmental sequence? *Journal of Methods and Measurement in the Social Sciences*, *7*, 23–51.

Hertler, S. C. (2017). Beyond birth order: The biological logic of personality variation among siblings. *Cogent Psychology*, *4*, 1–18.

Kennair, L. E. O. (2014). Evolutionary psychopathology and life history: A clinician's perspective. *Psychological Inquiry*, *25*, 346–351.

Mealey, L. (1995). The sociobiology of sociopathy: An integrated evolutionary model. *Behavioral and Brain Sciences*, *18*, 523–599.

Penke, L., Denissen, J. J., & Miller, G. F. (2007). The evolutionary genetics of personality. *European Journal of Personality*, *21*, 549–587.

Schmitt, D. P., & Shackelford, T. K. (2008) Big Five traits related to short-term mating: From personality to promiscuity across 46 nations. *Evolutionary Psychology*, *6*, 246–282.

Sih, A., Bell, A. M., Johnson, J. C., & Ziemba, R. E. (2004). Behavioral syndromes: An integrative overview. *Quarterly Review of Biology*, *79*, 241–277

Sinervo, B., & Calsbeek, R. (2010). Behavioral concepts of selection. In Westneat, D. F., & Fox, C. W. (Eds.), *Evolutionary Behavioural Ecology*. New York: Oxford University Press.

Stearns, S. C. (1989). The evolutionary significance of phenotypic plasticity. *Bioscience*, *39*, 436–445.

van der Linden, D., Dunkel, C. S., & Petrides, K. V. (2016). The General Factor of Personality (GFP) as social effectiveness: Review of the literature. *Personality and Individual Differences*, *101*, 98–105.

West-Eberhard, M. J. (2003). *Developmental plasticity and evolution*. New York: Oxford University Press.

11 Personality, Health and Death

Revisiting Friedman et al. (1993)

Margaret L. Kern

BACKGROUND TO THE STUDY

The 1970s and 1980s were challenging times for personality psychology. Critiques led to doubt as to whether personality traits mattered. The controversy grew, in part, from short-term studies that found inconsistencies across contexts and situations. However, even though the same person may act differently in different situations, if there are consistent between-person differences that predict meaningful life outcomes across eras of life – such as career success, marriage, social contribution and physical health – then these differences are potentially something to pay attention to. In their classic study, Friedman et al. (1993) focused on one such outcome – how long people live.

Personality has long been believed to be relevant to physical health. In the ancient Grecian era, Hippocrates, Galen and their protégés suggested that both temperament and health arose from four humours – bodily fluids that impacted how a person thought and functioned (Friedman, 2007). For instance, an apathetic person was thought to have an excess of phlegm and was at risk for rheumatism; an excess of melancholy led to sadness, depression, degenerative diseases and cancer; the sanguine person was healthy, with a ruddy, optimistic personality.

The 20th century brought a growing number of attempts to scientifically link individual differences with physical and mental health outcomes, with the focus primarily on risks arising from negative characteristics. Psychoanalytic theories suggested that diseases such as ulcers and asthma arose from unconscious psychological conflicts. The middle of the century brought attention to the Type A behaviour pattern, characterized by hostility, aggression, ambition, impatience and competitiveness, which was believed to increase risk for heart disease. This was followed by suggestions of a cancer-prone personality (Type C) and other disease-prone types. Yet subsequent studies found little consistent evidence for such type-disease association. Reviewing hundreds of studies, a meta-analysis suggested that it is not that specific personality types link to specific diseases, but rather that there are general sets of characteristics, such as hostility, aggression, and depression, that increase risk for multiple diseases (i.e., a disease-prone personality; Friedman & Booth-Kewley, 1987). Complementing these negative characteristics, Friedman (1991) suggested the self-healing personality, consisting of characteristics such as optimism, extraversion, sociability and hardiness, which results in good health over time.

DETAILED DESCRIPTION OF THE STUDY

THEORY

From a biopsychosocial framework, health is multidimensional, including physical, psychological, social, cognitive and functional domains. It is not simply a state at a single point at time, but rather an ongoing process of breakdown and repair, which ebbs and flows across life. Notably, there are individual differences in how those processes unfold across the lifespan, impacted by who we are, what we experience and what we do, which results in some people being more resilient than others.

The study of such processes requires longitudinal data that include both personality and long-term health information. Studies need to be well planned and maintained over time, intensive, systematic and methodologically well conducted, and be sufficiently long enough to observe developmental processes as they unfold (Block, 1993). Notably, across the 20th century, a number of such studies were conducted. Studies from around the world have followed cohorts over many years, subsequently archiving the data and making it available to other researchers (see Friedman, Kern, Hampson, & Duckworth, 2014 and Kern, Benson, Larson, Forrest, Bevans, & Steinberg, 2016 for summaries of studies that included personality information), opening the possibility to study the lives of people as they naturally unfolded over time.

METHODOLOGY

In 1990, Friedman obtained funding from the US National Institute of Aging to use archival study, the Terman Life Cycle Study, to examine lifespan predictors of mortality. The Terman Study began in 1921 as a descriptive study of children with high intelligence quotients (IQ). Lewis M. Terman (one of the early developers of IQ testing) and his colleagues recruited children from across California. Children were nominated by teachers, underwent a variety of intellect tests, and were included in the study if they had a minimal IQ of 135. Over the next five years, some siblings were added, resulting in a final sample of 1528 participants (856 males, 672 females), born primarily between 1904 and 1915. The sample included a significant proportion of females, which was quite unusual for the historical period.

At baseline (1921–22, average age 11), teachers, parents and the children completed various questionnaires, reporting on the children's demographic background, achievements, intellect, health, interests, educational history and psychosocial functioning. The project resulted in two descriptive books (Cox, 1926; Terman, 1925). In the mid-1930s, Terman and his colleagues decided to see if they could follow up with the participants. By 1940, they had managed to re-engage most of the original sample. The participants were subsequently followed throughout their lives, completing written assessments every five to ten years. The questionnaires contained a very broad range of variables, including physical and mental health, social relationships, marriage and family histories, military participation, a variety of psychological variables, educational and occupational information, health behaviours, perceptions of ageing, honours and achievements, and failures and challenges. Participants also contributed letters, pictures, stories, artwork, books and more. The quantitative data were coded, digitized and archived through the Henry A. Murray Data Archives (https://murray.harvard.edu/). The original data (including qualitative and other uncoded information) remain stored at Stanford University.

Complementing the archived data, Friedman and his colleagues collected death certificates, providing an objective indicator of how long participants lived (or an indication that they were still alive) and cause of death. Then, using the archival data, they identified variables that were theoretically relevant to personality theory. At baseline, parents and teachers rated the children on 25 different trait dimensions (e.g., 'will power and perseverance'), comparing the child to others of the same age on an 11-point scale. The researchers considered the extent to which each trait rating theoretically aligned with the Big Five personality dimensions (Extraversion, Agreeableness, Conscientiousness, Neuroticism, Openness/Intellect; John & Srivastava, 1999) and statistically analysed the items. This process resulted in six personality dimensions: conscientiousness/social dependability, motivation/self-esteem, cheerfulness/humour, sociability, energy and permanency of moods (i.e., low neuroticism). They then used two analytic approaches to estimate mortality risk: survival analysis, which estimates the probability of dying at any given age, and logistic regression, which predicts a dichotomous outcome (in this case, being alive versus dead at age 70). Analyses were conducted for the full sample and separately by gender.

FINDINGS

Not surprisingly, risk of death increased with age, and females had a longevity advantage over males. Controlling for age and gender, there were two significant child personality predictors: conscientiousness and cheerfulness. Across seven decades, a person rated in the highest quartile on conscientiousness had a significantly lower risk of dying at any given age than a person rated in the lowest quartile. For instance, a 20-year-old conscientious male had about a 73% chance of still being alive at age 70, compared to a 67% chance of remaining alive at age 70 for an unconscientious male (81% versus 76% for females). In contrast, cheerfulness predicted greater mortality risk. Interestingly, although conscientiousness was protective across genders, effects were stronger for males. In addition, emotional stability showed some signs of being protective for males – it was not related to length of life for females.

IMPACT OF THE STUDY

The Friedman et al. (1993) study was the first to find that personality could predict longevity across the lifespan. The idea that personality traits could have such long-reaching impact was striking. The study triggered several areas of theory and research that have developed and evolved over the past 25 years to create a lifespan perspective of personality development, which demonstrates that personality has both theoretical and practical significance.

THE BENEFITS OF ARCHIVAL STUDIES

The Friedman et al. (1993) study involved secondary analysis of an existing data-set (archived personality information) combined with the primary creation of new data (mortality information based upon the death certificate details). While the study was not the first to conduct secondary analyses with existing data, it did suggest the value that existing data might have for studying the longer-reaching impact of personality.

To study lifespan questions, collecting adequate data would extend well beyond the lifetime and resources of a single investigator. Further, existing studies represent a major investment by previous researchers. Considerable time, resources and effort were put into developing the studies, recruiting participants and following them over time. Many studies that were conducted across the 20th century managed to retain a large proportion of the sample across numerous decades. It is a tribute to both the researchers and the participants to learn as much from the data as possible. Fortunately, lifespan datasets are increasingly available to researchers.

Any single archival study is limited in numerous ways, including cohort and historical effects, the measures that the researchers chose to include, attrition (participants who leave the study) and missing data (Tomlinson-Keasey, 1993). The studies are often poorly documented. Studies often comprise a selective sample, such that results may not generalize to broader populations. Considerable work often has to be done to understand the participants, data and context of the study; select relevant variables; recode items to adequately address research questions; and run and make sense of analyses (see Andersen, Prause, & Cohen Silver, 2011, for a guide to using secondary data for psychological research).

Despite the many challenges, existing longitudinal studies provide opportunities to consider change and development over time, control for various confounding variables, and explore different contextual factors across development. Studies such as the Terman study and the Harvard Grant Study have converged on similar findings (Friedman & Martin, 2011; Vaillant, 2012). In short, archived data make it possible to address lifespan questions that cannot be addressed in short-term and cross-sectional studies (Block, 1993; Elder, Pavalko, & Clipp, 1993; Martin & Friedman, 2000; Tomlinson-Keasey, 1993). As Mroczek (2014) reflected, 'long term longitudinal studies are like mature trees ... like a century-old oak, such studies are rare resources and can add to our knowledge base in ways newer longitudinal studies cannot' (p. 1472).

LIFESPAN APPROACHES TO PERSONALITY AND HEALTH

The Friedman et al. (1993) study crossed disciplines, drawing on medicine, behavioural science, and personality, social and developmental psychology to unpack when and how individual differences impact life outcomes. Length of life provides a clear, valid and reliable measure of one's ultimate physical health. Health outcomes, especially longevity, are hard to predict, and thus effect sizes are typically very small. For instance, it is common for people with high blood pressure to take a baby aspirin to reduce risk for heart disease. The effect size for this is $r = .02$ (Meyer et al., 2001) – statistically trivial, but from a medical perspective, meaningful. The small effect sizes reflect that a lot contributes to one's health, including genetic, biological, psychological, social and environmental factors. Two individuals can come from similar backgrounds and experience very different outcomes, whereas two other people with dissimilar backgrounds can share the same outcomes. Different factors accumulate and interact to impact how long a person lives and what he or she dies from. Within this complexity, personality matters, as illuminated by the Friedman et al. (1993) study.

Even as studies began to examine psychological characteristics, the focus was primarily on negative emotional variables, such as hostility, depression and neuroticism. The Friedman et al. (1993) study turned to positive variables, for the first time suggesting the protective effect of conscientiousness. Indeed, studies have demonstrated that the Big Five model, despite numerous limitations, provides a useful framework for considering the broader impact of personality across the lifespan. The five factors have been linked to physical health, psychological well-being, social relationships, job performance, community participation, health-related behaviours, political participation, anti-social behaviour, education and socioeconomic status and political participation, amongst other outcomes (Ozer & Benet-Martínez, 2006; Roberts, Kuncel, Shiner, Caspi, & Goldberg, 2007; Roberts, Lejuez, Krueger, Richards, & Hill, 2014).

Still, such links are not always consistent or straightforward, pointing to the need for the deep, long, theory-based studies that Friedman et al. conducted. For instance, links between neuroticism and mortality find it to be protective, risky, or unrelated (see Kern & Friedman, 2016 for a review). Through his work with the eight-decade Harvard Grant Study, Vaillant (2012) reflected that many initial findings that were supported cross-sectionally were not maintained across time, and that understanding impacts on health and other outcomes over time requires piecing together multiple pieces of information over time to reveal a person's life. Understanding when a trait may or may not be protective depends on having appropriate data collected over long periods of time. The characteristics that impact one's health can only be understood within the context of the person's trajectory across life.

MECHANISMS AND MODERATORS

Finding links between childhood conscientiousness and longevity raised the question of why the two might be connected. This began a series of studies by Friedman, his collaborators and a growing group of personality–health researchers. Theoretically, various pathways linking personality and health have been proposed, including health behaviours, social relationships, situation selection, experiences of and reactions to stress, and physiological pathways, as well as spurious associations arising from confounding variables (Chapman, Hampson, & Clarkin, 2014; Friedman, 2000; Hampson, 2008, 2012; Kern & Friedman, 2010; Smith, 2006).

First, health behaviours impact risk for various diseases and chronic conditions, with smoking/tobacco being the greatest risk factor for poor health outcomes (World Health Organization, 2009). Personality characteristics have been linked to the propensity to engage in behaviours that are more or less health-promoting. Conscientious individuals are more likely to engage in healthy behaviours (e.g., healthy diet, moderate exercise, not smoking, no or moderate alcohol intake, proactively caring for health) than individuals low in conscientiousness (Bogg & Roberts, 2004; Lodi-Smith et al., 2010). In contrast, neuroticism increases risk of smoking and other poor habits (Mroczek, Spiro, & Turiano, 2009; Shipley, Weiss, Der, Taylor, & Deary, 2007). Still, health behaviours explain only part of personality–health links, with considerable variance remaining after health behaviours are controlled. And even personality and behavioural links can be inconsistent. A 28-day study found that although conscientious individuals were less likely to smoke, if they did, they smoked more than their less conscientious peers (O'Connor, Conner, Jones, McMillan, & Ferguson, 2009). Stress and behaviours may interact in healthy or unhealthy ways.

Second, studies have demonstrated how important positive social relationships are for health (Tay, Tan, Diener, & Gonzalez, 2012; Taylor, 2011), and personality appears to influence how one socially interacts with others. For instance, across 94 studies, high agreeableness, emotional stability and conscientiousness related to greater investment in work, family, religion and volunteering social roles (Lodi-Smith & Roberts, 2007), which in turn support better social relationships. In contrast, hostility and aggression relate to greater risk of heart disease (Booth-Kewley & Friedman, 1987), and neuroticism increases risk of loneliness, which in turn increases risk for mental and physical health problems (Cacioppo, Hawkley, & Berntson, 2003).

Third, although people move in and out of different contexts, environments and situations, personality influences situations that a person selects or is drawn towards (Friedman, 2000). Such experiences accumulate in non-random ways (Caspi, Roberts, & Shiner, 2005), which may be more or less health-promoting. A conscientious, dependable person might be more likely to obtain a good job and succeed professionally, leading to occupational advancement, income stability and various associated benefits. Extraverted individuals are more likely to be active socially, have large social circles and satisfying friendships, express positive emotion, and are happier than less extraverted peers (cf. Smillie, Kern, & Uljarevic, 2018). Neuroticism correlates with subjectively and objectively experiencing a greater number of negative life events (Magnus, Diener, Fujita, & Pavot, 1993).

The social contexts that a person lives and works in also impact upon one's personality (Srivastava, John, Gosling, & Potter, 2003). Still, social contexts can result in mixed effects across individuals. For instance, extraversion shows inconsistent links with health and longevity. The sociability aspects of extraverted individuals result in better social relationships, but when peers engage in risky behaviours, it can increase risk of poor health and early mortality.

Fourth, personality impacts experiences with and perceptions of stress. While some stress is healthy, chronic high levels of stresses can disrupt homeostatic functioning, creating extra strain on the physiological system over time, and increasing risk of infections, illness, disease and breakdown (Kemeny, 2007). People frequently are drawn to or select their own stressful or unstressful environments (Caspi et al., 2005; Friedman, 2000), choosing or being pulled towards experiences that continue to shape who they are and their subsequent life experiences. For instance, neuroticism is linked to experiencing a greater number of stressful events and using maladaptive approaches to dealing with stress, whereas positive personality characteristics have been linked to healthier coping styles (Carver & Connor-Smith, 2010; Connor-Smith & Flachsbart, 2007; Segerstrom & O'Connor, 2012).

Relatedly, personality may impact various physiological mechanisms, including blood pressure, heart and brain function, neurotransmitters such as serotonin and cortisol, and immune responses. Hostility has been linked to greater physiological reactivity, heart disease and poor health (e.g., Miller et al., 1996), and facets of neuroticism (proneness towards depression and anxiety) correlate with higher levels of cortisol (an indicator of stress), slower recovery from illness, and greater risk of heart disease (e.g., Januzzi, Stern, Pasternak, & DeSanctis, 2000; Rugulies, 2002). In the Hawaii Personality and Health Study, across 40 years, low childhood conscientiousness predicted poor physiological functioning (Hampson, Edmonds, Goldberg, Dubanoski, & Hillier, 2013).

Stress and physiological pathways offer an interesting and promising intersection between individual differences and internal body processes. But directly testing such pathways is challenging, and most studies have only connected personality and physiological measures cross-sectionally. Correlations may be bidirectional or caused by other related variables. To truly establish how personality gets under the skin to impact one's health over time, longitudinal studies are needed that include personality, physiological measures across multiple time points, and valid and reliable health outcomes measured across life.

Finally, personality and health are most likely linked through a variety of spurious connections – confounding variables that impact *both* personality and health. Personality is influenced by numerous genetic and environmental factors (e.g., Jang et al., 2002; South & Krueger, 2014), some of which also impact one's health trajectory. Genetic factors may even interact with personality, such that traits manifest differently at different points in life, in different ways, for different people. Personality can also moderate and be moderated by other variables (e.g., Jaconelli, Stephan, Canada, & Chapman, 2013; Kern, Friedman, Martin, Reynolds, & Luong, 2009; Korotkov, 2008).

Over the past few decades, each of these theoretical pathways have received at least some empirical support. Studies often test single pathways, limited in part by the available data. But both theory and research are becoming increasingly complex.

THREE GENERATIONS OF PERSONALITY–HEALTH STUDIES

Friedman and colleagues (2014) suggested three generations of personality–health theory and research. In the first generation, evident in research on the Type A behaviour pattern, personality traits were thought to be markers or symptoms of various illnesses. Friedman and colleagues (1993) offered an early representation of a second generation of personality–health models, in which personality is conceptualized as a relatively stable factor that predicts health and illness outcomes through one or more pathways. Second-generation research has established the importance of personality across life, identified multiple probably pathways, and rigorously added empirical data to test various theoretical models. However, even as these various models and pathways are useful and necessary, they are insufficient for fully describing and understanding how personality and health intersect across life. Effect sizes are small and considerable variance remains, even in the best controlled studies. Such models fail to take into account shifts and changes in personality that occur across life, or how various factors accumulate, interact, or change over time.

To truly understand the web of factors that connect personality and health, models are needed that bring together multiple pathways and capture continuity, change, inter-relationships and complexity. Thus, personality and health theory and some research is turning towards a third generation of models, which are more sophisticated, complex and dynamic in nature. For example, Smith and colleagues (Smith, Baron, & Grove, 2014) suggested that risk accumulates over time through a dynamic interaction of individuals within their social contexts. The Life Course of Personality model suggests that different mechanisms matter at different time in life, which are moderated by aspects of the person and the social context (Shanahan, Hill, Roberts, Eccles, & Friedman, 2014).

Third-generation theories and models take personality–health research from simplistic analyses of static predictors and outcomes to sophisticated models that capture dynamic processes as they unfold across life, providing a systems-based approach. Still, testing such models is challenging. Dynamic processes cannot be tested with traditional statistical models used in psychology. Adequate data is needed that includes long time periods, repeated measures of relevant factors, and alternative ways of thinking about and analysing data. Research must combine theory with an openness for exploration, which in turn can inform our theoretical models.

The increasing availability of data combined with newer statistical methods make testing third-generation models more feasible. For instance, integrative data analysis directly pools multiple datasets at the item level (Hofer & Piccinin, 2009). Conceptually, studies can be linked through overlapping items, and then models can be extended using unique items from the different studies. Such work is still in its early stages, but suggests that integrative approaches may make it be possible to directly test well-defined lifespan theories, taking advantage of different sources of data to piece together full life course models.

INTERVENTION

Personality research has remained mostly detached from real world contexts (Mermelstein & Revenson, 2013), but there is growing interest in how personality research can be practically applied. A benefit of basic research on naturally occurring life trajectories is that it can provide insights into when and for whom interventions might be most effective, and areas that might be targeted for those with high-risk backgrounds or characteristics. For instance, a follow-up study with the Terman sample found that experiencing parental divorce as a child increased risk of early mortality (Schwartz et al., 1995). However, this risk was averted for those who developed a sense of personal satisfaction and achievement by middle age (Martin et al., 2002). Early adversity does not doom an individual to early mortality, and health-protective personality characteristics do not ensure long life. Building from this, intervention studies might look towards which factors are most risky (suggesting individuals that will benefit most from an intervention), and which factors reduce risk (pointing to potential places to intervene), and target those factors.

Personality is often described in terms of stable and consistent patterns of thought, behaviour and emotions, leading to the misconception that it does not change (Magidson, Roberts, Collado-Rodriguez, & Lejuez, 2014). But personality and its correlates can and do develop, change and evolve throughout life (Chapman et al., 2014; Mroczek, 2014). Life experiences, purposeful intervention, disease or injury, drugs, social interactions, environmental factors and one's interpretation of life experiences can impact upon who that person is, as well as the resulting life outcomes (Mroczek, 2014). For instance, in the Mills Longitudinal Study of women, marriage, work and marijuana consumption related to changes in social responsibility (a facet of conscientiousness) (Roberts & Bogg, 2004). Such findings raise questions around the possibilities for purposeful personality change (Chapman et al., 2014; English & Carstensen, 2014; Magidson et al., 2014; Mroczek, 2014). The benefits of conscientiousness suggest that it may be a beneficial trait to build in individuals and communities. However, it remains unclear whether it is beneficial or even possible to change conscientiousness itself, or rather specific facets, behaviours and pathways that it predicts.

As personality is most fluid early in life, interventions that develop health-promoting traits, behaviours and mindsets in children and adolescents may be more likely to have ongoing and cumulative benefits. Most work in this area has focused on facets of conscientiousness, such as self-regulation. Self-regulation emerges early in childhood, and predicts conscientiousness and its correlates, including healthy behaviours, high achievement, higher income, better physical and mental health, and less criminal behaviour (Duckworth & Seligman, 2017; Eisenberg, Duckworth, Spinrad, & Valiente, 2014). Various theories and interventions are being developed and tested to increase self-regulation (e.g., Duckworth, Gendler, & Gross, 2016; Inzlicht, Legault, & Teper, 2014). While promising, it is unclear which strategies may be most effective, especially over time.

Beyond specific facets, it may be more useful to target the various pathways linking conscientiousness and health, rather than the underlying personality trait. Reducing smoking, improving eating habits, encouraging physical activity and teaching people to be responsible workers and good citizens can result in health benefits, regardless of whether or not underlying personality traits actually change (Chapman et al., 2014). At the community level, conscientious behaviours can be encouraged through social structures, norms and policies (Ross & Nisbett, 1991; Thaler & Sunstein, 2008). Still, which pathways should be targeted is unclear, especially when more complex, dynamic models of personality and health are considered. Such approaches may be addressing symptoms rather than addressing the underlying causal factor, which can result in various unintended consequences.

Personality and health studies can also inform approaches to treatment. Adding a brief measure of personality to health records might point to patients who might be at increased risk, and help the doctor quickly understand some of the thoughts, feelings and attitudes of their patient, which in turn might help inform personal-ized care, individualized approaches to health and timely treatments (Chapman et al., 2014). Still, the extent to which personality-informed health care is possible and beneficial remains unknown (Israel & Moffitt, 2014).

The growing amount of work in this area demonstrates the growing practical applications of personality–health research. Still, which approaches to interven-tion will be most effective, sustainable and useful at individual and societal levels is unknown, and most likely depend upon the context and the individual. It is also unknown whether changes in a person's level of conscientiousness will corre-spond with the benefits that have been observed in correlational studies, which may be a function of genetic, environmental, or various other factors.

CRITIQUE OF THE STUDY

Although the Friedman et al. (1993) study has resulted in numerous insights and productive areas of theory, research and application, both the original study and others within personality–health are limited in numerous ways.

The Terman sample used in the study is quite unique, and care needs to be taken in generalizing findings to other populations. The participants were highly intelligent – comprising the top 2.5% of the population. Most were Caucasian and from a middle- to upper middle-class background. They represent a historical time period that is very different from today, impacted by the Great Depression, World War II, the Cold War, the technological revolution and shifting societal structures. Still, despite considerable homogeneity, the sample represents an important seg-ment of 20th century US society (Subotnik, Karp, & Morgan, 1989). Numerous studies published on the sample demonstrate that the experiences, trajectories and outcomes of the participants varied considerably. Some achieved great things, others never rose to their potential. Some lived long fulfilling lives, others died early from illness, combat, suicide and a variety of other causes. Some lived happy and meaningful lives, others struggled deeply with mental illness. Some were happily married, others were divorced, widowed, or always single. The intellectual and socioeconomic homogeneity of the sample has allowed greater focus on the many psychosocial factors that impact health and longevity, helping to identify phenomena that might not be visible in cross-section or short-term studies.

The measures themselves are far from ideal. The items and constructs reflect the interests of the researchers at the time rather than the constructs that we might want to study. Constructs were often indicated by a single item or a few items with poor reliability. The validated scales commonly used today did not exist. But the items that were included provide insights into human life that otherwise might be ignored. Modern studies are often conducted to answer a specific set of questions or hypotheses, and only include questions and measures relevant to those questions. In contrast, many of the existing longitudinal studies included a broad range of variables and constructs across numerous assessments, allowing exploration of diverse phenomena.

While the study was built on existing psychological theory, the analyses were exploratory. The authors looked for 'significant' associations, using p values as a heuristic for meaningful results. This made it possible to identify phenomena that otherwise would be overlooked or missed – avoiding Type 2 errors. There was little reason to believe that variables measured in childhood would be related to variables decades later, so significant findings point to interesting patterns that might be further tested and explored in other samples. However, this also raises the risk of over-interpreting significance (Type I errors).

Indeed, while the study found that cheerfulness predicted increased mortality risk, other studies find that cheerfulness, optimism, humour, positive affectivity and related characteristics predict better health outcomes, including longevity (Howell, Kern, & Lyubomirsky, 2007; Pressman & Cohen, 2005). The authors offered several possible explanations for the counter-intuitive result. Cheerful individuals may underestimate the danger of various risks (unrealistic optimism) and fail to follow medical advice, resulting in increased risk. Martin et al. (2002) explored this further, finding that cheerful children in the Terman sample were more likely to smoke, drink more and engage in risky hobbies than less cheerful children, but this failed to explain the cheerfulness–mortality link. Second, there may be distinctions between cheerful temperamental predispositions (as was measured in this study) and the tendency for optimistic individuals to engage in positive behaviours and to use more adaptive coping mechanisms. Indeed, numerous studies suggest that the benefits of optimism come from the behavioural patterns that optimistic individuals engage in, including healthier coping styles, proactively caring for their health, persisting in tasks, and deve-loping positive social relationships (Carver, Scheier, & Segerstrom, 2010). Still, the authors failed to acknowledge that the unexpected finding could be a function of the unreliable measures used, the selective nature of the sample, or capitalizing on chance.

The same critiques could be made of the conscientiousness finding. The authors discussed various reasons why conscientiousness might relate to longer life, grounding the finding in developmental theory, but failed to acknowledge that this could simply be a chance finding. But this provides an example of the process of science working as it should. Science is meant to be cumulative in nature, moving between theory development, testing the theory through a variety of methods across different samples, affirming or disconfirming prior findings, and iteratively refining theory and understanding over time. Others built upon the initial study, using a variety of samples, measures, time periods and study designs to test and replicate this link, repeatedly finding support for the original finding (Friedman & Kern, 2014; Kern & Friedman, 2008; Roberts et al., 2014).

Finally, the study, along with most personality–health studies that have followed from it, took a trait-based approach to personality. Self- and other-ratings on personality questions attempt to capture broad, relatively stable characteristics of the individual that summarize consistent behaviours, thoughts, and emotions across time and contexts (McAdams & Olson, 2010). The Big Five in particular has become the dominating model for personality–health research, as the model provides a useful heuristic framework for identifying possible associations, at a broad enough level to find consistent between-person patterns despite idiosyncratic differences (Smith & Williams, 1992). Many trait descriptions used within archival studies can be conceptually aligned to the broader factors, allowing conceptual replications and extensions of personality–health relations to occur across multiple studies, despite inconsistencies at the item level. This is evident in the Friedman et al. (1993) study – the 25 trait ratings by parents and teachers could be grouped into factors that resemble modern personality theories. Other studies measured the Big Five in very different ways, which at the statement level are incomparable, but align at the broader factor level (see Kern, Hampson, Goldberg, & Friedman, 2014 for an example of aligning studies at the item level). By using broad dispositional traits, personality–health research has also made a clear case for the importance of personality. Differences in these broad factors can predict life outcomes that individuals and societies care about, including education, employment, marriage, behaviour, health and length of life (Friedman & Kern, 2014; Ozer & Benet-Martinez, 2006; Roberts, Kuncel, Shiner, Caspi, & Goldberg, 2007).

But the almost exclusive focus on dispositional traits has had the unintended consequence that many misunderstand what personality is. Personality is seen as traits alone, primarily represented by the Big Five. Traits fail to capture the dynamic and contextualized nature of individual behaviours, thoughts, feelings and motivations (McAdams & Olson, 2010; Mischel, 2004). From a lifespan perspective, personality unfolds through a dynamic interplay of traits, characteristic adaptations, goals and motivations, and one's narrative about his or her journey (McAdams & Olson, 2010). Even as third-generation personality–health models attempt to incorporate greater dynamism and complexity, they are still primarily grounded in the trait-based perspective, failing to take into account the deeper levels of the person.

CONCLUSIONS

The Friedman et al. (1993) study could be considered a well-targeted fishing expedition, which illustrates an ingenious application of existing data within the fertile waters of psychological theory. When Friedman began working with the Terman data, there had already been over 70 studies and books written on the sample. Friedman added an objective indicator of mortality, along with an extensive background of studying and thinking about personality–health associations. The study became a turning point in Friedman's career. For the next 20 years, Friedman, his students and his collaborators continued to explore psychosocial predictors of mortality, explanatory pathways and increasingly sophisticated models, publishing numerous papers and culminating in a book (Friedman & Martin, 2011). It also triggered work by numerous others, leading to a community of life-span personality–health researchers.

The study showed the value that exploratory analyses with archival data could play in identifying phenomena that otherwise would have been missed. Amidst the social–personality crisis, the study clearly suggested that personality traits did indeed matter. A large literature now shows that personality has both theoretical and practical significance. The question is no longer whether personality matters, but rather when, for whom, under what conditions and how. Such questions have led to an increasingly sophisticated understanding and approach of personality, health and development, which will continue to evolve for years to come.

FURTHER READING

Chapman, B. P., Hampson, S., & Clarkin, J. (2014). Personality-informed interventions for healthy aging: Conclusions from a National Institute on Aging work group. *Developmental Psychology, 50*, 1426–1441.

Friedman, H. S., & Kern, M. L. (2014). Personality, well-being, and health. *Annual Review of Psychology, 65*, 719–742.

Friedman, H. S., & Martin, L. R. (2011). *The longevity project: Surprising discoveries for health and long life from the landmark eight-decade study*. New York: Hudson Street Press.

Ozer, D. J., & Benet-Martinez, V. (2006). Personality and the prediction of consequential outcomes. *Annual Review of Psychology, 57*, 401–421.

REFERENCES

Andersen, J. P., Prause, J., & Cohen Silver, R. (2011). A step-by-step guide to using secondary data for psychological research. *Social and Personality Psychology Compass, 5*, 56–75.

Block, J. (1993). Studying personality the long way. In D. C. Funder, R. D. Parke, C. Tomlinson-Keasey, & K. Widaman (Eds.), *Studying lives through time: Personality and development*. Washington, DC: American Psychological Association.

Bogg T., & Roberts, B. W. (2004). Conscientiousness and health-related behaviors: A meta-analysis of the leading behavioral contributors to mortality. *Psychological Bulletin, 130*, 887–919.

Booth-Kewley, S., & Friedman, H. S. (1987). Psychological predictors of heart disease: A quantitative review. *Psychological Bulletin, 101*, 343–362.

Cacioppo, J. T., Hawkley, L. C., & Berntson, G. G. (2003). The anatomy of loneliness. *Current Directions in Psychological Science, 12*, 71–74.

Carver, C. S., & Connor-Smith, J. (2010). Personality and coping. *Annual Review of Psychology, 61*, 679–704.

Carver, C. S., Scheier, M. F., & Segerstrom, S. C. (2010). Optimism. *Clinical Psychology Review, 30*, 879–889.

Caspi, A., Roberts, B. W., & Shiner, R. L. (2005). Personality development: Stability and change. *Annual Review of Psychology, 56*, 453–484.

Chapman, B. P., Hampson, S., & Clarkin, J. (2014). Personality-informed interventions for healthy aging: Conclusions from a National Institute on Aging work group. *Developmental Psychology, 50*, 1426–1441.

Connor-Smith, J. K., & Flachsbart, C. (2007). Relations between personality and coping: A meta-analysis. *Journal of Personality and Social Psychology, 93*, 1080–1107.

Cox, C. M. (1926). *The early mental traits of 300 geniuses: Genetic studies of genius. Volume 2*. Stanford, CA: Stanford University Press.

Duckworth, A. L., Gendler, T., & Gross, J. (2016). Situational strategies for self-control. *Perspectives on Psychological Science, 11*, 35–55.

Duckworth, A. L., & Seligman, M. E. P. (2017). The science and practice of self-control. *Perspectives on Psychological Science, 12*, 715–718.

Eisenberg, N., Duckworth, A. L., Spinrad, T. L., & Valiente, C. (2014). Conscientiousness: Origins in childhood? *Developmental Psychology, 50*, 1331–1349.

Elder, G. H., Jr., Pavalko, E. K., & Clipp, E. C. (1993). *Working with archival data: Studying lives (Quantitative applications in the social sciences)*. Newbury Park, CA: Sage.

English, T., & Carstensen, L. L. (2014). Will interventions targeting conscientiousness improve aging outcomes? *Developmental Psychology, 50*, 1478–1481.

Friedman, H. S. (1991). *Self-healing personality: Why some people achieve health and others succumb to illness*. New York: Henry Holt.

Friedman, H. S. (2000). Long-term relations of personality, health: Dynamisms, mechanisms, and tropisms. *Journal of Personality, 68*, 1089–1107.

Friedman, H. S. (2007). Personality, disease, and self-healing. In H. S. Friedman & R. C. Silver (Eds.), *Foundations of health psychology*. New York: Oxford University Press.

Friedman, H. S., & Booth-Kewley, S. (1987). The 'disease-prone personality': A meta-analytic view of the construct. *American Psychologist, 42*, 539–555.

Friedman, H. S., & Kern, M. L. (2014). Personality, well-being, and health. *Annual Review of Psychology, 65*, 719–742.

Friedman, H. S., Kern, M. L., Hampson, S. E., & Duckworth, A. L. (2014). A new lifespan approach to conscientiousness and health: Combining the pieces of the causal puzzle. *Developmental Psychology, 50*, 1377–1389.

Friedman, H. S., & Martin, L. R. (2011). *The longevity project: Surprising discoveries for health and long life from the landmark eight-decade study*. New York: Hudson Street Press.

Friedman, H. S., Tucker, J., Tomlinson-Keasey, C., Schwartz, J. Wingard, D., & Criqui, M. H. (1993). Does childhood personality predict longevity? *Journal of Personality and Social Psychology, 65*, 176–185.

Hampson, S. E. (2008). Mechanisms by which childhood personality traits influence adult well-being. *Current Directions in Psychological Science, 17*, 264–268.

Hampson, S. E. (2012). Personality processes: Mechanisms by which personality traits 'get outside the skin'. *Annual Review of Psychology, 63*, 315–339.

Hampson, S. E., Edmonds, G. W., Goldberg, L. R., Dubanoski, J. P., & Hillier, T. A. (2013). Childhood conscientiousness relates to objectively measured adult physical health four decades later. *Health Psychology, 32*, 925–928.

Hofer, S. M., & Piccinin, A. M. (2009). Integrative data analysis through coordination of measurement and analysis protocol across independent longitudinal studies. *Psychological Methods, 14*, 150–164.

Howell, R., Kern, M. L., & Lyubomirsky, S. (2007). Health benefits: Meta-analytically determining the impact of well-being on objective health outcomes. *Health Psychology Review, 1*, 83–136.

Inzlicht, M., Legault, L., & Teper, R. (2014). Exploring the mechanisms of self-control improvement. *Current Directions in Psychological Science, 23*, 302–307.

Israel, S., & Moffitt, T. E. (2014). Conscientiousness in primary care: An opportunity for disease prevention and health promotion. *Developmental Psychology, 50*, 1475–1477.

Jaconelli, A., Stephan, Y., Canada, B., & Chapman, B. P. (2013). Personality and physical functioning among older adults: The moderating role of education. *The Journals of Gerontology: Series B: Psychological Sciences and Social Sciences, 68B*, 553–557.

Jang, K. L., Livesley, W. J., Angleitner, A., Riemann, R., & Vernon, P. A. (2002). Genetic and environmental influences on the covariance of facets defining the domains of the five-factor model of personality. *Personality and Individual Differences, 33*, 83–101.

Januzzi, J. L., Stern, T. A., Pasternak, R., & DeSanctis, R. W. (2000). The influence of anxiety and depression on outcomes of patients with coronary artery disease. *Archives of Internal Medicine, 160*, 1913–1921.

John, O. P., & Srivastava, S. (1999). The Big Five trait taxonomy: History, measurement, and theoretical perspectives. In L. Pervin & O. P. John (Eds.), *Handbook of personality: Theory and research* (2nd ed.). New York: Guilford Press.

Kemeny, M. E. (2007). Psychoneuroimmunology. In H. S. Friedman & R. C. Silver (Eds.), *Foundations of health psychology*. New York: Oxford University Press.

Kern, M. L., Benson, L., Larson, L., Forrest, C. B., Bevans, K. B., & Steinberg, L. (2016). The anatomy of developmental predictors of healthy lives study (TADPOHLS). *Applied Developmental Science, 20*, 135–145.

Kern, M. L., & Friedman, H. S. (2008). Do conscientious individuals live longer? A quantitative review. *Health Psychology, 27*, 505–512.

Kern, M. L., & Friedman, H. S. (2010). Why do some people thrive while others succumb to disease and stagnation? Personality, social relations, and resilience. In P. S. Fry & C. L. M. Keyes (Eds.), *Frontiers of resilient aging*. New York: Cambridge University Press.

Kern, M. L., & Friedman, H. S. (2016). Health psychology. In T. A. Widiger (Ed.), *The Oxford handbook of the Five Factor Model of personality*. Oxford: Oxford University Press.

Kern, M. L., Friedman, H. S., Martin, L. R., Reynolds, C. A., & Luong, G. (2009). Personality, career success, and longevity: A lifespan analysis. *Annals of Behavioral Medicine, 37*, 154–163.

Kern, M. L., Hampson, S. E., Goldberg, L. R., & Friedman, H. S. (2014). Integrating prospective longitudinal data: Modeling personality and health in the Terman Life Cycle and Hawaii Longitudinal studies. *Developmental Psychology*, *50*, 1390–1406.

Korotkov, D. (2008). Does personality moderate the relationship between stress and health behavior? Expanding the nomological network of the five-factor model. *Journal of Research in Personality*, *42*, 1418–1426.

Lodi-Smith, J., Jackson, J., Bogg, T., Walton, K., Wood, D., Harms, P., & Roberts, B. W. (2010). Mechanisms of health: Education and health-related behaviours partially mediate the relationship between conscientiousness and self-reported physical health. *Psychology and Health*, *25*, 305–319.

Lodi-Smith, J., & Roberts, B. W. (2007). Social investment and personality: A meta-analysis of the relationship of personality traits to investment in work, family, religion, and volunteerism. *Personality and Social Psychology Review*, *11*, 68–86.

Magidson, J. F., Roberts, B. W., Collado-Rodriguez, A., & Lejuez, C. W. (2014). Theory-driven intervention for changing personality: Expectancy value theory, behavioral activation, and conscientiousness. *Developmental Psychology*, *50*, 1442–1450.

Magnus, K., Diener, E., Fujita, F., & Pavot, W. (1993). Extraversion and neuroticism as predictors of objective life events: A longitudinal analysis. *Journal of Personality and Social Psychology*, *65*, 1046–1053.

Martin, L. R., & Friedman, H. S. (2000). Comparing personality scales across time: An illustrative study of validity and consistency in a large archival data set. *Journal of Personality*, *68*, 85–110.

Martin, L. R., Friedman, H. S., Tucker, J. S., Tomlinson-Keasey, C., Criqui, M. H., & Schwartz, J. E. (2002). A life course perspective on childhood cheerfulness and its relationship to mortality risk. *Personality and Social Psychology Bulletin*, *28*, 1155–1165.

McAdams, D. P., & Olson, B. D. (2010). Personality development: Continuity and change over the life course. *Annual Review of Psychology*, *61*, 517–542.

Mermelstein, R. J., & Revenson, T. A. (2013). Applying theory across settings, behaviors, and populations: Translational challenges and opportunities. *Health Psychology*, *32*, 592–596.

Meyer, G. J., Finn, S. E., Eyde, L. D., Kay, G. G., Moreland, K. L., Dies, R. R., ..., & Reed, G. M. (2001). Psychological testing and psychological assessment. *American Psychologist*, *56*, 128–165.

Miller, T. Q., Smith, T. W., Turner, C. W., Guijarro, M. L., & Hallet, A. J. (1996). Meta-analytic review of research on hostility and physical health. *Psychological Bulletin*, *119*, 322–348.

Mischel, W. (2004). Toward an integrative science of the person. *Annual Review of Psychology*, *55*, 1–22.

Mroczek, D. K. (2014). Personality plasticity, healthy aging, and interventions. *Developmental Psychology*, *50*, 1470–1474.

Mroczek, D. K., Spiro, A., & Turiano, N. A. (2009). Do health behaviors explain the effect of neuroticism on mortality? Longitudinal findings from the VA Normative Aging Study. *Journal of Research in Personality*, *43*, 653–659.

O'Connor, D. B., Conner, M., Jones, F., McMillan, B., & Ferguson, E. (2009). Exploring the benefits of conscientiousness: An investigation of the role of daily stressors and health behaviors. *Annals of Behavioral Medicine*, *37*, 184–196.

Ozer, D. J., & Benet-Martinez, V. (2006). Personality and the prediction of consequential outcomes. *Annual Review of Psychology*, *57*, 401–421.

Pressman, S. D., & Cohen, S. (2005). Does positive affect influence health? *Psychological Bulletin*, *131*, 925–971.

Roberts, B. W., & Bogg, T. (2004). A longitudinal study of the relationships between conscientiousness and the social-environmental factors and substance-use behaviors that influence health. *Journal of Personality*, *72*, 325–354.

Roberts, B. W., Kuncel, N. R., Shiner, R., Caspi, A., & Goldberg, L. R. (2007). The power of personality: The comparative validity of personality traits, socioeconomic status, and cognitive ability for predicting important life outcomes. *Perspectives on Psychological Science*, *2*, 313–345.

Roberts, B. W., Lejuez, C., Krueger, R. F., Richards, J. M., & Hill, P. L. (2014). What is conscientiousness and how can it be assessed? *Developmental Psychology*, *50*, 1315–1330.

Ross, L., & Nisbett, R. E. (1991). *The person and the situation*. New York: McGraw–Hill.

Rugulies, R. (2002). Depression as a predictor for coronary heart disease: A review and meta-analysis. *American Journal of Preventative Medicine*, *23*, 51–61.

Schwartz, J. E., Friedman, H. S., Tucker, J. S., Tomlinson-Keasey, C., Wingard, D. L., & Criqui, M. H. (1995). Sociodemographic and psychosocial factors in childhood as predictors of adult mortality. *American Journal of Public Health*, *85*, 1237–1245.

Segerstrom, S. C., & O'Connor, D. B. (2012). Stress, health and illness: Four challenges for the future. *Psychology & Health*, *27*, 128–140.

Shanahan, M. J., Hill, P. L., Roberts, B. W., Eccles, J., & Friedman, H. S. (2014). Conscientiousness, health, and aging: The life course of personality model. *Developmental Psychology*, *50*, 1407–1425.

Shipley, B. A., Weiss, A., Der, G., Taylor, M. D., & Deary, I. J. (2007). Neuroticism, extraversion, and mortality in the UK Health and Lifestyle Survey: A 21-year prospective cohort study. *Psychosomatic Medicine*, *69*, 923–931.

Smillie, L. D., Kern, M. L., & Uljarevic, M. (2018). Extraversion: Description, mechanisms, and development. In D. P. McAdams, R. L. Shiner, & J. L. Tackett (Eds.), *Handbook of personality development*. New York: Guilford Press.

Smith, T. W. (2006). Personality as risk and resilience in physical health. *Current Directions in Psychological Science*, *15*, 227–231.

Smith, T. W., Baron, C. E., & Grove, J. L. (2014). Personality, emotional adjustment, and cardiovascular risk: Marriage as a mechanism. *Journal of Personality*, *82*, 502–514.

Smith, T. W., & Williams, P. G. (1992). Personality and health: Advantages and limitations of the five-factor model. *Journal of Personality*, *60*, 395–423.

South, S. C., & Krueger, R. F. (2014). Genetic strategies for probing conscientiousness and its relationship to aging. *Developmental Psychology*, *50*, 1362–1376.

Srivastava, S., John, O. P., Gosling, S. D., & Potter, J. (2003). Development of personality in early and middle adulthood: Set like plaster or persistent change? *Journal of Personality and Social Psychology*, *84*, 1041–1053.

Subotnik, R. F., Karp, D. E., & Morgan, E. R. (1989). High IQ children at midlife: An investigation into the generalizability of Terman's Genetic Studies of Genius. *Roeper Review*, *11*, 139–144.

Tay, L., Tan, K., Diener, E., & Gonzalez, E. (2012). Social relations, health behaviors, and health outcomes: A survey and synthesis. *Applied Psychology: Health and Well-being*, *5*, 28–78.

Taylor, S. E. (2011). Social support: A review. In H. S. Friedman (Ed.), *The Oxford handbook of health psychology*. New York: Oxford University Press.

Terman, L. M. (1925). *Genetic studies of genius: I: Mental and physical traits of a thousand gifted children*. Stanford, CA: Stanford University Press.

Thaler, R. H., & Sunstein, C. R. (2008). *Nudge: Improving decisions about health, wealth, and happiness*. New Haven, CT: Yale University Press.

Tomlinson-Keasey, C. (1993). Opportunities and challenges posted by archival data sets. In D. C. Funder, R. D. Parke, C. Tomlinson-Keasey, & K. Widaman (Eds.), *Studying lives through time: Personality and development*. Washington, DC: American Psychological Association.

Vaillant, G. E. (2012). *Triumphs of experience: The men of the Harvard Grant Study*. Cambridge, MA: Belknap Press.

World Health Organization. (2009). *Global health risks: Mortality and burden of disease attributable to selected major risks*. Retrieved from http://apps.who.int/iris/bitstr eam/10665/44203/1/9789241563871_eng.pdf (accessed 26 June 2018).

12 Realistic Ratings of Personality

Revisiting Funder (1995)

Jeremy C. Biesanz

BACKGROUND TO THE STUDY

O ne of the major problems in personality research is how to measure its constructs accurately. Many constructs such as personality traits are theoretical and not possible to assess and measure precisely and without error. Scientific research requires some actual measurement, even if imperfect, and impressions of personality are the primary assessment tool used by the field. Our impression of another's personality provides a framework to explain their past behaviours over time and different situations. This framework allows us to anticipate, understand and predict their future behaviour, albeit imperfectly. Impressions of individual differences are important and have consequences for both ourselves and for others. For the field of personality psychology, meaningful and important individual differences that are broad, consistent, coherent and stable are fundamental building blocks for scientific inquiry. The existence of personality traits and ability to perceive, with at least some degree of accuracy, such relatively consistent patterns of thought, emotion and behaviour was initially taken as inherent and obvious truths and uncontroversial premises. For instance, in attempting to catalogue these important individual differences and understand their structure, the lexical hypothesis posits that these salient and important individual differences become encoded into natural language (Allport, 1937; for a review see Chapter 5 and Saucier & Goldberg, 1996). Based upon this hypothesis, Allport and Odbert (1936) exhaustively examined the English natural language for words that can be used to describe another person with the goal of trying to understand the broader categories of relevant and important individual differences (see Chapter 2). The lexical hypothesis makes two critical assumptions. First, that there indeed are socially relevant individual differences that are important to observe, understand and useful to convey to others when describing someone. Second, that we are able perceive these individual differences with at least some degree of accuracy. If our perceptions of others are neither useful nor accurate, there would be no practical utility or benefit in conveying this information to others. However, both of these premises have come under serious question and critical examination for decades in the 20th century with doubts raised about both the importance of individual differences in predicting behaviour as well as the accuracy in understanding such individual differences in others. An understanding of the crises that arose in questioning these premises is important for placing Funder's (1995) study in context and appreciating its subsequent impact.

Are our impressions of others accurate? Questions on both the accuracy of assessments of personality as well as about individual differences in the ability to judge more accurately the personality of others has a long and rich history in psychology (e.g., Adams, 1927; Allport, 1937; Taft, 1955; Vernon, 1933). This line of research started with the premise, similar to that of the lexical hypothesis, that we can, with some degree of accuracy, understand the personality and important attributes of others. Given this premise, the natural question for personality psychologists was whether some individuals are better than others at accurately perceiving others. If so, who are these individuals and can we identify them? Determining who is a 'good judge' of personality would be useful for selecting interviewers and clinicians as well as helping inform the development of potential treatments to improve the accuracy of assessments and to incorporate that into training protocols. However, this extensive line of research on this topic ground to a rather abrupt halt in the 1950s when Lee Cronbach wrote a series of devastating and rather impenetrable articles criticizing how researchers were measuring individual differences in the accuracy of personality judgments (e.g., Cronbach, 1955). Research to that point essentially labelled a person a good 'judge' by comparing impressions measured on rating scales to some standard such as the self-report of the person being judged or the social consensus regarding that person. Accuracy was assessed by squaring the difference between ratings and the accuracy standard with lower values indicating greater accuracy. Unfortunately many different measurement artifacts could influence accuracy measured in this manner (e.g., rating everyone highly on a scale or rating everyone similarly to the average person). Although Cronbach proposed solutions and an approach to disentangling these measurement artifacts, these solutions required more complicated assessment protocols, more effort on the part of researchers, greater quantitative expertise on the part of the analyst, and were likely quite disheartening to researchers at the time. With most research to that point in time under a cloud of uncertainty, researchers in the field of personality interested in assessing accuracy and the good judge could have embraced Cronbach's critiques and restarted research programmes using these newly proposed analytical methods. Instead there was a profound pivot away from the question of accuracy and interpersonal perception.

The impact of Cronbach's (1955) critique dramatically accelerated a trend started with Asch (1946) that is reviewed in depth review in Funder (1999, pp. 57–60). Following a conference that led to an edited book (Tagiuri & Petrullo, 1958), a number of prominent researchers moved away from questions of accuracy directly and focused instead on questions of *process*. This switch obviated the need to engage with Cronbach's critique of accuracy research. Instead of worrying about whether perceptions of another person were indeed accurate, it was much easier to study how people form impressions based on artificial stimuli such as vignettes or word lists. On the surface this movement seemed practical, logical and efficient. The study of impression formation is conceptually cleaner and simpler when the stimulus is constant for all participants and there is no need to determine if the impression formed accurately reflects another's actual personality. As Funder (1995) notes, the accuracy problem was 'solved' by simply bypassing it.

The second major challenge to fundamental assumptions in personality psychology was encompassed by Mischel's (1968) critique of assessments of broad individual differences (see also Chapter 6 and Guion & Gottier, 1965). Noting that correlations between assessments of personality and behaviour as well as assessments of behaviour across situations and time were generally low, Mischel argued that there was not evidence for strong generalities in behaviour. This, he argued, cast doubt on the utility of personality traits as a construct and as a consequence we should examine contextual assessments and focus instead on understanding the sources of specificity of behaviour. In other words, we should question why people behave the way they do within a specific situation. Although Mischel's argument was nuanced, there was a bottom-line interpretation that was echoed by many at the time – the effect size for assessments of personality appears small (especially after you square the correlation) so therefore personality does not matter in predicting behaviour.

In the decades following Mischel's critique, a number of detailed rebuttals to critical elements of his argument emerged. Funder and Ozer (1983) demonstrated that effect sizes in personality research corresponded with those of classic social psychological experiments. As the convention at the time was not to report effect sizes in experimental work, this equivalence was not obvious to experimentalists who focused primarily on the mere existence of significant results. Abelson (1985) argued how even apparently small effect sizes could have profound, important and valuable outcomes. Ozer (1985) noted that for observational designs typically used in personality, the raw correlation, not the squared correlation, is the measure of shared variance between two assessments such as self-reports of personality and behaviour, an important distinction in the interpretation of correlations in observational research that is often overlooked even today. Finally, building on Tupes and Christal (1961/1992) and the lexical hypothesis, the emergence of the Big Five factor structure of personality provided a unifying framework for personality researchers (for reviews see Goldberg, 1993; John & Srivastava, 1999). These rebuttals, along with additional accumulated evidence over the decades, culminated with Kenrick and Funder (1988) who argued that substantial self–other agreement and consensus among raters exists on measures of personality traits. These levels of agreement and consensus cannot be explained away as products of biases, cognitive errors, stereotypes, or other theoretically trivial explanations. In other words, these large levels of self–other agreement and consensus among informants or observers reflect underlying individual differences – there is, indeed, something there and this something reflects important and stable individual differences.

At the same time, the argument for the existence of important and meaningful individual differences rests on the accuracy of personality assessments – impressions of our own personality (self-reports) and impressions of others that we know well (informant reports). These personality assessments were the fundamental building blocks on which the lexical hypothesis and the Big Five structure of personality were built. The levels of agreement and consensus that were observed across diverse and large samples were not consistent with trivial alternative explanations. Yet, if those building blocks were to weaken or be removed, then the entire theoretical structure supporting large parts of the science of personality would weaken and potentially collapse. Chipping away at this foundation and these fundamental building blocks was the growth industry uncovering and documenting errors and biases in judgments (see Krueger and Funder, 2004, for a brief review). This long and ever-growing list of errors and biases undoubtedly accounted for research psychologists outside of personality questioning the use of self-reports and judgments of others and avoiding building substantive theories based on these data sources (e.g., see Funder, 1983). It was in the context of this tension between personality psychologists building theories and structure based on judgments (self and other) and the overwhelming documentation by cognitive and social psychologists that biases and errors in judgments are ubiquitous and substantial that Funder (1995) published the *Realistic Accuracy Model*.

DETAILED DESCRIPTION OF THE STUDY

Funder (1995) is not an empirical article and there are no studies, experiments or data. Instead this theoretical review paper is a call to action for personality psychology coupled with the outline of a research roadmap. After a review of the history of accuracy research and the intensifying focus on error and bias, Funder outlines the Realistic Accuracy Model (RAM) and examines in detail the implications of this model. There are four main components or elements to the article: an argument on why the field should explicitly examine accuracy, a practical definition of accuracy and the assessment of accuracy, a theoretical model on the process of forming accurate impressions, and research questions that the field should examine which arise naturally from the theoretical model.

ACCURACY VS. ERROR

Successful academic careers and entire research literatures have been built demonstrating the prevalence and variety of cognitive biases and errors. Krueger and Funder (2004) provided a partial list of 42 errors of judgment studied by social psychologists since 1985. Focusing on this long list of errors and biases suggests that the human observer is dangerously flawed and perceptions cannot be trusted or relied upon. Funder (1995) argues that a complementary programme of research focusing on accuracy is needed – when and for whom are perceptions more accurate? The key to understanding this argument and perspective is that accuracy and bias can be unrelated conceptually and empirically. Eliminating bias may not change accuracy as they are *not* flip sides of the same coin. It is for precisely this reason that James (1897) expressed discomfort with focusing solely on shunning error. As Figure 12.1 illustrates, all combinations of high and low accuracy and bias can coexist. The mere existence of bias – or the magnitude of it – does not inform us of the existence or magnitude of accuracy except at the extreme theoretical limits. Thus the existence of reliable and replicable biases and errors in judgments and impressions does not inform us of the accuracy of our impressions of others. Personality psychologists need to systematically examine and document the levels of accuracy in impressions of personality traits and dimensions.

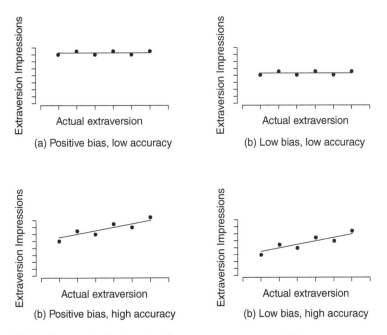

Figure 12.1   Potential relationships between accuracy and bias.

HOW SHOULD WE THINK OF ACCURACY?

The answer to this philosophical question has profound implications for the study of personality and person perception. To document and assess accuracy requires a clear and practical definition of accuracy. A number of different frameworks had been proposed over the years that were often not useful or practical for personality as a science. For instance, the *constructivist* perspective examines accuracy as a social construction (e.g., consensus among observers) and the actual personality of the person in question is, in a certain manner, irrelevant. If everyone agrees that Jack is annoying, then he is truly and really annoying. If Jack would be friendly and sociable and a pleasure to have around within other contexts and social environments, those alternative and unobserved realities are not considered under this perspective. All that matters is the consensus such as it exists currently. The *pragmatic* perspective defines accuracy in relation to how well assessments allow one to function and successfully interact with that person. Jack's personality is, in a certain sense, not relevant as the only concern is how well do judgments of Jack's personality allow one to interact successfully with Jack. In contrast, Funder defined *realistic* accuracy as a broader construct. Making the explicit assumption that personality exists – that there is something there to actually perceive – the Realistic Accuracy Model starts with the premise that complete accuracy cannot be achieved. Assessing someone's personality without error is neither conceptually possible nor empirically feasible. In the language of psychometrics, personality is a latent variable – a construct that can be assessed but only with some degree of measurement error. Realistic accuracy compares assessments of personality to a composite that includes as broad an array of criteria as possible (e.g., self-reports, informant-reports, behavioural measures). These criteria ideally represent a realistic assessment of someone's personality across contexts, time and perspectives. This perspective provides the functional definition of personality as *personality is as personality does*. The empirical assessment of accuracy of impressions and ratings of personality is then simply the observed correspondence between those impressions and assessments and the multifaceted and broad realistic criteria of personality – what the person has done.

THE THEORETICAL MODEL: HOW ARE ACCURATE IMPRESSIONS MADE?

RAM describes the process through which an accurate impression is made. Mirroring Brunswick's (1956) lens model, four necessary conditions must be met for an accurate impression to be formed. First, the target must engage in behaviours that are *relevant* to his or her personality. These behaviours must, in turn, be made *available* to the perceiver who then *detects* and then appropriately *utilizes* them when forming impressions. Omitting any step in this sequence or breaking this chain would not allow the perceiver to form an accurate impression. In other words, each of these conditions is necessary but not sufficient for an accurate impression of the target. Careful consideration of the sequence of events necessary for an accurate impression to be formed highlights the incredible fragility of accurate impressions. What is remarkable is not the existence of bias but that any level of accuracy can be achieved at all.

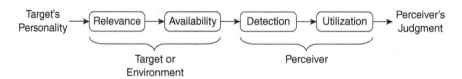

Figure 12.2 Realistic Accuracy Model of the process of accurate personality judgment from Funder (1995).

WHAT ARE THE IMPLICATIONS OF THE REALISTIC ACCURACY MODEL?

Given the apparent fragility of accurate impressions, it is clear from RAM, and the process outlined in Figure 12.2, that altering any one of these paths will change the accuracy of impressions. For instance, if targets engage in more relevant behaviours, then this should, all else being equal, increase the accuracy of impressions. This suggests that there are specific research programs that should examine the extent to which there exists variation in these paths, or specific moderators that influence each of these paths. Four primary potential moderators emerge from considering RAM.

- **Good target**. If some individuals provide more relevant cues or make more information available to perceivers, then accuracy would be enhanced for these individuals. In other words, the paths associated with *relevance* and *availability* may vary systematically across individuals resulting in individual differences with respect to the accuracy with which they are perceived.

- **Good judge**. If some individuals are better able to detect and utilize the information that targets provide, then their impressions of others should be more accurate. In other words, if the paths associated with *detection* and *utilization* are stronger for some individuals, these individuals would be able to form more accurate impressions than others.

- **Good trait**. Accuracy may be greater for some traits. The paths associated with *relevance* and *availability* may be greater for some traits which would lead to more accurate impressions for those traits.

- **Good information**. The quality and quantity of information should clearly impact the level of accuracy in personality judgments. Judgments based on more and higher quality information should be more accurate than judgments based on less and lower quality information.

These basic moderators may also interact with each other. Funder (1995) argued that personality researchers need to examine these potential moderators and interactions to parallel the research on errors and bias. Accurate impressions of others can be achieved. However, when are impressions more accurate? Under what circumstances are impressions likely to be more or less accurate? By focusing on the process through which accurate impressions are (must be) made, RAM provided a clear roadmap for researchers to follow and specific questions to address.

IMPACT OF THE STUDY

One immediate impact of Funder (1995) was the conceptual liberation of the term *accuracy* when considering personality judgments. Researchers could study and report on bias and error but there was a strong tendency – one that continues to a certain extent today – to discourage the use of the term *accuracy* in empirical work on personality judgments. Instead, researchers were encouraged to use more methodologically specific terms such as self-other agreement and consensus. RAM provided a coherent and rational framework for examining accuracy – and being able to describe that work as focused on accuracy – without falling into the philosophical trap of needing to determine someone's 'true' personality. Yet, beyond this linguistic reclamation, RAM provided researchers with a familiar and versatile framework to use. By defining the criterion to examine impressions as *realistic*, in that it maps on to a broad set of criteria that describes a person across time and contexts, RAM functionally equated realistic accuracy with construct validity. Questions on the accuracy of personality judgments are equivalent to those on the validity of a perceiver's impressions. Even if questions on accuracy may seem initially conceptually difficult, daunting, or feel unfamiliar, questions on validity are familiar. Assessing realistic accuracy is simply assessing the validity of the perceiver's impressions.

ASSESSING THE MODERATORS

ARE SOME INDIVIDUALS MORE ACCURATE IN THEIR JUDGMENTS ('GOOD JUDGE')?

The good judge is the individual whose impressions correspond with realistic criteria, such as reports of personality completed by the target or by individuals close to the target or a behavioural measure. A meta-analytic review of the early literature by Davis and Kraus (1997) found modest relationships between assessments of individual differences (e.g., intelligence and adjustment) and assessments of judgmental accuracy. Letzring (2008) found indirect evidence of the good judge. Impressions by outside observers were more accurate as the number of good judges in an interaction increased, suggesting that good judges provide a context that allows targets to make more relevant cues available to outside observers. There is an accumulating body of research suggesting that the good judge does exist and that there are meaningful individual differences in how accurately one judges the personality of others (e.g., Christiansen, Wolcott-Burnam, Janovics, Burns, & Quirk, 2005; Colman, Letzring, & Biesanz, 2017; Rogers & Biesanz, 2018). The social accuracy model (SAM; Biesanz, 2010), designed specifically to directly assess individual differences in interpersonal perception, has repeatedly demonstrated that there are reliable individual differences in the good judge. Some perceivers' initial impressions, after just 3 minutes of interacting with another person, are more realistically accurate than others'. However the variability in realistic accuracy across judges appears relatively modest compared to the variability across targets (good target) and dyadic accuracy. Interestingly, this does not appear to be a static effect. Encouraging perceivers to form accurate impressions does indeed increase the realistic accuracy of their impressions (Biesanz and Human, 2010). Interacting with more attractive targets – even targets that one perceives as more attractive than others do – increases the realistic accuracy of their impressions as well (Lorenzo, Biesanz, & Human, 2010). These results are consistent with the malleability of the *detection* and *utilization* paths in RAM. Overall, these results suggest that there are indeed broad individual differences in realistic accuracy associated with the good judge. Some individuals do indeed form impressions that correspond with realistic criteria more than others and the accuracy of impressions can be enhanced with appropriate motivation.

ARE SOME INDIVIDUALS MORE ACCURATELY JUDGED BY OTHERS ('GOOD TARGET')?

The good target is an individual who expresses their personality in a way that facilitates realistically accurate personality judgments. This can include providing others with highly accurate or relevant cues, making more of these relevant cues available to others, or expressing them in a way that facilitates cue detection or utilization. Emerging evidence strongly supports expressive accuracy (the good target) as a broad, fundamental individual difference – a critical element of our personality and defining of who we are. The evidence for the good target as a fundamental individual difference is the strong associations across diverse contexts. First, expressive accuracy is stable over time (Biesanz & West, 2000; Biesanz, West, & Graziano, 1998) – for example, good targets in adolescence also tend to be good targets in adulthood (Colvin, 1993). Second, individuals who were accurately perceived in an initial interaction were also accurately perceived by close others (e.g., through written essays; Stewart & Biesanz, 2017).

ARE SOME TRAITS MORE ACCURATELY JUDGED THAN OTHERS ('GOOD TRAIT')?

Some traits may be more visible or observable and thus lead to higher levels of accuracy (Beer & Watson, 2008; Funder & Colvin, 1997; Kenrick & Stringfield, 1980; Watson, Hubbard, & Wiese, 2000). Vazire (2010) expanded this basic idea, arguing for the self–other knowledge asymmetry (SOKA) model. In brief, Vazire argues that the availability of relevant cues may be limited for outside observers but accessible to the self. As a consequence, self–other agreement and other measures of realistic accuracy should be lower for traits that outside observers are not able to directly observe. For instance, when Jack experiences anxiety his heart rate may rise dramatically. This rapid beating would be rather difficult to detect by outside observers but the incessant pounding would be quite salient to him. Recent work examining the SOKA model has found evidence supporting such asymmetries (e.g., Beer and Vazire, 2017; Carlson, Vazire, & Oltmanns, 2013). This perspective and these results suggest that one needs to carefully consider which sources of information one should aggregate and use when assessing realistic accuracy.

DOES INCREASING INFORMATION ENHANCE ACCURACY ('GOOD INFORMATION')?

Impressions based on thin slices of information are remarkably accurate. For instance, watching very brief videos (Ambady, Hallahan, & Rosenthal, 1995; Borkenau & Liebler, 1992), perusing someone's dorm room (Gosling et al., 2002), reading a Facebook profile (Back et al., 2010), or learning someone's musical preference (Rentfrow & Gosling, 2006) or daily goals (Dunlop, McCoy, & Staben, 2017) all can lead to accurate impressions of basic broad personality traits. However, does increasing information lead to increased accuracy? Cross-sectional work shows that longer-term acquaintances have greater consensus and self–other agreement (Biesanz, West, & Millevoi, 2007). Systematic experimental work has documented how accuracy increases from initially very thin observational slices with greater exposure and information (e.g., Blackman & Funder, 1998; Borkenau, Wolcott-Burnam, Janovics, Burns, & Quirk, 2004; Carney, Colvin, & Hall, 2007). This careful experimental work demonstrates clearly how the accuracy of very initial impressions increases quickly, but appears to develop more slowly over longer periods of time.

CRITIQUE OF THE STUDY

The core elements of Funder (1995) have received no serious criticisms or critiques. The focus on realistic accuracy, compared to other forms of accuracy such as pragmatic accuracy or consensus, is a philosophical approach and choice that has often been adopted either implicitly or explicitly by researchers in the field. The only serious critique of RAM has emerged recently (Allik, 2017; Allik, de Vries, & Realo, 2016). The criticisms raised by Allik and colleagues do not lie with the call to investigate accuracy or with RAM's theoretical model outlined in Figure 12.2, but rather primarily with the focus and attention devoted to examining moderators of accuracy. Referencing Connelly and Ones' (2010) meta-analysis, the differences in self–other agreement across the Big Five personality traits are modest relative to the overall correlational levels. This suggests that perhaps the good trait is not important and that traits do not differ that meaningfully with respect to accuracy. For information, it is clear that accuracy increases dramatically, but Allik (2017) argues that after ~20 minutes the empirical evidence suggests that further observation does not enhance accuracy. This is consistent with the cross-sectional data from Biesanz, West and Millevoi (2007) that demonstrate that self–other and consensus correlations increase by ~.01 per year of acquaintanceship after this rapidly increasing initial window. This slow maturational change in accuracy over long periods of time is consistent with the differences in accuracy levels between relatively new acquaintances and long-term married couples. Outside of the window of initial impressions, information seems to have relatively little impact on accuracy, suggesting that this moderator has little influence on levels of accuracy. With respect to the other two main moderators of accuracy, Allik (2017) notes that very few individual difference measures correlate with levels of accuracy, consistent with the meta-analytic findings of Davis and Kraus (1997), which suggests that there is relatively little difference among individuals with respect to perceptive accuracy (i.e., the good judge). The overall thrust of the critique provided by Allik, de Vries and Realo (2016) and Allik (2017) is that the search for moderators of accuracy is akin to arguing whether or not Everest is taller than Mauna Kea. Everest is higher than Mauna Kea if you reference against sea level, but if you consider the natural base of each mountain, Mauna Kea is ~500 meters taller. The differences in the heights of the two mountains is dwarfed by the absolute magnitude of each. For personality, accuracy in impressions exists across all of the broad personality domains and Allik and colleagues argue that the impact of moderators of accuracy are modest compared to the existence of the overall magnitude of the levels of accuracy in perceiving broad dispositions.

CONCLUSIONS

For a major theoretical paper that is now over two decades old, Funder (1995) has aged remarkably well. The basic philosophical premise of realistic accuracy has emerged as arguably the most common framework for considering and reporting accuracy. In part, this reflects the tight association between realistic accuracy and examining the validity of impressions. An abbreviated version of this classic paper is condensed in Funder (2012) and an expanded version was published as a readable and accessible book (Funder, 1999). Recently edited volumes on accuracy in personality judgments include Ambady and Skowronski (2008) and Hall, Mast and West (2016). Finally, Rogers and Biesanz (2018) reassesses the good judge and demonstrates across four large samples how assessments of the good judge are dependent on the good target and provides some of the first evidence how there are strong interactions across moderators of accuracy that are consistent with predictions from RAM.

FURTHER READING

Ambady, N., & Skowronski, J. (2008). *First impressions*. New York: Guilford Press.

Funder, D. C. (1999). *Personality judgment: A realistic approach to person perception*. San Diego, CA: Academic Press.

Funder, D. C. (2012). Accurate personality judgment. *Current Directions in Psychological Science, 21*(3), 177–182.

Hall, J., Mast, M., & West, T. (2016). *The social psychology of perceiving others accurately*. Cambridge: Cambridge University Press.

REFERENCES

Abelson, R. P. (1985). A variance explanation paradox: When a little is a lot. *Psychological Bulletin, 97*, 129–133.

Adams, H. F. (1927). The good judge of personality. *Journal of Abnormal and Social Psychology, 22*, 172–181.

Allik, J. (2017). The almost unbearable lightness of personality. *Journal of Personality, 86*, 109–123.

Allik, J., de Vries, R. E., & Realo, A. (2016). Why are moderators of self–other agreement difficult to establish? *Journal of Research in Personality, 63*, 72–83.

Allport, G. W. (1937). *Personality: A psychological interpretation*. Oxford: Holt.

Allport, G. W., & Odbert, H. S. (1936). Trait-names: A psycho-lexical study. *Psychological Monographs, 47*, i–171.

Ambady, N., Hallahan, M., & Rosenthal, R. (1995). On judging and being judged accurately in zero-acquaintance situations. *Journal of Personality and Social Psychology, 69*, 518–529.

Ambady, N., & Skowronski, J. (2008). *First impressions*. New York: Guilford Press.

Asch, S. E. (1946). Forming impressions of personality. *Journal of Abnormal and Social Psychology, 41*, 258–290.

Back, M. D., Stopfer, J. M., Vazire, S., Gaddis, S., Schmukle, S. C., Egloff, B., & Gosling, S. D. (2010). Facebook profiles reflect actual personality, not self-idealization. *Psychological Science, 21*, 372–374.

Beer, A., & Vazire, S. (2017). Evaluating the predictive validity of personality trait judgments using a naturalistic behavioral criterion: A preliminary test of the self–other knowledge asymmetry model. *Journal of Research in Personality, 70*, 107–121.

Beer, A., & Watson, D. (2008). Asymmetry in judgments of personality: Others are less differentiated than the self. *Journal of Personality, 76*, 535–560.

Biesanz, J. C. (2010). The social accuracy model of interpersonal perception: Assessing individual differences in perceptive and expressive accuracy. *Multivariate Behavioral Research, 45*, 853–885.

Biesanz, J. C., & Human, L. J. (2010). The cost of forming more accurate impressions accuracy-motivated perceivers see the personality of others more distinctively but less normatively than perceivers without an explicit goal. *Psychological Science, 21*, 589–594.

Biesanz, J. C., & West, S. G. (2000). Personality coherence: Moderating self–other profile agreement and profile consensus. *Journal of Personality and Social Psychology, 79*, 425–437.

Biesanz, J. C., West, S. G., & Graziano, W. G. (1998). Moderators of self–other agreement: Reconsidering temporal stability in personality. *Journal of Personality and Social Psychology, 75*, 467–477.

Biesanz, J. C., West, S. G., & Millevoi, A. (2007). What do you learn about someone over time? The relationship between length of acquaintance and consensus and self–other agreement in judgments of personality. *Journal of Personality and Social Psychology, 92*, 119–135.

Blackman, M. C., & Funder, D. C. (1998). The effect of information on consensus and accuracy in personality judgment. *Journal of Experimental Social Psychology, 34*, 164–181.

Borkenau, P., & Liebler, A. (1992). Trait inferences: Sources of validity at zero acquaint-ance. *Journal of Personality and Social Psychology, 62*, 645–657.

Borkenau, P., Wolcott-Burnam, S., Janovics, J. E., Burns, G. N., & Quirk, A. (2004). Thin slices of behavior as cues of personality and intelligence. *Journal of Personality and Social Psychology, 86*, 599–614.

Brunswick, E. (1956). *Perception and the representative design of psychological experiments*. Berkeley, CA: University of California Press.

Carlson, E. N., Vazire, S., & Oltmanns, T. F. (2013). Self–other knowledge asymmetries in personality pathology. *Journal of Personality, 81*, 155–170.

Carney, D. R., Colvin, C. R., & Hall, J. A. (2007). A thin slice perspective on the accu-racy of first impressions. *Journal of Research in Personality, 41*, 1054–1072.

Christiansen, N. D., Wolcott-Burnam, S., Janovics, J. E., Burns, G. N., & Quirk, S. W. (2005). The good judge revisited: Individual differences in the accuracy of personality judgments. *Human Performance, 18*, 123–149.

Colman, D. E., Letzring, T. D., & Biesanz, J. C. (2017). Seeing and feeling your way to accurate personality judgments: The moderating role of perceiver empathic tenden-cies. *Social Psychological and Personality Science, 8*, 1–10.

Colvin, C. R. (1993). Judgable people: Personality, behavior, and competing explana-tions. *Journal of Personality and Social Psychology, 64*, 861–873.

Connelly, B. S., & Ones, D. S. (2010). An other perspective on personality: Meta-analytic integration of observers' accuracy and predictive validity. *Psychological Bulletin, 136*, 1092–1122.

Cronbach, L. J. (1955). Processes affecting scores on 'understanding of others' and 'assumed similarity'. *Psychological Bulletin, 52*, 177–193.

Davis, M. H., & Kraus, L. A. (1997). Personality and empathic accuracy. In W. J. Ickes (Ed.), *Empathic accuracy*. New York: Guilford Press.

Dunlop, W. L., McCoy, T. P., & Staben, O. (2017). From personal goals disclosed to personality judgments composed: Trait perceptions made on the basis of idiographic goals. *Journal of Research in Personality, 68*, 82–87.

Funder, D. C. (1983). The 'consistency' controversy and the accuracy of personality judgments. *Journal of Personality, 51*, 346–359.

Funder, D. C. (1995). On the accuracy of personality judgment: A realistic approach. *Psychological Review, 102*, 652–670.

Funder, D. C. (1999). *Personality judgment: A realistic approach to person perception*. San Diego, CA: Academic Press.

Funder, D. C. (2012). Accurate personality judgment. *Current Directions in Psychological Science, 21*, 177–182.

Funder, D. C., & Colvin, C. R. (1997). Congruence of others' and self-judgments of personality. In R. Hogan, J. Johnston, & S. Briggs (Eds.), *Handbook of personality psychology*. San Diego, CA: Academic Press.

Funder, D. C., & Ozer, D. J. (1983). Behavior as a function of the situation. *Journal of Personality and Social Psychology, 44*, 107–112.

Goldberg, L. R. (1993). The structure of phenotypic personality traits. *American Psychologist, 48*, 26–34.

Gosling, S. D., Ko, S. J., Mannarelli, T., & Morris, M. E. (2002). A room with a cue: Personality judgments based on offices and bedrooms. *Journal of Personality and Social Psychology, 82*, 379–398.

Guion, R. M., & Gottier, R. F. (1965). Validity of personality measures in personnel selection. *Personnel Psychology, 18,* 135–164.

Hall, J., Mast, M., & West, T. (2016). *The social psychology of perceiving others accurately*. Cambridge: Cambridge University Press.

James, W. (1897). *The will to believe: And other essays in popular philosophy*. New York: Longmans, Green, and Company.

John, O. P., & Srivastava, S. (1999). The big five trait taxonomy: History, measurement, and theoretical perspectives. In L. A. Pervin & O. P. John (Eds.), *Handbook of personality: Theory and research*. New York: Guilford Press.

Kenrick, D. T., & Funder, D. C. (1988). Profiting from controversy: Lessons from the person–situation debate. *American Psychologist, 43,* 23–34.

Kenrick, D. T., & Stringfield, D. O. (1980). Personality traits and the eye of the beholder: Crossing some traditional philosophical boundaries in the search for consistency in all of the people. *Psychological Review, 87,* 88–104.

Krueger, J. I., & Funder, D. C. (2004). Towards a balanced social psychology: Causes, consequences, and cures for the problem-seeking approach to social behavior and cognition. *Behavioral and Brain Sciences, 27,* 313–376.

Letzring, T. D. (2008). The good judge of personality: characteristics, behaviors, and observer accuracy. *Journal of Research in Personality, 42,* 914–932.

Lorenzo, G. L., Biesanz, J. C., & Human, L. J. (2010). What is beautiful is good and more accurately understood: Physical attractiveness and accuracy in first impressions of personality. *Psychological Science, 21,* 1777–1782.

Mischel, W. (1968). *Personality and assessment*. New York: Wiley.

Ozer, D. J. (1985). Correlation and the coefficient of determination. *Psychological Bulletin, 97,* 307–315.

Rentfrow, P. J., & Gosling, S. D. (2006). Message in a ballad: The role of music preferences in interpersonal perception. *Psychological Science, 17,* 236–242.

Rogers, K. H., & Biesanz, J. C. (2018). Reassessing the good judge of personality. *Journal of Personality and Social Psychology*, Advance online publication.

Saucier, G., & Goldberg, L. R. (1996). The language of personality: Lexical perspectives on the Five-Factor Model. In J. S. Wiggins (Ed.), *The Five-Factor Model of personality: Theoretical perspectives*. New York: Guilford Press.

Stewart, J., & Biesanz, J. C. (2017). *Good targets in text: Individual differences in distinctive expressive accuracy through writing samples*. Poster session presented at the meeting of the American Psychological Society, May 2017, Boston, MA.

Taft, R. (1955). The ability to judge people. *Psychological Bulletin, 52,* 1–23.

Tagiuri, R., & Petrullo, L. (Eds.). (1958). *Person perception and interpersonal behavior*. Stanford, CA: Stanford University Press.

Tupes, E. C., & Christal, R. E. (1961/1992). *Recurrent personality factors based on trait ratings (USAF ASD Technical Report No. 61–97)*. Aeronautical Systems Division, Personnel Laboratory: Lackland Air Force Base, TX. (Reprinted as Tupes, E. C., & Christal, R. E. (1992). Recurrent personality factors based on trait ratings. *Journal of Personality, 60,* 225–251.)

Vazire, S. (2010). Who knows what about a person? The self–other knowledge asymmetry (SOKA) model. *Journal of Personality and Social Psychology, 98,* 281–300.

Vernon, P. E. (1933). Some characteristics of the good judge of personality. *Journal of Social Psychology, 4*, 42–57.

Watson, D., Hubbard, B., & Wiese, D. (2000). Self–other agreement in personality and affectivity: The role of acquaintanceship, trait visibility, and assumed similarity. *Journal of Personality and Social Psychology, 78*, 546–558.

13

Personality Traits as State Density Distributions

Revisiting Fleeson (2001)

John F. Rauthmann and
Manfred Schmitt

BACKGROUND TO THE STUDY

Personality psychology is often equated with the study of traits (see also Chapters 2, 3, 5). Traits are defined as enduring levels or patterns of affect, behavior, cognition and desire. They are believed to form a certain structure (e.g., the Big Five: Openness, Conscientiousness, Extraversion, Agreeableness, Neuroticism), be stable across time, and be able to describe any person. Often, traits are defined as abstract and decontextualized entities on which people differ from each other. While a lot of research (e.g., by Cattell, Eysenck, Goldberg, Costa and McCrae) has been devoted to understanding between-person differences and uncovering the structures of traits, equating personality psychology with a psychology of traits would fall short. Early 'differential psychology' (still used as a discipline label), as put forth by William Stern and Gordon Allport, focused on differences *between* people (inter-individual perspective) as well as differences *within* people (intra-individual perspective) in enduring variables (traits) as well as momentary variables (states). As such, differential psychology is a broad field focused on differences in stable or variable bio-psycho-social variables. This means that mechanisms, processes and dynamics going on within a person – across different situations and time – were also of interest to personality psychologists. Such a more process- and state-focused approach, however, got deemphasized more and more (much of state research, especially in interpersonal situations, was absorbed by social psychology and is still studied there), while interest in a structure- and trait-focused approach increased. This created a rift between structure- and process-focused approaches, which we have only recently started to bridge. One impressive and consequential paper demonstrating how a single synthetic approach could tie together structure- and process-focused approaches comes from Fleeson (2001). This paper demonstrated the possibility of merging both approaches, highlighted the merits of employing experience-sampling methods in people's daily lives, and spurred lines of research that focus on a more dynamic understanding of personality.

CORE CONTROVERSIES

To understand the merits of Fleeson's approach, we need to take a look at core controversies within personality psychology. Five are especially relevant:

1. Person vs. Situation

2. Consistency/Stability vs. Variability

3. Structure vs. Process

4. Nomothetic vs. Idiographic

5. Description vs. Explanation

The 'person vs. situation' controversy revolves around the question of whether, or to what extent, forces within the person (traits) or from outside (situations, environments) generate behavior (see Chapter 6). Mischel (1968) argued that traits did not predict or explain behavior well enough. Indeed, many scholars cite .30 as the supposedly small 'personality coefficient'. However, actual empirical evidence points towards the conclusions that (a) correlations around .30 can be quite meaningful (Gignac & Szodorai, 2016; Hemphill, 2003) and that (b) traits predict aggregated behavior often above the .30 threshold. Nonetheless, the so-called person–situation debate ensued where the power of personality was abdicated in favor of situations being stronger determinants of behavior. This led to increased efforts of personality psychologists to showcase the relevance of traits (Kenrick & Funder, 1988) and look into statistical interactions between traits and situations (Ekehammar, 1974). Today, the person–situation debate is resolved (Fleeson & Noftle, 2008, 2009) as psychologists have a better understanding how persons and situations are related (Rauthmann, in press) and demonstrated the power of personality in predicting a plethora of outcomes in different life domains (Ozer & Benet-Martínez, 2006; Roberts, Kuncel, Shiner, Caspi, & Goldberg, 2007).

Closely associated with the person–situation debate is the 'consistency/stability vs. variability' controversy. It has been repeatedly voiced that behaviors are neither consistent enough across different situations nor stable across time to warrant the concept of traits (Hartshorne & May, 1928). This argument has also been extended somewhat to the stability of traits, but an abundance of literature demonstrates their stability (Roberts & DelVecchio, 2000; Roberts, Walton, & Viechtbauer, 2006). Further, according to Fleeson and Noftle (2008), there are 36 different ways of quantifying consistency or stability, and each way reveals something different about personality. We have explored only a handful of these concepts so far, but all of these point towards the empirical reality that behaviors and traits are relatively consistent/stable.

Another controversy concerns 'structure vs. process', depending on what personality researchers are interested in. Partly in response to the person–situation debate, personality psychologists focused increasingly on broad, universal and stable categories of human individual differences (Costa & McCrae, 1992; Goldberg, 1990). In doing so, the Five-Factor Model of personality was uncovered in countless factor-analytical studies. In contrast, a different strand of personality research – concerned with within-person processes – got neglected. Originally, personality psychologists were interested in how a person fluctuated from moment to moment in their mental states and behaviors and how such fluctuation could be manifestations of their personalities. Also, they were interested in how personality functioned and operated. Such questions were not addressed in most research that occupied mainstream personality psychology. Fleeson (2004) was one of the first to try to integrate structure- and process-focused approaches, resulting eventually in a more comprehensive understanding of personality (Fleeson, 2012).

An important further controversy concerns 'nomothetic vs. idiographic' approaches. Briefly, a nomothetic approach seeks to uncover universal laws at the population-level, that is, insights that will generalize (under most circumstances) to almost all people. In contrast, an idiographic approach seeks to understand one person thoroughly, regardless whether the insights gleaned can be generalized to other persons or not. Thus, the controversy boils down to whether insights *can* or *should* be generalized to other people. Although it may seem as if nomothetic and idiographic approaches must be necessarily antithetically opposed, there are actually important distinctions to be made. First, there are strict idiographic and normative–nomothetic approaches, most closely resembling the extreme poles of the controversy: the former asserts that each person must be seen as a single, separate case that cannot be understood in terms of how the 'average' (normative) person is, while the latter maintains that people can be understood in terms of universally accepted variables that apply to all people. As an example, the normative–nomothetic approach would claim that each person can be described on the Big Five traits, while the strict idiographic approach would claim that for each person her/his own set of traits must be identified. For trait psychology, this means in essence distinguishing between common and personal traits, as Allport (1937) did. In addition to these extreme positions, there are two moderate positions that aim to strike a balance. First, aggregating–nomothetic approaches maintain that insights from strict idiographic analyses can be culled or aggregated to a higher level, yielding nomothetic insights. Concrete insights uncovered in many single cases may show some commonalities, and these can be used to form a new, abstract nomothetic law. Second, a moderate idiothetic approach claims that one could describe single persons idiographically, but this may still be done in a manner so as to later compare people inter-individually.

Notably, questions of 'structure vs. process' and 'nomothetic vs. idiographic' are in principle orthogonal, as Table 13.1 illustrates. As can be seen, there can be nomothetic structure-focused, nomothetic process-focused, idiographic structure-focused and idiographic process-focused research. The Big Five tradition falls into the nomothetic structure-focused cell, while research on within-person structures (Cattell, 1966) falls into the idiographic structure-focused cell. Lamiell (1981) claims that intra-individual processes are highly idiosyncratic and cannot be generalized across individuals, and thus falls into the idiographic process-focused cell. In contrast, Beck (1967) and Mathews and MacLeod (1994) maintain that personality processes operate similarly across individuals, and thus fall into the nomothetic process-focused cell.

Table 13.1   Crossing between 'structure vs. process' and 'nomothetic vs. idiographic'

Controversies	Structure	Process
Nomothetic (population-level)	• Inter-individual differences in traits (and their correlational structure) are studied across several persons	• Intra-individual processes are studied within several persons
	• Trait structures can be generalized across several persons	• Intra-individual processes can be generalized across several persons
Idiographic (individual-level)	• Intra-individual differences in trait expressions (and their correlational structure) are studied within a single person	• Intra-individual processes are studied within a single person
	• Trait structures cannot be generalized across several persons	• Intra-individual processes cannot be generalized across several persons

Closely associated with the 'structure vs. process' controversy is the difference in scientific aims of describing or explaining personality and individual differences. The structure-focused approach often amounts to descriptions of personality: in which ways are we different from each other? What are taxonomic classification systems of traits? Notably, some trait models are explicitly only concerned with description (Goldberg, 1990) and thus see traits as abstract summary descriptions of behavioral regularities. In contrast, other trait models (Eysenck, 1970) see traits as explanatory constructs that cause people's daily physiological processes, thoughts, feelings, motivations, behaviors, social interactions and life events (see Chapters 4, 7, 8). Thus, traits have been used in descriptive and explanatory functions – a distinction that Fleeson (2012) seeks to integrate (see 'Advances' below). In contrast, the process-focused approach aims to explain personality: how and why do individual differences emerge? How does a 'personality' operate in daily life? How does a person function in different situations? Personality theories will be most powerful when they attempt to describe and explain (Fleeson & Jayawickreme, 2015).

INTEGRATING STRUCTURE- AND PROCESS-ACCOUNTS
OF PERSONALITY

In his classic article on traits as density distributions of states, Fleeson (2001) advocates the integration of dynamic personality processes into structural personality trait models. These models assume that individual trait-levels do not change much across a person's lifespan. Indeed, meta-analyses of longitudinal studies have shown that mean-level (Roberts et al., 2006) and rank-order stability (Roberts & DelVecchio, 2000) are indeed remarkably high. Despite this support for the traditional trait model, Fleeson claims that traits provide only limited personality descriptions because short-termed intra-individual changes in behavioral manifestations of traits are ignored. These intra-individual changes, as Fleeson argues in line with dynamic personality theories (Mischel & Shoda, 1998), are systematic and lawful. They reflect adaptive reactions of an individual to specific situational opportunities and demands. For example, an extraverted person does not show extraverted behavior all the time but reacts flexibly to specific situation characteristics. Behavioral expressions of personality traits in specific situations indicate personality *states*. Fleeson proposes that comprehensive personality descriptions require the simultaneous consideration of both traits and states.

Fleeson defines traits as density distributions of the frequency with which states are expressed in a certain intensity. For example, the intensity of socializing with other people (on a response scale from 0 'not at all' to 6 'very strong') can be rated several times throughout the day by different people. Then intra-individual density distributions can be constructed for each person when examining how often a given person performed socializing with a certain intensity (0, 1, ..., 6) across all measurement occasions. Such density distributions summarize *individual* within-person trait-expressions in states. Several intra-individual density distributions from single individuals can be aggregated to an inter-individual density distribution. Such a density distribution is nomothetic and describes *average* within-person trait-expressions in states. Notably, both intra- and inter-individual density distributions describe and condense processes *within* people. All of these distributions have different parameters, pertaining to extreme values (minimum and maximum values), central tendencies (arithmetic mean, median, modus), spread (standard deviation, inter-quartile range) and shape (skewness, kurtosis). These parameters capture different aspects of the density distributions. For example, one person's intra-individual density distribution has a mean of 1.25 on socializing intensity, indicating that she/he is rather introverted. In contrast, another person has a mean of 3.11, indicating she/he is moderately extraverted. A third person has a mean of 5.55, indicating that she/he is rather extraverted. Thus, each person has a different overall shape of their intra-individual density distributions, and Fleeson (2001) has shown that these shapes remain stable across time. At the same time this means that there are inter-individual differences in intra-individual density distributions (each person has a different mean, standard deviation, etc.). Such inter-individual differences can, in a next step, be explained by traits. For example, inter-individual differences in trait-levels of extraversion should be associated with inter-individual differences in means of intra-individual density distributions of state-levels of extraversion. Put more simply, trait extraversion should predict state extraversion. This is exactly what Fleeson (2001) shows empirically for all Big Five traits.

An example illustration of three intra-individual and two inter-individual density distributions is given in Figure 13.1. As can be judged by the shape of the distributions on the left side of Figure 13.1, Person 1 is rather introverted, Person 2 moderately extraverted and Person 3 very extraverted. Now suppose several introverted people's as well as several extraverted people's intra-individual density distributions were aggregated. As can be seen on the far right side of Figure 13.1, one would obtain inter-individual density distributions for introverts and extraverts. These two distributions are different from each other, most notably in the average frequency of which intensities of extraversion states are expressed: introverts express less (white distribution) and extraverts more (grey distribution) state extraversion throughout their daily lives (more socializing, talking, etc.).

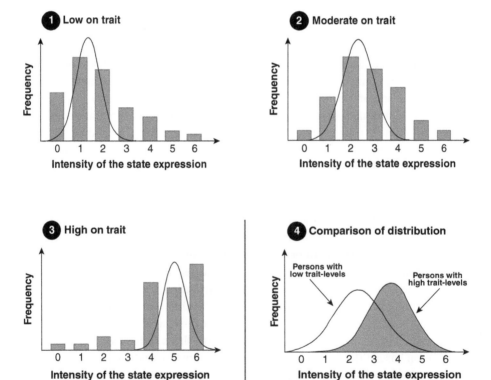

Figure 13.1 Fictitious examples of density distributions. _Left_: intra-individual density distributions; _right_: inter-individual comparison of aggregated intra-individual density distributions

Such a density distribution approach to personality can demonstrate several things that neither a structure- nor a process-focused approach can do on its own. First, state-levels of an individual can deviate from the corresponding trait-level and often do so. In other words, at many different times throughout the day, we are in our states not necessarily the persons we are in our traits. Second, the trait-level often captures to a large degree the average, most frequent, or most typical state-level of a person. In other words, there are at least moderate inter-individual correlations between traits and states (see Rauthmann, Horstmann, & Sherman, in press). Third, small deviations of state-levels from the trait-level occur more frequently than large deviations. This means, for instance, that a moderately extraverted person with an extraversion trait-level of 4 on a 7-point scale will most often display level 4 behavior and more often level 3 and level 5 behavior as compared to level 2 or level 6 behavior. Nevertheless, substantial deviations of state-levels from the trait-level happen and should therefore be included in the description of an individual's personality.

DETAILED DESCRIPTION OF THE STUDY

THEORY

Fleeson's (2001) definition of traits as density distributions of states comes with several assumptions that were each tested in the research program reported in the article. The first assumption predicts that individuals express their personality trait-levels on all behavioral levels. This means, for example, that even a person with an extremely low extraversion trait-level (level 1 on a 7-point scale) sometimes shows extremely extraverted behavior (level 7). The sizeable variability of behavior may occur in reaction to pronounced differences between situations or because of different temporarily activated goal-processes within a person. An introverted person, for example, can behave like an extravert in situations that strongly demand extraverted behavior for reaching an important goal such as impressing a manager during a job interview or meeting an attractive person at a party.

Second and in line with the traditional trait model, it was assumed that the average behavioral manifestation of a trait is highly stable and predictable even though each single behavioral manifestation is not. In other words, the means of intra-individual density distributions of states can be used to index the individual trait-level to some degree.

According to the third assumption, the shape of the density distribution of states entails unique details of an individual's personality. In addition to the mean of the distribution, its standard deviation (state variability), skewness (asymmetry of state-trait deviations) and kurtosis (tailedness of state-trait deviations) convey valuable personality information. State variability as the most important parameter from the perspective of dynamic personality theories reflects a person's responsiveness (sensitivity, reactivity) to situational cues and characteristics.

For example, the presence versus absence of other people may affect extraverted behavior more strongly in some individuals than in others. Fleeson (2001) assumed that all parameters of the density distribution vary systematically and in a stable manner between individuals. We will next describe the three studies that Fleeson (2001) conducted for testing his assumptions.

STUDY 1 OF FLEESON (2001)

Forty-six students reported personality and affect states five times a day on 13 consecutive days. Self-reports were delivered via hand-held computers. At each daily measurement occasion (noon, 3 p.m., 6 p.m., 9 p.m., midnight), participants were asked to indicate their behavior and feelings during the last hour. Students were asked, for example: 'During the previous hour, how well does "talkative" describe you?' Students answered all adjective items on 7-point scales (from 1 to 7). Five personality and two affectivity constructs were measured with four adjectives each: Extraversion (*talkative*), Agreeableness (*cooperative*), Conscientiousness (*organized*), Emotional Stability (*perturbable*), Intellect (*intelligent*), Positive Affect (*excited*), and Negative Affect (*distressed*). Additionally, students indicated how many other people were present during the last hour (0, 1–3, 4–10, more than 10). This information was collected because the number of people present in a situation was assumed to explain the variability of extraverted behavior but not the variability of the remaining states. At the end of the last daily measurement occasion, students also provided personality and affectivity trait self-descriptions. Using the same adjectives that were employed for measuring personality and affect states, students were asked to self-describe how they are in general. Finally, at the end of the last day of the study, participants also completed a standard Big Five Inventory and the Positive and Negative Affect Scale (PANAS; Watson, Clark, & Tellegen, 1988). In sum, each participant provided (up to) 65 state measures (13 days x 5 measurement occasions) and 14 trait measures for seven constructs (Big Five, Positive and Negative Affect). In addition, each set of state measures included the number of other people that were present during the hour before self-reports were provided. These data were used for testing the main assumptions to be tested in Fleeson's (2001) first study.

WITHIN-PERSON VARIABILITY OF STATES

The first assumption stated that individuals express their personality trait-level on all behavioral levels and that for this reason, individual state variability will be substantial. This assumption was tested via three comparisons.

The first comparison pitted the average individual personality state variability (standard deviation) against the total personality state variability across all individuals at all occasions of measurement. This comparison revealed that the individual personality state variability was lower as compared to the total personality state variability, but not much, with the individual standard deviation roughly amounting to .90 and the total stand deviation roughly amounting to 1.20.

This result clearly confirms Fleeson's claim that personality states and their variability across situations contain important personality information over and above personality trait-levels.

Second, the average individual personality state variability (standard deviation) was compared to the average affect state variability. This comparison was performed because personality constructs have mostly been conceptualized as traits, whereas affect constructs have mostly been conceptualized as states. Quite surprisingly in view of these conceptualizations, the average personality state variability was almost equal to the average affect state variability. This result shows that personality states can vary across situations as much as affective states do.

Third, the average individual personality and affect state variability was compared to the trait-level variability between individuals. The trait-level variability was determined both with the average state-level of a person (mean of the state density distribution) and the direct trait measures. The results of both comparisons converged and showed that the average intra-individual state variability was larger than the average inter-individual trait variability. This means that 'individuals differ from themselves over time at least as much as they differ from each other at the average level' (Fleeson, 2001, p. 1016).

STABILITY OF STATES

The second assumption stated that individual trait-levels are stable and predictable whereas single behavioral manifestation (states) are not. Both parts of the assumption were clearly supported by the data. The average correlation between randomly selected states ranged from .28 (Conscientiousness) to .54 (Intellect), with the average correlation across all Big Five constructs amounting to .39. By contrast, the split-half correlation between the average personality states ranged from .87 (Conscientiousness) to .94 (Agreeableness and Intellect), with an average of .91. These results replicate previous findings (Epstein, 1979, 1980) and fully support Fleeson's second assumption.

INDIVIDUAL DIFFERENCES AND STABILITY OF STATE DISTRIBUTIONS

The third assumption predicted that, in addition to the mean of the state density distribution, its shape as described by the standard deviation, skewness and kurtosis would vary systematically and in a stable manner between individuals. This assumption received mixed support. Split-half correlations of the standard deviation were substantial, ranging from .55 (Emotional Stability) to .67 (Conscientiousness), with an average of .59. Split-half correlations of skewness (average = .47) and kurtosis (average = .26) were much lower, suggesting that these parameters contain a limited proportion of systematic variance. By contrast, individual differences in state variability seemed to be reliable. Moreover, they generalized to some extent across traits. Specifically, the average correlation of state variability across traits was .38 suggesting that individuals differ not only in their trait-specific situational reactivity but also in their general reactivity.

INDIVIDUAL DIFFERENCES IN SITUATIONAL REACTIVITY

This interpretation was tested directly by regressing the state variability of all personality constructs on the time of the day and the number of other persons that were present during the hour before the measurement of personality states. Analyses revealed significantly unique effects both of the time of the day and the number of persons present. Confirming the construct validity of the state measures, the strongest effects were obtained for extraversion state variability. However, significant albeit smaller average effects were also found for the number of persons present on the state variability of the remaining four personality traits. This means that the number of persons present cannot only explain how extraverted a person behaves but also, for example, how conscientiously a person behaves in a specific situation. Together, these results suggest that individuals differ reliably in their reactivity to situational cues. Moreover, this reactivity is not fully trait-specific (limited to situations that match the trait) but generalized to some extent across traits.

STUDY 2 OF FLEESON (2001)

The second study was conducted to rule out the possibility that the substantial stabilities obtained in Study 1 for the mean and the standard deviation of the state density distribution were due to idiosyncratic definitions of the adjectives used for measuring personality and affect. Attaching idiosyncratic meanings to adjectives like *adventurous* (Extraversion), *trustful* (Agreeableness), *responsible* (Conscientiousness), *vulnerable* (Emotional Stability), or *creative* (Intellect) might generate systematic but irrelevant variance between individuals and artificially inflate trait stability. A second purpose of Study 2 was increasing the reliability of the parameters of the state density distribution by increasing the number of measurement occasions from 2 weeks (Study 1) to 3 weeks. Third, Study 2 used different adjectives for measuring the personality constructs in order to test the robustness of the results of Study 1.

The sample consisted of 29 students who were asked to self-report their behavior (but not their feelings) five times a day over a period of 20 or 22 days. Ten students delivered self-reports via hand-held computers, as in Study 1. The remaining participants used paper and pencil. Students were asked to report their behavior during 3 hours (rather than 1 hour as in Study 1) before each measurement occasion. Five adjectives measured each of the Big Five personality constructs and these adjectives were different from those used in Study 1. Importantly, students were provided with standard definitions of all 25 adjectives and were instructed to learn and remember these definitions. This procedure aimed at replacing idiosyncratic adjective meanings with standard meanings shared by all participants.

Despite these methodological changes, Study 2 replicated the results of Study 1. Importantly, the average intra-individual state variability was again similar in size to the trait-level variability between individuals (as determined in an independent sample). Moreover, the average stability (split-half correlation) of the mean (≈ .96) and the standard deviation (≈ .79) of the state density distribution were high and even higher than in Study 1. By contrast, the average stability of skewness (.44) and kurtosis (.22) remained unaffected by increasing the number of items and measurement occasions. In fact, they were even slightly lower than in Study 1 (.47 and .26).

STUDY 3 OF FLEESON (2001)

Study 3 tested whether high state variability, high stability of this variability and high stability of the average state were, at least partly, due to idiosyncratic scale usage. This might be a possibility because only the high end (7) of the 7-point scale was anchored with the specific adjective used for measuring behavior (*talkative*) or affect. The low end of the scale (1) was not anchored and might therefore have been given idiosyncratic meaning. For instance, some individuals might have equated the low end of the scale with a low degree of the adjective (*somewhat talkative*) and others with its opposite (*silent*). Just like idiosyncratic meanings of adjectives (see Study 2), idiosyncratic scale usage generates systematic but irrelevant variance between individuals and artificially inflates state variability and trait stability. In order to address this problem, both high and low ends of the adjective scales were anchored in Study 3 (1/*silent* vs. 7/*talkative*) turning the previously unipolar adjective scales into bipolar scales.

The sample consisted of 30 students who reported their behavior and feelings five times a day over a period of 21 days. Twelve participants used hand-held computers, 18 paper and pencil. Prior to the experience sampling part of the study, participants self-reported their Big Five trait-levels using the same items used for the assessment of states. The experience sampling procedure was similar to Study 2 with three exceptions. First, bipolar items were used. Second, students reported their behavior since the last measurement occasion. Third, six instead of five items were used for each construct.

Despite differences in material, results were similar to those of Study 1 and 2. Importantly, average within-person state variability (quantified by the standard deviation) amounted to about 70% of the total variability across all participants and measurement occasions and was similar in size to the trait variability between individuals. Moreover, the two most important parameters of the individual state density distribution – level (mean) and variability (standard deviation) – were again very high, amounting to an average of .96 and .86, respectively, across individuals and constructs.

IMPACT OF THE STUDY

Over a period of eight decades before Fleeson's (2001) article appeared, structure- and process-focused personality theories competed for the best explanation of human behavior. Structure-focused theories searched for a limited number of broad traits that could describe stable personality differences between individuals both parsimoniously and comprehensively. The Big Five personality model is a prominent product of this endeavor (Digman, 1989). Many studies have demonstrated that broad personality traits are not only remarkably stable both normatively and relatively but also capable of predicting aggregated behavior (Epstein, 1979, 1980) and life outcomes (Roberts et al., 2007).

The trait approach was criticized by process-focused personality theorists who demonstrated empirically that single behaviors belonging to the same trait correlated only weakly among each other (Hartshorne & May, 1928) and could not be predicted well from traits (Mischel, 1968). Accordingly, process-focused personality researchers argued that any explanation of behavior needs to take into account that humans react flexibly to situational demands, that characteristics of the person and characteristics of the situation interact (Ekehammar, 1974), that behavior reflects individual 'if–then signatures' (Mischel & Shoda, 1995), and that for these reasons human behavior changes systematically across situations.

For long, the structure- and the process-focused approaches were considered irreconcilable. Fleeson's research suggests that this may not be the case. Not only are trait theories and dynamic theories compatible, they even complement each other and together achieve a more accurate description of personality than each alone. The studies conducted by Fleeson (2001) consistently showed that behavior varies systematically within individuals. At the same time, aggregates of behavior are highly stable and describe reliably how a person feels, thinks and behaves in general. In conclusion, Fleeson's (2001) article convincingly demonstrates that an integration of structure- and process-focused personality theories is not only possible but superior to what each of them is capable of performing alone. It thus ushered in a new more *integrative* era of personality science (Baumert et al., 2017).

CRITIQUE OF THE STUDY

The immense influence on personality psychology notwithstanding, there are also critical aspects of the density distribution approach. Notably, these critical aspects are currently being picked up by personality psychologists already. First, most research has used people's self-reports of personality states in experience sampling. These may approximate, but are not actual behavior. Thus, several findings may suffer from common method variance (stemming from the self being the rater for states and traits), possibly artificially inflating associations. However, this is not a problem if researchers are explicit in the aim of studying people's self-concepts. Second, the exact underlying processes and mechanisms (which can be biophysiological, perceptual, cognitive, motivational, intentional, volitional, regulatory, behavioral, or social-interactional) that constitute, drive, generate, or explain density distributions are poorly understood as of yet. However, this is gradually changing (Baumert et al., 2017). Third, it was initially not quite clear what *exactly* a trait is and how density distributions 'capture' traits. Fleeson himself has offered his Whole Trait Theory (see 'Advances' below) to remedy this. Lastly, while a density distribution approach is based on the same principles as Classical Test Theory (where a 'true' trait score may be buried in a distribution of scores measured at different occasions), it is not a formalized theory of traits, states, or their relations. The lack of a formal representation (in mathematical formulae) is counteracted somewhat by the conceptual advancement and heuristic nature of the approach. Nonetheless, a density distribution approach as well as its successor Whole Trait Theory will need to be formalized more strongly at some point which will also make hypothesis-testing more stringent.

ADVANCES

Fleeson extended his density distribution approach to a Whole Trait Theory (WTT: Fleeson, 2012; Fleeson & Jayawickreme, 2015), which is based on over 15 years of research on integrating states and traits (Fleeson, 2004; Fleeson & Gallagher, 2009; Fleeson & Law, 2015). Density distributions of states have several properties that make them well suited to integrate structure- and process-focused research strands: empirical research has shown that they (a) summarize mental and behavioral states efficiently across measurement occasions (by using an average); (b) can be used to understand structures (between-person differences in averages of distributions) and processes (within-person differences manifested in dispersions of distributions); (c) may be constructed ideographically (for one person only) as well as nomothetically (across several persons); (d) are relatively stable across time within persons; (e) are substantially associated with self-ratings of traits; and (f) predict later mental and behavioral states.

Based on these properties, Fleeson sought to devise a theory that would be able to study 'whole traits', not just parts of them. Thus, WTT needed to integrate 'classic' trait-theoretical and social-cognitive models to fully understand traits. Classic trait-models are concerned with the descriptive of personality and its structure. Social-cognitive models are concerned with the dynamic cognitive, affective, motivational and regulatory processes that underlie, drive and explain a trait and its functioning. In reconciling both approaches to understanding personality, Fleeson proposed to view a trait as being made up of $Trait_{DES}$ (the descriptive side of the trait) and $Trait_{EXP}$ (the explanatory side of the trait). $Trait_{DES}$ and $Trait_{EXP}$ thus represent different but connected aspects of a trait – much like two sides of a coin. WTT maintains that $Trait_{DES}$ (a measured density distribution) can be *causally* explained by $Trait_{EXP}$ (goals of a person).

Figure 13.2 provides a schematic representation of Fleeson's WTT. $Trait_{EXP}$ consists of several dynamic elements that are in constant flux. Environmental stimuli provide input for sensory perception which, in turn, spurs further explicit and implicit cognitive, affective, motivational and regulatory information processing. These processes function as mediating variables between the input from the environment and output, the latter being manifest or overt behavior that may again impact the environment. These ongoing processes and feedback loops in $Trait_{EXP}$ are mirrored in $Trait_{DES}$ because density distributions change and shift around as a function of what is going on in $Trait_{EXP}$. Fleeson and Jayawickreme (2015) list

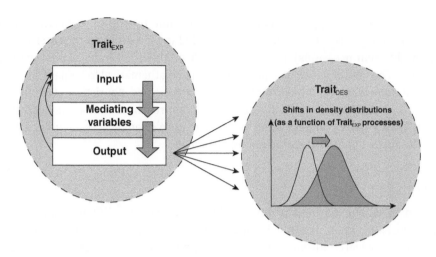

Figure 13.2 Whole Trait Theory.

several dynamic processes (interpretative, motivational, stability-inducing, temporal and random-error processes) in Trait$_{EXP}$ that can impact Trait$_{DES}$. Thus, Trait$_{DES}$ may, in certain ways, stand in the service or be 'tools' of underlying processes (goals: McCabe & Fleeson, 2016). For example, McCabe and Fleeson (2012) found that variance in density distribution parameters could be substantially explained by variance in social-cognitive mechanisms. However, the exact nature of these processes and how they constitute traits remains to be further elucidated (Baumert et al., 2017).

WTT is holistic as it seeks to integrate structures (Trait$_{DES}$) and processes (Trait$_{EXP}$) in the hope of fully understanding traits. Nonetheless, there are desiderata for future theorizing and research. First, when looking at Table 13.1, it can be noted that WTT is more concerned with the nomothetic branches of structure- and process-focused approaches. This is not necessarily a limitation as it is not clear if (or to what extent) idiographic analyses would actually coalesce into nomothetic insights. However, examining the generalizability of idiographic structures and processes to nomothetic ones remains an empirical question that WTT would need to tackle more strongly. Second, WTT is very inclusive and integrative, but at the same time risks a lack of precise predictions. As WTT stands now in literature, it is hard to think of tests that would falsify it as it is more a meta-theoretical framework to understand traits – which is a good first step towards a more integrative science of personality (Baumert et al., 2017; Wrzus & Roberts, 2016).

BIGGER PICTURE

Fleeson's concepts can be put into a bigger picture when looking at other trait models that also seek to understand states and traits. Here, we briefly highlight the latent state-trait theory (LSTT) and the non-linear interactions of persons and situations model (NIPS).

LATENT STATE-TRAIT THEORY (LSTT)

Fleeson's (2001) definition of traits as density distributions of states shares many ideas with latent state-trait theory (LSTT; Steyer & Schmitt, 1990; Steyer, Schmitt, & Eid, 1999). LSTT assumes that every behavior is shaped by at least three factors, the trait to which the behavior belongs, the situation in which behavior occurs, and the interaction between the trait (person) and the situation. The situation effect and the person × situation interaction effect are responsible for deviations of states (behavior) from the trait. These ideas are virtually identical to Fleeson's (2001) ideas. Unlike Fleeson's model of traits as density distributions of states, LSTT provides a formal definition of traits and states. Consistent with Classical Test Theory (CTT), which is a latent trait theory, LSTT defines latent traits as conditional expectations given the person (the behavior you would expect if you only knew which person is considered). Although statistically more formal, this definition of latent traits is conceptually identical to Fleeson's (2001) idea that traits are average states. Importantly, LSTT also provides a formal definition of latent states. Latent states are conditional expectations given the person and the situation. In other words, latent states are the 'best guess' of how a particular person will behave in a particular situation. Any deviation from this conditional expectation (best guess) is defined as measurement error in LSTT. The advantage of these formal definitions is that they can be translated into a structural equation model in which latent states are shaped by the latent trait, the latent situation and person × situation interaction, and measurement error. Such a model is testable and it can be applied to any personality indicator. Importantly, it can be estimated for any behavioral expression of a trait how strongly it is influenced by the trait, the situation and person × situation interactions, and unknown causes unrelated to the trait (measurement error). Because all variables are elements of a simultaneous model, they can be linked to other variables and imbedded in a multivariate network of traits and situations.

NON-LINEAR INTERACTIONS OF PERSONS AND SITUATIONS MODEL (NIPS)

WTT and LSTT can model traits and states without knowledge of the properties of the situation in which the state was expressed. This is a clear advantage in cases where the measurement of situation characteristics is impossible or costly (but see Rauthmann, Sherman, & Funder, 2015a, 2015b). Yet without knowledge of situational characteristics and their varying levels, it remains impossible to determine which situational factors interact with which person factors, how the interactions are shaped, and which psychological mechanisms drive them.

A recently proposed person × situation interaction model addresses these limitations (Schmitt et al., 2013). The model makes three assumptions. First and in line with previous person × interaction models (Ekehammar, 1974; Marshall & Brown, 2006), it assumes that personality traits and situation characteristics are functionally equivalent in their impact on behavior. For example, a person can feel anxious (state) in a specific situation because she/he is an anxious person (anxiety trait-level) or because the situation is threatening (anxiety-inducing situation characteristic-level). Because of this assumption, the model is primarily suited for interactions between functionally equivalent person characteristics and situation characteristics such as trait anxiety and situational threat or trait aggression and situational provocation. Second, the new model makes specific assumptions about the shape of the person × situation interaction. It assumes that interactions follow a logistic function. A logistic function is a specific nonlinear function and more realistic as compared to assumptions of previous models. It implies that traits have a stronger impact on behavior in weak situations and a weaker impact in strong situations. Strong situations are defined by high or low levels on the relevant situation characteristic. In the case of threat, strong situations can be a little threatening (low level) or very threatening (high level), both being instances of strong situations. Weak situations are situations with a moderate level of the relevant characteristic (moderate threat). Strong situations are restrictive, leaving little room for individual differences in behavior and thus little room for effects of personality traits. Weak situations are less restrictive and leave more room for individual differences and personality effects to manifest. Because personality traits and situation characteristics are functionally equivalent, the model also defines strong and weak persons. Strong persons are persons with low or high personality trait levels. Weak persons are persons with moderate trait levels. Strong persons are less influenced by situation effects as compared to weak persons. For example, a highly anxious person tends to feel afraid in many situations even if they differ in threat. Accordingly, a person with a low trait anxiety level does not feel afraid even in situations that contain considerable threat. By contrast, a person with a moderate trait anxiety level will react more strongly to the specific situational threat level.

The NIPS stresses the importance of persons, situations and their interactions in shaping behavior. The density distribution approach does not make any assumptions of the situations in which the personality states were measured, while LSTT and NIPS require the modeling of situation-dependent state factors. However, LSTT does not require actual measurements of situations, while the NIPS does.

SITUATIONAL TAXONOMIES

A deeper understanding of how personality manifests in states necessitates that psychologists know how to measure situation characteristics. Recently, different situational taxonomies have been proposed (see an overview in Horstmann, Rauthmann, & Sherman, 2017), with the Situational Eight DIAMONDS taxonomy proving especially useful for personality research (Jones et al., 2017; Rauthmann et al., 2014; Rauthmann, Jones, & Sherman, 2016; Sherman et al., 2015). Future studies should routinely seek to assess person and situation characteristics simultaneously.

CONCLUSIONS

Fleeson's density distribution approach and its extension by Whole Trait Theory clearly advanced personality science. As outlined at the beginning of this chapter, several core controversies have bedeviled personality research for quite some time (and in certain cases still continue to do so). The density distribution approach touches upon all of them and explicitly tries to provide an integration. The result is an understanding of personality traits and states that permits the reconciliation of structure- and process-focused accounts of inter- and intra-individual differences. Several other researchers have adopted Fleeson's ideas for their own research. The use of experience sampling and ambulatory assessment technology has risen since the millennium. This occurred thanks to technological advances, but also thanks to approaches – such as those from Fleeson – that require sampling people's mental processes and behaviors in their daily lives.

FURTHER READING

Baumert, A., Schmitt, M., Perugini, M., Johnson, W., Blum, G., Borkenau, P., ... Wrzus, C. (2017). Integrating personality structure, personality process, and personality development. *European Journal of Personality, 31*, 503–528.

Fleeson, W. (2012). Perspectives on the person: Rapid growth and opportunities for integration. In K. Deaux & M. Snyder (Eds.), *The Oxford handbook of personality and social psychology*. New York: Oxford University Press.

Fleeson, W., & Jayawickreme, E. (2015). Whole Trait Theory. *Journal of Research in Personality, 56*, 82–92.

REFERENCES

Allport, G. (1937). *Personality: A psychological interpretation*. New York: Holt.

Baumert, A., Schmitt, M., Perugini, M., Johnson, W., Blum, G., Borkenau, P., ... Wrzus, C. (2017). Integrating personality structure, personality process, and personality development. *European Journal of Personality, 31*, 503–528.

Beck, A. T. (1967). *Cognitive therapy and the emotional disorders*. New York: Meridian.

Blum, G., & Schmitt, M. (2017). The Nonlinear Interaction of Person and Situation (NIPS) Model and its values for a psychology of situations. In J. F. Rauthmann, D. C. Funder, & R. Sherman (Eds.), *The Oxford handbook of psychological situations*. Oxford: Oxford University Press.

Cattell, R. B. (1966). The data box: Its ordering of total resources in terms of possible relational systems. In R. B. Cattell (Ed.), *Handbook of multivariate experimental psychology*. Chicago, IL: Rand McNally.

Costa, P. T., & McCrae, R. R. (1992). *Revised NEO Personality Inventory (NEO-PI-R) and NEO Five-Factor Inventory (NEO-FFI) professional manual*. Odessa, FL: Psychological Assessment Resources.

Digman, J. M. (1989). Five robust trait dimensions: Development, stability, and utility. *Journal of Personality, 57*, 195–214.

Ekehammar, B. (1974). Interactionism in personality from a historical perspective. *Psychological Bulletin, 81*, 1026–1048.

Epstein, S. (1979). The stability of behavior: I. On predicting most of the people much of the time. *Journal of Personality and Social Psychology, 37*, 1097–1126.

Epstein, S. (1980). The stability of behavior: II. Implications for psychological research. *American Psychologist, 35*, 790–806.

Eysenck, H. J. (1970). *The structure of human personality*. London, UK: Methuen.

Fleeson, W. (2001). Towards a structure- and process-integrated view of personality: Traits as density distributions of states. *Journal of Personality and Social Psychology, 80*, 1011–1027.

Fleeson, W. (2004). Moving personality beyond the person–situation debate: The challenge and the opportunity of within-person variability. *Current Directions in Psychological Science, 13*, 83–87.

Fleeson, W. (2012). Perspectives on the person: Rapid growth and opportunities for integration. In K. Deaux & M. Snyder (Eds.), *The Oxford handbook of personality and social psychology*. New York: Oxford University Press.

Fleeson, W., & Gallagher, P. (2009). The implications of big-five standing for the distribution of trait manifestation in behavior: Fifteen experience-sampling studies and a meta-analysis. *Journal of Personality and Social Psychology, 97*, 1097–1114.

Fleeson, W., & Jayawickreme, E. (2015). Whole Trait Theory. *Journal of Research in Personality, 56*, 82–92.

Fleeson, W., & Law, M. K. (2015). Trait manifestations as density distributions: The role of actors, situations, and observers in explaining stability and variability. *Journal of Personality and Social Psychology, 109*, 1090–1104.

Fleeson, W., & Noftle, E. E. (2008). Where does personality have its influence? A supermatrix of consistency concepts. *Journal of Personality, 76*, 1355–1385.

Fleeson, W., & Noftle, E. E. (2009). In favor of the synthetic resolution to the person–situation debate. *Journal of Research in Personality, 43*, 150–154.

Gignac, G. E., & Szodorai, E. T. (2016). Effect size guidelines for individual differences researchers. *Personality and Individual Differences, 102*, 74–78.

Goldberg, L. R. (1990). An alternative 'description of personality': The Big-Five factor structure. *Journal of Personality and Social Psychology, 59*, 1216–1229.

Hartshorne, H., & May, M. A. (1928). *Studies in the nature of character: Vol. 1 – Studies in deceit*. New York: Macmillan.

Hemphill, J. F. (2003). Interpreting the magnitude of correlation coefficients. *American Psychologist, 58*, 78–79.

Horstmann, K. T., Rauthmann, J. F., & Sherman, R. A. (2017). The measurement of situational influences. In V. Zeigler-Hill & T. K. Shackelford (Eds.), *The Sage handbook of personality and individual differences*. Los Angeles, CA: Sage.

Jones, A. B., Brown, N. A., Serfass, D. G., & Sherman, R. A. (2017). Personality and density distributions of behaviors, emotions, and situations. *Journal of Research in Personality, 69*, 225–236.

Kenrick, D. T., & Funder, D. C. (1988). Profiting from controversy: Lessons from the person–situation debate. *American Psychologist, 43*, 23–34.

Lamiell, J. T. (1981). Toward an idiothetic psychology of personality. *American Psychologist, 36*, 276–289.

Marshall, M. A., & Brown, J. D. (2006). Trait aggressiveness and situational provocation: A test of the traits as situational sensitivities (TASS) model. *Personality and Social Psychology Bulletin, 32*, 1100–1113.

Mathews, A., & MacLeod, C. (1994). Cognitive approaches to emotion and emotional disorders. *Annual Review of Psychology, 45*, 25–50.

McCabe, K. O., & Fleeson, W. (2012). What is extraversion for? Integrating trait and motivational perspectives and identifying the purpose of extraversion. *Psychological Science, 23,* 1498–1505.

McCabe, K. O., & Fleeson, W. (2016). Are traits useful? Explaining trait manifestations as tools in the pursuit of goals. *Journal of Personality and Social Psychology, 110,* 287–301.

Mischel, W. (1968). *Personality and assessment.* New York: Wiley.

Mischel, W., & Shoda, Y. (1995). A cognitive-affective system theory of personality: Reconceptualizing situations, dispositions, dynamics, and invariance in personality structure. *Psychological Review, 102,* 246–268.

Mischel, W., & Shoda, Y. (1998). Reconciling processing dynamics and personality dispositions. *Annual Review of Psychology, 49,* 229–258.

Ozer, D. J., & Benet-Martínez, V. (2006). Personality and the prediction of consequential outcomes. *Annual Review of Psychology, 57,* 401–421.

Rauthmann, J. F. (in press). Person–situation interactions. In B. J. Carducci (Editor-in-Chief & Vol Ed.), *The Wiley–Blackwell encyclopedia of personality and individual differences: Vol. II – Research methods and assessment techniques.* Hoboken, NJ: John Wiley & Sons.

Rauthmann, J. F., Gallardo-Pujol, D., Guillaume, E. M., Todd, E., Nave, C. S., Sherman, R. A., Ziegler, M., Jones, A. B., & Funder, D. C. (2014). The situational eight DIAMONDS: A taxonomy of major dimensions of situation characteristics. *Journal of Personality and Social Psychology, 107,* 677–718.

Rauthmann, J. F., Horstmann, K., & Sherman, R. A. (in press). Do self-reported traits and aggregated states capture the same thing? A nomological lens model approach. *Social Psychological and Personality Science.*

Rauthmann, J. F., Jones, A. B., & Sherman, R. A. (2016). Directionality of person–situation transactions: Are there spill-overs among and between situation experiences and personality states? *Personality and Social Psychology Bulletin, 42,* 893–909.

Rauthmann J. F., Sherman R. A., & Funder D. C. (2015a). Principles of situation research: Towards a better understanding of psychological situations. *European Journal of Personality, 29,* 363–381.

Rauthmann, J. F., Sherman, R. A., & Funder, D. C. (2015b). New horizons in research on psychological situations and environments. *European Journal of Personality, 29,* 419–432.

Roberts, B. W., & DelVecchio, W. F. (2000). The rank-order consistency of personality traits from childhood to old age: A quantitative review of longitudinal studies. *Psychological Bulletin, 126,* 3–25.

Roberts, B. W., Kuncel, N. R., Shiner, R., Caspi, A., & Goldberg, L. R. (2007). The power of personality: The comparative validity of personality traits, socioeconomic status, and cognitive ability for predicting important life outcomes. *Perspectives on Psychological Science, 2,* 313–345.

Roberts, B. W., Walton, K. E., & Viechtbauer, W. (2006). Patterns of mean-level change in personality traits across the life course: A meta-analysis of longitudinal studies. *Psychological Bulletin, 132,* 1–25.

Schmitt, M., & Blum, G. (2017). The Nonlinear Interaction of Person and Situation (NIPS) Model and its values for a psychology of situations. In J. F. Rauthmann, D. C. Funder, & R. Sherman (Eds.), *The Oxford handbook of psychological situations.* Oxford: Oxford University Press.

Schmitt, M., Gollwitzer, M., Baumert, A., Blum, G., Geschwendner, T., Hofmann, W., & Rothmund, T. (2013). Proposal of a nonlinear interaction of person and situation (NIPS) model. *Frontiers in Psychology in Personality Science and Individual Differences, 4*, 499.

Sherman, R. A., Rauthmann, J. F., Brown, N. A., Serfass, D. S., & Jones, A. B. (2015). The independent effects of personality and situations on real-time expressions of behavior and emotion. *Journal of Personality and Social Psychology, 109*, 872–888.

Steyer, R., & Schmitt, M. (1990). The effects of aggregation across and within occasions on consistency, specificity, and reliability. *Methodika, 4*, 58–94.

Steyer, R., Schmitt, M., & Eid, M. (1999). Latent state-trait theory and research in personality and individual differences. *European Journal of Personality, 13*, 389–408.

Watson, D., Clark, L. A., & Tellegen, A. (1988). Development and validation of brief measures of Positive and Negative Affect: The PANAS scales. *Journal of Personality and Social Psychology, 54*, 1063–1070.

Wrzus, C., & Roberts, B. W. (2016). Processes of personality development in adulthood: The TESSERA framework. *Personality and Social Psychology Review, 21*, 253–277.

14 The Dark Side of Personality

Revisiting Paulhus and Williams (2002)

Virgil Zeigler-Hill and David K. Marcus

BACKGROUND TO THE STUDY

There are various aspects of personality that are generally considered beneficial in terms of helping individuals navigate their complex social environments. For example, individuals who are 'agreeable' experience a variety of social benefits (see Graziano & Tobin, 2018, for a review). However, there are also 'darker' aspects of personality that tend to be socially aversive because they involve characteristics such as the tendency to manipulate or deceive others, a willingness to exploit others and a lack of concern for the welfare of others (e.g., Marcus & Zeigler-Hill, 2015; Zeigler-Hill & Marcus, 2016). These dark aspects of personality have garnered a tremendous amount of empirical attention over the past 15 years. This rapidly expanding body of literature owes a considerable debt to the work of Paulhus and Williams (2002), which focused attention on the similarities and differences between the personality traits of narcissism (characterized by grandiosity, entitlement and superiority), psychopathy (characterized by callousness, impulsivity and interpersonal antagonism) and Machiavellianism (characterized by charm and manipulativeness). These three traits have been found to be associated with a wide range of important outcomes, including interpersonal hostility, sexually aggressive behavior, a lack of concern for others, the tendency to deceive others and the willingness to manipulate or exploit others.

Paulhus and Williams (2002) focused on narcissism, psychopathy and Machiavellianism because they were highly prominent traits that were socially aversive yet still fell within the normal range of functioning (i.e., they were subclinical in nature). Further, each of these traits had its own extensive research literature that had developed in relative isolation from other traits (e.g., the Big Five dimensions of personality; see Chapter 5), which may have contributed to *construct creep* (i.e., the tendency for researchers who are focused on a particular construct to expand the scope of that construct; Jones & Paulhus, 2011). Interest in the connections between these three traits actually originated with McHoskey, Worzel and Szyarto (1998), who focused primarily on the similarities between psychopathy and Machiavellianism but also included their connections with narcissism. Paulhus and Williams (2002) expanded the work of McHoskey et al. by synthesizing the independent bodies of research concerning narcissism, psychopathy and Machiavellianism and coining the term 'Dark Triad' to refer to this constellation of traits.

Although there are similarities between the Dark Triad traits (e.g., the willingness to manipulate and exploit others), they are considered to represent empirically distinct constructs because there are also important differences between these traits (e.g., Lee & Ashton, 2005; Paulhus & Williams, 2002). For example, narcissism has strong ties to self-enhancement, whereas psychopathy is only weakly associated with self-enhancement and Machiavellianism is unrelated to self-enhancement (Paulhus & Williams, 2002). The programme of research concerning the Dark Triad that was initiated by Paulhus and Williams (2002) has had a tremendous impact on the psychological literature as evidenced by its nearly 1000 citations and the more than 300 scholarly works that have explicitly focused on the determinants and correlates of the Dark Triad since its publication. In this chapter, we provide a review of the impact that Paulhus and Williams (2002) has had on the literature so far as well as suggest some avenues for future research.

DETAILED DESCRIPTION OF STUDY

Paulhus and Williams (2002) examined the possibility that narcissism, psychopathy and Machiavellianism constituted a Dark Triad of personality traits. This was accomplished by administering standard measures of these constructs along with other instruments designed to capture broad aspects of personality and intellectual ability to a sample of 245 college students. The measures of narcissism, psychopathy and Machiavellianism had moderate correlations with each other in this sample showing that an individual who reported a high score for one of these traits was also likely to report relatively high scores for the other traits. However, there were both similarities and differences in the associations that the Dark Triad personality traits had with other constructs. For example, the Dark Triad personality traits had similar negative associations with the personality trait of agreeableness but often had divergent associations with the personality trait of neuroticism (i.e., psychopathy was negatively associated with neuroticism, whereas narcissism and Machiavellianism were not associated with neuroticism). The conclusion reached by Paulhus and Williams (2002) was that the Dark Triad personality traits were distinct constructs that had important similarities to each other but were far from interchangeable.

NARCISSISM

Narcissism refers to exaggerated feelings of grandiosity, vanity, self-absorption and entitlement (e.g., Morf & Rhodewalt, 2001). There has been continued interest in narcissism since Freud (1914/1957) introduced the construct to the psychological literature (see Dowgwillo, Dawood, & Pincus, 2016, for a review). Although extreme levels of narcissism are considered to constitute a form of personality pathology known as *narcissistic personality disorder* (American Psychiatric Association, 2013), the interest in narcissism extends to subclinical manifestations of this trait (see Miller & Campbell, 2008, for the distinctions between clinical and subclinical conceptualizations of narcissism). In fact, the Dark Triad literature has focused almost exclusively on the subclinical manifestation of narcissism that considers it to be a normally distributed personality trait in the general population. Narcissism is considered a 'dark' personality trait because it interferes with various aspects of interpersonal functioning and contributes to a range of negative social outcomes (e.g., Dowgwillo et al., 2016). The general image of narcissism that has emerged from the literature includes inflated self-views, a willingness to manipulate or exploit others, defensiveness, heightened reactivity to self-esteem threats (e.g., failure, rejection) and a tendency to engage in unethical behavior.

There are a large number of instruments that assess narcissism such as the Narcissistic Admiration and Rivalry Questionnaire (Back et al., 2013), the Pathological Narcissism Inventory (Pincus, Ansell, Pimentel, Cain, Wright, & Levy, 2009), and the Hypersensitive Narcissism Scale (Hendin & Cheek, 1997). However, the most frequently used instrument for measuring narcissism is the Narcissistic Personality Inventory (NPI; Raskin & Hall, 1979, 1981). There are multiple versions of the NPI but the most popular consists of 40 items that are presented in a forced-choice format such that respondents must best describe themselves using either a narcissistic statement (e.g., 'I like to be the center of attention') or a non-narcissistic statement (e.g., 'I prefer to blend in with the crowd'). There has been considerable debate concerning the factor structure of the NPI with several alternative factor structures being suggested (e.g., Ackerman et al., 2011; , 1987; Raskin & Terry, 1988). One consistent pattern that has emerged from this debate is that the NPI is a multidimensional instrument that consists of one or more factors that capture the *agentic* aspects of narcissism (which tend to be associated with indicators of psychological health) and one or more factors that capture the *antagonistic* aspects of narcissism (which are often linked with relatively poor psychological adjustment; e.g., Brown, Budzek, & Tamborski, 2009). Despite the multidimensional nature of the NPI, most studies concerning the Dark Triad have focused exclusively on the overall composite NPI score rather than distinguishing among the subscales of the NPI. Although the use of a composite score for the NPI simplifies the presentation of results, neglecting the specific factors may be problematic due to the differences among those factors.

PSYCHOPATHY

Psychopathy is considered the most malevolent of the Dark Triad traits (Furnham, Richards, & Paulhus, 2013; Muris, Merckelbach, Otgaar, & Meijer, 2017). Although there is controversy regarding the nature and essential components of psychopathy, there is general agreement that psychopathy includes 'certain key affective (e.g. remorselessness), interpersonal (e.g. superficial charm), and behavioral (e.g. irresponsibility) features, oftentimes in conjunction with considerable antiso-cial conduct' (Edens & McDermott, 2010, p. 32). The concept of psychopathy can be traced to the beginning of the 19th century, with the term 'psychopathic per-sonality' being introduced around the turn of the 20th century (see Arrigo & Shipley, 2001, for a historical review). Cleckley (1941/1988) is generally credited with initiating the modern conceptualization and study of psychopathy. In *The Mask of Sanity*, Cleckley (1941/1988) presented detailed case histories of psycho-pathic patients at an in-patient psychiatric facility and provided a list of 16 diagnostic criteria for psychopathy. These criteria can be divided into three general categories: 'chronic behavioral deviance' (e.g., 'inadequately motivated antisocial behavior'), 'emotional-interpersonal deficits' (e.g., 'untruthfulness and insincerity'), and 'positive adjustment' (e.g., 'absence of "nervousness" or psycho-neurotic manifestations'; Patrick, 2006, p. 612).

There are various difficulties associated with the measurement of psychopathy because individuals with high levels of psychopathy are deceitful, may have an incentive to misrepresent their psychopathic traits, and often lack insight into their own personalities (Lilienfeld & Fowler, 2006). In response to these chal-lenges, Hare developed the Psychopathy Checklist (PCL; Hare, 1980) and the Psychopathy Checklist-Revised (PCL-R; Hare, 2003). The PCL and the PCL-R are clinician-rating scales that are scored based on a semi-structured interview that is performed in conjunction with a file review. Although the development of the PCL was informed by Cleckley's checklist, it did not include the items that focused on positive adjustment. The file review generally limits PCL-based research to insti-tutionalized samples, most typically incarcerated samples. It has been recognized during recent years that psychopathy can be conceptualized as a normally distrib-uted personality trait that exists to varying extents in community samples (e.g., Marcus, John, & Edens, 2004). As a result, although it is considered the 'gold stand-ard' measure of psychopathy (Lynam & Gudonis, 2005), the PCL-R is not ideal for studying subclinical manifestations of psychopathy, which are the focus of most studies concerning the Dark Triad. Instead, Dark Triad researchers have often used the Self-Report Psychopathy Scale-III (SRP-III; Paulhus, Hemphill, & Hare, 2009), which is based on the PCL-R.

The triarchic conceptualization of psychopathy (Patrick, Fowles, & Krueger, 2009) is one of the most influential recent approaches to understanding psychop-athy. This model posits that prototypical psychopathy consists of a combination of disinhibition, meanness and boldness. The inclusion of boldness – which includes fearlessness, low anxiety and social influence – in this model of psychopathy hark-ens back to Cleckley's attention to the positive adjustment components of psychopathy. The instruments that have been used to assess psychopathy in Dark Triad research (e.g., the SRP-III) generally do not tap into this boldness compo-nent. There are, however, other self-report scales, such as the Psychopathic Personality Inventory-Revised (PPI-R; Lilienfeld & Widows, 2005) and the TriPM (Patrick, 2010) that can be used in future Dark Triad research to assess all three of these triarchic components.

MACHIAVELLIANISM

In contrast to narcissism and psychopathy, which have their origins in the clinical literature, Machiavellianism is exclusively a non-clinical construct that takes its name from Niccolò Machiavelli, whose 16th-century book *The Prince* described the sort of manipulative and calculating interpersonal strategies that he thought were necessary for individuals to be able to seize or maintain power. Christie and Geis (1970) introduced the construct of Machiavellianism to the psychological literature. Machiavellianism is characterized by a selfish orientation, the strategic manipulation of others and a cynical view of human nature. Individuals with high levels of Machiavellianism use whatever means are necessary to accomplish their goals (e.g., manipulation, deception, exploitation; see Jones, 2016, for a review). Even though individuals with high levels of Machiavellianism are more likely than others to lie, cheat and betray their allies, they do not routinely engage in extreme forms of antisocial behavior such as physical violence (Jones & Paulhus, 2009).

The most common instrument for capturing Machiavellianism is the MACH-IV (Christie & Geis, 1970). This self-report scale consists of items that concern various aspects of interpersonal manipulation. The MACH-IV is generally considered to be a unidimensional measure but there has been some recent reexamination of its underlying factor structure (e.g., Kessler, Bandelli, Spector, Borman, Nelson, & Penney, 2010; Rauthmann & Will, 2011). Despite concerns about some of the MACH-IV items being outdated (e.g., Bagozzi et al., 2013; Jones & Paulhus, 2009; Rauthmann & Will, 2011) and the availability of alternative instruments for measuring Machiavellianism (e.g., the MACH* [Rauthmann, 2013], Workplace Machiavellianism [Kessler et al., 2010]), the MACH-IV continues to be commonly used in studies concerning the Dark Triad. As with narcissism and psychopathy, it may be problematic to rely on self-report instruments when attempting to capture Machiavellianism because individuals with high levels of Machiavellianism may be reluctant to provide honest assessments of their own personality traits. One alternative may be the development of an instrument that could be completed by individuals who are familiar with the target (e.g., friends, romantic partners, family members, co-workers). However, this approach would have its own set of limitations (e.g., limited insight into the motivations of the target, limited information concerning the behaviors of the target; see Jones, 2016, for a discussion of this issue).

IMPACT OF THE STUDY

Although Paulhus and Williams (2002) originally stressed the unique qualities of each of the Dark Triad traits, measures of these three traits are consistently positively correlated with one another. In their meta-analysis of 118 studies, Muris and colleagues (2017) reported a large correlation between Machiavellianism and psychopathy ($r = .58$) as well as moderate correlations between Machiavellianism and narcissism ($r = .34$) and between psychopathy and narcissism ($r = .38$).

Muris et al. (2017) suggested that Machiavellianism and psychopathy both involve 'malicious interpersonal behavior' (p. 188), which accounts for the high correlation between these two traits. Although narcissism may be interpersonally aversive, malice does not appear to be an essential component of this trait. Furthermore, vulnerability and insecurity are often found in narcissism, but are not components of Machiavellianism or psychopathy, which may explain why narcissism is less strongly related to the other two dark traits. Of course, this pattern of relations is not consistent across all studies and situations. For example, interpersonal perceptions of psychopathy and narcissism were more closely related to one another than either was to Machiavellianism among college students engaged in a cooperative task (Rauthmann, 2012).

Since Paulhus and Williams (2002), researchers have used a variety of methods to identify the source of the shared variance among these traits in order to identify the core of the Dark Triad (Furnham, Richards, Rangel, & Jones, 2014). Most of the traits that have been nominated as being at the heart of the Dark Triad are closely related traits that are derived from different personality or psychopathology frameworks. Low agreeableness (Egan & McCorkindale, 2007; Jakobwitz & Egan, 2006), low honesty-humility (e.g., Ashton & Lee, 2001; Book, Visser, & Volk, 2015; Lee & Ashton, 2005), and high callousness (Jones & Paulhus, 2011) have all been identified as being at the core of the Dark Triad. Using a structural equation model, Jones and Figueredo (2013) found that the combination of callousness and manipulativeness explained the associations among the Dark Triad traits, which is a finding that Marcus, Preszler and Zeigler-Hill (2018) recently replicated using network analysis. Thus, the core of the Dark Triad may be a lack of concern for others – except to the extent that they can be used to meet one's own needs and desires. The disagreement and confusion concerning the true core of the Dark Triad may be due, at least in part, to the distinct presentation of each trait. For example, each Dark Triad trait is linked with manipulative qualities but individuals with high levels of Machiavellianism tend to be far more calculating in their use of manipulation than individuals with high levels of narcissism or psychopathy, who tend to be more impulsive (e.g., Book et al., 2015; Jones & Figueredo, 2013).

Paulhus and Williams (2002) suggested that researchers interested in any component of the Dark Triad should consider assessing all three Dark Triad personality traits in order to determine the unique contributions made by each of them (see Furnham et al., 2014). Although there are advantages associated with assessing all three Dark Triad traits, this approach also presents a potential concern because the instruments that are typically used to measure these traits are all at least somewhat lengthy, which may lead to fatigue for the respondents (Jones, 2016). To address this issue, relatively concise instruments such as the Dirty Dozen (Jonason & Webster, 2010) and the Short Dark Triad (SD3; Jones & Paulhus, 2014) have been developed. The brevity of these measures led to some limitations but comparisons of the psychometric properties and utility of these two instruments have suggested that the SD3 should be the preferred instrument for researchers wanting to employ a brief measure of the Dark Triad (Lee et al., 2013;

Maples, Lamkin, & Miller, 2014). Some particularly harsh criticisms of the Dirty Dozen have even gone so far as to describe it as something akin to a 'cautionary tale' for the development of instruments that are too brief to adequately represent the bandwidth of complex constructs such as the Dark Triad traits (Miller, Few, Seibert, Watts, Zeichner, & Lynam, 2012).

To capture the unique contributions of each Dark Triad trait, it is important to employ statistical approaches that account for their shared variance (see Furnham et al., 2014). The most common strategy for accomplishing this has been to enter all three Dark Triad traits into a simultaneous multiple regression analysis. Although this approach has the benefit of being relatively simple, it likely underestimates the associations that the Dark Triad traits have with outcomes because overlapping variance is not accounted for when calculating effect sizes. Other approaches – such as Structural Equation Modelling (SEM) – have been used to better account for the shared variance between the Dark Triad traits but these approaches may overestimate their overlap. Furnham et al. (2014) proposed Set Theory – which is a mathematical approach that uses family sets and truth tables to determine connections between constructs – as a strategy for dealing with the overlap between the Dark Triad traits. Although they do so in different ways, the goal of each of these strategies is to account for the shared variance between the Dark Triad traits in such a way that it is possible to disentangle the unique contributions of each trait.

ORIGINS OF THE DARK TRIAD

To develop a more complete understanding of the Dark Triad traits, it may be helpful to consider their potential evolutionary origins. Several evolutionary approaches have been applied to understanding personality processes including life history theory, costly signalling theory, mutation load, flexibly contingent shifts in strategy according to environmental conditions, environmental variability in fitness optima and frequency-dependent selection (see Buss, 2009, for a review). Personality processes have tremendous implications for how individuals manage various life tasks (e.g., gaining access to mates, navigating status hierarchies) with some individuals – such as those with high levels of the Dark Triad traits – using manipulative and exploitative strategies to accomplish their social goals (Jonason & Webster, 2010; O'Boyle, Forsyth, Banks, & McDaniel, 2012). The idea underlying these evolutionary perspectives is that the self-serving, manipulative and exploitative strategies that characterize the Dark Triad traits may be adaptive under certain conditions.

One of the earliest scholars to advocate for an evolutionary perspective for any of the Dark Triad traits was Mealey (1995), who suggested that psychopathy may be the expression of a frequency-dependent life strategy that is selected in response to varying environmental circumstances. The argument for frequency-dependence involves a dynamic equilibrium such that high levels of psychopathy are advantageous as long as the frequency of psychopathy remains relatively low in the general population. That is, a small number of individuals may be able to benefit from adopting a socially parasitic strategy that is focused on deception, manipulation and exploitation as long as the vast majority of individuals adopt a strategy that emphasizes trust and cooperation. Under these conditions, individuals with psychopathic tendencies may experience considerable fitness benefits. However, the advantages that accompany psychopathy would decline if the frequency of psychopathy increased because other individuals would become more vigilant for the detection of 'cheaters'. Although the frequency-dependence explanation of psychopathy has some appeal, it has been criticized for various problems, including the heritability estimates of psychopathy (e.g., Crusio, 1995; Stoltenberg, 1997) and the failure to consider other explanations for psychopathy that may be more parsimonious (Crusio, 2004; see Glenn, Kurzban, & Raine, 2011, for a review of evolutionary perspectives on psychopathy).

Another approach to understanding the origins of the Dark Triad traits has been to consider their links with life history strategies which concern how individuals resolve the various trade-offs that must be made due to time and energy limitations (e.g., Kaplan & Gangestad, 2005). These trade-offs focus on: (1) somatic effort vs. reproductive effort; (2) parental effort vs. mating effort; (3) quality of offspring vs. quantity of offspring; and (4) future reproduction vs. present reproduction. This perspective argues that individuals differ along a continuum with regard to the reproductive strategies they employ to resolve these trade-offs (e.g., Buss, 2009). At one end of the continuum are those individuals who adopt a *fast* life history strategy in which emphasis is placed on short-term benefits with less concern for long-term outcomes (e.g., individuals focus on producing a relatively large quantity of offspring with little concern given to how to care for them). At the other end of the continuum are those individuals who adopt a *slow* life history strategy in which emphasis is placed on long-term benefits (e.g., individuals produce fewer offspring but they invest more resources in raising them).

Dark Triad traits are often associated with the adoption of a relatively fast life history strategy (e.g., Figueredo, Wolf, Gladden, Olderbak, Andrzejczak, & Jacobs, 2009; Jonason, Koenig, & Tost, 2010; Jonason, Webster, Schmitt, Li, & Crysel, 2012). Specifically, the Dark Triad traits have been associated with opportunistic, short-term mating strategies (e.g., one-night stands; Jonason, Li, Webster, & Schmitt, 2009; Jonason, Luevano, & Adams, 2012; Jonason, Valentine, Li, & Harbeson, 2011) as well as deceptive and manipulative mating behaviors (e.g., mate poaching, infidelity; Jonason & Buss, 2012; Jonason, Li, & Buss, 2010). However, McDonald, Donnellan and Navarrete (2012) argued for a more nuanced perspective with only certain aspects of the Dark Triad being associated with a fast life history strategy (e.g., the impulsive antisociality facet of psychopathy, the entitlement/exploitativeness facet of narcissism). This more nuanced perspective is consistent with the observation that individuals with high levels of narcissism tend to be perceived as more attractive than those with high levels of psychopathy or Machiavellianism (Rauthmann & Kolar, 2013). Furthermore, Machiavellianism does not appear to have a unique association with short-term mating strategies beyond its overlap with narcissism and psychopathy (e.g., Jonason, Luevano, et al., 2012). Taken together, these results suggest the possibility that the Dark Triad traits may represent specialized adaptations that allow individuals to exploit particular niches within society such as those concerning opportunistic mating (e.g., Furnham et al., 2013).

INTERPERSONAL CORRELATES OF THE DARK TRIAD

The Dark Triad is associated with a wide array of behaviors and life outcomes (see Furnham et al., 2013, for a review). We cannot address the full breadth of research concerning the relationships between the Dark Triad and life outcomes in this brief review so we will focus primarily on certain aspects of interpersonal behavior. The Dark Triad traits tend to have similar – but not identical – associations with a range of aversive outcomes, including a tendency to engage in aggressive behavior (Jones & Paulhus, 2010), use coercive strategies to obtain desired resources (Zeigler-Hill, Southard, & Besser, 2014), engage in counterproductive work behaviors (O'Boyle et al., 2012), employ hostile interpersonal styles (Jones & Paulhus, 2011; Southard, Noser, Pollock, Mercer, & Zeigler-Hill, 2015), focus on self-advancement with relatively little concern for others (Zuroff, Fournier, Patall, & Leybman, 2010), deceive others (Baughman, Jonason, Lyons, & Vernon, 2014), and admit to prejudice against outgroup members (e.g., Hodson, Hogg, & MacInnis, 2009; Jones, 2013).

Although many of the results concerning the Dark Triad provide an unpleasant view of these traits, other studies reveal that the Dark Triad traits may be beneficial or at least neutral in certain areas of life. For example, these traits may be helpful for individuals pursuing leadership positions especially when they are combined with factors such as intelligence and physical attractiveness (Furnham, 2010), which raises the possibility that there may be 'successful' manifestations of these traits such as the 'successful psychopath' (e.g., Hall & Benning, 2006). Despite some of the benefits that accompany these traits (e.g., greater comfort engaging in self-promotion), it appears that these traits may have at least some costs. For example, the Dark Triad traits may help individuals 'get ahead' in the workplace in the short term but they often impede their ability to 'get along' with others, which may be detrimental to their long-term success (e.g., Hogan, 2007).

There are clear similarities between the Dark Triad traits but important differences between these traits have emerged as well. For example, psychopathy is associated with the use of aggression in response to physical threats (Jones & Paulhus, 2011), whereas narcissism tends to be associated with aggression following threats concerning self-esteem (e.g., Bushman & Baumeister, 1998) and Machiavellianism does not have consistent associations with aggression following any sort of provocation (Jones, 2016). Machiavellianism is generally characterized by a cautious and deliberate approach to social interactions (Jones, 2016) that is quite different from the impulsive behavior that characterizes both psychopathy (Hart & Dempster, 1997) and narcissism (Vazire & Funder, 2006). The caution that is associated with Machiavellianism may explain why it is uniquely associated with unethical behaviors that involve long-term planning and require self-control such as white collar crimes (e.g., embezzlement; see Jones, 2016, for a review) and plagiarism (Williams, Nathanson, & Paulhus, 2010). In contrast, psychopathy tends to be linked with unethical behaviors that are impulsive in nature, such as aggression (Glenn & Raine, 2009) and exam copying (Nathanson, Paulhus, & Williams, 2006).

Each of the Dark Triad traits has been found to be associated with various forms of sexual aggression, such as sexual coaxing (e.g., Jones & Olderbak, 2014) and sexual harassment (e.g., Zeigler-Hill, Besser, Morag, & Campbell, 2016). However, only narcissism (e.g., Baumeister, Catanese, & Wallace, 2002; Bushman, Bonacci, van Dijk, & Baumeister, 2003; Zeigler-Hill, Enjaian, & Essa, 2013) and psychopathy (e.g., Harris, Rice, Hilton, Lalumiere, & Quinsey, 2007; Jones & Olderbak, 2014; Knight & Guay, 2006) have been associated with sexual coercion (cf. McHoskey, 2001). The patterns that have emerged from these studies suggest that individuals with high levels of narcissism are sometimes willing to resort to sexually coercive behaviors following rejection (e.g., they behave as if they have been deprived of a sexual experience to which they believe they are entitled), whereas individuals with high levels of psychopathy are willing to use an array of aversive tactics (including aggression) to create and take advantage of perceived sexual opportunities. The unique aspects of the Dark Triad traits (e.g., the caution that characterizes those with high levels of Machiavellianism) may suggest particular 'dark niches' that increase reproductive fitness through the use of specific types of manipulative and exploitative sexual strategies (e.g., Harris et al., 2007; Jonason & Buss, 2012; Jonason & Kavanagh, 2010; Jonason et al., 2011).

One possible explanation for the socially aversive behaviors that characterize the Dark Triad traits is that individuals who possess these traits have at least some difficulty understanding the mental states of others (e.g., Jonason & Krause, 2013; Vonk, Zeigler-Hill, Ewing, Mercer, & Noser, 2015) and deficiencies in the ability to empathize with others (Jonason, Lyons, Bethell, & Ross, 2013; Wai & Tiliopoulos, 2012). It is important to note that these deficiencies were more consistent across studies for psychopathy and Machiavellianism than they were for narcissism. Although difficulty understanding or caring about the mental states of others may have various negative consequences (e.g., impaired social relationships), it may also be associated with some benefits under the appropriate circumstances because this may reduce the likelihood that one's own emotions would interfere with the ability to manipulate or exploit others. For example, individuals who experience guilt during laboratory-based economic tasks often make decisions that lead to poorer financial outcomes for themselves (e.g., Ketelaar & Au, 2003). This suggests that these 'deficits' may have some benefits for those with high levels of the Dark Triad traits.

The general pattern that emerges from this large body of research is that the Dark Triad traits may represent variations of something akin to a 'cheater strategy' to the extent that they use different blends of dishonesty, intimidation and grandiosity to manipulate and exploit others (Jonason & McCain, 2012; Jonason, Webster, et al., 2012; Lee & Ashton, 2005). Although all three of the Dark Triad traits are relatively 'dark', it is important to note that narcissism appears to be somewhat 'lighter' – at least in some respects – than psychopathy and Machiavellianism (e.g., Furnham et al., 2013; Rauthmann & Kolar, 2012). For example, individuals with high levels of psychopathy and Machiavellianism tend to express fewer moral concerns than individuals with high levels of narcissism (Arvan, 2013; Glenn, Iyer, Graham, Koleva, & Haidt, 2009).

CRITIQUE OF THE STUDY

Paulhus and Williams (2002) is a seminal paper because it has generated considerable research and focused attention on dark personality traits at a time when interest in 'positive psychology' was really starting to emerge. However, the selection of these three traits was based on their shared social aversiveness and the amount of previous research attention they had generated. Other than perhaps following the 'rule of three' (Dundes, 1968), there is no intrinsic reason why the set of dark personality traits should be limited to a triad. In fact, Chabrol, Van Leeuwen, Rodgers and Séjourné (2009) have provided compelling evidence that sadism belongs with these other traits, creating a 'Dark Tetrad'. We have argued that there are numerous additional dark traits that merit study and that could be included in the types of studies that have examined the Dark Triad (e.g., Marcus & Zeigler-Hill, 2015; Zeigler-Hill & Marcus, 2016). Some of these traits, such as perfectionism and dependency, are not necessarily antagonistic, but can often be associated with destructive and even violent outcomes (see Flett, Hewittt, & Sherry, 2016, and Bornstein, 2016, for reviews of the dark aspects of perfectionism and dependency, respectively). However, even if the term 'dark' is limited to antagonistic traits, there are still a host of traits that might be considered along with the Dark Triad, including spitefulness (Marcus, Zeigler-Hill, Mercer, & Norris, 2014) and greediness (Seuntjens, Zeelenberg, van de Ven, & Breugelmans, 2015). Authoritarianism (see Ludeke, 2016, for a review) is perhaps the most noteworthy trait to currently be excluded from the Dark Triad. At a time when there are growing concerns about rising levels of authoritarianism in many countries. including the United States (e.g., the election of totalitarian leaders, support for fascist political groups), it is worth remembering that authoritarianism is likely responsible for more misery, suffering and death than all three of the Dark Triad traits combined.

CONCLUSIONS

We believe that research concerning the darker aspects of personality has advanced our understanding of human behavior. Paulhus and Williams (2002) made a vital contribution to this area of the literature when they initiated the process of identifying the similarities and differences between the personality traits that would come to be known as the Dark Triad. Although research concerning the

Dark Triad has certainly attracted a great deal of interest in recent years, it is our hope that continued advancements in the conceptualization and measurement of the darker aspects of personality will lead to an even deeper understanding of socially aversive behaviors in the years to come. We look forward to future innovations concerning the study of the darker aspects of personality.

FURTHER READING

Barry, C. T. (2011). *Narcissism and Machiavellianism in youth: Implications for the development of adaptive and maladaptive behavior*. Washington, DC: American Psychological Association.

Campbell, W. K., & Miller, J. (2011). *Handbook of narcissism and narcissistic personality disorder: Theoretical approaches, empirical findings, and treatment*. Hoboken, NJ: Wiley.

Furnham, A., Richards, S. C., & Paulhus, D. L. (2013). The Dark Triad of personality: A 10 year review. *Social and Personality Psychology Compass, 7*, 199–216.

Zeigler-Hill, V., & Marcus, D. K. (2016). *The dark side of personality: Science and practice in social, personality, and clinical psychology*. Washington, DC: American Psychological Association.

REFERENCES

Ackerman, R. A., Witt, E. A., Donnellan, M. B., Trzesniewski, K. H., Robins, R. W., & Kashy, D. A. (2011). What does the narcissistic personality inventory really measure? *Assessment, 18*, 67–87.

American Psychiatric Association (2013). *Diagnostic and Statistical Manual of Mental Disorders* (5th ed.). Washington, DC: American Psychiatric Publishing.

Arrigo, B. A., & Shipley, S. (2001). The confusion over psychopathy (I): Historical considerations. *International Journal of Offender Therapy and Comparative Criminology, 45*, 325–344.

Arvan, M. (2013). A lot more bad news for conservatives, and a little bit of bad news for liberals? Moral judgments and the dark triad personality traits: A follow-up study. *Neuroethics, 6*, 51–64.

Ashton, M. C., & Lee, K. (2001). A theoretical basis for the major dimensions of personality. *European Journal of Personality, 15*, 327–353.

Back, M. D., Küfner, A. C. P., Dufner, M., Gerlach, T. M., Rauthmann, J. F., & Denissen, J. J. A. (2013). Narcissistic admiration and rivalry: Disentangling the bright and dark sides of narcissism. *Journal of Personality and Social Psychology, 105*, 1013–1037.

Bagozzi, R. P., Verbeke, W. J., Dietvorst, R. C., Belschak, F. D., van den Berg, W. E., Wouter, E. B., & Rietdijk, W. J. (2013). Theory of mind and empathic explanations of Machiavellianism: A neuroscience perspective. *Journal of Management, 39*, 1760–1798.

Baughman, H. M., Jonason, P. K., Lyons, M., & Vernon, P. A. (2014). Liar liar pants on fire: Cheater strategies linked to the Dark Triad. *Personality and Individual Differences, 71*, 35–38.

Baumeister, R. F., Catanese, K. R., & Wallace, H. M. (2002). Conquest by force: A narcissistic reactance theory of rape and sexual coercion. *Review of General Psychology*, *6*, 92–135.

Book, A., Visser, B. A., & Volk, A. A. (2015). Unpacking 'evil': Claiming the core of the Dark Triad. *Personality and Individual Differences*, *73*, 29–38.

Bornstein, R. F. (2016). Interpersonal dependency. In V. Zeigler-Hill & D. K. Marcus (Eds.), *The dark side of personality: Science and practice in social, personality, and clinical psychology*. Washington, DC: American Psychological Association.

Brown, R. P., Budzek, K., & Tamborski, M. (2009). On the meaning and measure of narcissism. *Personality and Social Psychology Bulletin*, *35*, 951–964.

Bushman, B. J., & Baumeister, R. F. (1998). Threatened egotism, narcissism, self-esteem, and direct and displaced aggression: Does self-love or self-hate lead to violence? *Journal of Personality and Social Psychology*, *75*, 219–229.

Bushman, B. J., Bonacci, A. M., van Dijk, M., & Baumeister, R. F. (2003). Narcissism, sexual refusal, and aggression: Testing a narcissistic reactance model of sexual coercion. *Journal of Personality and Social Psychology*, *84*, 1027–1040.

Buss, D. M. (2009). How can evolutionary psychology successfully explain personality and individual differences? *Perspectives on Psychological Science*, *4*, 359–366.

Chabrol, H., Van Leeuwen, N., Rodgers, R., & Séjourné, N. (2009). Contributions of psychopathic, narcissistic, Machiavellian, and sadistic personality traits to juvenile delinquency. *Personality and Individual Differences*, *47*, 734–739.

Christie, R., & Geis, F. (1970). *Studies in Machiavellianism*. New York: Academic Press.

Cleckley, H. (1941/1988). *The mask of sanity* (5th ed.). St Louis, MO: Mosby.

Crusio, W. E. (1995). The sociopathy of sociobiology. *Behavioral and Brain Sciences*, *18*, 552.

Crusio, W. E. (2004). The sociobiology of sociopathy: An alternative hypothesis. *Behavioral and Brain Sciences*, *27*, 154–155.

Dowgwillo, E. A., Dawood, S., & Pincus, A. L. (2016). The dark side of narcissism. In V. Zeigler-Hill & D. K. Marcus (Eds.), *The dark side of personality: Science and practice in social, personality, and clinical psychology*. Washington, DC: American Psychological Association.

Dundes, A. (1968). The number three in American culture. In A. Dundes (Ed.), *Every man his way: Readings in cultural anthropology*. Englewood Cliffs, NJ: Prentice–Hall.

Edens, J. F., & McDermott, B. E. (2010). Examining the construct validity of the Psychopathic Personality Inventory-Revised: Preferential correlates of fearless dominance and self-centered impulsivity. *Psychological Assessment*, *22*, 32–42.

Egan, V., & McCorkindale, C. (2007). Narcissism, vanity, personality, and mating effort. *Personality and Individual Differences*, *43*, 2105–2115.

Emmons, R. A. (1987). Narcissism: Theory and measurement. *Journal of Personality and Social Psychology*, *52*, 11–17.

Figueredo, A. J., Wolf, P. S. A., Gladden, P. R., Olderbak, S. G., Andrzejczak, D. J., & Jacobs, W. J. (2009). Ecological approaches to personality. In D. M. Buss & P. H. Hawley (Eds.), *The evolution of personality and individual differences*. New York: Oxford University Press.

Flett, G. L., Hewitt, P. L., & Sherry, S. S. (2016). Deep, dark, and dysfunctional: The destructiveness of interpersonal perfectionism. In V. Zeigler-Hill & D. K. Marcus (Eds.), *The dark side of personality: Science and practice in social, personality, and clinical psychology*. Washington, DC: American Psychological Association.

Freud, S. (1914/1957). On narcissism: An introduction. In J. Strachey (Ed. & Trans.), *The standard edition of the complete psychological works of Sigmund Freud* (Vol. 7). London: Hogarth Press.

Furnham, A. (2010). *The elephant in the boardroom: The causes of leadership derailment*. London: Palgrave Macmillan.

Furnham, A., Richards, S. C., & Paulhus, D. L. (2013). The Dark Triad of personality: A 10 year review. *Social and Personality Psychology Compass, 7*, 199–216.

Furnham, A., Richards, S., Rangel, L., & Jones, D. N. (2014). Measuring malevolence: Quantitative issues surrounding the Dark Triad of personality. *Personality and Individual Differences, 67*, 114–121.

Glenn, A. L., Iyer, R., Graham, J., Koleva, S., & Haidt, J. (2009). Are all types of morality compromised in psychopathy? *Journal of Personality Disorders, 23*, 384–398.

Glenn, A. L., Kurzban, R., & Raine, A. (2011). Evolutionary theory and psychopathy. *Aggression and Violent Behavior, 16*, 371–380.

Glenn, A. L., & Raine, A. (2009). Psychopathy and instrumental aggression: Evolutionary, neurobiological, and legal perspectives. *International Journal of Law and Psychiatry, 32*, 253–258.

Graziano, W. G., & Tobin, R. M. (2018). Agreeableness: A three-level integration. In V. Zeigler-Hill & T. K. Shackelford (Eds.), *The Sage handbook of personality and individual differences: Volume 3 – Applications of personality and individual differences*. London: Sage.

Hall, J. R., & Benning, S. D. (2006). The 'successful' psychopath: Adaptive and subclinical manifestations of psychopathy in the general population. In C. J. Patrick (Ed.), *Handbook of psychopathy*. New York: Guilford Press.

Hare, R. D. (1980). A research scale for the assessment of psychopathy in criminal populations. *Personality and Individual Differences, 1*, 111–117.

Hare, R. D. (2003). *Manual for the Revised Psychopathy Checklist* (2nd ed.). Toronto, ON: Multi-Health Systems.

Harris, G. T., Rice, M. E., Hilton, N. Z., Lalumiere, M. L., & Quinsey, V. L. (2007). Coercive and precocious sexuality as a fundamental aspect of psychopathy. *Journal of Personality Disorders, 21*, 1–27.

Hart, S. D., & Dempster, R. J. (1997). Impulsivity and psychopathy. In C. D. Webster & M. A. Jackson (Eds.), *Impulsivity: Theory, assessment, and treatment*. New York: Guilford Press.

Hendin, H. M., & Cheek, J. M. (1997). Assessing hypersensitive narcissism: A reexamination of Murray's Narcissism Scale. *Journal of Research in Personality, 31*, 588–599.

Hodson, G., Hogg, S. M., & MacInnis, C. C. (2009). The role of 'dark personalities' (narcissism, Machiavellianism, psychopathy), Big Five personality factors, and ideology in explaining prejudice. *Journal of Research in Personality, 43*, 686–690.

Hogan, R. (2007). *Personality and the fate of organizations*. Mahwah, NJ: Erlbaum.

Jakobwitz, S., & Egan, V. (2006). The Dark Triad and normal personality traits. *Personality and Individual Differences, 40*, 331–339.

Jonason, P. K., & Buss, D. M. (2012). Avoiding entangling commitments: Tactics for implementing a short-term mating strategy. *Personality and Individual Differences, 52*, 606–610.

Jonason, P. K., & Kavanagh, P. (2010). The dark side of love: The Dark Triad and love styles. *Personality and Individual Differences, 49*, 611–615.

Jonason, P. K., Koenig, B., & Tost, J. (2010). Living a fast life: The Dark Triad and Life History Theory. *Human Nature, 21*, 428–442.

Jonason, P. K., & Krause, L. (2013). The emotional deficits associated with the Dark Triad traits: Cognitive empathy, affective empathy, and alexithymia. *Personality and Individual Differences, 55*, 532–537.

Jonason, P. K., Li, N. P., & Buss, D. M. (2010). Costs and benefits and the Dark Triad: Implications for mate poaching and mate retention tactics. *Personality and Individual Differences, 48*, 373–378.

Jonason, P. K., Li, N. P., Webster, G. W., & Schmitt, D. P. (2009). The Dark Triad: Facilitating short-term mating in men. *European Journal of Personality, 23*, 5–18.

Jonason, P. K., Luevano, V. X., & Adams, H. M. (2012). How the Dark Triad traits predict relationship choices. *Personality and Individual Differences, 53*, 180–184.

Jonason, P. K., Lyons, M., Bethell, E. J., & Ross, R. (2013). Different routes to limited empathy in the sexes: Examining the links between the Dark Triad and empathy. *Personality and Individual Differences, 54*, 572–576.

Jonason, P. K., & McCain, J. (2012). Using the HEXACO model to test the validity of the Dirty Dozen measure of the Dark Triad. *Personality and Individual Differences, 53*, 935–938.

Jonason, P. K., Valentine, K. A., Li, N. P., & Harbeson, C. L. (2011). Mate-selection and the Dark Triad: Facilitating a short-term mating strategy and creating a volatile environment. *Personality and Individual Differences, 51*, 759–763.

Jonason, P. K., & Webster, G. D. (2010). The Dirty Dozen: A concise measure of the Dark Triad. *Psychological Assessment, 22*, 420–432.

Jonason, P. K., Webster, G. D., Schmitt, D. P., Li, N. P., & Crysel, L. (2012). The antihero in popular culture: Life history theory and the Dark Triad personality traits. *Review of General Psychology, 16*, 192–199.

Jones, D. N. (2013). Psychopathy and Machiavellianism predict differences in racially motivated attitudes and their affiliations. *Journal of Applied Social Psychology, 43*, E367–E378.

Jones, D. N. (2016). The nature of Machiavellianism: Distinct patterns of misbehavior. In V. Zeigler-Hill & D. K. Marcus (Eds.), *The dark side of personality: Science and practice in social, personality, and clinical psychology*. Washington, DC: American Psychological Association.

Jones, D. N., & Figueredo, A. J. (2013). The core of darkness: Uncovering the heart of the Dark Triad. *European Journal of Personality, 27*, 521–531.

Jones, D. N., & Olderbak, S. G. (2014). The associations among dark personalities and sexual tactics across different scenarios. *Journal of Interpersonal Violence, 29*, 1050–1070.

Jones, D. N., & Paulhus, D. L. (2009). Machiavellianism. In M. R. Leary & R. H. Hoyle (Eds.), *Handbook of individual differences in social behavior*. New York: Guilford Press.

Jones, D. N., & Paulhus, D. L. (2010). Different provocations trigger aggression in narcissists and psychopaths. *Social Psychological and Personality Science, 1*, 12–18.

Jones, D. N., & Paulhus, D. L. (2011). Differentiating the Dark Triad within the interpersonal circumplex. In L. M. Horowitz & S. Strack (Eds.), *Handbook of interpersonal psychology: Theory, research, assessment, and therapeutic interventions*. New York: Wiley.

Jones, D. N., & Paulhus, D. L. (2014). Introducing the Short Dark Triad (SD3): A brief measure of dark personality traits. *Assessment, 21*, 28–41.

Kaplan, H. S., & Gangestad, S. W. (2005). Life history theory and evolutionary psychology. In D. M. Buss (Ed.), *The handbook of evolutionary psychology*. Hoboken, NJ: Wiley.

Kessler, S. R., Bandelli, A. C., Spector, P. E., Borman, W. C., Nelson, C. E., & Penney, L. M. (2010). Re-examining Machiavelli: A three-dimensional model of Machiavellianism in the workplace. *Journal of Applied Social Psychology, 40*, 1868–1896.

Ketelaar, T., & Au, W. T. (2003). The effects of feelings of guilt on the behaviour of uncooperative individuals in repeated social bargaining games: An affect-as-information interpretation of the role of emotion in social interaction. *Cognition and Emotion, 17*, 429–453.

Knight, R. A., & Guay, J. P. (2006). The role of psychopathy in sexual coercion against women. In C. J. Patrick (Ed.), *Handbook of psychopathy*. New York: Guilford Press.

Lee, K., & Ashton, M. C. (2005). Psychopathy, Machiavellianism, and narcissism in the Five-Factor model and the HEXACO model of personality structure. *Personality and Individual Differences, 38*, 1571–1582.

Lee, K., Ashton, M. C., Wiltshire, J., Bourdage, J. S., Visser, B. A., & Gallucci, A. (2013). Sex, power, and money: Prediction from the Dark Triad and honesty-humility. *European Journal of Personality, 27*, 169–184.

Lilienfeld, S. O., & Fowler, K. A. (2006). The self-report assessment of psychopathy: Problems, pitfalls, and promises. In C. J. Patrick (Ed.), *Handbook of psychopathy*. New York: Guilford Press.

Lilienfeld, S. O., & Widows, M. R. (2005). *Psychopathic Personality Inventory Revised (PPI-R): Professional manual*. Lutz, FL: Psychological Assessment Resources.

Ludeke, S. (2016). Authoritarianism: Positives and negatives. In V. Zeigler-Hill & D. K. Marcus (Eds.), *The dark side of personality: Science and practice in social, personality, and clinical psychology*. Washington, DC: American Psychological Association.

Lynam, D. R., & Gudonis, L. (2005). The development of psychopathy. *Annual Review of Clinical Psychology, 1*, 381–407.

Maples, J. L., Lamkin, J., & Miller, J. D. (2014). A test of two brief measures of the Dark Triad: The Dirty Dozen and the Short Dark Triad. *Psychological Assessment, 26*, 326–331.

Marcus, D. K., John, S. L., & Edens, J. F. (2004). A taxometric analysis of psychopathic personality. *Journal of Abnormal Psychology, 113*, 626–635.

Marcus, D. K., Preszler, J., & Zeigler-Hill, V. (2018). A network of dark personality traits: What lies at the heart of darkness? *Journal of Research in Personality, 73*, 56–62.

Marcus, D. K., & Zeigler-Hill, V. (2015). A big tent of dark personality traits. *Social and Personality Psychology Compass, 9*, 434–446.

Marcus, D. K., Zeigler-Hill, V., Mercer, S., & Norris, A. L. (2014). The psychology of spite and the measurement of spitefulness. *Psychological Assessment, 26*, 563–574.

McDonald, M. M., Donnellan, M. B., & Navarrete, C. D. (2012). A life history approach to understanding the Dark Triad. *Personality and Individual Differences, 52*, 601–605.

McHoskey, J. W. (2001). Machiavellianism and sexuality: On the moderating role of biological sex. *Personality and Individual Differences, 31*, 779–789.

McHoskey, J. W., Worzel, W., & Szyarto, C. (1998). Machiavellianism and psychopathy. *Journal of Personality and Social Psychology, 74*, 192–210.

Mealey, L. (1995). The sociobiology of sociopathy: An integrated evolutionary model. *Behavioral and Brain Sciences, 18*, 523–599.

Miller, J. D., & Campbell, W. K. (2008). Comparing clinical and social-personality conceptualizations of narcissism. *Journal of Personality*, *76*, 449–476.

Miller, J. D., Few, L. R., Seibert, A., Watts, A., Zeichner, A., & Lynam, D. R. (2012). An examination of the Dirty Dozen measure of psychopathy: A cautionary tale about the costs of brief measures. *Psychological Assessment*, *24*, 1048–1053.

Morf, C. C., & Rhodewalt, F. (2001). Expanding the dynamic self-regulatory processing model of narcissism: Research directions for the future. *Psychological Inquiry*, *12*, 243–251.

Muris, P., Merckelbach, H., Otgaar, H., & Meijer, E. (2017). The malevolent side of human nature: A meta-analysis and critical review of the literature on the Dark Triad (narcissism, Machiavellianism, and psychopathy). *Perspectives on Psychological Science*, *12*, 183–204.

Nathanson, C., Paulhus, D. L., & Williams, K. M. (2006). Predictors of a behavioral measure of scholastic cheating: Personality and competence but not demographics. *Contemporary Educational Psychology*, *31*, 97–122.

O'Boyle, E. H., Forsyth, D. R., Banks, G. C., & McDaniel, M. A. (2012). A meta-analysis of the Dark Triad and work behavior: A social exchange perspective. *Journal of Applied Psychology*, *97*, 557–579.

Patrick, C. J. (2006). Back to the future: Cleckley as a guide to the next generation of psychopathy research. In C. J. Patrick (Ed.), *Handbook of psychopathy*. New York, NY: Guilford Press.

Patrick, C. J. (2010). *Triarchic Psychopathy Measure (TriPM). PhenX Toolkit Online assessment catalog.* Retrieved from www.phenxtoolkit.org/index.php?pageLink=browse. protocoldetails&id=121601.

Patrick, C. J., Fowles, D. C., & Krueger, R. F. (2009). Triarchic conceptualization of psychopathy: Developmental origins of disinhibition, boldness, and meanness. *Development and Psychopathology*, *21*, 913–938.

Paulhus, D. L., Hemphill, J. F., & Hare, R. D. (2009). *Self-report psychopathy scale (SRP-III)*. Toronto, ON: Multi-Health Systems.

Paulhus, D. L., & Williams, K. M. (2002). The Dark Triad of personality: Narcissism, Machiavellianism, and psychopathy. *Journal of Research in Personality*, *36*, 556–563.

Pincus, A. L., Ansell, E. B., Pimentel, C. A., Cain, N. M., Wright, A., & Levy, K. N. (2009). Initial construction and validation of the Pathological Narcissism Inventory. *Psychological Assessment*, *21*, 365–379.

Raskin, R., & Hall, C. S. (1979). A Narcissistic Personality Inventory. *Psychological Reports*, *45*, 590.

Raskin, R., & Hall, C. S. (1981). The narcissistic personality inventory: Alternate form reliability and further evidence of construct validity. *Journal of Personality Assessment*, *45*, 159–162.

Raskin, R., & Terry, H. (1988). A principal-components analysis of the Narcissistic Personality Inventory and further evidence of its construct validity. *Journal of Personality and Social Psychology*, *54*, 890–902.

Rauthmann, J. F. (2012). The Dark Triad and interpersonal perception: Similarities and differences in the social consequences of narcissism, Machiavellianism, and psychopathy. *Social Psychological and Personality Science*, *3*, 487–496.

Rauthmann, J. F. (2013). Investigating the MACH-IV with item response theory and proposing the trimmed MACH*. *Journal of Personality Assessment*, *95*, 388–397.

Rauthmann, J. F., & Kolar, G. P. (2012). How 'dark' are the Dark Triad traits? Examining the perceived darkness of narcissism, Machiavellianism, and psychopathy. *Personality and Individual Differences, 53*, 884–889.

Rauthmann, J. F., & Kolar, G. P. (2013). The perceived attractiveness and traits of the Dark Triad: Narcissists are perceived as hot, Machiavellians and psychopaths not. *Personality and Individual Differences, 54*, 582–586.

Rauthmann, J. F., & Will, R. (2011). Proposing a multidimensional Machiavellianism conceptualization. *Social Behavior and Personality, 39*, 391–404.

Seuntjens, T. G., Zeelenberg, M., Van de Ven, N., & Breugelmans, S. M. (2015). Dispositional greed. *Journal of Personality and Social Psychology, 108*, 917–933.

Southard, A. C., Noser, A. E., Pollock, N. C., Mercer, S. H., & Zeigler-Hill, V. (2015). The interpersonal nature of dark personality features. *Journal of Social and Clinical Psychology, 34*, 555–586.

Stoltenberg, S. F. (1997). Heritability estimates provide a crumbling foundation. *Behavioral and Brain Sciences, 20*, 525–532.

Vazire, S., & Funder, D. C. (2006). Impulsivity and the self-defeating behavior of narcissists. *Personality and Social Psychology Review, 10*, 154–165.

Vonk, J., Zeigler-Hill, V., Ewing, D., Mercer, S., & Noser, A. E. (2015). Mindreading in the dark: Dark personality features and theory of mind. *Personality and Individual Differences, 87*, 50–54.

Wai, M., & Tiliopoulos, N. (2012). The affective and cognitive empathic nature of the dark triad of personality. *Personality and Individual Differences, 52*, 794–799.

Williams, K. M., Nathanson, C., & Paulhus, D. L. (2010). Identifying and profiling scholastic cheaters: Their personality, cognitive ability, and motivation. *Journal of Experimental Psychology: Applied, 16*, 293–307.

Zeigler-Hill, V., Besser, A., Morag, J., & Campbell, W. K. (2016). The Dark Triad and sexual harassment proclivity. *Personality and Individual Differences, 89*, 75–79.

Zeigler-Hill, V., Enjaian, B., & Essa, L. (2013). The role of narcissistic personality features in sexual aggression. *Journal of Social and Clinical Psychology, 32*, 186–199.

Zeigler-Hill, V., & Marcus, D. K. (2016). A bright future for dark personality features? In V. Zeigler-Hill & D. K. Marcus (Eds.), *The dark side of personality: Science and practice in social, personality, and clinical psychology*. Washington, DC: American Psychological Association.

Zeigler-Hill, V., Southard, A. C., & Besser, A. (2014). Resource control strategies and personality traits. *Personality and Individual Differences, 66*, 118–123.

Zuroff, D. C., Fournier, M. A., Patall, E. A., & Leybman, M. J. (2010). Steps toward an evolutionary personality psychology: Individual differences in the social rank domain. *Canadian Psychology, 51*, 58–66.

Author Index

Subject Index

Page numbers in *italics* refer to tables.